ueRsicut[...]
Cingitur bona nagula · Arce hinu bin ta[...]
recta atque diuina · omni   parte
struitur sca sed ula   ben   aunita
summa iusta ac min·   IR·
uinther benedictum beata · sacnoser neserta
fide fundata certa · uinis quae corpora[...]
spe salutis ornata · Xpo regina apta
caritate perfecta · solir luce amicta
ianus unum qua turbata · semplex simul doct[...]
qua uis fluctibr consa · unde cumque inuicta
nuptas quoque panata · Uere negadis aula
regno no sponsa · uanis gemmis onnata
domus diues plena · gregis Xpi cauta
super petra na confirmata · patre summo scnata
nec non ut nea uena · Uirtute ualde secunda
ex aegypto transducta · haec ma[...] inta[...]
erce ciuitas firma · letia creme bunda
fortis atque munita · uerbo di subacta
gloriosa ac digna ·
supra montem
posita

io 30 of the Antiphonary, reproduced by permission of the Ambrosian
rary

the
antiphonary
of bangor

F
L

MICHAEL CURRAN, MSC

the
antiphonary
of bangor

AND THE
EARLY IRISH MONASTIC LITURGY

IRISH ACADEMIC PRESS

This Book was typeset by Datamove
(Ireland) Ltd for the Irish Academic
Press, Kill Lane, Blackrock, Co. Dublin.

© Michael Curran 1984

Printed in Ireland

ISBN 0-7165-0338-7

CONTENTS

PREFACE

The Latin liturgies continue to attract the interest and scholarly research of historians and theologians. In recent years there has been a vast amount of work done on the edition and study of the texts of these liturgies, and in the history of the liturgy in its cathedral and monastic traditions. Among them, by comparison, the early Irish liturgy has been somewhat neglected. It is hoped that this book will not only help fill a lacuna but also stimulate further research into an area of the Latin liturgy where much remains yet to be done.

It is a pleasant duty for me to express my thanks to all who have helped me in my work. I am deeply indebted to Dom Jordi Pinnell, O.S.B., of the Liturgical Institute of St Anselm in Rome, both for the example of his own research into the Western liturgies, always a source of inspiration, and especially for his guidance and encouragement, without which I would have neglected many areas of research. My thanks are also due in a special way to Fr Martin McNamara, M.S.C., who has offered innumerable suggestions and helpful criticism out of his own store of knowledge of the early Irish Church. I should like to thank the Liturgical Institute of St Anselm for the resources and availability of its library, and also the librarians and staffs of the Biblioteca Nazionale, Rome; Trinity College, Dublin; the Royal Irish Academy, Dublin; and the National Library, Dublin.

ABBREVIATIONS

AB   *The Antiphonary of Bangor. An Early Irish Manuscript in the Ambrosian Library at Milan,* ed. F. E. Warren, 2 vols. Part I Facsimile, Part II Amended Text: HBS 4 and 10 (London 1893).

A CPs   *Collectae Psalmorum, Series Africana,* ed. A. Wilmart and L. Brou, *The Psalter Collects from V-VIth Century Sources*: HBS 83 (London 1949) 72–111.

AH   *Analecta Hymnica Medii Aevi,* ed. G. M. Dreves, C. Blume and H. M. Bannister, 55 vols (Leipzig 1886–1922). Cited by vol. and page.

Am   Books of the Ambrosian Liturgy:
 — Be   *Sacramentarium Bergomense,* ed. A. Paredi: Monumenta Bergomentia VI (Bergamo 1962).
 — Bi   *Das ambrosianische Sacramentar von Biasca,* ed. O. Heiming: Corpus Ambrosiano Liturgicum II. Liturgiewissenschaftliche Quellen und Forschungen 51 (Münster Westfalen 1968).
 — M   *Manuale Ambrosianum* I–II, ed. M. Magistretti: Monumenta Veteris Liturgiae Ambrosianae II–III (Milano 1905).

Bishop, *Note* E. Bishop, 'Liturgical Note', in: *The Prayer Book of Aedeluald the Bishop, commonly called the Book of Cerne,* ed. A. B. Kuypers (Cambridge 1902) 234–283.

CC   *Corpus Christianorum, Series Latina* (Turnholti 1954ff).

Ce   Books of the Irish (Celtic) Liturgy:
 — S   *The Stowe Missal,* ed. G. F. Warner: HBS 32 (London 1915).
 — see also: AB, ILH, T.

CLA   E. A. Lowe, *Codices Latini Antiquiores. A palaeographical Guide to Latin Manuscripts prior to the ninth Century.* 10 vols (Oxford 1934–1963).

CSEL   *Corpus Scriptorum Ecclesiasticorum Latinorum* (Vienna 1866ff).

DACL   *Dictionnaire d'archéologie chrétienne et de liturgie,* ed. F. Cabrol and H. Leclercq (Paris 1907–1953).

De ps. usu   *De psalmorum usu liber,* attributed to Alcuin: PL 101, 466–508.

Ga   Books of the Gallican Liturgy:
 — B   *The Bobbio Missal. A Gallican Mass-Book,* ed. E. A. Lowe: HBS 58 (London 1920).
 — C   *Das irische Palimpsest Sakramentar im Clm 14429 der Staatbibliotek München,* ed. A. Dold: Texte und Arbeiten 53–54 (Beuron 1964).
 — F   *Missale Francorum,* ed. L. C. Mohlberg, L. Eizenhofer and P. Siffrin: Rerum Ecclesiasticarum Documenta, Fontes II (Roma 1957).

– G   *Missale Gothicum*, ed. L. C. Mohlberg: Rerum Ecclesiasticarum Documenta, Fontes V (Roma 1961).

– V   *Missale Gallicanum Vetus*, ed. L. C. Mohlberg, I . Eizenhöfer, and P. Siffrin: Rerum Ecclesiasticarum Documenta, Fontes III, (Roma 1958).

– Mone   *Die Mone-Messen*, ed. L. Eizenhöfer, in: Ga V, p. 61–69.

Gamber, *Codices*   K. Gamber, *Codices Liturgici Latini Antiquiores*: Spicilegii Friburgensis Subsidia I 1–2. 2 vols (Freiburg Schweiz 1968). Cited by number, unless the page is expressly indicated.

Gougaud, *Christianity*   L. Gougaud, *Christianity in Celtic Lands* (London 1932).

Gr C   *Das Sacramentarium Gregorianum nach dem Aachener Urexemplar* ed. H. Lietzmann: Liturgiegeschichtliche Quellen 3 (Münster Westfalen 1921).

HBS   *Henry Bradshaw Society* (London 1891ff).

I CPs   *Collectae Psalmorum, Series Italica*, in: *The Psalter Collects from V–VIth Century Sources*, ed. A. Wilmart and L.Brou: HBS 83 (London 1949) 174–227.

ILH   *The Irish Liber Hymnorum*, ed. with Translations, Notes and Glossary by J. H. Bernard and R. Atkinson, 2 vols: HBS13–14 (London 1898). Cited by vol. and page.

Kenney, *Sources*   J. F. Kenney, *The Sources for the Early History of Ireland. An Introduction and Guide*. Vol. I *Ecclesiastical* (New York 1929). Cited by page unless otherwise indicated.

Lib. sac.   Ps.– Aluin, *Liber Sacramentorum*: PL 101, 446–466.

M 12 sup   *Das Sakramentar im Schabcodex M 12 sup. der Biblioteca Ambrosiana*, ed. A. Dold: Text = e und Arbeiten 43 (Beuron 1952).

Manz   G. Manz, *Ausdrucksformen der lateinischen Liturgiesprache bis ins elfte Jahrhundert*: Text = e und Arbeiten I 1 (Beuron 1941). Cited by number unless the page is expressly indicated.

MGH   *Monumenta Germaniae Historica* (Berlin 1826ff).

Mo   Books of the Spanish (Mozarabic) Liturgy:

– BR   *Breviarium Gothicum secundum regulam beati Isidori*, ed. F. de Lorenzana (Madrid 1776): PL 86. Cited by column of Migne.

– CPs   *Liber Orationum Psalmographus. Colectas de Salmos del antiguo Rito Hispánico*, ed. J. Pinell: Monumenta Hispaniae Sacra, Serie Litúrgica IX (Barcelona – Madrid 1972).

– Gil   *The Mozarabic Psalter*. ed. J. P. Gilson: HBS 30 (London 1905).

– Hor   *Liber Horarum*, ed. in part by J. Pinell, 'Las horas vigiliares del oficio monacal hispánico', *Liturgica* 3: Scripta et Documenta 17 (Montserrat 1966) 197–340.

– LO   *Le Liber Ordinum en usage dans l'Eglise visigothique et mozarabe d'Espagne du V au XI siècle*, ed. M. Férotin: Monumenta Ecclesiae Liturgica 5 (Paris 1904).

– LS   *Le Liber Mozarabicus Sacramentorum et les manuscrits mozarabes*, ed. M. Férotin: Monumenta Ecclesiae Liturgica 6 (Paris 1912).

– M   *Missale Mixtum secundum regulam beati Isidori dictum mozarabes* ed. A. Lesley (Roma 1775): PL 85. Cited by column of Migne.

– Or   *Oracional Visigótico*, ed. J. Vives and J. Claveras: Monumenta Hispaniae Sacra I (Barcelona 1946).

– Vesp.Mat.   *Le orazioni vespertine e mattutine ispaniche*. Vol. II *I Testi*, ed. J. Pinell (Romae, *pro manuscripto*, 1968). We will refer to this by numbered item for prayers otherwise unedited.

Norberg, *Versification* D. Norberg, *Introduction à l'Ètude de la versification latine médiévale*: Acta Universitatis Stockholmiensis. Studia Latina Stockholmiensia V (Stockholm 1958).

OF   Ps.— Alcuin, *Officia per ferias*: PL 101, 510–612.

PG   *Patrologiae Cursus completus, Series Graeca*, ed. J. P. Migne (Paris 1857ff).

PL   *Patrologiae Cursus completus, Series Latina*, ed. J. P. Migne (Paris 1844ff).

PLS   *Patrologiae Latinae Supplementum*, ed. A. Hamman.

PRIA   *Proceedings of the Royal Irish Academy* (Dublin).

Regensburg   *Das berliner Doppelblatt eines Sakramentars (MS lat. fol. 877) in northumbrischer Schrift aus Regensburg*, in: Ga F, Beigabe V, p. 71–79.

Rot.Rav.   *Der Rotulus von Ravenna*, in: Ve, Beigabe I, p. 173–178.

Ryan, *Irish Monasticism*   J. Ryan, *Irish Monasticism. Origins and Early Developments* (Dublin and Cork 1931).

SC   *Sources Chrétiennes*, ed. H. de Lubac, J. Danielou and C. Montdesert (Paris).

Stokes, VT   W. Stokes, *The Tripartite Life of Saint Patrick with other Documents relating to that Saint*. 2 vols (London, Rolls Series, 1887).

Szövérffy, Analen   J. Szövérffy, *Die Analen der lateinischen Hymnendichtung*. Vol. I *Die Lateinischen Hymnen bis zum Ende des 11. Jahrhunderts* (Berlin 1964).

T   'Das turiner Bruckstück der ältesten irischen Liturgie', ed. W. Meyer, *Nachrichten von der königl. Gesellschaft der Wissenschaften zu Göttingen. Phil.— historische Klasse* (1903) 163–214.

Ve   *Sacramentarium Veronense*, ed. L. C. Mohlberg, L. Eizenhöfer and P. Siffrin: Rerum Ecclesiarum Documenta, Fontes I (Roma 1966).

Walker   G. S. M. Walker, *Sancti Columbani Opera*: Scriptores Latini Hiberniae II (Dublin 1957).

Warren I–II   *The Antiphonary of Bangor*. Part I and Part II (See AB). Cited by page.

INTRODUCTION

Our knowledge of the Irish or 'Celtic' liturgy is due almost entirely to the survival of two manuscripts, namely, the Antiphonary of Bangor and the Stowe Missal. They have been studied by countless scholars, and on their basis the structures and characteristic traits of the Irish liturgy have been frequently expounded. The Antiphonary, in addition, has often been referred to as an important source in general studies of the liturgy, especially of the divine office, and it has been used in the study of specific questions, such as the early history of Latin hymnody, the Old Latin text and liturgical use of the canticles, the history of the *Gloria in excelsis* and *Te Deum*, and so on. The question might well be asked: What more is there to be said on the subject of the Antiphonary?

It seemed to me that some fundamental questions regarding its origins in seventh-century Ireland and regarding its sources in detail remained to be answered. No all-embracing study of it has been undertaken since the work of edition and detailed commentary of it carried out by F.E. Warren in the last century, and it has remained in many respects an enigmatic book. It is at once an antiphonary, a collectary, and a hymnary, evidently a compilation made from the collections of collects, hymns, and antiphons that were available at Bangor at the time of its composition. But what are the ultimate sources of all this material? Are the originals genuinely Irish or are they 'purely Gallican', as has often been maintained? Answers to these questions should throw some extra light on the cultural and liturgical situation of Ireland in the seventh century.

Our investigation has been directed mainly to an area that has been largely neglected in the study of the early Irish liturgy. In the work of the early authorities in this field, such as Warren and Gougaud, the emphasis was placed on the ritual elements that were characteristic of the Celtic rite, and on the external aspects of worship, such as church architecture, sacred objects and ornaments. The long-established tradition regarding the Gallican origin of the Irish Church seemed to be confirmed by some common traits observed between the Celtic and Gallican rites, such as the number of hours celebrated in the office and the number of psalms said at certain hours. As a result, the presumption that the Antiphonary is a Gallican document was created and accepted. A.A. King continued the same approach to the Irish liturgy, and in his view also the Antiphonary is at once 'purely Celtic' and 'still wholly Gallican'.[1] At times, the term 'Gallican' is, for these authors, purposely vague, meaning simply 'non-Roman'; at other times it appears to mean Gallican in the strict sense of belonging to Gaul.[2] The classification of the Antiphonary as Gallican in the broad sense is unsatisfactory, because it is quite evidently non-Roman.

Our study will reveal to what extent it is Gallican in the strict sense.

The neglect of the *texts* used in the Irish liturgy and the need to study them more carefully have become apparent.[3] It is from the texts of prayers and hymns that we can discover the characteristic 'genius' of this liturgy, as of any other liturgy. The present investigation aims, therefore, to explain as fully as possible the origin and sources of the hymns and collects preserved in the Antiphonary, to understand how the Irish authors treated the sources they were using, how original they were and what their capacity was to grasp and express the mysteries of Christianity in their liturgical prayer. The scope of our investigation is intentionally limited to the hymns and collects, which will be studied in Part One and Part Two respectively of this work. We are not going to delve into such specialized questions as the textual history of the *Gloria in excelsis*, the *Te Deum* or the Apostles' Creed, all of which are found in the Antiphonary. The peculiarly Irish text of some of the Old Testament canticles found here has been studied by H. Schneider; we will simply take account of his conclusions and suggestions. Our remarks on the antiphons will be few; sources for some of them have been indicated by F.E. Warren in his annotated edition.[4] Our first task is to determine the sources of the hymns and collects in so far as this is now possible. The term 'source' is taken in a broad sense, to include not only direct literary sources of individual pieces, but also parallel expressions and ideas found in the liturgical or patristic texts of the Western Churches generally. In this way it will be possible to situate the Antiphonary in the context of the Irish Church and of the ecclesiastical tradition of the West.

Great pioneering work in the study of the texts of the Irish liturgy was made by E. Bishop[5] and G. Manz,[6] and frequent reference will be made especially to the latter's collection. One of the most important results of Bishop's *Note* was the discovery of certain 'Spanish symptoms' in the prayers of the *Book of Cerne* and in Irish liturgical texts.[7] We will see that the Antiphonary contains a number of Spanish prayers and other 'symptoms', and in this way add further to the evidence that is coming to light today regarding the influence of Spain on Ireland in the seventh century. This influence was not limited to the liturgy, but included a wide range of literary, artistic and commercial relationships.[8] But contact between Ireland and the Continent was not limited to Spain. We will see that certain items in the Antiphonary have their source in northern Italian writings. This is what might have been expected, in view of the position of Bobbio as one of the most important Irish centres on the continent in the seventh century; relations between it and Ireland would naturally have continued during the period we are investigating. Relations with Gaul were re-opened through the mission of Columban and the foundation of Luxeuil and other Irish centres in France and Germany. This explains how certain Gallican sources could influence the composition of various items in the Antiphonary.

12

The sources I have used, including all the books of prayer representing the distinct liturgical traditions, are listed above. Mixed sacramentaries, the later Gregorian and Gelasian books, have not been used, with the exception of those eighth-century Gelasians which contain prayers for the hours identical with or close to those given in the Antiphonary. My reading of patristic writings has been, of necessity, fragmentary and incomplete; it includes the early Hiberno-Latin biblical commentaries and some writings of certain Fathers who are known to have been used in Ireland in the seventh century. The few discoveries I have made in this area are less the result of systematic reading than of following up an occasional hint or guess.

The present study deals with a collection of texts used in the liturgy of the monastery of Bangor in northern Ireland in the seventh century. This monastery was founded in the year 555 by St Comgall on the southern shore of Loch Laoigh, now Belfast Lough.[9] Comgall was a native of the Pictish kingdom of Dal n-Araidhe, which corresponds roughly to modern Co. Antrim. He received his monastic training in Leinster under Fintan of Clonenagh, from whom he inherited a discipline and a rule noted in the Irish tradition for its severity. In spite of this rigorous asceticism, many disciples gathered around Comgall, the most renowned of whom was undoubtedly Columbanus, who was to become the great missionary and founder of monasteries at Luxeuil and Bobbio. Comgall himself participated in the missionary thrust of his community, working along with his friend Colmcille among the Scots and Picts of Scotland. His monastery at Bangor flourished and in the seventh century it became one of the great centres of Irish monastic culture. In the course of our study we will have occasion to consider the hymn composed in praise of its first fifteen abbots and another hymn composed in praise of its rule of life.

The Antiphonary is a codex of thirty-six leaves written at Bangor between the years 680–691.[10] It was composed in three parts, according to a pre-arranged plan. The first part (ff.1–17ᵛ) was set aside for canticles and hymns. The second part (ff.18–28ᵛ) contains two groups of collects, the first group comprising two sets of collects for all the hours of the office, the second group containing seven sets of collects for various parts of the morning office. The third part (ff.30–36) is a heterogeneous collection of texts: hymns, antiphons, and collects which do not form any complete set, but are meant for various liturgical occasions.

The first edition of the manuscript was by Muratori,[11] and many other complete or partial editions have followed. The best edition is the monumental work of F.E. Warren in two volumes of text, introduction and detailed commentary.[12] In the course of our study we will take up again the 'traces of Hispano-Gallican influence' and the many other points of interest to which he first drew attention. A new edition of the hymns and some of the rhythmical prayers was made by C. Blume for the *Analecta Hymnica Medii Aevi*; for this edition he also made use of the other

Irish manuscripts in which they occur.[13] Then in 1941 a new edition of the entire manuscript was made by Ezio Franceschini, whose aim was to supply for the deficiencies of Warren's emended text by reproducing the original as faithfully as possible.[14] Finally, we may note that L. Brou included in an appendix to his edition of the Psalter Collects those collects of the Antiphonary which are composed on the basis of the psalms.[15]

Mention must be made here of another Irish manuscript, now in Turin, which is contemporary and almost totally parallel to the Antiphonary.[16] W. Meyer thought it to be of slightly earlier date than the Antiphonary, but E.A. Lowe judges it to have been written at the beginning of the eighth century in Ireland.[17] Due to the loss of its outer sheet it is known as the Turin Fragment; yet almost the entire original has been preserved in the three bifolia remaining. Of the twenty items it contains, all except four collects are found in the Antiphonary, and a comparison of the two reveals that both go back to common originals.[18]

In this study we will have recourse especially to Warren's facsimile edition. We will not, however, take account of peculiarities of spelling which do not affect the intended meaning or the structure of a verse. Many of these peculiarities show the Irish character of the manuscript, but they do not necessarily prove the Irish origin of any particular item in which they occur. A number of the hymns and collects are also found in other manuscripts and where critical editions exist we will use them.

Already prior to the issue of Warren's annotated edition, W.C. Bishop contributed an important study in which he compared the Bangor morning office with the Ambrosian office of lauds.[19] We will return to this question in the third part of our study. The Antiphonary was, of course, the major source for Dom Gougaud's study of the office of the Celtic Church.[20] He observed how the collects for the various hours express the mystical meaning proper to each hour, and he drew attention to certain points of agreement between the Irish monastic office and the monastic office at Arles. In his view the Antiphonary is 'encore purement gallican',[21] that is, non-Roman.

The best study of the purpose for which the Antiphonary was composed was made by F. Cabrol.[22] He examined different theories and possibilities regarding its nature and function, and concluded that it was the book used for the office by the president of the choir, who would normally have been the abbot. With this book, along with the psalter and Bible, he was able to direct the entire office throughout the whole year and recite the collects in their appropriate places. Many items in the manuscript were not strictly required for the abbot to fulfill his role as president, such as the canticles, hymns, and antiphons. But these, as well as other items, may have been included on his personal recommendation, or to suit his particular fancies and inclinations. The result is 'to a considerable degree a personal and chance production: priest's or prior's or abbot's liturgical handbook it doubtless was, but it appears to have been at the same time his common-place book'.[23]

14

We now turn our attention once more to the texts of this renowned manuscript. But first a word needs to be said about the method of exposition which we have adopted. It would have been possible to present the results of our enquiry in a systematic way, giving in turn the distinct Irish, Spanish, Gallican and Italian elements that went into the making of the book. But this method has not been chosen, and systematic considerations are reserved for the concluding chapter in each part of our study. The method chosen, a more analytical and lapidary one, was suggested by the nature of the manuscript and alone could do justice to its contents. It is not a homogeneous book but a collection of the most varied and disparate units, each of which had its own history before its incorporation into the manuscript. This is evidently true of the hymns, but it is not less true of the collects; the latter are arranged in series, each of which has its own characteristics differentiating it from all the others. The scribes of the Antiphonary copied these hymns and sets of collects as they found them, written apparently on distinct *libelli*. Generally speaking, there is no internal connection between these distinct units, and they will be considered separately in distinct chapters. As a result, there will be little or no connection, in the first two parts of our study, between one chapter and the next, but an attempt will be made to remedy this inconvenience in the concluding chapters.

PART I

THE HYMNS OF THE ANTIPHONARY

CHAPTER ONE

EARLY IRISH VERSE

Many hymns of the early Irish Church have been preserved in two eleventh-century manuscripts of the Irish *Liber Hymnorum*.[1] They were composed in Latin and Irish for the liturgy and piety of early Christian Ireland during the course of about four hundred years. In the two manuscripts referred to, which are antiquarian rather than liturgical in character, each hymn is prefaced by an introduction which speaks of the occasion which prompted its composition. These prefaces are largely legendary and little reliance can be placed on their attribution of certain hymns to well-known early authorities such as St Hilary, St Secundinus or St Columcille. Nevertheless, some of the hymns have a great antiquity, among them the *Altus Prosator* attributed to St Columcille[2] and the *Amra Choluim Chille*, or 'Eulogy of Columcille', attributed to Dallán Forgaill,[3] chief of the Irish poets and a contemporary of the saint. Other hymns are of special interest as showing the development of Latin versification in Ireland, a development which reached its perfection in the eighth century with Colmán mac Murchon's hymn to St Michael, *In trinitate spes mea*,[4] and especially with Cúchuimne's hymn in praise of the Blessed Virgin, *Cantemus in omni die*.[5]

For the early period, that is, roughly the first hundred years of Hiberno-Latin versification, we are largely indebted to the Antiphonary of Bangor. Of the dozen hymns it contains, only two occur again in the *Liber Hymnorum*, namely, *Hymnum dicat turba fratrum* and *Audite omnes amantes*, the two most popular and widely attested hymns of the early Irish Church. A few of the hymns are found also in other manuscripts, as we shall see; others occur only in the Antiphonary, a fact that gives a special importance to its witness for the early period. We shall, therefore, study all these hymns of the Antiphonary in detail and endeavour to discover their several sources of origin, inspiration and thought, and to set in clearer light the inclination and capacity of the Irish for verse as the favoured medium of expression.

The Antiphonary is characterized by an abundance of verse. The twelve hymns which it contains deal with a variety of subjects in a variety of metres. There are two hymns, mainly narrative, about the life of Christ; one on the dogma of the Trinity; three in praise of particular saints, and one in praise of the martyrs in general; a communion hymn; a hymn for the blessing of the paschal candle; two hymns in praise of Bangor and its abbots; and, finally, a hymn for the office of midnight, this one imported from the continent. Besides, there is a great number of rhythmical collects and antiphons for the daily hours and for the various parts of the morning office. This wide variety was to continue to characterize Irish hymnody in the centuries after the composition of the Antiphonary, and the Irish preference for verse was not without influence in the subsequent development of the liturgy in the Franco-Germanic world.

The urge for Latin versification was not an entirely new development attributable to the introduction of Christianity and the beginnings of the monastic movement. It was, rather, the co-natural expression in the new Latin dress of the native literary tradition of pre-Christian Ireland. The native discipline of learning was transmitted orally, and its custodians formed a special learned class, the *filid* (seers or poets), who were honoured and respected by all because of the divine gifts that were theirs by heredity.[6] They were masters of the entire complex of native learning, comprising history and heroic tales, genealogy, topography, and law. Much of this material was formulated in verse to facilitate memory and oral transmission. The *fili* would not only retain the ancient laws, sagas and heroic tales. His long years of training would enable him to be a competent poet in his own right, able to compose such things as eulogies in honour of his patron, the king, and satires against his enemies. The introduction of the Latin alphabet in the fifth century and its adoption by the Order of Poets and the law schools as the new vernacular alphabet resulted in the first written Irish literature in the sixth century. In certain versified sections of the law tracts and genealogies, as well as in certain other fragments of poems, we still possess some of this earliest written verse.

We shall see in the course of our study that these early vernacular verse-forms have been imitated in certain Latin compositions included in the Antiphonary. The structure of this verse has still not been fully explained, but at least we know that it was an accentual type of verse; it consisted of certain 'rhythmical patterns' and used plentiful alliteration as a means of ornamentation and for binding phrases together.[7] The Irish poets discovered the rich possibilities of rhyme and stanzaic division soon after the introduction of Latin literature, and they exploited these possibilities in quite an original and masterly way in their accentual poetry.[8] Then from the seventh century onwards the poets introduced a new structural principle for Irish poetry. Based on syllable counting rather than on accent or stress, this principle was a further imitation of the structure of Latin syllabic or so-called rhythmical verse. It continued to be used in Ireland for a thousand years in a great variety of metres, always embellished with alliteration and rhyme. The ancient accentual principle continued to be used as well, at least until the ninth century.

The early hostility of the learned class of *filid* to the new Latin learning was gradually giving way to a more positive attitude. Soon there were noblemen and *filid* in the monasteries and through monastic education there were learned Christians in the highest ranks of society. The integration of the old and new orders was the special achievement of the sixth and seventh centuries and it is vividly illustrated in the person of St

Columcille (d. 597), nobleman and poet; in the *Amra* composed in his honour we meet the old accentual verse put at the service of the new order of Christianity. From the seventh century onwards the monks set about the task of recording the traditional body of learning and setting it in the context of Christian history.[9] The monastic movement not only gave a new impetus to scholarly work in Latin and Irish, but it also greatly influenced the emergence of a new lyrical and personal type of poetry. Many examples of this lyrical poetry, which includes nature poetry and poems of solitude and exile, have come down to us in the manuscripts composed and copied in the monasteries.[10] But the great task of the versifiers lay in the recording or original composition of the law tracts, genealogies, calendars of saints, even works of history. Since prose was not held in great esteem in the Irish tradition, the old and the new types of verse were used as the favoured literary medium for every subject thought worthy of study.[11]

The extensive use of verse in the Antiphonary is, therefore, a reflection of the importance attached to verse in Ireland as the privileged medium of literary expression for every subject. Among the hymns we find the use of various kinds of metre for narrative, dogmatic, doxological and lyrical purposes; here also the native eulogy is found in a new Latin dress, in the *Audite* panegyrics in honour of St Patrick, St Comgall and St Camelacus. Many of the collects themselves have been imposed in verse. And in both hymns and collects we will find echoes of the old rhythmical, alliterative type of verse, which continued to be used along with the new syllabic metres until the end of the Old Irish period.

Only two hymns in the Antiphonary are written in quantitative metre, *Hymnum dicat turba fratrum* and *Ignis creator igneus*. The others may be termed rhythmical, in the various senses of this word.[12] We will now consider each of the hymns in turn, with a view to explaining or illustrating their origin and content and placing them in the general context of Latin hymnody.[13] Observations on their liturgical use will generally be reserved for the third part of our study, where we will be dealing expressly with the office at Bangor.

CHAPTER TWO

HYMNUM DICAT TURBA FRATRUM

We begin with the first hymn transcribed in the Antiphonary and also the most famous. Written in quantitative metre, trochaic tetrameter catalectic, it is one of two hymns in our manuscript which have the life of Christ as their theme. The *Hymnum dicat* has come down to us in ten manuscripts dating from the seventh to the thirteenth century; for the purpose of our study we will use the text of A. Feder's critical edition.[1] In the Antiphonary (AB 2), the hymn is entitled *Ymnum Sancti Hilari de Christo*; five other manuscripts also attribute it to Hilary (of Poitiers), as does Hincmar of Rheims (802–882) when on two occasions he cites a number of verses from it in his work *De una et non trina deitate*.[2] The external evidence for its attribution to Hilary is, therefore, quite strong. But the manuscript tradition is either exclusively Irish or at least connected with an Irish centre of influence, so that internal evidence for or against Hilary's authorship is of decisive importance here.

Since the last century, scholars have been divided in their judgement as to the place of origin and authorship of this hymn. Chief among those who ascribed it to Hilary, some with certainty, others with some probability, were: Bernard and Atkinson,[3] C. Blume,[4] A.S. Walpole,[5] A. Feder,[6] and J.F. Kennedy.[7] They argued:

(a) The manuscript tradition is exclusively in favour of Hilary.

(b) The metre of the hymn is the same as in Hilary's *Adae carnis gloriosae*.[8]

(c) There are a few instances of parallel rhyming expressions within a single line in both *Hymnum dicat* and *Adae carnis*:

Gaudet aris, gaudet templis, gaudet sanie victimae,
Gaudet falsis, gaudet stupris, gaudet belli sanguine.
(*Adae carnis* 3: AH 50, 8)
Multa parvus, multa adultus signa fecit caelitus.
Pane quino, pisce bino quinque pascit milia.
Galli cantus, galli plausus proximum sentit diem.
(*Hymnum dicat* 20, 27, 67)

(d) The word *falsa* is used in both as a noun, with the meaning 'falsehoods':

GAUDET FALSIS (*Adae carnis* 3)

FALSIS GRASSATUR (*Hymnum dicat* 34)

(e) The hymn is certainly not Irish — there is nothing like it in metre or language in the whole extent of Irish hymnody.[9] Yet its popularity in Ireland was rivalled only by the hymn *Audite omnes* in honour of St Patrick.[10] This popularity can best be explained on the basis of the genuine authorship of Hilary.

In spite of these authorities and the arguments they have put forward, opposition to Hilarian authorship has grown steadily, and today there is no one to my knowledge who upholds it. The genuineness of the attribution to Hilary was already denied by F.E. Warren,[11] who regarded it as a fifth- or sixth-century continental production. Then W. Meyer put forward what he considered decisive arguments against authenticity based on the metre,[12] and his argument has been developed and expanded by M. Simonetti.[13] They argue:

(a) The manuscript attributions to Hilary are inconclusive. Many unreliable ascriptions are found in early Irish sources, and it is noteworthy that all the manuscripts of the hymn are Irish or connected with Irish tradition. The attribution to Hilary is understandable in view of his renown as a hymn-writer. But here as elsewhere in doubtful cases the argument has to be decided on internal evidence.

(b) The hymn cannot have been written by Hilary, and this for metrical reasons. The chief difference is the presence in *Adae carnis*, as a constant structural feature, of a secondary caesura in the first half-line; this is not found in *Hymnum dicat*.[14] There are also some breaches of quantity, which are surprising in view of the author's good acquaintance with the old quantitative metre, especially his observance of the dipody law, the use of elision and avoidance of hiatus. For these reasons, Meyer assigned it to the fifth or sixth century, and did not exclude the possibility that 'this Irish hymn'[15] may actually have been written in Ireland.

(c) Simonetti argues that the metrical difference pointed out by Meyer is only one element in the fundamental stylistic difference between *Hymnum dicat* and the three authentic hymns of Hilary. It is not a question merely of a secondary metrical difference between *Hymnum dicat* and *Adae carnis*, but a matter of an entirely different *usus scribendi* in the authentic hymns of Hilary. The difference is such that it is unthinkable that he be the author of *Hymnum dicat*.[16]

(d) The comparison made by Feder between the Arezzo hymns and the writings of Hilary revealed so many agreements of language and ideas that these hymns must be accepted as the genuine compositions of Hilary.[17] There are no such points of agreement between the *Hymnum dicat* and the works of Hilary; the few parallel instances of rhyming phrases are not sufficient to prove the authorship of Hilary in this case.

These arguments of Meyer and Simonetti are conclusive and they are accepted by recent writers on the subject. But disagreement continues with regard to assigning it a place and time of origin. Simonetti argues, on the basis of the manuscript tradition and especially from what he considers as the use of ritornello (*Hymnum dicat* 71–72), in favour of an Irish origin.[18] He rightly regards as insufficient and aprioristic the argument against an Irish origin based on the quantitative nature of the metre; he points out that *Ignis creator igneus* (AB 9) is both quantitative and Irish, and he also regards *Sancti venite* (AB 8) as substantially quantitative.[19]

More recent writers, however, do not accept Simonetti's conclusion, because of the absence of any Irish characteristic of language or style. J. Szövérffy, following W. Bulst, regards it as a Gallican hymn, written probably in the fifth century.[20] The attribution of the hymn to Hilary may, according to this view, be regarded as a sign of its foreign origin and a factor which helps to explain its popularity in Ireland. The present writer's conclusion regarding the origin of the hymn will be given in due course. I would simply draw attention here to a more important factor in its popularity, that is, the fine quality of the hymn itself – *ille hymnus pulcherrimus*, in Bede's words[21] – and the indubitable fact that it struck a sympathetic chord in the Irish spirit.

Hymnum dicat is one of a number of early hymns which celebrate the life of Christ from his birth to his death and glorification.[22] Three of these hymns are closely related: both *Hymnum dicat* and Fortunatus' *Pange lingua* drew inspiration from the hymn of Prudentius (*Cath.* IX), and there is some trace of direct contact between them as well. All three are composed in trochaic tetrameter catalectic, with two lines to each stanza in *Hymnum dicat* and three lines to each stanza in the other two. Again, the author of *Ab ore verbum*, a Spanish hymn of uncertain date, was well acquainted with both *Pange lingua* and *Hymnum dicat*. The Irish *Praecamur patrem* is quite singular and will be considered separately later. But, before we begin a more detailed analysis of *Hymnum dicat*, we will compare it in summary fashion to each of the other hymns we have mentioned.

(a) *A solis ortus*

There is a good measure of agreement in both hymns regarding the events spoken about, as might be expected in hymns dealing with the life of Christ. But there is no direct contact whatever in thought or language between the two; the metre of *A solis ortus* is iambic dimeter. There is a greater wealth of detail in *Hymnum dicat*, even though Sedulius draws a fuller picture of the nativity scene (st.6–7; this receives one line – 13 – in *Hymnum dicat*) and he speaks at much greater length about the various miracles of Christ (st.12–18).

(b) *Cath.* IX

Both begin in parallel fashion with an invitation to praise, but then they go their several ways in commemorating the life of Christ. Prudentius goes directly from the nativity scene (19–21, followed by a renewed invitation to praise: 22–27) to the miracle of Cana (28–30), whereas our hymn devotes some space (14–22) to the events leading from the birth of Christ to the beginning of his public mission. The miracles of Christ are treated of at length by Prudentius (28–69), but only very briefly in *Hymnum dicat* (20–28), which, however, gives much more space to narrating the details of the passion, death and resurrection of Christ (31–48). The descent of Christ is fully treated by Prudentius (82–103), but is not mentioned in

Hymnum dicat. The conclusions again have something in common.

(c) *Pange lingua*

Fortunatus is more concerned with the theological implications of redemption and with his lyrical praise of the cross than with narrative detail about the life of Christ. When he gives some details, for example, when he describes the infant in the manger (st.5), there is no agreement with *Hymnum dicat.* But there is one phrase which is quite singular and common to both, as we shall see.

(d) *Ab ore verbum*

Following two introductory strophes on the Incarnation, *Ab ore* goes on to the narrative and theology of the passion and from there on it agrees quite closely with *Hymnum dicat,* not only in the order of events, but sometimes also in expression. Even though *Ab ore verbum* was formally inspired by *Pange lingua,*[23] it has a closer material agreement with *Hymnum dicat,* as may be seen from the following comparison.

	Hymnum dicat	*Ab ore*
Sufferings and trial of Jesus	37–38	3
Crucifixion and death	39–42	4–5
Events after crucifixion	43–44	6
Descent into hell		7
Burial of Jesus	45–46	
Soldiers are terrified	47–50	8
Resurrection and meeting with women	51–56	9–10
Meeting with disciples	57–58	11
Gift of the Spirit and commission	59–64	12
Return of Christ and conclusion	65–72	13–23

The author of *Ab ore verbum* was, apparently, familiar with *Hymnum dicat*; he followed its order and drew on some of its expressions, as indeed he also did from other sources.[24] This is not the only evidence for the presence and knowledge of *Hymnum dicat* in Spain, as we shall see presently. We can now proceed to a more detailed study of the hymn.

The hymn opens with an invitation to praise Christ the King:

hymnum dicat turba fratrum, hymnum cantus personet;
Christo regi concinentes laudem demus debitam.

What is meant exactly by *turba fratrum,* the faithful in general or a monastic community, is hard to say; the expression could mean either.[25] As we noted, Prudentius began his *Cath.*IX in a similar way:

Da, puer, plectrum, choraeis ut CANAM fidelibus
dulce carmen et melodum, gesta Christi insignia.
Hunc camena nostra solum pangat, hunc LAUDET lyra.

CHRISTUS est, quem REX sacerdos adfuturum protinus
infulatus CONCINEBAT voce corda et tympano,
spiritum caelo influentem per medullas hauriens.

22. Psallat altitudo caeli, psallite omnes angeli,
quidquid est virtutis usquam psallat in LAUDEM Dei,
nulla linguarum silescat, vox et omnis CONSONET.

The response of our author to his opening invitation takes the form of a collection of lyrical expressions of praise in that litanic form so frequently encountered in Irish prayers:

3. Tu dei de corde verbum, tu via, tu veritas,
Iesse virga tu vocaris, te leonem legimus.

Dextra patris, mons et agnus, angularis tu lapis,
sponsus idem vel columba, flamma, pastor, ianua.

Such a concentration of honorific titles for Christ is rare in Latin hymnody, but it agrees with the Irish liking for litanic-type prayers in which consecutive discourse is abandoned in favour of brief descriptive phrases.[26] The idea of *verbum de corde patris* is favoured by Prudentius; it is found in his Cath.IX 10:

corde natus ex parentis ante mundi exordium,

and is of frequent occurrence in his poems; it was also used by Venantius Fortunatus.[27] All the titles found for Christ in our hymn are, with the exception of two (*veritas, flamma*), found also among the titles which constitute the hymn *De epithetis salvatoris nostri* attributed to the fifth-century Gallican poet Orientius, but many more are also found there.[28]

The narrative proper now begins;the point of departure is the temporal birth of the eternal Christ, by whom all things were created:

7. In prophetis inveniris nostro natus saeculo,
ante saecla tu fuisti factor primi saeculi.

Factor caeli, terrae factor, congregator tu maris,
omniumque tu creator, quae pater nasci iubet.

The antithesis between the eternal and temporal nature of Christ, as well as his work in creation, are constant themes in hymnody; for example, Prudentius,*Cath.*IX 10–14:

Corde natus ex parentis ANTE MUNDI EXORDIUM,
alfa et O cognominatus, ipse fons et clausula
OMNIUM quae sunt fuerunt quaeque post futura sunt.
Ipse iussit, et CREATA. dixit ipse et FACTA sunt
TERRA CAELUM fossa PONTI trina rerum machina.

Again, the theme is found in Hilary, *Ante saecula qui manens* 1 – 2 (AH 50, 4):

ANTE SAECULA qui manens
semperque nate, semper ut est pater,
namque te sine quomodo
dici, ni pater est, quod pater sit potest?

Bis nobis genite deus,
Christe, dum innato nasceris a deo,
vel dum corporeum et deum
mundo te genuit virgo puerpera.

26

The same theme is found in one of the hymns used at Arles in the time of
St Caesarius, *Rex aeterne domine* (AH 51, 5):

Rex aeterne domine,
rerum CREATOR OMNIUM,
qui eras ANTE SAECULA
semper cum patre filius.

The theme returns in some Spanish hymns,[29] but the text of Prudentius
remains closest to that of *Hymnum dicat*, with its *fons omnium quae sunt,
creata, facta, terra, caelum, fossa ponti.*

The events of the incarnation, nativity, the visit of the Magi are now
mentioned in very simple terms:

11. Virginis receptus membris Gabrielis nuntio
crescit alvus prole sancta, nos monemur credere

Rem novam nec ante visam, virginem puerperam:
tunc magi stellam secuti primi adorant parvulum.

This passage is also a reflection of Prudentius, *Cath.*IX 19–20:

O beatus ortus ille, VIRGO CUM PUERPERA
edidit nostram salutem feta sancto spiritu.

Another Spanish hymn, *Sacer octavarum dies* (AH 25, 67; AH 27, 117),
speaks of the nativity in similar terms:

2. Spiritu COMPLETUR ALVUS incorruptae virginis
pariens quae mansit caelebs VIRGOQUE PUERPERA;
illibatam genetricem proles casta eligit.

But the theme of the virginal conception and birth is frequently found in
hymns,[30] although comparison with other texts reveals no striking
similarity of language.

The hymn goes on to speak of the gifts offered by the magi, the jealousy
of Herod, the martydom of the innocents, and the flight into Egypt. The
language is simple and easy-flowing as the narrative proceeds and there is
nothing worthy of note by way of comparison.

The return from Egypt to Nazareth is followed by a reference to many
miracles worked by Jesus as an infant, doubtless reflecting some
apocryphal infancy Gospel. The next two stanzas describe in general terms
the miracles or signs worked by Christ:

21. Quae latent et quae leguntur coram multis testibus,
praedicans caeleste regnum dicta factis adprobat.

Debiles facit vigere, caecos luce inluminat,
verbis purgat leprae morbum, mortuos resuscitat.

The phrase used here to describe the nature of Jesus' preaching, *dicta factis
adprobat*, returns in a Spanish hymn for St Caecilia, *Incliti festum pudoris*
(AH 27, 140):

5. Sed beata virgo FACTIS DICTA prorsus COMPROBANS.

We shall see that the same idea occurs a number of times in the hymn in
honour of St Patrick, *Audite omnes* (AB 13), in describing that saint's

27

ministry. Two expressions in the second stanza cited above seem to have been borrowed from Prudentius, *Cath*.IX:

47. Lazarum IUBET VIGERE reddito spiramine.
66. PURGAT AD PRAECEPTA CHRISTI crassa quaeque obstacula.

The phrase *caecos luce inluminat* may have been inspired by St Ambrose, *Hic est dies verus dei* (AH 50, 16):

2.Fidem refundans perfidis
CAECOSQUE VISU ILLUMINANS.

The next stanza, which treats of the miracle of Cana, has been regarded by some as an interpolation, because of certain metrical faults and obscurity of language.[31] If it is an interpolation, it must have been an early one, because it is found in all the manuscripts:

25. Vinum quod deerat hydriis, mutari aquam iubet,
nuptiis mero retentis propinando poculo.[32]

Pane quino, pisce bino quinque pascit milia
et refert fragmenta cenae ter quaternis corbibus.

This last stanza was probably influenced by Prudentius, *Cath* IX 58–60:

Ferte qualis TER QUATERNIS ferculorum FRAGMINA!
Adfatim REFERTA iam sunt adcubantium milia
quinque panibus peresis et gemellis piscibus.

The word *corbes* was used by Prudentius instead of *fercula* to describe the same miracle in another poem.[33]

The author of our hymn now leads us into the narrative of the Passion. The betrayal by Judas is followed by the capture and trial of Jesus:

33. Innocens captus tenetur nec repugnans ducitur,
sistitur, falsis grassatur offerendus Pontio.

This stanza was used in one well-known formulary of the Spanish *preces*, which also begins, like our hymn, by enumerating some titles of Christ:

Preces. Ad te redemptor ... P. *Et miserere.*[34]

1. Dextera patris, lapis angularis,
via salutis, ianua caelestis,
ablue nostri maculas delicti.

4. INNOCENS CAPTUS, NEC REPUGNANS DUCTUS,
testibus FALSIS, impiis damnatus,
quos redemisti tu conserva Christe.

The word *sistitur* of our hymn is also found in Prudentius, *Cath*.IX 42:

SISTITUR rivus cruore qui fluebat perpeti,

and in the sense of 'standing one's trial' in Prudentius, *Perist*.II 53:

Laurentium SISTI iubet.

The trial and suffering of Jesus are described in a few words, which will later be developed in *Ab ore verbum*.[35] The crucifixion follows:

39. Scandere crucem iubetur innocens pro noxiis,
morte carnis, quam gerebat, mortem vincit omnium.

Tum deum clamore magno patrem pendens invocat;
mors secuta membra Christi laxat stricta vincula.

Vela templi scissa pendunt, nox obscurat saeculum;
excitantur de sepulchris dudum clausa corpora.

We may note the use of the word *scandere* in Prudentius,[36] and a few
Spanish instances of the expression *mortem morte vincere*.[37] The third
stanza seems to have influenced the author of *Ab ore verbum prolatum*.[38]
But the most interesting line here is 42, which is connected linguistically
and thematically with certain lines of the *Pange Lingua* (AH 50, 71):

5. Vagit infans inter arta conditus praesaepia,
MEMBRA pannis involuta virgo mater adligat,
et pedes manusque crura STRICTA pingit fascia.

9. Flecte ramos, arbor alta, tensa LAXA viscera,
et rigor lentescat ille, quem dedit nativitas ,
ut superni MEMBRA regis mite tendas stipite.

Because of the correspondence of *laxat stricta vincula* and *tensa laxa
viscera*, V. Buzna suggested that perhaps Venantium Fortunatus is the
author of *Hymnum dicat*.[39] But if he were the author, he would surely have
avoided the few metrical errors which are found in our hymn. Besides,
Fortunatus, even if he did borrow the theme from another source, has fully
mastered it. The expression in *Hymnum dicat* is somewhat
cumbersome,with two objects for the verb *laxat*: *mors laxat membra, stricta
vincula*. This has the appearance of being a borrowed expression rather
than an original one. Fortunatus, of course, may have borrowed in turn
from *Hymnum dicat*. But since the expression is so singular, and
Fortunatus appears to be the more original of the two, there is some
probability that the author of *Hymnum dicat* depends here on Fortunatus
and that he has borrowed from him a theme which was given a more
natural and convincing expression in the *Pange lingua*. If this is the case, it
gives us a *terminus a quo* for the composition of the *Hymnum dicat*, that is,
the end of the sixth century.

The burial of the body of Jesus by Joseph (vv. 45–46) is followed by the
order given by Annas to guard the tomb:

47. Milites servare corpus Annas princeps praecipit,
ut videret, si probaret Christus, quod spoponderat.

Angelum dei trementes veste amictum candida,
quo candore claritatis vellus vicit sericum.

The rare word *spopondere* occurs in Prudentius, *Cath*.IX 26:

quem profetarum fideles paginae SPOPONDERANT.

And the phrase *candore vincere vellus* surely reflects Prudentius,
Quicumque Christum quaeritis (*Cath*.XII 5):

Haec stella, quae solis rotam
VINCIT DECORE ac lumine.

The narrative continues with the resurrection of Christ (vv. 51–52), his apparition to the women, whom he salutes and fills with joy (53–54), his apparition to the disciples (57–58), to whom he gives the precepts of the law and the divine Spirit (59–60). The Holy Spirit is described as *trinitatis vinculum*, an idea I have not been able to trace to any patristic source.[40] The commission given to the apostles to go and baptize all nations (61–62) introduces the conclusion,which speaks of the life of the baptized and their expectation of eternal life with Christ. It also shows that the hymn was meant to be sung in the early morning:

> 63. Mystica fide revelat tinctos sancto spiritu,
> fonte tinctos, innovatos, filios factos dei.
>
> Ante lucem, turba fratrum, concinamus gloriam,
> qua docemur nos futuros sempiterno saeculo.

These verses bring to mind the words of Cyprian, when he urges his people to pray during the night. He says that in Christ we are always in the day and should always pray, even at night, which for us is also the day. He continues:

> Per Dei indulgentiam recreati spiritaliter et renati imitemur
> quod futuri sumus: habituri in regno sine interventu noctis solum
> diem, sic nocte quasi in luce vigilemus; oraturi semper et acturi
> gratias Deo, hic quoque orare et gratias agere non desinamus.[41]

The final three stanzas have been regarded by some as being either wholly or partly later interpolations.[42] They speak of the morning prayer by way of a comparison: just as the cock-crow announces the coming day, so the *turba fratrum* proclaims in song and prayer the future life, God's majesty, and the reign of Christ:

> 67. Galli cantus, galli plausus proximum sentit diem,
> nos cantantes et precantes, quae futura credimus.
>
> Inmensamque maiestatem concinamus iugiter,
> ante lucem nuntiemus Christum regem saeculo.
>
> Ante lucem decantantes Christo regi domino
> et, qui in illum recte credunt, regnaturi cum eo.[43]

The doxology, found in all the manuscripts save one, is a rhythmical 'ambrosian' stanza (4 x 8pp), and it is an obvious interpolation:

> Gloria patri ingenito, gloria unigenito
> simul cum sancto spiritu in sempiterna saecula.

The same doxology is used at the conclusion of two other hymns in the Antiphonary: *Ignis creator igneus* (AB 9), written in iambic dimeter, and *Mediae noctis tempus est* (AB 10), a rhythmical version of iambic dimeter (4 x 8pp). The doxology is in place only after the latter hymn and in Blume's edition it is found at the conclusion of this hymn (AH 51, 4), even though it is not found in the earliest manuscripts, apart from the Antiphonary, and is given only in two of the later manuscripts (Farfa, *saec.* 10–11).

Otherwise, the use of this doxology is peculiar to Spain, where it is found after a number of hymns:

(a) *Te lucis auctor personant* (AH 27, 87)

This hymn is found in one tenth-century Spanish MS and in a number of non-Spanish MSS (*saec.* 10–12). In the Spanish MS and in one of the others (*Cod. Trev.* 1404, *saec.* 10) the doxology is:

Gloria patri ingenito, gloria (semperque T) unigenito,
una (simul T) cum sancto spiritu in sempiterna saecula.

Blume thought it doubtful whether the hymn is Spanish at all.

(b) *Sol angelorum respice* (AH 27, 111)

This hymn is found in one tenth-century Spanish MS and in Mo Br. Blume thought that this hymn 'ist sicherlich spätere Zuthat bzw. Entlehnung'. The doxology is given in Br and it is identical with that found in AB, except that it has *una cum* instead of *simul cum*.

(c) *Christe qui lux es et dies* (AH 51, 21–22; AH 27, 23)

This hymn is found in numerous MSS, but only three give our doxology: the ILH, two Spanish MSS and Mo Br. A number of different doxologies are given in the other MSS. The Irish and Spanish reading agree, except that once again the ILH has *simul cum* instead of *una cum*. This agreement is all the more interesting in view of the fact that the hymn is not Spanish or Irish, but Gallican.

The doxology is, therefore, apart from the three exceptions noted (two Farfa MSS and *Cod.Trev.*), peculiar to Spanish and Irish texts. The Spanish characters of the doxology is witnessed to by the expression *Pater ingenitus*, which was a great favourite in Spain and was often used in conjunction with it correlative *Filius unigenitus*.[44] The doxology is probably of Spanish origin and it may have come to Ireland attached to one or other of the hymns which contain it in the Irish and Spanish sources, that is, *Christe qui lux es et dies* or *Mediae noctis tempus est*. Then, in Ireland, the doxology was erroneously attached to two hymns composed in quantitive metre, *Ignis creator igneus* and *Hymnum dicat*.

We shall now make some further observations regarding the origin of *Hymnum dicat*. Until recently, I accepted the Gallican origin of this hymn as advocated by most authorities on the subject, even though I would date it to the end of the sixth century rather than to the fifth. But I gradually began to realize that there is no evidence to support this view, that, in fact, it is a typical instance of what I have come to regard as a Gallican 'prejudice' regarding the origins of the Irish liturgy. Its Irish origin has been rejected on the grounds that nothing like it in metre, style or language can be found in the whole field of Hiberno-Latin versification. This objection to the Irish origin of *Hymnum dicat* is ill-founded. It does not take sufficient cognizance of a well-documented fact, namely, that the Irish were quite capable of producing a singular work of art, that, indeed, their genius manifested itself precisely in individuality, in the unexpected, in the pursuit of 'the strange, the odd, the rare'.[45] The absence from our hymn of such Irish symptoms as rhyme and alliteration need cause no surprise in the case of a sixth-century work; they are equally absent from *Sancti venite* and *Audite omnes amantes*. the Irish origin of which there can be no doubt.

The manuscript tradition is already a significant pointer to the Irish origin of *Hymnum dicat*. Apart from this, the Irish authorship of the hymn is arguable from the manner in which it fits in so well with what we know of the general situation of Irish monasticism. Other hymns in the Antiphonary show that the Irish monks were anxious to master the traditional Latin metres, to imitate the form and style of such a master as Ambrose and to apply the traditional metres to new purposes. Is it not entirely in character for them to draw inspiration from Prudentius' hymn on the life of Christ, to imitate its structure and content? It seems to me beyond doubt that *Hymnum dicat* is a hymn inspired by that of Prudentius, a work of imitation, yet not slavish but free, creative and original throughout.

Furthermore, the summary comparison we made above[46] between *Hymnum dicat* and other early hymns on the life of Christ revealed that our hymn is characterized by a wealth of detail coupled with the absence of elaborate and sustained description of any one scene or episode. The syntax is simple and direct, the events of the life of Christ are compressed into a few words, and we get the impression that the author feared that the poetic impact would be lost by further elaboration. In illustration, I quote that section of the hymn which goes from the Incarnation through to the public life of Christ (vv. 11–24):

Virginis receptus membris Gabrielis nuntio
crescit alvus prole sancta, nos monemus credere

Rem novam nec ante visam, virginem puerperam.[47]
tunc magi stellam secuti primi adorant parvulum,

Offerentes tus et aurum digna regi munera.
mox Herodi nuntiatum; invidens potentiae

Tum iubet parvos necari, turbam fecit martyrum.
fertur infans occulendus, Nili flumen quo fluit.

Qui refertur post Herodem nutriendus Nazareth.[48]
multa parvus,[49] multa adultus signa fecit caelitus,

Quae latent et quae leguntur coram multis testibus,
praedicans caeleste regnum dicta factis adprobat.

Debiles facit vigers, caecos luce inluminat,
verbis purgat leprae morbum, mortuos recusitat.

Not all Hiberno – Latin verse is distinguished by such economy of expression. But this hymn has a quality of directness and simplicity which make it comparable to early Irish vernacular lyrical poetry. Kuno Meyer expressed, in a classical statement, the qualities of the nature poetry of the Celts:

In Nature Poetry the Gaelic muse may vie with that of any other nation. Indeed, these poems occupy a unique position in the literature of the world. To seek out and watch and love Nature, in its tiniest phenomena as in its grandest, was given to no people so early and so fully as to the Celts. Many hundreds of Gaelic and Welsh poems testify to this fact. It is a characteristic of these poems that in none of them do you get an elaborate or sustained description of any scene or scenery, but rather a succession of pictures and images which the poet, like an impressionist, calls up before us by light and skilful touches. Like the Japanese, the Celts were always quick to take an artistic hint; they avoid the obvious and the commonplace; the half-said thing to them is is dearest.[50]

The author of *Hymnum dicat* also prefered the concrete to the abstract, he wrote 'a succession of pictures and images' rather than a sustained description of any scene and he also shows his ability in 'light and skilful touches'.

Furthermore, the subject of the hymn is not without significance in forming a balanced judgement of its origin. The kingship of Christ was one of the favourite themes of early Irish piety,[51] and here we have a hymn in praise of Christ the King.[52]

In conclusion, I believe that *Hymnum dicat* was written by an Irishman at the end of the sixth century. Our analysis of the hymn has not revealed any striking parallel with other Irish works, but the subject-matter and style, such as the litanic character of the opening stanzas of praise as well as the concrete and simple language of the narrative, are such as could quite conceivably come from an Irish author. Arguments against Irish authorship based on consideration of metre, language and style are unconvincing. The Irish were willing and prepared to learn the traditional Latin metres, both quantitative and rhythmical, and to use them for purposes either long established or entirely new in the area of Latin hymnody.

Prudentius had written a hymn on the life of Christ in trochaic tetrameter catalectic. An Irishman got to know this hymn and liked it so much that he decided to write a similar work, one that would be at once simpler and more in keeping with the needs and aspirations of Irish prayer. The author was also probably acquainted with certain other hymns of Prudentius, he knew the *Pange lingua* of Fortunatus (written *c.* 570) and he appears to have been influenced by at least one particular phrase of St Ambrose. Although he did borrow occasional ideas and terms from Prudentius, his chief source was the Gospel narrative itself. It was on its basis that he fashioned his hymn in a language that is generally free-flowing, simple and original throughout. Only at the beginning and end, influenced probably by Prudentius, did he give full lyrical expression to his sentiments of praise for Christ, whose life and signs form the main subject of the hymn.

The popularity of the hymn in Ireland testifies to the signal success of the author; the hymn became the favourite expression of Irish piety and prayer of Christ the King. They, or perhaps the author himself, gave St Hilary the honour of writing it, and no doubt this too contributed to its authority and popularity. Irish monks propagated it in Britain and on the continent from the seventh century onwards. It was known and cited by

Hincmar of Rheims and by Bede, and its presence was felt in Spain possibly as late as the tenth century. Where precisely it was written, whether at Bangor or Luxeuil or elsewhere, we cannot say. But it was a centre in which the Latin culture of the Church had made a decided impact[53] and it was written by a man who was at once a scholar, a poet, and one whose faith and piety were rooted in the New Testament. Written for the morning prayer of the *turba fratrum*, the hymn was to become one of their greatest treasures for all occasions and situations.

CHAPTER THREE

AUDITE OMNES AMANTES AND AUDITE BONUM EXEMPLUM

We will take these two hymns[1] together at this point, for a number of reasons. Both are rhythmical imitations of the trochaic tetrameter catalectic; in other words, their quantitative model was a hymn like *Hymnum dicat*, if not that hymn itself. Secondly, they are two of the oldest Irish hymns, if we can take the absence in them of any use of rhyme as an indication of their antiquity.[2] And, thirdly, they have some claim to be taken together on the grounds of common authorship.

Both hymns imitate the structure of the quantitative model, in as much as:

(a) The lines consist of 8p + 7pp. Some exceptions to this structure, for example (8p + 7p).

Audite omnes 22:
Apostolorum exémplum formamque praebet bónis
Audite bonum 3:
Ieiunus et mansuétus kastus hic servit déo

may mean that the quantitative model was of the classical type, which freely admitted disyllables at the line-ends.[3] But some few disyllabic line-endings are also found in *Hymnum dicat*.[4]

(b) Except for the paroxytone at the caesura, and the proparoxytone at the line – end, all possible varieties of accentuation are found in the rest of the line. This also is an imitation of the quantitative model.[5]

(c) Both frequently commence the lines with a trisyllabic paroxytone word, for example, *Audite*. There is no example of this in *Hymnum dicat* or in any hymn which observed the dipody-law which forbade the use of words like -/-- or --- (three long syllables) to commence the line. Therefore, the model was in our case either a hymn of the irregular archaic type or the imitation of the regular model was imperfect.[6] In this second case, the structural model could again have been *Hymnum dicat*.

We will first take each hymn individually and return later to their relationship.

1. AUDITE OMNES AMANTES

In early Irish literature there are many references and witnesses to the popularity of *Audite omnes*, but they do not date earlier than the seventh century.[7] At that time the Legend of St Patrick was beginning to take shape and our hymn became part of that legend. We are given all the picturesque details of its composition in the ninth-century Irish *Tripartite Life* of St Patrick, and in the eleventh-century prefaces to the hymn in the Irish *Liber Hymnorum*.[8] There the hymn is attributed to St Secundinus, who was an important figure in Irish Church of the fifth century. We know very little with certainty about St Secundinus and the relationship between himself and St Patrick.But the origins and even the precise destination of the hymn *Audite omnes* cannot be discussed without raising the vexed question of the historical Patrick and the historical Secundinus.

Two divergent views are at present held by Patrician scholars in relation to St Patrick. The generally accepted view is that Patrick's apostolate in Ireland dated from A.D. 432–461; that Secundinus, Auxilius and Iserinus were sent to Ireland in 439 as bishops to help Patirck in his mission; that Secundinus died in 447 at the age of seventy-two; that his name was gaelicized to Sechnall and his see reputed to be Domnach Sechnaill, that is, the church (*dominica*) of Sechnall, which became modern Dunshaughlin, in Co. Meath. As a contemporary of St Patrick, he could have written this hymn in his honour. This view is based on the testimony of the ancient Annals.[9]

According to another view, represented today by J. Carney, the 'obvious' reading of the Annals is a fabrication inspired by an apologetic in favour of Armagh and its primacy in the Irish Church. The reason given for this primacy is the foundation of the see by St Patrick, who made it the centre of his apostolate to the Irish. He is, indeed, portrayed as the only apostle of the Irish. But behind this re-writing of history certain traces of the true historical situation remain, and certain inconsistencies and duplications in the sources are explicable in its light. Critical investigation shows that Secundinus was in Ireland before Patrick, that he was bishop of Armagh from A.D. 444, when that see was founded, until his death in 457. The historical Patrick very probably had no connection with Armagh; he came in 456 and died in 493, after a very successful mission in the centre and west of Ireland. It follows that Secundinus could not have written this hymn in praise of Patrick. It was attributed to him as part of the general aim to exalt Patrick and 'to depress Secundinus in the interest of Patrick'.[10] Patrick's coming was put back to 432 so as to give him sole credit for the conversion of the Irish; Secundinus and the other bishops were made his subordinates and Secundinus was represented as having composed a panegyric in praise of the great Apostle of the Irish.

It is sufficient for our purpose to have stated these two divergent views. The tradition of Secundinus' authorship is first witnessed in the Calendar of Oengus, written around A.D. 800.[11] The 'orthodox' school of Patrician scholars has argued that 'there is no valid reason for doubting the authorship of Secundinus',[12] and has marshalled positive arguments in his favour. Others have taken up the suggestion of M. Esposito, who claimed that the hymn 'may, in fact, have been composed at any time between the middle of the fifth and the middle of the seventh centuries'.[13]

36

The arguments in favour of authenticity may be summarized as follows.

(a) The praise of Patrick is not extravagant; when set in the context of Patrick's apostolate in Ireland, it becomes understandable as an enthusiastic defence of Patrick by a friend and associate against the attacks made on Patrick by his enemies at home in Britain. There is ample evidence in Patrick's own writings of the opposition to him and his mission, the contempt with which he was regarded, and the accusations of ignorance, incompetence and vain-glory made against him.[14] Seen in this context, the language is understandable and it is, in fact, sober and restrained by comparison with what is found in the lives of Patrick written from the seventh century onwards.[15]

(b) St Patrick is spoken of throughout as being still alive and references to his eternal reward are in the future tense; this indicates a contemporary author.

(c) 'A fifth century date is suggested also by the language and metre of the hymn, and by the Old Latin biblical text which its author had in his mind'.[16]

The arguments against a fifth-century date are diametrically opposed to the above arguments.

(a) The praises of Patrick are extravagant and contrast so sharply with the realities of Patrick's life, as depicted in his *Confession*,[17] that it is highly unlikely they were written by a contemporary.

(b) The argument based on the present tense used throughout the hymn is unconvincing. It is a 'dramatic expedient',[18] and something similar is found in *Audite bonum exemplum*.

(c) The linguistic connection between the hymn and *Confession* are so close that one must have borrowed from the other. But Patrick was hardly likely to borrow from this extravagant panegyric; moreover, a detailed comparison shows that the *Confession* is the original document.[19]

A point made by MacNeill in favour of the authorship of Secundinus might be used to show that a fifth-century date is very unlikely. He argued[20] that if the hymn is contemporary, and he accepts that it is, it must have been written by one of the band of missionaries who came from overseas to Ireland. It cannot have been written by a native Irishman in the fifth century, when the state of Latin culture must have been rudimentary in the extreme. The missionary in question is, according to unanimous tradition, Secundinus. But is the hymn, in fact, contemporary? With the growth of the monastic movement in the sixth century, Latin began to be cultivated in the native soil of the monastic schools and some of the hymns in the Antiphonary and *Liber Hymnorum* were written in that century. Now, *Audite omnes* is a full-blooded panegyric in the native tradition of eulogy and its author is more likely to have been an Irishman than a foreign missionary. And since it is a highly skillful composition, a sixth-century date, rather than a fifth-century one, is what we should expect for its composition.

Who, then, composed the hymn, if Secundinus did not? Carney has drawn attention to a marginal note in the Book of Armagh which identifies it as *Ymnus Colman Alo*. This note was occasioned by an item in the *Notulae* appended to Tirechán's seventh-century Life of St Patrick in the Book of Armagh. The *Notulae* deal with the 'four honours' of Patrick in Ireland, the third of which is:

Ymnum eius per totum tempus (*scil.* sollemnitatis eius) cantari.[21]

The marginal note referred to identifies *ymnum eius* as *ymnus Colman Alo*. The hymn in question can be none other than *Audite omnes* because it is distinguished from the *Lorica*, or *Canticum eius scotticum*, which is the subject of the fourth honour. Carney has argued[22] that these words, *Ymnus Colman Alo*, can only mean either of two things: that the hymn is one in honour of Colmán Alo, which is evidently not the case here, or that it is a hymn written by Colmán Alo, which must be the sense in this case.[23] When the fiction of the authorship of Secundinus was created in the eighth century, a story was invented to explain the special connection of Colmán with the hymn; he is represented as given to reciting it.[24]

Colmán Alo, a friend and contemporary of St Colmcille, was the founder of the monastery of Lann Eala, from which he got his name Alo (Elo). Like many of his contemporaries, he was esteemed for his sanctity and learning,[25] and his association with the poet and scholar St Colmcille adds a touch of likelihood to Carney's suggestion that he is the author of our hymn. He died *c.* 612, so that if he is the author, the hymn dates from the end of the sixth or the begining of the seventh century.

There are many points of contact in language and ideas betweem *Audite omnes* and the writings of St Patrick, as G.F. Hamilton has shown.[26] Even though this relationship is an established fact, it will not be entirely unprofitable to go over the ground again and make a more detailed comparison than has so far been made. It will appear in this way how far the author went in borrowing from the Patrician documents, what principle guided him in his use of these sources, and what his interests were with regard to his hero.We will quote from the hymn only such verses as appear interesting for our purpose; our quotations from the Patrician documents will be from Bieler's edition.[27]

The hymn is an alphabetical one, with twenty-three stanzas which commence with successive letters of the alphabet, and with four lines to each stanza. The Irish were very fond of this alphabetical structure, and many of these hymns commence with the word *Audite*.

The hymn begins with an invitation addressed to all to pay attention to the poet as he tells the virtues of the great Patrick:

Audite omnes amantes Deum sancta mereta
viri in Christo beati Patrici episcupi
quomodo bonum ob actum similatur angelis
perfectamque propter vitam aequatur apostolis.

The poet introduces from the begining one of his favorite themes: the comparison of Patrick with the apostles. It is a theme which recurrs throughout the hymn; for example:

10. super quem aedificatur ut Petrus aecclesia
cuiusque apostolatum a Deo sortitus est
in cuius porte adversum inferni non praevalent.

21. Fidelis Dei minister insignisque nuntius
apostolicum exemplum formamque praebet bonis.

27. quem Deus misit ut Paulum ad gentes apostolum.

81. Xp(istu)s illum sibi elegit in terris vicarium.

This comparison is already implicit in Patrick's writings, in which he vigorously defends his divine call to be apostle and bishop among a barbarous people, in order to convert them to the true faith. To this end Patrick frequently uses the language used by St Paul in speaking of the special grace given to him to convert the gentiles. For example:

*Epist.*1. Patricius peccator indoctus scilicet Hiberione constitutus episcopum me esse fateor. Certissime reor a Deo accepi id quod sum. Inter barbaras itaque gentes habito proselitus et profuga ob amorem Dei; testis est ille si ita est. Non quod optabam tam dure et tam aspere aliquid ex ore meo effundere; sed cogor zelo Dei, et veritas Christi excitavit, pro dilectione proximorum atque filiorum; pro quibus tradidi patriam et parentes et animam meam usque ad mortem. Si dignus sum vivo Deo meo docere gentes etsi contempnor aliquibus.

*Epist.*6. Non usurpo. Partem habeo cum his quos advocavit et praedestinavit evangelium praedicare in persecutionibus non parvis usque ad extremum terrae, etsi invidet inimicus per tyrannidem Corotici, qui Deum non veretur nec sacerdotes ipsius,quos elegit et indulsit illis summam divinam sublimem potestatem,quos ligarent super terram ligatos esse in caelis.

*Conf.*37. Non mea gratia, sed Deus qui vincit in me et resistit illis omnibus, ut ego veneram ad Hibernas gentes evangelium predicare et ab incredulis contumelias perferre.

*Conf.*56. Ecce nunc commendo animam meam fidelissimo Deo meo, pro quo legationem fungor in ignobilitate mea, sed quia personam non accepit et elegit me ad hoc officium ut unus essem de suis minimis minister.

These are but a few examples of a constant theme in the writings of Patrick; it was precisely his answer to those who attacked him and tried to subvert his mission.[28] But in Patrick's mind the grace given to him constantly sugests his own unworthiness, his sinfulness and lack of merit. There is nothing of this complementary theme in the hymn; right from the start the author is anxious to praise Patrick's merits and perfect life,[29] and in this he gives us an insight into the way he used his sources. In his own eyes, Patrick is *Patricius peccator*:

*Conf.*1. Ego Patricius peccator rusticissimus et minimus omnium fidelium et contemptibilis apud plurimos....Deum enim verum ignorabam et Hiberione in captivitate adductus sum cum tot milia hominum − SECUNDUM MERITA MEA, quia a Deo recessimus et praecepta eius non custodivimus et sacerdotibus nostris non oboedientes fuimus.

*Conf.*44. Et scio ex parte quare VITAM PERFECTAM EGO NON EGI sicut et ceteri credentes.

The themes of the fear of God and fidelity in the faith are found associated both in the hymn –

9. Constans in Dei timore et fide inmobilis
29. Humilis Dei ob metum spiritu et corpore,

and in the writings of Patrick, in very similar terms:

*Conf.*16. Sed postquam Hiberione deveneram ... magis ac magis accedebat amor Dei et timor ipsius et fides augebatur et spiritus agebatur.
*Conf.*44. Confiteor Deo meo, ... ex quo cognovi eum a iuventute mea crevit in me amor Dei et timor ipsius, et usque nunc favente Domino fidem servavi.
Dictum I. Timorem Dei habui ducem itereris mei per Gallias atque Italiam, etiam in insolis quae sunt in mari Terreno.

The imagery of the fisherman used to illustrate his ministry -

13. Dominus illum elegit ut doceret barbaras
nationes et piscaret per doctrinae retia
et de saeculo credentes traheret ad gratiam
Dominum qui sequerentur sedem ad etheream,

is a biblical theme which had been used by Patrick himself:

*Conf.*40. Idcirco itaque oportet quidem bene et diligenter PISCARE, sicut Dominus praemonet et docet dicens: 'Venite post me et faciam vos fieri piscatores hominum'.... Unde autem valde oportebat RETIA nostra tendere, ita ut multitudo copiosa et turba Deo caperetur et ubique essent clerici qui baptizarent et exhortarent populum indigentem et desiderantem.[30]

Patrick's ministry in Ireland was a difficult one, involving much suffering and hard work. Our hymn speaks of this work and of the great reward in store for Patrick:

19. Navigi huius laboris tum opere praetium
cum Christo regni caelestis possessurus gaudium.

31. cuiusque iusta in carne Christi portat stigmata
in cuius sola sustentans gloriatur in cruce.

90. cuius ingentis laboris percepturus praemium.

Patrick had written at length about his difficulties and sufferings, even his desire for martyrdom:

*Conf.*26. Et quando temptatus sum ab aliquantis senioribus meis, qui venerunt, et peccata mea, contra LABORIOSUM EPISCOPATUM MEUM, utique ille die fortiter impulsus sum ut caderem hic et in aeternum.
*Conf.*35.Longum est autem totum per singula enarrare LABOREM MEUM vel per partes. Breviter dicam qualiter piissimus Deus de servitute saepe liberavit et de periculis duodecim qua periclitata est anima mea, praeter insidias multas et quae verbis exprimere non valeo.
*Conf.*57. Unde autem retribuam illi pro omnibus quae retribuit mihi.... Nimis cupio et paratus eram ut donaret mihi bibere calicem eius, sicut indulsit et caeteris amantibus se.
*Conf.*59. Et si aliquid boni umquam imitatus sum propter Deum meum, quem diligo, peto illi det mihi ut cum illis proselitis et captivis pro nomine suo effundam sanguinem meum.

40

Indeed, Patrick never suggests that he experienced any of the honour and glory which, according to our poet, was given to him by all:

25. Gloriam habet cum Christo honorem in saeculo
qui ab omnibus ut Dei veneratur angelus.
45. Maximus namque in regno caelorum vocabitur.

In his own estimation, Patrick is *minimus omnium fidelium et contemptibilis apud plurimos* (*Conf*.1). Especially in *Conf*.51–55, he speaks of the hardship and dangers which were his daily lot. For example:

Conf.51. Inter vos et ubique pergebam causa vestra in multis periculis etiam usque ad extremas partes.
Conf.52. (Reges) comprehenderunt me cum comitibus meis et illa die avidissime cupiebant interficere me, sed tempus nondum venerat, et omnia quaecumque nobiscum invenerunt rapuerunt illud et me ipsum ferro vinxerunt.
Conf.54. Ecce testem Deum invoco in animam meam quia non mentior:neque ut sit occasio adulationis vel avaritiae scripserim vobis neque ut HONOREM spero ab aliquo vestro; sufficit enim honor qui nondum videtur sed corde creditur.
Conf.55. Cotidie spero aut internicionem aut circumveriri aut redigi in servitutem sive occasio cuiuslibet.

Our poet is careful to add that in spite of all this glory and honour Patrick's humility was unimpaired:[31]

29. Humilis Dei ob metum spiritu et corpore.

His ministry is described in the hymn as an indefatigable dedication to preaching the Gospel, administering baptism, and strengthening those who have believed with the heavenly food of the Eucharist. His preaching is not in word only but also in deed; he is a living witness and example to the faithful. This theme is developed at length, especially in lines 33–68; we will give a few salient lines and show how they stand in relation to the *Confession*.

37. Kastam qui custodit carnem ob amorem Domini
quam carnem templum paravit sanctoque Spiritui
a quo constanter cum mundis possedetur actibus
quam et hostiam placentem vivam offert Domino.
Conf.44. Semet ipsum non credo quamdiu fuero in hoc corpore mortis, quia fortis est qui cotidie nititur subvertere me a fide et praeposita CASTITATE RELIGIONIS NON FICTAE usque in finem vitae meae Christo Domini meo, sed caro inimica semper trahit ad mortem, id est ad inlecebras inlicitate perficiendas.
Conf.34. Unde ergo indefessam gratiam ago Deo meo, qui me fidelem servavit in die temptationis meae ita ut hodie confidenter offeram illi sacrificium ut HOSTIAM VIVENTUM ANIMAM MEAM Christo Domino meo, qui me servavit ab omnibus angustiis meis.

The substance of Patrick's missionary activity is expressed in two central stanzas of the hymn:

45. Maximus namque in regno caelorum vocabitur
qui quod verbis docet sacris factis adimplet bonis.

49. Nomen Domini audenter adnuntiat gentibus
quibus lavacri salutis aeternam dat gratiam
pro quorum orat delictis ad Deum cotidie
pro quibus ut Deo dignas immolatque hostias.

The expression *verba factis adimplet* may have been suggested by a similar expression in *Hymnum dicat* 22: *dicta factis adprobat*. Patrick frequently refers to the great numbers baptized by him.[32] This baptismal activity follows his announcement of the name of God:

*Conf.*14. In mensura itaque fidei Trinitatis oportet distinguere,sine reprehensione periculi notum facere donum Dei et consolationem aeternam, sine timore fiducialiter DEI NOMEN UBIQUE EXPANDERE, ut etiam post obitum meum exaggelias relinquere fratribus et filiis meis quos in Domino ego baptizavi tot milia hominum.

His frequent prayer, spoken about by Patrrck himself, will later become lengendary and a source of inspiration for his followers in the Irish Church. Our hymn returns to it again:

85. Ymnos cum apocalypsi salmosque cantat Dei,[33]
quosque ad aedificandum Dei tractat populum.

*Conf.*16. Sed postquam Hiberione deveneram - cotidie itaque pecora pascebam et frequens in die orabam - magis ac magis accedebat amor Dei et timor ipsius et fides augebatur et spiritus agebatur,ut in die una usque ad centum orationes et in nocte prope similiter, ut etiam in silvis et monte manebam, et ante lucem excitabar ad orationem per nivem per gelu per pluviam, et nihil mali sentiebam neque ulla pigritia erat in me -sicut nunc video, quia tunc spiritus in me fervebat.

Patrick is the true and faithful shepherd, who feeds his flock with the true catholic doctrine; the substance of this teaching is the dogma of the blessed Trinity and the divinity of Christ.

57. Pastor bonus et fidelis gregis evangelici
quem Deus Dei elegit custodire populum
suamque pascere plebem divinis dogmatibus
pro qua a Christi exemplo suam tradit animam.

69. Sacrum invenit thesaurum sacro in volumine
salvatorisque in carne deitatem pervidet.

73. Testis domini fidelis in lege catholica
cuius verba sunt divinis condita oraculis.

87. quam legem in trinitate sacri credit nominis
tribusque personis unam docetque substantiam.

Patrick also spoke of his people as the Lord's flock; it is for this flock that he gives up his life and everything:

*Epist.*12. Ecce oves tuae circa me laniantur atque depraedantur. . . . Lupi rapaces deglutierunt gregem Domini, qui utique Hiberione cum summa diligentia optime crescebat.

*Epist.*1. Cogor zelo Dei, et veritas Christi excitavit, pro dilectione proximorum atque filiorum, PRO QUIBUS TRADIDI patriam et parentes et ANIMAM MEAM usque ad mortem.

He is the faithful witness of the true faith,[34] and his preaching of it, as is evident from his writings, was inspired by the Scriptures:

Conf.58. Oro Deum ut det mihi perseverantiam et dignetur ut reddam illi TESTEM FIDELEM usque ad transitum meum propter Deum meum.

Conf.4. Quem confitemur et adoramus unum Deum IN TRINITATE SACRI NOMINIS.

Conf.14. In mensura itaque fidei Trinitatis oportet distinguere,... fiducialiter Dei nomen ubique expandere.

Epist.5. Iniqui dissipaverunt LEGEM TUAM, Domine, quam in supremis temporibus Hiberione optime benigne plantaverat atque instructa erat favente Deo.

The author of our hymn, however, has credited Patrick with more perfect knowledge of Scripture than he claimed for himself:

Conf.9. Quapropter olim cogitavi scribere, sed et usque nunc haesitavi; timui enim ne incederem in linguam hominum, quia non didici sicut et ceteri, qui optime itaque iura et sacras litteras utraque pari modo combiberunt et sermones illorum ex infantia nunquam mutarunt, sed magis ad perfectum semper addiderunt. Nam sermo et loquela nostra translata est in linguam alienam.

As a result of this scriptural basis of his preaching, Patrick's words bear fruit when planted in the minds and hearts of the faithful:

77₁ Verus cultor et insignis agri evangelici
cuius semina videntur Christi evangelia
quae divino serit ore in aures prudentium
quorumque corda ac mentes sancto arat Spiritu.

But his care extends beyond the preaching of the word to the everyday needs of the young Church:

61. Quem pro meretis salvator provexit pontificem
ut in caelesti moneret clericos militiae
caelestem quibus annonam erogat cum vestibus
quod in divinis inpletur sacrisque affatibus.[35]

81. Xp(istu)s illum sibi elegit in terris vicarium
qui de gemino captivos liberat servitio
plerosque de servitutei quos redemit hominum
innumeros de zaboli absolvit dominio.

Patrick had spoken about his efforts to free the Christians taken captive by Coroticus and his men; the latter are themselves in the captivity of the devil:

Epist.3. Misi epistolam cum sancto presbytero quem ego ex infantia docui, cum clericis, ut nobis aliquid indulgerent de praeda vel de CAPTIVIS baptizatis quos ceperunt; cachinnos fecerunt de illis.

Epist.4. Idcirco nescio quid magis lugeam: an qui interfecti vel quos ceperunt vel quos zabulus graviter inlaqueavit. Perenni poena gehennam pariter cum ipso mancipabunt, quia utique qui facit peccatum servus est et filius zabuli nuncupatur.

Epist.14. Consuetudo Romanorum Gallorum christianorum: mittunt viros sanctos idoneos ad Francos et ceteras gentes cum tot milia solidarum ad REDIMENDOS

CAPTIVOS baptizatos. Tu potius interficis et vendis illos genti externae ignoranti Deum; quasi in lupinar tradis membra Christi.

We have already drawn attention to the numberless (*innumeri*) converts which, according to Patrick, were made by him. The term itself is found in

*Epist.*2. quos (Chistianos) ego IN NUMERO Deo genui atque in Christo confirmavi.

*Epist.*16. O speciosissimi atque amantissimi fratres et filii quos in Christo genui enumerare nequeo, quid faciam vobis?

The hymn concludes by speaking of the reward which Patrick will receive for his labours; it reflects Patrick's own expectation, and the terms of the reward were used by himself in relation to those unfortunate converts who had been captured and slain:

91. cuius ingentis laboris percepturus praemium
cum apostolis regnabit sanctus super Israel.

*Epist.*17–18. Deo gratias, creduli baptizati, de saeculo recessistis ad paradisum... Vos ergo REGNABITIS CUM APOSTOLIS et prophetis et martyribus.

We can now sum up what we know regarding the hymn *Audite omnes*. It is very doubtful that this was 'the first hymn that was made in Ireland',[36] if it was written not by Secundinus, but, as seems most likely, by an Irish author. One does not succeed in writing such a fine composition on a first attempt. But it is, nevertheless, of early origin; this is indicated by the absence of rhyme and the perfection of the metrical form, which in later compositions tended to change to a simple count of syllables. Its quantitative model may have been *Hymnum dicat*, which was composed or at least know in Ireland towards the end of the sixth century; two expressions of *Audite omnes* may have been drawn from there.[37] For its content it depends largely on the writings of Patrick; the author drew extensively on them and created a glowing portrait of Patrick as apostle and bishop of the Irish Church. His divine mission, his apostolic zeal and activity, his holiness and the success of his apostolate are particularly stressed. There is very little historical detail in the hymn. The author's aim was not to write history but rather a eulogy of Patrick, whose perfect life and work is crowned with success in the conversion of the Irish. The author occasionally used Patrick's own words in a sense opposite to that intended by Patrick, and accommodated them to his purpose. The result is a picture of Patrick which is not fully historical, but rather the expression of the esteem in which he was held by the author and by the Irish Church in the sixth and seventh centuries. Finally, the author may have been Colmán Alo; if this is so, we can date the hymn to the end of the sixth or the beginning of the seventh century.

2. AUDITE BONUM EXEMPLUM

We have already spoken about the metrical similarity between *Audite omnes* and this hymn in honour of St Camelacus. There are, besides, certain other similarities of structure and language between them[38] which are worth noting.

(a) Both hymns are alphabetical; both begin with *Audite*, they have *Kastus* (*Kastuṁ*) for initial K, *Quem* for initial Q, and *Xps* for initial X. But whereas in *Audite bonam* there are four lines in each stanza and it is the stanzas that are alphabetically arranged, in *Audite omnes* there are only two lines in each stanza and it is the half-lines that begin with successive letters of the alphabet. Since there are only twenty-three letters in the alphabet, an extra half-line had to be added in the last stanza outside the alphabetical arrangement, to make twenty-four half-lines or six stanzas.

(b) In both hymns the X line has a syllable too many, giving us a unique case of elision:

Audite omnes	*Audite bonum*
81. Xps illum sibi elegit	6.Xps illum insinuavit.

(c) Bernard noted the frequent use of the enclitic *que* in *Audite omnes*.[39] It is used twice in the much shorter *Audite bonum:*

4. Noctibus at*que* diebus orat dominum suum
5.Regem dominum aspexit salvatorem*que* suum

(d) *Audite bonum* also speaks of Camelacus, who was a fifth-century contemporary of St Patrick, as if he were still alive, except in the final two stanzas where he is spoken as of being in his eternal home.

(e) The praise of Patrick in *Audite omnes,* which is eight times as long as *Audite bonum,* is more elaborate and fittingly greater than that given to Camelacus. But there are a few parallel expressions of eulogy in both:

Audite omnes	*Audite bonum*
7.sanctumque cuius sequuntur EXEMPLUM MIRIFICUM	
47. BONO praecedit EXEMPLO formamque fidelium	1. Audite BONUM EXEMPLUM benedicti pauperis
56. sed IN ADVERSIS LAETATUR cum pro Christo patitur	3. LAETATUR IN PAUPERTATE mitis·est in omnibus
89. Zona domini praecinctus DIEBUS AC NOCTIBUS sine intermissione Deum ORAT DOMINUM	4. NOCTIBUS ATQUE DIEBUS ORAT DOMINUM suum
92. Cum apostolis REGNABIT sanctus super Israel	6. In paradiso REGNABIT cum sancto Elizaro

All of these similarities may indicate either that *Audite bonum* is an imitation of *Audite omnes* or that both were written by the same author.[40] The shorter hymn draws a warm and attractive picture of Camelacus, who is characterized above all by humility, gentleness and joyful fidelity in the service of God. Mention is made more than once of his poverty:

1. benedicti pauperis
3. laetatur in paupertate
6. regnabit cum sancto Elizaro

This association with Lazarus anticipates the later tradition which speaks of him as Patrick's leper,whatever may have been the basis for this name.[41]

In Tirechan's Life of Patrick, Camulacus is named as one of many bishops ordained by Patrick and to him is given the episcopal see of Raithin, modern Rahen in Co. Offaly.[42] His church at Raithin later (c. 595) became the site of a monastic foundation under St Mo-Chuta,who subsequently founded the monastery of Lismore in Co. Waterford when he and his monks were forced to leave Raithin. It is interesting to hear that it was during a visit to Colmán Alo at Lynally that St Mo-Chuta was urged by Colmán to settle in Raithin, which is only a few miles distant from Lynally. He founded a monastery and a leper-colony there.[43] Colmán Alo appears as the instigator of this enterprise, which leads us to surmise that the new foundation at Raithin may have been due to his own particular regard for Camelacus.It is possible that the new monastery and its leper-colony was a memorial and tribute to Camelacus, the first bishop of Raithin, who was remembered for his evangelical poverty and possibly for his care for lepers, if not already regarded as a leper himself. We are thus led to surmise that Colmán composed a hymn in honour of Camelacus. The indications for this conclusion are slight in themselves, but when we add to them the independent evidence of his authorship of *Audite omnes* and the similarity between the two hymns, we can conclude with some probability that he is the author of both hymns.

Little further need be said regarding the content of *Audite bonum*. The language is extremely simple and consists mostly of adjectives which describe the virtues of the saint:

2. Exemplum praebet in toto, fidelis in opere,
gratias Deo (Domini: AH 51, 321) agens, hylaris in omnibus.

3. Ieiunus et mansuetus, kastus hic servit Deo,
laetatur in paupertate, mitis est in omnibus.

4. Noctibus atque diebus orat dominum suum,
prudens, iustus ac fidelis, quem cognati diligunt.

The final two stanzas speak of his vision of Christ the Saviour and of the eternal life which he has received. He has been placed in Abraham's bosom,[44] and will reign in the company of Lazarus .

CHAPTER FOUR

SANCTI VENITE AND PRAECAMUR PATREM

We will consider, once again, these two hymns[1] in a single chapter because they have a similar metrical form, being rhythmical imitations of iambic trimeter (5p + 7pp). The quantitative model is imitated more or less perfectly, in as much as:[2]

(a) There was a tendency in quantitative metre to avoid disyllables at the end of the long lines, which, therefore, ended in polysyllabic proparoxytone words ('iambic cadence'). This tendency is regularly observed in *Sancti venite*, with only two exceptions to it: *déo* (2,2) and *déo* (4,1); but out of the eighty-four lines of *Praecamur patrem*,twenty-three end in paroxytones.

(b) There is a caesura after the fifth syllable and the half-line ends in a paroxytone; the only exception is *Praecamur patrem: caélitus* (37,1).

(c) The iambic trimeter line could never begin with a trisyllabic proparoxytone; the second syllable had to be long and, consequently, it was accentuated in trisyllabic words. In *Sancti venite*, this rule is perfectly imitated; five initial trisyllabic words end in paroxytones. But of the thirty initial trisyllables in *Praecamur patrem*, five are proparoxytones: *ténebrae* (7,1), *sáliet* (22,2), *fúnere* (24,2), *tótidem* (25,1), *éxtricat* (33,3).

Sancti venite is, therefore, a perfectly rythmical hymn,[3] but *Praecamur patrem* is so careless about the accentual structures even in the final cadence that its system is little more than a count of syllables, divided by a caesura after the fifth. In the manuscript, each stanza of *Sancti venite* is written without distinction of lines or half-lines, whereas the stanzas of *Praecamur patrem* are written as four lines (5, 7, 5, 7); we will transcribe the stanzas of both hymns as two long lines. *Sancti venite* appears to be the older of the two. It does not employ either rhyme or alliteration, which are a marked feature of *Praecamur patrem*, and the sensitivity shown in it for the structural laws of the quantitative model sets it alongside *Audite omnes* and *Audite bonum*. This early rhythmical poetry quickly developed in Ireland into pure syllabism, with abundant use of rhyme and alliteration, and *Praecamur patrem* marks an intermediate stage in this development.[4]

1. SANCTI VENITE

The hymn was probably composed in the sixth century. The picturesque and fictional occasion of its composition is given in the *Leabhar Breac* (*saec.* 14) preface to the *Audite omnes amantes*.[5] It was used as a communion hymn, as the title in the Antiphonary indicates:'a hymn (to be sung) while the priests are communicating'.

It is a eucharistic hymn of fine theological and devotional quality. In content it is to a large extent based on the communion chants found in early Irish liturgical documents and fragments.[6] This is immediately apparent from the opening lines:

Sancti venite Christi corpus sumite
sanctum bibentes quo redempti sanguine.

This is the theme of several communion chants:[7]

AB.G.S. Hoc sacrum CORPUS DOMINI et SALVATORIS SANGUINEM SUMITE vobis in vitam perennem (aeternam S), alleluia.

G.S. VENITE, commedite panem meum, alleluia, et BIBITE vinum quod miscui vobis, alleluia.

S. Regnum caeli cum pace, alleluia,
plenum odorem vitae, alleluia,
novum carmen cantate, alleluia,
omnes SANCTI VENITE, alleluia,

The second stanza corresponds to an antiphon in the Antiphonary:

2. Salvati Christi corpore et sanguine,
a quo refecti laudes dicamus deo.

AB 115. REFECTI CHRISTI CORPORE ET SANGUINE, tibi semper, domine, DICAMUS ALLELUIA.

The third stanza can be compared to another antiphon in the Antiphonary and to a postcommunion prayer:

3. Hoc sacramento corporis et sanguinis
omnes exuti ab inferni faucibus

AB 109. CORPUS domini accepimus et SANGUINE eius potati sumus; AB OMNI MALO non timebimus, quia dominus nobiscum est.

G.S. Gratias tibi agimus, domine, sancte pater, omnipotens aeterne Deus, qui nos CORPORIS ET SANGUINIS Christi filii tui communione satiasti, tuamque misericordiam humiliter postulamus, ut HOC tuum, domine, SACRAMENTUM non sit nobis reatus ad penam, sed intercessio salutaris ad veniam.

In the next four stanzas the Eucharist is related to the sacrifice of Christ on the cross, and to the sacrifices of the Old Law which foreshadowed the sacred mysteries:

4. Dator salutis Christus filius Dei,
mundum salvavit per crucem et sanguinem.

5. Pro universis immolatus Dominus,
ipse sacerdos existit et hostia.[8]

6. Lege praeceptum immolari hostias
qua adumbrantur divina misteria.

7.Lucis indultor et salvator omnium,
praeclarum sanctis largitus est gratiam.

These themes are not found in the Irish communion chants; but one manuscript gives a proper chant for Christmas, which speaks of the birth of the great King, Christ the Saviour of the world, who is celebrated in the Eucharist:

G. Nos oportet celebrare, alleluia,
magni regis in natale, alleluia,
Christum mundi salvatorem, alleluia,
sacrosancto sanguine.

Through reception of the heavenly Bread and living Fountain, with the proper dispositions of faith and purity of intention, the Lord bestows his salvation, protection and eternal life:

8. Accedunt omnes pura menti creduli,
sumant aeternam salutis custodiam.

9. Sanctorum custos rector quoque dominus,
vitae perennis largitor credentibus.

10. Caelestem panem dat esurientibus
de fonte vivo praebet sitientibus.

AB.G.S. Hoc sacrum corpus domini et salvatoris sanguinem, alleluia, SUMITE VOBIS IN VITAM PERENNEM (aeternam S), alleluia.

AB.G.S. Hic est PANIS VIVUS qui DE CAELO descendit, alleluia, qui manducat ex eo VIVET IN AETERNUM, alleluia.

S. PANEM CAELI dedit eis dominus, alleluia, panem angelorum manducavit homo, alleluia.

The whole of Columban's *Instructio* 13 is a development of this theme: Christ is the bread and fountain of life, whom we are invited to eat and drink. He is not speaking specifically of the Eucharist, but it is not far from his thought.[9]

The conclusion of the hymn brings out the escatological dimension of the eucharistic celebration:

11. Alfa et O(mega) ipse Christus dominus,
venit venturus iudicare homines.

This expectation is also found in the communion antiphons:

G.S. Paenitentiam agite, alleluia, adpropinquavit enim regnum caelorum, alleluia.

G.S. Venite benedicti patris mei, alleluia, possedete regnum, alleuia, quod vobis paratum est ab origine mundi, alleluia.

The identification of Christ as *Alfa et Omega* occurs in a number of hymns, and the reference to the coming of Christ reflects the language of the Apostles' Creed.[10]

The preface to *Audite omnes* in the *Leabhar Breac* would lead us to believe that *Sancti venite* was a very popular eucharistic hymn in mediaeval Ireland. But, strangely enough, it is not found in the Irish *Liber Hymnorum* or in any other Irish manuscript. Its Irish origin would appear certain,[11] and it must be one of the earlist Irish Latin hymns, along with *Hymnum dicat, Audite omnes amantes* and *Audite bonum exemplum.*

2. PRAECAMUR PATREM

THIS HYMN IS QUITE DIFFERENT FROM *Sancti venite* in subject-matter and language. It is a long and in places difficult hymn on the life of Christ. Its Irish origin is evident for a number of reasons:

(a) The language of the hymn shows points of contact with other early Hiberno-Latin texts, in particular the writings of Columban and the Irish biblical commentaries.

(b) The orthography is Irish. This is true not just for such forms as *polump nodoso* for *polum nodoṣo* (7,2), *loquatur* for *locatur* (15,1), which are found throughout. It is also true for the contraction of *ii* into *i* as one final syllable, something which is taken into account in reckoning the correct syllabic length of the lines.[12]

(c) There is a great variety of rhyme and assonance, which is used in most stanzas, but is not governed by any strict rule or pattern.[13] There is also some alliteration.

(d) The hymn shows a liking for latinized Greek words, among which the form *Cincris* for Pharaoh; the Irish had a marked tendency to include a smattering of Greek and Hebrew words in their Latin writings.[14]

The hymn has a complex structure. Apart from the introduction (1–4) and conclusion (41–42), it is divided into two parts by a sharp transition from stanza 15 to 16. But the organic unity of the hymn, called into question by C. Blume, has been adequately established by M. Simonetti.[15] In the first main section (4–15) the central theme is the light of creation and salvation. The creation of light on the first day is contrasted thematically with the Incarnation of the eternal light. The contrast is not one between the Old and New Testaments. Rather, on the one hand, there is the (natural) light which dispels the primordial darkness of the world, and, on the other hand, the Word of God, who is the source of light and salvation for the world and for mankind. The contrast is developed in pairs of stanzas. In its language and ideas this first part has many points of contact and similarity with the morning and evening hymns of the Western Church generally, beginning with St Ambrose and Prudentius. The second main section (16–39) develops at length, mainly in narrative form, the salvific action of the Word-Light Incarnate. In this section there are some definite parallels with the writings of Columban, the hymns of Venantius Fortunatus, a Sermon of Caesarius of Arles and an apocryphal account of the descent into Hell, probably the Gospel of Nicodemus.

The introduction is a brief statement of the dogma of the Trinity. Part of the second stanza has been cut away in the MS and has been restored conjecturally by Blume (AH 51, 271):

1. Praecamur patrem regem omnipotentem
et Iesum Christum sanctum quoque spiritum.

2. Deum in una perfectum s(ubstantia),
trinum p(ersona, unum in essentia).

3. Universorum fontis iubar luminum
aethereorum et orbi lucentium.

This third stanza, which probably speaks of Christ rather than of the divinity as the 'ray of the source of all lights', introduces the main theme. It is developed in pairs of stanzas.

4. Hic enim dies velut primogenitus
caeli ab arce mundi moli micuit.

5. Sic verbum caro factum a principio
lumen aeternum missum patre saeculo.

We have here a favourite theme of the morning and evening hymns of the Latin liturgies. Ambrose, for example, in his *Splendor paternae gloriae* (AH 50, 11), has many terms and ideas comparable to those used in the first five stanzas of our hymn:

1. Splendor paternae gloriae,
de luce lucem proferens,
lux lucis et FONS LUMINIS,
diem DIES illuminans.

2. Verusque sol illabere,
MICANS nitore perpeti,
IUBARQUE sancti spiritus,
infunde NOSTRIS SENSIBUS.

3. Votis VOCEMUS ET PATREM,
patrem perennis gloriae,
PATREM POTENTIS gratiae,
culpam releget lubricam.

The same theme is found in the early Gallican hymns known by Caesarius and Aurelian of Arles; for example (AH 51, 10):

1. Aeterne lucis conditor,
lux ipse totus et DIES
noctem nec ullam sentiens,
natura lucis perpetim.

2. Iam cedit pallens proximo
diei nox adventui,
obtendens lumen siderum
adest et clarus lucifer.

Similarly, another hymn mentioned by Caesarius (AH 51, 21):

1.Christe qui lux es et DIES
noctis tenebras detegis,
lucifer, lucem proferens,
LUMEN beatum praedicans.

It is also a recurring theme in the 'Gregorian' evening hymns.[16]

In the next two stanzas of our hymn we are told that this eternal Light dispelled the primordial darkness of the world and also vanquished the old enemy, the author of death:

6. Illeque proto vires adimens chao
tum inproviso noctem pepulit mundo.

7. Ita veterno iste hoste subacto
polum nodoso solvit mortis vinculo.

In certain evening hymns also the night is a sign of the primordial chaos:

Prudentius,*Cath.*V 1 – 4:
Inventor rutili, dux bone, luminis,
qui certis vicibus tempora dividis,
merso sole CHAOS ingruit horridum,
lucem redde tuis, Christe, fidelibus!

The 'Gregorian' evening hymn (AH 51, 34):

1. Lucis creator optime,
lucem dierum proferens,
primordiis lucis novae
mundi parans originem;

2. qui mane iunctum vesperi
diem vocari praecipis,
taetrum CHAOS illabitur,
audi preces cum fletibus.

The contrast between the two activities of Christ, in creation and redemption, is restated in the next two stanzas of our hymn:

8. Tenebrae super ante erant abissum
quam radiaret primus dies dierum.

9. Hoc quam prodiret vera lux mortalia
contexit alta corda ignorantia[17]

The identification of Christ as *dies dierum* is found in the sixth-century Gallican morning hymn *Deus qui caeli lumen es.*[18]

The hymn now goes on to speak about the historical action of Christ, the eternal day, in the Old Testament; the pairing of stanzas continues:

10. Eodem die rubrum ut aiunt mare
post tergum liquit,[19] liberatus Israhel.

11. Per hoc docemur mundi acta spernere
et in deserto virtutum consistere.

The early Irish Church was very much attracted to the ideal of 'desert' monasticism, and the monks sought to realize this ideal in their own country, by seeking the desert in lonely places and islands around the coast. One expression of this ideal, which comes close to that found in our hymn, is given in the seventh-century Ps.-Hieronymus, *Commentarius in Evang. Marci* (Mk 4, 34–37):

Illi enim digni erant audire mysteria in penetrali intimo sapientiae, qui remotis cogitationum malorum tumultibus, IN SOLITUDINE VIRTUTUM PERMANEBANT.[20]

The next pair of stanzas restate the same event in other terms. The cruel Pharaoh (Cincris) is drowned and the people sing the praises of God, their fiery leader. We also are asked to praise God, who has delivered us from our enemies. Then the entire section is summed up and concluded in two stanzas which set in contrast the two 'days' of creation and of salvation:

14. Et sicut ille lucis fit initium
ita et iste salutis exordium.

15. Locatur primus in tenore diei
secundus vero in calore fidei.[21]

The second main section of the hymn speaks of the historical accomplishment of salvation through Christ. It begins with the Incarnation:

16. In fine mundi post tanta misteria
adest salvator cum grandi clementia.

In fine mundi is a phrase which is frequently used by the Irish commentators when speaking of the Incarnation or of the second coming of Christ.[22] The entire stanza finds a close parallel in Ps.-Hieronymus, *Comm. in Ev. Marci* (Mk 1,7):

Non est digna 'sola gratia' procumbens in baptismo solvere corrigiam calciamentorum eius, id est, MYSTERIUM INCARNATIONIS Dei. Calx enim extrema pars est corporis. IN FINE enim ad iustitiam ADEST SALVATOR incarnatus.[23]

The elements proclaim the presence of him who was foretold by the prophets; the divine Son is born as man:

18. Natus ut homo mortali in tegmine
non deest caelo manens in trinitate.

These lines are clearly related in an immediate way to a passage in Columban, whatever may be said regarding the priority of one over the other:

*Epist.*5, 13. Christus enim SALVATOR noster verus Deus aeternus sine tempore et VERUS HOMO absque peccato in tempore est, . . . qui NATUS IN CARNE, NEQUAQUAM DEERAT CAELO, MANENS IN TRINITATE.[24]

The nativity is narrated in terms borrowed from Caesarius of Arles and Venantius Fortunatus:

19. Vagit in pannis veneratur a magis
fulget in stellis adoratur in caelis.

20. Statura vili continetur praesepi
cuius pugillo potest orbis concludi.

Caesarius, *Sermo* 194

Hodie magos ab oriente venientes usque ad locum geniti salvatoris stella Christum quaerentibus monstratura perduxit. Spectatur SUB HUMILI TEGURIO sacra NATIVITAS (cf. stanza 17: NATUS . . . MORTALI IN TEGMINE): ADORATUR IN PANNIS QUI FULGET IN STELLIS. . . Inter amplexas genetricis INCLUDITUR qui CAELUM TERRAMQUE CONPLECTITUR.[25]

Venantius Fortunatus, *Pange lingua* 5 (AH 50, 771)

VAGIT infans inter arta conditus praesaepia,
membra PANNIS involuta virgo mater adligat,
et pedes manusque crura stricta pingit fascia.

Three other hymns attributed to Fortunatus may also have influenced our author when he wrote *cuius pugillo potest orbis concludi.*[26]

The miracles of Christ are now narrated, but briefly (21–25). The language is somewhat less concrete than that of *Hymnum dicat*, but elaborate description is also avoided here and the author shows his liking for 'the half-said thing' so dear to the Irish poets. Parallels with other sources are not great or numerous, but the more interesting will be indicated in the notes.

21. Primumque signum portendit discipulis
aquae conversae in sapore nectaris.[27]

22. Tum per prophetam conpletur ut dictum est[28]
saliet claudus ut cervus perniciter.

23. Planaque fatur absoluto vinculo
lingua mutorum imperante domino.[29]

24. Surdi sanantur caeci atque leprosi
funere truso suscitantur mortui.

25. Totidem panes quinque dividit virum
saturaturis proculdubio milibus.[30]

In spite of these works of mercy, Christ was met with envy and hatred; a council was held against him, who is 'the angel of the great council',[31] and he was treated like an outlaw.

30. Tandem humano traditur iudicio,
mortali rege damnatur perpetuus.

31. Cruci confixus polum mire concutit,
lumenque solis tribus obtendit horis.

32. Saxa rumpuntur velum scinditur templi,
vivi consurgunt de sepulchris mortui.

It is possible to discern here a certain influence of the early Gallican hymns known to Caesarius and Aurelian. The events narrated are, of course, those found in the Gospel, but the manner of expressing them is peculiarly similar in both: the subjection of the eternal one to a mortal judgement, the darkness expressed by *obtendere lumen* and the miraculous events which followed the death of Christ.[32]

The descent of Christ is then related. The author appears to have drawn his material directly, for the most part, from the Gospel of Nicodemus and given it an original rendering. At any rate he is not dependent on the accounts of the descent found in other hymns, for example those of Prudentius and Venantius Fortunatus.[33] We will first give the text of the hymn, making some incidental remarks in the notes, and then we will compare it to the text of the Gospel of Nicodemus.

33. Conrosum nodis annis fere milibus
extricat senis[34] inferi feralibus[35]

34. (Tunc) protoplaustum, (lacri) mosa suboli
abiecta mali morte saeva ultrice.[36]

35. Quemque antiquum paradiso incolam
recursu suo clementer restituit.[37]

54

36. Exaltans caput universi corporis
in trinitate locavit ecclesiae.[38]

37. In hoc caelitus iubet portas principes
regi cum socis aeternales pandere.

The descent of Christ into Hell is narrated in the second part of the Gospel of Nicodemus.[39] It is told by two witnesses of the event, Karinus and Leucius, sons of Simeon; they had been raised from the dead by Christ. They are brought to Jerusalem and charged by the high-priests to write an account of what happened. They begin their account by telling of the great light which suddenly shone in the underworld, where they lay in deep darkness with all the fathers. Then 'the father of the whole human race', all the patriarchs and prophets rejoiced and identified the light as the eternal light which had been promised them. Isaiah, Simeon and John the Baptist give their witness to the promised redeemer. Then the story continues:

Cap.3. Et cum haec audisset PROTOPLASTUS Adam pater, quia in Iordane baptizatus est Iesus, exclamavit ad filium suum Seth: Enarra filiis tuis patriarchis et prophetis omnia quae a Michaele archangelo audisti, quando te transmisi ad portas PARADISI, ut depraecareris deum quatenus transmitteret tibi angelum suum ut daret tibi oleum de arbore misericordiae, ut perungeres corpus meum, cum essem infirmus. Tunc Seth appropinquans sanctis patriarchis et prophetis dixit: Ego Seth cum essem orans dominum ad portas paradisi, ecce angelus domini Michael apparuit mihi dicens: Ego missus sum ad te a domino; ego sum constitutus super CORPUS HUMANUM. Tibi dico enim, Seth, noli lacrimare lacrimis orando et deprecando propter oleum ligni misericordiae, ut perungeres patrem tuum Adam pro dolore corporis sui, quia nullo modo poteris ex eo accipere nisi in novissimis diebus et temporibus, nisi quando completi fuerint QUINQUE MILLIA ET QUINGENTI ANNI.[40] Tunc veniet super terram amantissimus dei filius AD RESUSCITANDUM CORPUS ADAE ET CORPORA MORTUORUM, et ipse veniens in Iordane baptizabitur.... Tunc descendens in terras amantissimus dei filius Christus Iesus INTRODUCET PATREM NOSTRUM ADAM IN PARADISUM ad arborem misericordiae.[41]

Cap.4. (*Inferus* addresses Satan) Et si perduxeris illum ad me, omnes qui sunt hic IN CRUDELITATE CARCERIS CLAUSI ET IN INSOLITIS VINCULIS PECCATORUM CONSTRICTI, solvet et AD VITAM DIVINITATIS SUAE perducet in aeternum.[47]

Cap.5. Et cum haec ad invicem loquerentur Satan princeps et inferus, subito facta est vox ut tonitruum et spiritualis clamor:TOLLITE PORTAS PRINCIPES VESTRAS,ET ELEVAMINI PORTAE AETERNALES, ET INTROIBIT REX GLORIAE... Et facta est vox magna ut tonitruum dicens: TOLLITE PORTAS... Haec dicente David ad inferum, supervenit in forma hominis dominus maiestatis, et aeternas tenebras illustravit et INDISSOLUBILIA VINCULA DISRUPIT, et invictae virtutis auxilium visitavit nos sedentes in profundis tenebris delictorum et in umbra mortis peccatorum.[43]

Cap.8. Et extendit dominus manum suam dixit: Venite ad me sancti mei omnes, qui habetis imaginem et similitudinem meam. Qui per lignum et diabolum et mortum damnati fuistis, modo videte per lignum DAMNATUM DIABOLUM ET MORTEM... Et extendens dominus manum suam fecit signum crucis super Adam et super omnes sanctos suos, et TENENS DEXTERAM ADAE ASCENDIT AB INFERIS,ET OMNES SANCTI SECUTI SUNT EUM.[44]

Cap.9. Dominus autem tenens manum Adae tradidit Michaeli archangelo, et omnes sancti sequebantur Michaelem archangelum, et INTRODUXIT OMNES IN PARADISI gratiam gloriosam. Et occurrerunt eis obviam duo viri vetusti dierum. Interrogati a sanctis: Qui estis vos qui in inferis mortui nondum fuistis et IN PARADISO corpore COLLOCATI estis? Respondens unus ex eis dixit: Ego sum Enoch. . . .[45]

Cap. 10. (The repentant thief explains his presence in paradise) Cum haec a me audivit (*scil.* angelus), statim aperiens introduxit me et COLLOCAVIT me ad dexteram paradisi dicens: Ecce modicum sustine et ingredietur OMNIS GENERIS HUMANI PATER ADAM CUM OMNIBUS FILIIS SUIS SANCTIS ET IUSTIS post triumphum et gloriam ascensionis Christi domini curcifixi. Haec omnia verba latronis audientes, omnes sancti patriarchae et prophetae una voce dixerunt: Benedictus dominus omnipotens, pater aeternorum bonorum et pater misericordiarum, qui talem gratiam peccatoribus tuis dedisti et in gratiam paradisi reduxisti et in tua pinguia pascua: quia haec est spiritualis vita certissima. Amen. Amen.[46]

This is the story which evidently provided our author with his material, even though his rendering of it is condensed and personal. The *pinguia pascua* of paradise suggested to him an additional stanza in praise of the Good Shepherd:

38. Errantem propris evehens centesimam
supernis ovem humeris ovilibus.

The complex stucture of this stanza is reminiscent of the equally tortuous account of the parable given by Prudentius.[47] It is followed by the concluding stanza of this second part of the hymn, with a look to the future coming of Christ in judgment:

39. Quem expectamus adfuturum iudicem
iustum cuique opus suum reddere.

The conclusion expresses the author's wonder at these great gifts of God, as told in the hymn; his sense of inadequacy to offer anything in return, or indeed to speak about them at all-this in the forty-first stanza! All that is left to him is a simple request for mercy; this is the greatest thing man can do:

40. Rogo quam tantis talibusque donariis
vicem condigne possumus rependere?[48]

41. Quid tam mortales temptamus micrologi
narrare, quivit quae nullus edicere?[49]

42. Solum oramus hoc idemque maximum:
nostri aeterne miserere domine. Alleluia.

We can now, by way of conclusion, sum up what we know of the hymn *Praecamur patrem*. The Antiphonary is the only MS in which the hymn is contained and it is not mentioned in any other Irish document.[50] Towards the end of the seventh century some thought it was of Apostolic origin, according to the heading it received in AB: *Ymnum apostolorum ut alii dicunt*. That its author was Irish is certain, and a date of composition in the

56

late sixth century is indicated on grounds of metre and content.[51] Can we determine its origin any more precisely?

The parallels between the hymn and the Epistles of Columban could be explained in a number of ways. Firstly, I think we can safely exclude the authorship of Columban; the parallels are too occasional and fragmentary to support that possibility. Therefore, either Columban himself was influenced by the language and ideas of the hymn or the author of the hymn was influenced by Columban's Epistles. The first alternative is the more acceptable. It gives us a sixth-century date for the hymn,[52] a date suggested also by the metrical and rhyming system.

Now, if Columban was familiar with the hymn, it is reasonable to suppose that he knew it in Ireland before he and his companions left on their pilgrimage around the year 590. The author manifests a good acquaintance with a wide variety of continental material: the hymns of Ambrose, Prudentius, Fortunatus and other early Gallican hymns. He had also read at least one of the Sermons of Caesarius and the apocryphal Gospel of Nicodemus. He seems to have composed his hymn at some date between 570, date of Fortunatus' *Pange lingua*,[53] and 590. The question is, could an Irish scholar acquire such a good knowledge of continental sources in Ireland itself at the end of the sixth century? It is quite possible that he could and, in fact, likely that he did. The monastic school had been established for about fifty years, and such masters as Columban and Columcille would have been anxious to acquire as many manuscripts as possible for their libraries. Even though the possibility of the hymn having been written at Luxeuil cannot be absolutely ruled out, it seems more likely to have been written in Bangor itself. We must remember that the only manuscript of the hymn comes from Bangor. Here, a century later, the author was no longer known and some thought the hymn was of apostolic origin. This tradition confirms its antiquity but it scarcely proves that it was imported from an Irish centre on the continent. The Irish commentaries, on the other hand, cannot be used as proof of its composition in Ireland. They give supporting evidence for Irish authorship, but the earliest of them is half a century later than our hymn.

With its broad sweeping vision of the history of salvation from the day of creation to the second coming of Christ, the hymn is in many ways the most striking and original of all the hymns in the Antiphonary. It is more elaborate in thought and execution than *Hymnum dicat*, and it loses something by comparison in terms of simplicity and realism. The traditional symbolism of light appealed very much to the author. Christ is the eternal Light sent into the world in creation and in the work of salvation. Yet, while remaining God and Eternal King, the Saviour is very much a man, one full of clemency and love for the lost sheep. His saving deeds are told in a manner which shows what good Latin poetry an Irish author could produce at the end of the sixth century and what the person and saving work of Christ meant for him. His conception of the history of salvation was formed on the basis of Scripture and on the knowledge of the great authors of the Western tradition, some of whom we have indicated as direct sources of inspiration. But the author's expression of the traditional themes remains quite original throughout.

CHAPTER FIVE

IGNIS CREATOR IGNEUS

The Ambrosian tradition of hymnody is represented in the Antiphonary by this hymn 'for the blessing of the candle'.[1] It is formally 'Ambrosian' in as much as it consists of eight stanzas in iambic dimeter, with four lines in stanza. In vocabulary also there are many parallels with the hymns and other writings of St Ambrose, and G. Mercati suggested, on the basis of these formal and material similarities, that it is a genuine hymn of St Ambrose.[2] But there is one basic metrical difference between this hymn and the genuine hymns of St Ambrose, in that it is not the classical type of iambic dimeter used by him but rather the archaic type which admitted the use of a spondee in the second foot. Mercati was aware of this metrical difference, but he held that St Ambrose could have changed his style occasionally. W. Meyer, on the other hand, was convinced that this metrical difference alone excludes the possibility of Ambrosian authorship of our hymn.[3]

Irish authorship was ruled out by W. Meyer because of the quantitative metre,[4] but this *a priori* is not tenable in view of the Irish origin of *Hymnum dicat* and the ability of Columban, at least when he settled on the Continent, to write classical verse.[5] In favour of its Irish origin there is, apart from the manuscript tradition, the frequent alliteration and irregular rhyme.[6]

The hymn is a finely constructed one, and the depth of thought blended to the poetic expression of symbolic themes reveals an author of no mean quality.[7] Already in the first stanza the main themes are announced: God as author of *light*, *fire*, *life* and *salvation*. These themes are then developed and illustrated, with particular reference to the paschal themes of the Easter vigil: the deliverance from Egypt, with the column of fire and the burning bush, the Easter celebration of the Church, with the paschal candle and its rich symbolism. In the first part of the hymn the author shows that he is steeped in the symbolic theology which found its classical expression in the hymns of Ambrose[8] and in the evening hymn of Prudentius, *Cath*. V. Indeed, our author probably knew well this hymn of Prudentius. The final three stanzas draw on the speculation about the bee and its activity as expressed in the blessing of the paschal candle, in particular the blessing contained in the Gelasian sacramentary. We will now examine the hymn in greater detail.

1. Ignis creator igneus,
lumen donator luminis
vitaque vitae conditor,
dator salutis et salus.[9]

As we have said, this stanza introduces us into the mainstream of Western hymnody, beginning with St Ambrose. Mercati drew attention to its similarity to the Ambrosian morning hymn (AH 50, 11):

> 1. Splendor paternae gloriae,
> de luce lucem proferens,
> lux lucis et FONS LUMINIS,
> diem dies inluminans.

We may also compare it to Ambrose's hymn for the Epiphany (AH 50, 15):

> 1. Illuminans altissimus
> micantium astrorum globos,
> pax, VITA, LUMEN, veritas,
> Iesu, fave precantibus.

But it is especially in the Spanish hymns that we find these favourite themes developed. For example, the evening hymn of Prudentius, *Cath.* V:

> 1. INVENTOR rutili, dux bone, LUMINIS,
> qui certis vicibus tempora dividis,
> merso sole chaos ingruit horridum,
> lucem redde tuis, Christe, fidelibus!

Or again, the morning hymn of Prudentius, *Cath*.II:

> 1. Nox et tenebrae et nubila,
> confusa mundi et turbida,
> lux intrat, albescit polus,
> Christus venit, discedite!

> 25. Sol ecce surgit IGNEUS;
> piget pudescit paenitet
> nec teste quisquam lumine
> peccare constanter potest.

Prudentius began one of his hymns, *Cath*.X, with the invocation

> Deus, IGNEE FONS animarum

and this fire-theme returns again in his hymn for St Laurence, *Peristeph*.II 393–396:

> Sic IGNIS aeturnus deus
> (nam Christus IGNIS verus est)
> is ipse conplet LUMINE
> iustos et urit noxios.

These classical themes were continued in later Spanish hymns[10] which, though they cannot be regarded as sources for our hymn, show how widespread these ideas were. Indeed, the immediate source of inspiration for our author may well have been the Gelasian *Benedictio cereï*:

> GeV 426 Deus, MUNDI CONDITOR, AUCTOR LUMINIS, SIDERUM FABRICATOR,
> Deus qui iacentem mundum in tenebris luce perspicua retexisti,
> Deus per quem ineffabili potentia OMNIUM CLARITAS SUMPSIT EXORDIUM, ... tibi
> Deo FULGORE FLAMMARUM placita luminaria exhibemus.[11]

The illustration of the basic themes is commenced in the second stanza. The occasion for which the hymn was intended is mentioned and this introduces the theme of *light*:

2. Ne noctis huius gaudia
vigil lucerna deserat,
qui hominem non vis mori
da nostro lumen pectori.

The joyful night referred to can be none other than the night of the Easter vigil; this will become clearer in subsequent stanzas. We may note what appears to be the definite influence of Prudentius, *Cath.*V 137–144:

Nos festis trahimus per pia GAUDIA
NOCTEM conciliis votaque prospera
certatim VIGILI congerimus prece
extructoque agimus liba sacrario.

PENDENT mobilibus LUMINA funibus,
quae suffixa micant per laquearia,
et de languidulis fota natantibus
lucem perspicuo flamma iacit vitro.

This could explain the use of the word *lucerna*, meaning an oil-lamp, in our hymn, which was intended for the blessing of the paschal candle. But, once again, we should observe how close our hymn is to the language of the Gelasian *Benedictio*:

GeV 426 Deus, mundi conditor, ... te in tuis operibus invocantes, IN HAC SACRATISSIMA NOCTIS VIGILIA de donis tuis cereum tuae suppliciter offerimus maiestati. ... Magnum igitur mysterium, et NOCTIS HUIUS mirabile sacramentum, dignis necesse est laudibus cumulari.

The power and symbolism of light and fire in the deliverance from Eygpt of the people, under the leadership of Moses, is now recalled:

3. Ex Aegypto migrantibus
indulges geminam[12] gratiam:
nubis velamen exhibes,
nocturnum lumen porrigis.

4. Nubis columna per diem
venientem plebem protegis,
ignis columna ad vesperum
noctem depellis lumine.[13]

5. E flamma famulum provocas,
rubum non spernis spineam,
et cum sis ignis concremens
non uris quod inluminas.[14]

Again we can indicate parallels in the Gelasian blessing and in Prudentius:

GeV 427 FLAMMAE lux quippe dicenda est per quam potestas Deitatis MOYSI apparere dignata est, quae de terra servitutis populo exeunti salutifero lumine ducatum EXHIBUIT... Nam ut, praecedente huius LUMINIS GRATIA tenebrarum horror excluditur, ita, Domine, lucescente maiestatis tuae imperio, peccatorum sarcinae diluuntur.[15]

Prudentius, *Cath*.V 25 – 32
Splendent ergo tuis muneribus, pater,
flammis nobilibus scilicet atria
absentemque diem lux agit aemula,
quam NOX cum lacero VICTA FUGIT peplo.

Sed quis non rapidi luminis arduam
manantemque deo cernat originem?
Moses nempe DEUM SPINIFERO IN RUBO
vidit conspicuo lumine FLAMMEUM.

The concluding three stanzas of our hymn speak in symbolic terms of the new *life* and *salvation* given to the Church through the Easter mystery. The basis of the symbolism is provided by the paschal candle and its light; the mention of the wax leads into the activity and productivity of the bee, which is symbolically applied in two stanzas:

6. Fuco depasto nubilo
tempus decoctis sordibus
fervente sancto spiritu
carnem lucere ceream.[16]

7. Secretis iam condis favi[17]
divini mellis alitus;
cordis repurgans intimas
verbo replesti cellulas,[18]

8. examen ut foetus novi
ore praelectum Spiritu[19]
relictis caelum sarcinis
quaerat securis pinnulis.[20]

The first of these three stanzas may have been influenced by Prudentius' morning hymn, *Cath*.II, which proclaims that it is now *time* to renounce the dark and evil things of night and to live in the light of day:

1. Nox et tenebrae et NUBILA,
confusa mundi et turbida,
lux intrat, albescit polus,
Christus venit, discedite!

57. Intende nostris sensibus
vitamque totam dispice;
sunt multa FUCIS inlita
quae LUCE PURGENTUR TUA.

61. Durare nos tales iube
quales REMOTIS SORDIBUS
NITERE pridem iusseras
Iordane tinctos flumine.

But we can see above all in this section of the hymn the influence of the Gelasian blessing, which in its second part speaks of the symbolism of the candle and of the bee's fruitful industry:

62

GeV 427 Ad huius ergo festivitatis reverentiam FERVORE SPIRITUS descendentes, quantum devotio humana exigit, tibi Deo fulgore flammarum placita luminaria exhibemus, ut dum haec fide integra persolvuntur, creaturae tuae etiam praeconia extollantur.... Nam ut, praecedente huius luminis gratia, tenebrarum horror excluditur, ita, Domine, lucescente maiestatis tuae imperio, peccatorum SARCINAE diluuntur. Quum igitur huius substantiae miramur exordium, apum necesse est laudemus originem. Apes vero sunt frugales in sumptibus, in procreatione castissimae. Aedificant CELLULAS cereo liquore fundatas quarum humanae peritiae ars magistra non coaequat. Legunt pedibus flores, et nullam damnum in floribus invenitur. Partus non edunt, sed ORE LEGENTES CONCEPTI FETUS REDDUNT EXAMINA, sicut exemplo mirabili Christus ore paterno processit. Fecunda est in his sine partu virginitas, quam utique Dominus sequi dignatus carnalem se matrem habere virginitatis amore constituit. Talia igitur, Domine, digne sacris altaribus tuis munera offeruntur, quibus te laetari religio Christiana non ambigit.

There is no reference in the Gelasian blessing to the more detailed activity of the bees, which was symbolically interpreted by our author, who sees special significance in the storing of honey in the hidden recesses of the honey comb and in the flight of the newly born swarm with their little wings (*pinnuli*). The basis of his symbolical interpretation of this activity was probably provided for him in this case by the *Exultet*:

Ga G 225 ... dispersaeque per agros, libratis paululum PINNIBUS, cruribus suspensis insidunt, (prati) ore legere flosculos. Oneratis victualibus suis ad castra remeant, ibique aliae inaestimabili arte cellulas tenaci glutino instruunt, aliae LIQUANTIA MELLA STIPANT, aliae vertunt flores in ceram, aliae ore natos fingunt, aliae collectis e foliis nectar includunt.... O vere beata nox ... in qua TERRENIS CAELESTIA iunguntur.[21]

Addressing himself directly to God, the author of our hymn expresses his thought on the basis of his material from the blessings of the paschal candle: 'You store up the nourishment of divine honey in the secret recesses of the honey-comb: purifying the innermost cells of the heart, you fill them with your word, so that the swarm of new offspring, begotten by the word and the Spirit, may leave behind the things of earth and soar towards heaven on carefree wings'. This is a fine expression of a deeply experienced reality of the early Church on Easter night. The neophytes are then born into the Christian life. They are the new 'swarm' of the Church, prepared by the sacraments of initiation to live without fear their new life which has its goal in heaven. At the time the hymn was composed there must still have been a large number of candidates for initiation at Easter and our author would have experienced for himself the deep religious meaning and symbolic implication of the whole paschal celebration. He wished to express something of this in his hymn, and he did so by bringing into full prominence certain themes found implicitly in the blessings of the paschal candle. As a result, his hymn for the blessing of the (paschal) candle is even more paschal in its content than the prose blessings on which it largely depends. For Alcuin it was simply a 'paschal hymn' without qualification.[22]

In conclusion, we can say that *Ignis creator igneus* was written by an Irish author and was meant for the blessing of the paschal candle on Easter night. We might compare it in this respect to the *Sancti venite*, which was to be sung 'while the priests were communicating'. And just as the source of the *Sancti venite* was at hand in the early Irish communion antiphons, so also *Ignis creator* draws its chief inspiration and content from the blessing *Deus mundi conditor* and, to a lesser extent, from the *Exultet*. But in the first part of the hymn the author shows his acquaintance with a wider range of sources, notably the hymns of Ambrose and some of Prudentius' hymns, in particular the latter's evening hymn, *Cath*.V.

We cannot say whether or not the hymn entirely replaced the prose formulas for the blessing of the paschal candle in the Irish practice, or, indeed, whether any of the latter were ever used in Ireland. They could well have been known here, at least from the early seventh century, but instead of using them an Irish comunity such as Bangor might have preferred the hymn[23] and the collect *In nocte tu fuisti columna ignis domine* (AB 127).

Certain indications, however, favour Bobbio rather than Bangor as the place where the hymn was composed. The survival of an independent MS from Bobbio, the studied imitation of the metrical structure and language of Ambrose's hymns, and the author's familiarity with the Italian blessings of the paschal candle all point in this direction. If the formula *Deus mundi conditor* is of Roman origin,[24] we have to do with a unique case of Roman influence in the composition of the material contained in the Antiphonary; but by the early seventh century the ancient Roman sacramentary, the 'pre-Gelasian', would have been known in northern Italy and Gaul,[25] and the blessing *Deus mundi conditor* would have been easily available in Bobbio.

Ignis creator igneus is a good example of the Irish inclination to transform traditional liturgical material in order to suit their own particular tastes,[26] in this case, their preference for verse rather than prose. Even if this entails a certain lack of appreciation of the qualities of such a classical piece of liturgical prose as the Gelasian blessing, nevertheless, the tradition of the liturgy is received and expressed in a new and living way. The author of the hymn was deeply influenced by that tradition and he used a traditional metre to give to the blessing of the paschal candle what was, for him, the most fitting literary expression.

A Note on *Mediae Noctis Tempus Est*

This early sixth-century Gallican hymn, which was used for the office of nocturns at Arles, is indicated for the midnight office in the Antiphonary.[27] It must have been brought to Bangor from a Columbanian centre on the Continent in the seventh century. It has recently been studied in detail by M. Simonetti and we have nothing to add to his conclusions.[28] It is a rhythmical imitation of the Ambrosian verse form and in content also it is closely dependent on the Ambrosian tradition. We will deal later with its position in the Bangor office.

CHAPTER SIX

SPIRITUS DIVINAE LUCIS

This hymn, which was destined for matins on Sundays,[1] was not printed by C. Blume in his *Hymnodia Hiberno-Celtica* and neither was it included by J. Szövérffy in his list of hymns of the Antiphonary.[2] The reason is that it can be regarded as a 'hymn' only in the general sense, according to which compositions like the *Te Deum* were universally regarded as hymns in the early Church. In form it consists simply of a varying number of phrases strung together without any regard for equality in length, and without any rythmical pattern whatever. At times it is difficult, even impossible, to make any sense of the 'stanzas' or to break them up into meaningful clauses. In content it is an expression of the dogma of the blessed Trinity and it was regarded by Kenney as 'a rythmical prose adaptation of the language of the creeds'.[3]

The key to a further understanding of the origin and form of this hymn was revealed to me as I read M. Simonetti's fine analysis of the hymns of Marius Victorinus.[4] I was immediately struck by the similarities between these hymns and *Spiritus divinae lucis*. Both have the same characteristics, the same strange form, the same obscurity of language. On further examination of the writings of Victorinus,[5] I soon found that *Spiritus divinae* is based almost entirely on these writings.

We will first review in brief outline the characteristics of the three hymns of Victorinus, as given by Simonetti. These are:

(a) They have no regular or recognizable metre: 'non hanno struttura metrica; sono divisi in versetti di varia estensione, tutti conchiusi in sé e senza collegamento sintattico con gli altri' (p.371).

(b) Each verse or 'stanza' in the second and third hymn is followed by a refrain.

(c) Certain key words are repeated within the individual verses: 'colpisce la tendenza ai construtti simmetrici, alle studiate represe, ai ricercati accostamenti di termini e di concetti' (p.374).

(d) Victorinus has a liking for Greek words. Strangely enough, the author of *Spiritus divinae* resisted this practice, which should have appealed to an Irish author.

(e) In the third hymn there is a gradual build-up of complexity in the verses: 'si comincia con una certa regolaritá, versetti brevi che a mano a mano si fanno sempre piú complessi, ma ad un certo punto l'alternanza diventa capricciosa, et troviamo affiancati, uno di seguito all'altro, versetti di dimensioni molto diverse' (p.374).

(f) The language is obscure.

(g) Another feature of the hymns of Victorinus not mentioned by Simonetti is the constant changing, in hymns II and III, from direct address to God or to one of the three divine Persons to indirect speech about God or about one of the divine Persons.

Each of these characteristics, apart from the use of Greek words, is found in our hymn. We find the same absence of metre, the use of a refrain, the repetition of certain expressions (this is not such a marked feature of our hymn, but we have repetitions of *divinae lucis gloriae, lumen de lumine, in una substantia, unigenitus et primogenitus, nunc cepit*), the gradual build-up in complexity, the obscurity of language, and the changing of address and indirect speech. There is no need for us to illustrate these characteristics at this point; they will become apparent as we go through the hymn and examine its contents in the light of writings of Victorinus.

The hymn depends in detail on the *Adversus Arium libri IV* of Victorinus. In this work there is a vast number of texts which serve to illustrate the meaning of our hymn; we have selected a number which will suffice to throw some light on it and show the manner in which our author was influenced by his model.

> 1. Spiritus divinae lucis gloriae:
> Respice in me, domine.

It is not the Holy Spirit who is addressed here as a distinct Person, but the three divine Persons who are one God and one Spirit. This is one of Victorinus's favourite ideas: he proves the consubstantiality of the three hypostases by showing, among other things, that they are one Spirit. For example:

> I 12,1 – 3 Si deus spiritus et Iesus spiritus et sanctus Spiritus spiritus, ex una sunstantia tria. Homoousion ergo tria.

Victorinus develops this theme on a number of occasions; for example, in this text:[6]

> I 7,12 – 8,25 Quod spiritus deus est, dictum est: 'Spiritus deus est', et quod filius 'spiritus est vivificans'. . . . Et iterum quod ipse Christus, qui filius patris, et ipse est spiritus sanctus:'Iesus stabat et clamabat: si quis est qui sitit, veniat et bibat. Qui credit in me, quemadmodum dixit scriptura, flumina ex ventre ipsius manant aquae viventis'. Est istuc quidem dictum de illo, qui accipit spiritum, qui accipiens spiritum efficitur venter effundens flumina aquae viventis. . . . Venter igitur, qui accipit spiritum, et ipse spiritus venter, a quo manant flumina aquae viventis, sicut scriptura dicit. 'Hoc autem dixit de spiritu'. . . . Sed rursum iterum flumina spiritus, venter autem, ex quo flumina, Iesus; Iesus enim est spiritus. Iam ergo Iesus venter, de quo flumina spiritus. Sicuti enim a gremio patris et 'in gremio' filius, sic a ventre filii spiritus. Homoousioi ergo tres et idcirco in omnibus unus deus. . . . Quod omnes tres spiritus, iam dixit: 'deus spiritus est'. . . . Spiritus autem sanctus spiritus manifeste.

The second stanza is a threefold address and the refrain:

> 2. Deus veritatis, domine deus sabaoth, deus Israhel:
> Respice in me, domine.

Victorinus loves to use such triads, in which to express what he regards as distinct properties or attributes of the divine persons; for example, at the begining of Hymn III:

2 – 5 Deus, Dominus, Sanctus Spiritus:
O beata Trinitas.

14 – 17 Spiritus operationum, spiritus ministeriorum, spiritus gratiarum:
O beata Trinitas.

30 – 33 Fons, flumen, Inrigatio:
O beata Trinitas.

38 – 41 Exsistentia, Vita, Cognitio:
O beata Trinitas.

42 – 45 Caritas, Gratia, Communicatio:
O beata Trinitas .

In our hymn, however, the triad is not meant to express distinct properties of Father, Son and Holy Spirit, but simply various appelations of God as such.

3. Lumen de lumine referimus filium patris
sanctumque spiritum in una substantia:
Respice in me, domine.

The use of *lumen de lumine* as a proof of consubstantiality is naturally found also in Victorinus. We will give simply one text:[7]

II 3,27-34.44-47 Accipiamus et Christum et esse substantiam, et de patre eius esse substantiam, quippe cum sit et ipse LUMEN DE LUMINE, deus de deo, spiritus, logos 'per quem facta sunt omnia', et cum sit ita, ut usque ad mysterium corporale substantia sua venire voluerit, de quo dictum ab Apostolo: 'Et non secundum Christum, quia in illo habitat omnis plenitudo divinitatis corporaliter' quod est ousiodos... Hoc si ita est, et substantia pater et filius, et una substantia, et de patre substantia, et simul substantia, et semper et ex aeterno simul pater et filius, eadem simulque substantia, hoc est homoousion.

4. Unigenitus et primogenitus a te obtinemus
redemptionem nostram:
Respice in me, domine.

It will suffice to cite two texts to show how central this thought is in Victorinus; the first simply states that Jesus is *unigenitus et primogenitus*; the second draws some theological consequences from this in a typically complicated way:[8]

IV 18 39 – 42 Si spiritus sanctus prudentia est et intellectus et scientia et doctrina, Christus est sine dubio, quia ipse est ab aevo, id est ex aeterno, et PRIMOGENITUS, et, quod est amplius, UNIGENITUS.

I 35,6 – 39 Quis igitur iste filius? Ipse, inquit 'in quo habemus REDEMPTIONEM per sanguinem ipsius, remissionem peccatorum nostrorum'. Iste quis est? Qui natus est ex Maria. . . . Si igitur in filio habemus spem, et ipse per sanguinem suam redemit nos, ipse autem imago est dei, imago ergo filius est dei. An ego dico istud? Non solus, sed et Paulus. Quomodo enim dicit? 'Primogenitus omnis creaturae'. Quis primogenitus? Filius. Quis Filius? Filius qui ex Maria. Quis filius ex Maria? 'Primigenitus totius creaturae'. Quis totius creaturae primigenitus? Qui imago dei est.... Si filius dei redemit nos per sanguinem suum, qui de Maria filius est, et, si ipse imago est dei, dei est filius. Si enim totius creaturae primigenitus, necessario filius. Numquid alius? Absit. Unigenitus enim dei filius. Necesse est ergo eundem ipsum esse filium, et imaginem, et eum qui de Maria. Quomodo enim imago dei filius, si non primigenitus totius creaturae? Et quomodo imago dei, qui filius de Maria, post omnia facta, natus est? Manifestum ergo quod ipse primigenitus. Quid vero? Quod natum est de Maria, non creatura est? Sed si filius dei, imago dei, ante omnem creaturam natus est, et ante ipsum qui ex Maria, natus est. Qui igitur ante omnem creaturam natus est, ipse est in eo qui de Maria natus est. Manifestum igitur quod ipse unigenitus.

5. Natus es sancto spiritu ex Maria virgine
in id ipsum in adoptionem filiorum
qui tibi procreati ex fonte vivunt:
Respice in me, domine.

The verses begin to get more complex. The virginal birth of Christ in time is dealt with by Victorinus in the text cited immediately above (I 35,6 – 39). He also has the following close parallel to our text:

I 56,41 – 42 Natus est igitur Iesus Christus secundum carnem de Maria, et ex sancto spiritu, virtute altissimi.

The expression *id ipsum* is used with great frequency by Victorinus,[10] in the sense of 'the same thing', 'identical','identically','by that very fact'. The combination *in id ipsum* occurs in

I 29,29 tu in id ipsum incurris (translated by Hadot: 'tu t'esposes aux mêmes difficultés', p.273), quod metuis in homoousio.

The phrase *in id ipsum in adoptionem filiorum* stresses the connection between adoptive sonship and the birth of Jesus. The sense is stronger than: 'Just as you were born of the virgin, so also the baptized are your (!) adopted sons'. There is a closer identity of sonship between Jesus and the baptized, who are sons only *in that very one* born by the Holy Spirit of the Virgin Mary. We can also see in the repetition of the preposition *in* (*in id ipsum ... in adoptionem*) an indication of the activity of the Holy Spirit in the mystery of rebirth in baptism, similar to his activity in the birth of Jesus. This is suggested by some passages in Victorinus:

I 12,29 – 32 Omne mysterium hoc est: pater inopernas operatio, filius operans operatio in id quod est generare, sanctus autem spiritus operans operatio IN ID QUOD EST REGENERARE.

I 17,24 – 27 Totius mysterii virtus in baptismo est, eius potentia in accipiendo spiritu, utique spiritu sancto. Hoc si ita est dictum est: vos in spiritu estis, utique quem sanctus spiritus dedit vobis.

Victorinus enlarged on the relationship and distinction between the *natural sonship* of Jesus and our *adoptive sonship* especially in this text:[11]

I 10,4 – 15 Quod non sic filius, quemadmodum nos: nos enim adoptione filii, ille natura, etiam quadam adoptione filius et Christus, sed secundum carnem: 'ego hodie genui te'; si enim istud, solum hominem filium habet, sed: 'ante Abraham ego sum' dicens, quod natura filius erat primum, declaravit. Non igitur Photinianum dogma verum. Deinde nos 'non gentes solum', sed et 'qui dispersi sunt filii'. Dei igitur filius Christus, filii et nos; sed nos per adoptionem, nos per Iesum Christum, nos ut filii dispersi. Num et Christus sic filius? Natura igitur Iesus filius, nos adoptione filii. Quod natura filius, et ipse dicit saepe. . . .

6. Heredes et coheredes Christi tui,
in quem et per quem cuncta creasti,
quia in praedestinatione a saeculis
nobis est deus Iesus qui nunc cepit:[12]
Respice in me, domine.

We have to go to Victorinus's commentaries on Paul's epistles to find his treatment of this consequence of adoptive sonship, that we are heirs and co-heirs with Christ[13]. But we find in his books *Adv. Arium* the constant affirmation of the doctrine *in quem* (*in quo*) *et per quem omnia* as expressing the divinity of the Son and the creation of all things by him:

I 35,2 – 3 Quid est Logos? Per quem omnia, et in quo omnia, et in quem omnia.[14]

The eternity of the Son, his existence before the creation of the world and before he became man, is a fundamental doctrine of Victorinus, in opposition to the principle *fuit quando non fuit* of the Arians.[15] In opposition to this eternal existence, there is the temporal birth of Jesus, his beginning in time. This is expressed in the words of our hymn:

II 2,6 – 19 Deus, ut inquunt, esse est; Christus, item, esse, sed COEPIT tamen. VERUM HOC EST. Sed istud esse quod coepit, ab eo coepit, quod fuit aliquo modo fuisse, ut omnia divina et a divinis orta, potentia semper sunt ac fuerunt. . . . An illud credibile est aut fas est dicere, ex nihilo vel factum vel natum esse Christum quem dicimus dei filium, qui est dominus maiestatis, et cetera quae supra diximus et in aliis libris. Hoc vero postrema haeresis dicit, cui similis et illa est quae vel a Maria dicit coepisse Christum, vel quae non ipsum Logon induisse carnem, sed assumpsisse hominem, ut eum ipse Logos regeret, atque hoc Marcellus, quod superius autem Photinus.

7. Unigenitus ex mortuis deus
obtinens corpus claritatem dei
manens in saecula saeculorum rex aeternorum:
Respice in me, domine.

The author does not depend here on Victorinus; he has simply joined together certain scriptural references to Christ,[16] quite without regard for the meaning of the stanza as a whole. The resultant obscurity was probably intended directly, as an imitation of the style of Victorinus.

8. Quia nunc cepit qui semper fuit naturae tuae
filius divinae lucis gloriae tuae,
qui est forma et plenitudo divinitatis tuae frequens:
Respice in me, domine.

In this stanza the effort of the author achieves the summit of obsurity, and at the same time succeeds in concentrating some of the favourite ideas of Victorinus. We have already illustrated the phrase *nunc cepit qui semper fuit* (stanza 6). We have also considered the category *filius naturae*, when we discussed Victorinus's teaching on adoptive sonship and its relationship to the natural sonship of Christ (stanza 5). The conception of the Son as *forma Dei* is one of the fundamental categories of the theology of Victorinus: the Father is the substance, *esse*, to which the Son is consubstantial by being the *forma*, *logos*, *agere* or *actio* in relation to the *esse*. This implies the mutual presence in the other of Father and Son, the superiority of the Father and the action of the Son in creation and revelation.[17] Out of many possible texts[18] we will cite one as an example:

> I 53,9 – 15 Filius forma est patris, ... substantia quaedam subsistens, in qua apparet et demonstratur quod occultatum et velatum est in alio. Deus autem et velatum quiddam est. Nemo enim videt deum. Forma igitur filius, in qua videtur deus.

The expression *plenitudo divinitatis* (Col.2,9) is also, of course, used and explained by Victorinus. For example:[19]

> I 25,2 – 30 Si non homoousion, quomodo et pater et plenitudo, et filius?... Quod in eo inhabitat omnis plenitudo divinitatis corporaliter, hoc est in operatione substantialiter. In patre enim potentialiter omnia inhabitant, et idcirco Iesus logos, imago est dei patris.

What is meant by *frequens* (T: *frequerens*) is impossible to say. Perhaps it means that these expressions are found frequently in Scripture and in Victorinus.

> 9. Persona unigeniti et primogeniti
> qui est totus a toto
> diximus lux de lumine:
> Respice in me, domine.

Victorinus strenuously refused to use the term *persona* as the equivalent of *hypostasis*, as we shall see when we come to the next stanza. He used *persona* only once of Christ, and then only as the equivalent of *forma*.[20] But the expression *totus a (de, ex)toto* is a favourite one of his and he also uses it in association with the other expression, *lumen ex lumine*:

> I 9,6 – 7 Quomodo 'pater in me est et in patre', si non a patre substantiam habuisset et potentiam, genitus de toto totus?[21]

> I 13,6 – 9 Accedit etiam: si totus ex toto et lumen ex lumine et si omnia quae habet pater dedit filio – omnia autem sunt et substantia et potestas et dignitas – , aequalis patri.

> IV 29,17 – 22 Intelligendo autem totum quod pater est, pleroma exstitit genitus et ipse totus ex toto..., lumen ex lumine.... verum lumen ex vero lumine.... deus ex deo.[22]

The term *diximus* refers back to *lumen de lumine* of stanza 3, and this is surely a further imitation of the style of Victorinus, who frequently refers back to points already treated by himself, using such expressions as *diximus*, *docuimus*, and so forth.[23]

10. Et deum verum a deo vero se se confitemur,
tribus personis in una substantia:
Respice in me, domine.

This concluding stanza, a brief expression of the substance of the dogma, was probably suggested by the profession of faith given by Victorinus at the end of his first book *Adv. Arium*, a formula which summarises his teaching and could serve as a paraphrase of our hymn:

I 47 CONFITEMUR igitur deum patrem omnipotentem, confitemur filium unigenitum Iesum Christum, deum de deo, lumen verum de lumine vero, formam dei, qui habet substantiam de dei substantia,natura, generatione filium, simul cum patre consubstantiatum, quod Graeci homoousion appellant, primogenitum ante constitutionem mundi et primogenitum ante omnem creaturam, hoc est et ante in substantiam veniendi et regenerationis et revivendi et reviviscendi, primogenitum a mortuis... Confitemur ergo et sanctum spiritum ex deo patre omnia habentem, to logo hoc est Iesu Christo tradente illi omnia, quae Christus habet a patre. Et isto huius modi modo et simul confitemur esse haec tria et isto quod unum et unum deum et homoousia ista et semper simul et patrem et filium et spiritum sanctum.

Haec tria, not *tres personae*! The purpose of Victorinus is to defend the dogma of Nicea and its implications: Father, Son and Holy Spirit are three distinct hypostases; they are consubstantial, homoousioi. He refused to use the word *persona*, so as to ward off any possible accusation of Patripassianism.[24] Instead he used concrete denominations, *haec tria*, or the more abstract *subsistentia* as the Latin equivalent of *hypostasis*.[25] His opposition to *persona* is expressed unequivocally:

I 11,15 – 18 Non oportet igitur dicere: duae personae, una substantia, sed: duo, pater et filius, ex una substantia, dante patre a sua substantia filio substantiam in hoc, in quo genuit filium et ex hoc homoousioi ambo.

I 41,26 – 29 Non enim oportet dicere, nec fas et dicere, unam esse substantiam, tres esse personas. Si enim istud, ipsa substantia et egit omnia et passa est. Patripassiani ergo et nos? Absit.

The author of the hymn, therefore, corrected Victorinus in this matter and used the long-accepted terminology: three persons in one substance.[26]

Finally, the expression *se se*, which has constituted an insoluble crux for the editors of the hymn,[27] can be explained as a maladroit borrowing from the writings of Victorinus. He uses it to show that the generation of the Son is an action identified with the divinity, not something external to God. In this sense, he claims, the Son generates himself, since he is identified with the will of God; the Father generates in as much as it is God who generates and, consequently, he is Father. Victorinus is typically obscure in his explanation of this idea, but evidently our author thought he understood him:

I 32,3 – 8 A SE SE movens pater, a SE SE generans filius, sed potentia patris SE SE generans filius: voluntas enim filius. Vide enim: si ipsa voluntas non est a SE SE generans, nec voluntas est. Sed quoniam dei est voluntas, equidem ipsa quae sit generans, generatur in deo, et ideo deus pater, voluntas filius, unum utrumque.[28]

The expression *deum verum a deo vero se se* of our hymn has its source in this idea of Victorinus, whether or not he would agree with this formulation of it. In the context the *se se* is both unnecessary and meaningless, inserted for enigmatic effect, and should at least have been followed by *generantem* to bring out the idea of Victorinus.

To sum up, *Spiritus divinae lucis* is based both in style and language on the works of Marius Victorinus. While Warren was justified in claiming that 'it does not exhibit sufficiently distinct characteristics to enable us to decide whether it is an Irish composition or an importation from the continent'[29] it now has all the appearance of being an Irish work of imitation. The author must have been fascinated by the style and obscure thought of Victorinus and conceived the desire to produce something equally good himself. And, indeed, this entire hymn is a vivid illustration of a particular trait of the Irish mentality at that time: their penchant for the rare and the difficult, their liking for strange words and authors, as exemplified in their adoption of the strange grammar of Virgilius Maro, in the language of the *Hisperica famina*, and in their pursuit of etymologies and explanations in the 'three sacred languages'. *Spiritus divinae lucis* is not a lost hymn of Victorinus – the word *persona* and the not only obsure but occasionally meaningless language excludes that possibility.

It is difficult to say whether our author came upon the works of Victorinus in Ireland or the Continent. At the end of the fourth century his writings were well known and admired at Milan, in neoplatonic circles, and in particular by St Augustine. They were taken to Spain around the year 400 as material for the fight against Priscillianism, but the Spanish clergy did not find them very helpful.[30] They may have been transmitted from Spain to Ireland, along with so many other works in the seventh century. But they may also have been discovered in northern Italy following the foundation of Bobbio and sent from there to Ireland.[31] It is also possible that the hymn was written by an Irish monk at Bobbio and sent from there to Bangor. Of these alternatives, I am inclined to favour the transmission to Ireland of the works of Victorinus, either from Bobbio or from Spain, and the composition of the hymn in Ireland itself, doubtless at Bangor, at some date in the seventh century. It has survived in three MSS and it must have attained a certain popularity in Ireland and in Irish foundations abroad as the hymn for matins on Sundays.

CHAPTER SEVEN

SACRATISSIMI MARTYRES

This hymn was meant for use 'on the feast of martyrs or on Saturdays for matins' and it is not found in any other MS apart from the Antiphonary.[1] There are nine stanzas in the hymn, with three lines and a refrain in each stanza. The lines, including the refrains, vary in length from eleven to fifteen syllables. There are only rare and uncertain traces of rhyme and alliteration.[2]

W. Meyer attempted to prove, with great brilliance and imaginative insight, that it is a strictly rhythmical hymn, written in anapaestic accentual feet, in imitation of certain Greek hymns in honour of the martyrs.[3] He remarked, firstly, that this hymn stands apart from the rest of Hiberno-Latin rhythmical poetry.[4] The lines, which are generally of twelve syllables, are built in accentual feet:

Sacratíssimi mártyres súmmi déi
tibi sáncti proclámant: allélúia

This anapaestic pattern is recognizable in many lines and it can easily be restored in some others; for example,

Armis spiritalibus munita mente

can be easily corrected to:

Spiritálibus ármis muníta ménte.

In Latin no word or line can end in an accentual anapaest, so that the final anapaest had to be replaced by another foot: the stress *muníta menté* is impossible and it becomes simply *muníta ménte*.

This type of anapaestic rhythmical line, though unheard of in Latin hymnody, was frequently used by the Greeks in their rhythmical poetry. Meyer wondered, therefore, whether *Sacratissimi martyres* was not a translation from a Greek original. He failed to discover this hypothetical original, but he did find the same anapaestic line used in hymns in praise of the martyrs, with *alleluia* also in the refrain.[5] The particular tone in which these hymns were written was called *autòs mónos*, which consisted of eight lines followed by a refrain. The lines varied in length from ten to twelve syllables and were all in anapaestic rhythm apart from the fifth line which was constructed of accentual iambs. Meyer considered the sixth line as particularly significant: it had twelve syllables and was frequently accented in exactly the same way as the lines of *Sacratissimi martyres* (in Meyer's view), that is, three anapaests followed by an amphibrac.[6] Meyer concluded that an Irishman heard a Greek hymn in praise of the martyrs composed in the tone *autòs mónos*, and conceived the desire to write something similar in Latin. To simplify the task, he chose one line of the

Greek hymn as his structural model and repeated it four times in each stanza. The last word of the fourth line is always *allélúia*.

Meyer's conclusion, which he regarded as certain,[7] has been accepted as such by subsequent authorities.[8] But I think this argument is unsatisfactory and inconclusive. In the first place, it is *a priori* unlikely that an Irish author of the seventh century would have known sufficient Greek to have understood and imitated a Greek hymn, even if he had occasion to hear one.[9] Naturally, every rule admits of exceptions and one cannot insist on this *a priori*. Above all, it is clear from the hymn itself and from the manner in which Meyer had to correct it to suit his hypothesis that the composition of the hymn in anapaestic accentual feet was never intended by the author. Meyer finds it easy to correct such lines as *Armis spiritalibus munita mente*, but it is difficult to appreciate how such 'scribal errors' were possible when, presumably, the same scibes knew the hymn by heart, since they chanted it every Saturday at matins. The fact that the scribes wrote *Armis spiritalibus munita mente* and that it was left uncorrected[10] is clear enough indication that an anapaestic rhythm never entered their minds. Was it intended by the original author and subsequently forgotten? The answer to this question is found in the hymn itself, where out of the total 36 lines only 19 have, without correction, an anapaestic rhythm. This total of nineteen anapaestic lines includes the seven repetitions of the refrain:

tibi sáncti proclámant (*al.* canébant): allélúia

and it includes such lines as:

4,3 qui cum ipsa crucís pateréntur mórte
5,1 Christe mártyrum tú es adiútor pótens
9,2 ut in ipsius glóriam cónsummémur

Seven of the remaining seventeen lines defy correction to an anapaestic rhythm,[11] and Meyer proposed correct readings for the other ten lines, which affect every stanza except the first.[12] I think it is unacceptable that the hymn could have become so totally corrupt between the time of its composition – some time in the seventh century, according to Meyer – and the date of its incorporation into the Antiphonary.

How, then, are we to explain the appearance of this strange rhythmical form, for which there is no model in Latin hymnody? First, it is necessary to point out that it is not so unique in form as has been supposed.[13] There are over twenty other items in the Antiphonary which correspond exactly, in rhythmical form, to the form used in our hymn. These other items are the many rhythmical collects and antiphons for the morning office at Bangor. The number of lines in these pieces can be either two, or three, or four; the number of syllables in each line can vary from ten to sixteen, but it is generally between ten and thirteen. Many of the lines have a partly anapaestic rhythm. We will give a few examples to show the similarity:

AB 85. *Collectio post evangelium*
Diluculo lucis auctore resurgente
exultémus in dómino devicta morte,

quo peccáta possımus semper obire
vitaeque ambulemus in novitate.

AB 87. *De martyribus*
Triumphálium mémores mártyrum tuorum
qui pro té tolleráre vixílla passionum,
praecamur ut per sancta merita ipsorum
nostrorum veniam mereamur peccatorum.

AB 99,1. *Antiphona super cantemus*
Educti ex Aegypto patres nostri
et pertransierunt pedibus rubrum mare,
dixerunt laudem domino nostro.

The key to the understanding of this rhythmical verse is not to be sought in rhythmic Greek models, but rather in native Irish vernacular versification. We referred in our first chapter to the 'rhythmical patterns' characteristic of Irish alliterative verse, the form which prevailed before the introduction of syllabic verse-forms from Latin hymnody. G. Murphy distinguishes two types of this early verse:[14] the older form of *retoiric* 'in which the rhythm of the lines varies greatly and no strict rule of alliteration prevails', and later poems 'composed in short lines of almost identical rhythm with regular alliteration'. He describes the form of these later poems more fully in these words:

> Each short line . . . commonly contains two or three stressed feet; the final foot in each line commonly has the rhythm ⁔ (though not in all examples), and a line of slightly different build may be used to mark off a section; there is commonly alliteration between words in each short line, and almost always between the last word of each short line and the first word of the next.[15]

Stress and alliteration were, therefore, the chief features of this early verse. But there are a number of poems which belong to the period of transition between the old accentual verse and the new syllabic metres, poems which contain some features of both types of verse.[16] These poems belong to the old tradition of accentual verse in the rhythm and irregular length of the lines. But the binding and decorative functions formerly served by alliteration are now ever more fully taken over by rhyme. This type of rhymed alliterative accentual verse continued to be used alongside the new syllabic metres for a long time.[17]

In seventh-century Ireland, therefore, there were two main types of vernacular Irish verse: the old 'rudely rhythmical' unrhymed alliterative verse, which continued to be cultivated in secular and ecclesiastical literature until about the ninth century, and the new syllabic verse which used rhyme and alliteration as its chief ornaments. A transitional stage in the development of the new metres is witnessed in certain poems which are still basically rhythmical rather than syllabic, but which show an incipient use of rhyme and a more sparing use of alliteration. I suggest that the hymn *Sacratissimi martyres* and the many other rhythmical pieces in the Antiphonary are structural imitations of those poems which we have classed as transitional. They are rhythmical, not syllabic, and they show that incipient use of rhyme and more sparing use of alliteration which characterizes the vernacular poems. They offer us a new, hitherto unsuspected, witness to the encounter of the native Irish tradition of verse with the new Christian Latin culture. This encounter resulted, on the one hand, in the new syllabic metres adapted for vernacular verse and, on the other hand, in the use of the old rhythmical form for Latin compositions, as exemplified in *Sacratissimi martyres* and the rhythmical collects and antiphons of the Antiphonary. In some of these pieces there is a plentiful use of alliteration, in others very little or none at all; in most there is a combination of rhythm and rhyme. They all mark the period of transition between the old alliterative verse to the new rhymed syllabic form, in so far as the irregular rhythmical line is still the basic feature. In the Irish prototype each short line had two or three stressed feet – the number varied even within the same poem.[18] In the Latin rhythmical pieces of the Antiphonary there are generally two stresses in each half-line, but occasionally we also find three stresses. And a greater variety of rhythmical patterns is possible in Latin than in Irish, in which the stress must always fall on the first syllable and a line could not begin with a rhythmical anapaest. In *Sacratissimi martyres* the most prevalent rhythmical pattern is the anapaestic; this is particularly marked in the first stanza. But it cannot have been the author's intention to construct his hymn of 'anapaestic feet'. This rhythm came to him implicitly in his very choice of the majestic words of the opening lines, words which express in superlative fashion the depth of his own feelings for the martyrs.[19] And it is only one of the many varieties of strict rhythmical feet (iambic, trochaic . . .) used in the course of the hymn. This variety does not destroy the overall rhythmical unity of the hymn, which goes forward on the basic rhythm, which even we today can appreciate in reading it, of two stresses in each half-line.

We can now see in detail how *Sacratissimi martyres* must be considered as rhythmical verse in the sense of the early tradition of Irish rhythmical verse. The number of syllables in each long line is not 'mostly twelve', as Meyer claimed; it is either eleven (9 lines), or twelve (10 lines), or thirteen (9 lines), but there are also lines of fourteen or fifteen syllables. There are some half-lines regarding which it is difficult to say whether they were meant to have two or three stresses; but these are rare cases, and what I consider to be subordinate stresses will be marked ˎ, while the main stress will be marked ˊ. As we go through the hymn, certain parallel expressions and ideas regarding the martyrs in other sources will be noted. Not much can be offered in this connection because of the very general content and the language of the hymn. It is a hymn in praise of the martyrs, but there are no detailed references to their sufferings or to their historical existence. This in itself is significant, since the Irish Church never experienced martyrdom in its own history. It is just as much a hymn in praise of Christ and of his power as manifested in the heroic fidelity of the martyrs.

Following his opening words, in which he expresses his admiration for the martyrs, their fortitude and strength, the author addresses Christ. The Lord is now glorified and surrounded by choirs of angels and martyrs, but he was the first to suffer and he gave his apostles the strength to follow him and be crucified with him. He is the strength of the martyrs; he gives them the Holy Spirit so that they may remain steadfast in the struggle and finally share in the reign of Christ and obtain the crown which awaits them.

> 1.Sacratíssimi mártyres súmmi déi,[20]
> bellatóres fortíssimi Chrísti régis,
> potentíssimi dúces exércitus déi,
> victóres in caélis déo canéntes: allelúia.[21]

Similar expressions of praise for the martyrs are found in other Irish sources:

> AB 124 Sancti et gloriosi, mirabiles atque POTENTES martyres, quorum in operibus gaudet dominus et in congregatione laetatur, intercessores optimi et FORTISSIMI protectores, mementote. . . .

Columban, *Epist*.5,17.

> De caetero, sancte papa et fratres, orate pro me, vilissimo peccatore, et meis comperegrinis, iuxta loca sancta et sanctorum cineres et praecipue iuxta Petrum et Paulum, viros similiter et magnos magni REGIS DUCES AC FORTISSIMOS campi felicissimi BELLATORES, DOMINUM CRUCIFIXUM cum cruore SEQUENTES, ut mereamur Christo haerere. . . .[22]

A similar 'militaristic' interpretation of the victory of the martyrs is also found in Ambrose's *Aeterna Christi munera*; he, however, goes into the detail of their sufferings.[23]

> 2. Excelsíssime Chríste caelórum déus,
> hirubín cui sédes cum pátre sácra,
> angelórum ibi et mártyrum fúlgiens chórus,
> tibi sáncti proclámant: allelúia.
>
> 3. Magnífice tú prior ómnium passus crúcem,
> qui devícta mórte refulsísti múndo,
> ascendísti ad caélos ad déxteram déi,
> tibi sáncti proclámant: allelúia.
>
> 4. Ármis spiritálibus muníta ménte[24]
> apóstoli sáncti te súnt secúti,
> qui cum ípsa crúcis pateréntur mórte
> tibi sáncti canébant: allelúia.
>
> 5. Christe mártyrum tú es adiútor pótens
> proeliántium sáncta pro túa glória,
> qui cum victóres exírent dé hoc saéculo
> tibi sáncti canébant: allelúia.
>
> 6. Inlústris tua dómine laudánda vírtus,
> qui per spíritum sánctum firmávit mártyres,
> qui constérnerent zábulum et mórtem víncerent,
> tibi sáncti canébant: allelúia.

7. Mánu dómini excélsa protécti
cóntra diabólum stetérunt firmáti,
sèmper trinitáti fîdem[25] tòto córde sérvantes,
tibi sáncti canébant: allelúia.

8. Vére regnántes erunt técum Christe déus,
qui passiónis mérito corónas hábent,
et centinário frúctu repléti gaúdent,[26]
tibi sáncti proclámant: allelúia.

9. Chrîsti dei grátiam súpplices obsecrémus,
út in ipsîus glóriam consummémur,
et in sáncta Hierúsalem civitáte déi
trinitáti cum sánctis dicámus: allelúia.

Sacratissimi martyres is an eloquent witness to the veneration of the martyrs in the early Irish Church. But it is more than that. It mirrors for us in the clearest manner the thoughts and aspirations of the Irish monastic movement, revealing the source of its strength and the goal to which it aspired.

God the Father is a remote figure, *Deus summus*, hidden behind the halo of glory which surrounds Christ the King. Christ is the most exalted King, *Christus Deus* (stanzas 2, 8, 9), surrounded by the radiant choir of angels and martyrs. His passion and death, his resurrection and ascension were a magnificent triumph, not only for himself but also for his followers. His glory does not remove him from his disciples: on the contrary, they share in his victory, carry on the battle against death and the devil, as God's army in the world, are strengthened by him through the Holy Spirit, until, finally, in total fidelity to the faith (*fides trinitatis*), they obtain the crown and reign with him.

The victory of the apostles and of the other martyrs was achieved through a struggle comparable to that of Christ, through spiritual armour, through strength and fidelity. There is not a word here about their love for Christ, or about salvation and holiness.[27] Rather, the martyrs are *fortified* by Christ and by the Holy Spirit so that they may crush the devil, overcome death and march victoriously out of this world.

This aspect of Christian existence, the spiritual combat with the devil and with sin, appealed in a marked degree to the Irish monastic spirit. Even though *red martyrdom*, which consisted 'in suffering tortures and death for the love of Christ, like the apostles' was never likely in Ireland, it was replaced by other types of martyrdom. *White martyrdom* was chosen by those 'who for the love of God renounce everything that they like, no matter what privations and troubles they may have to pass through'. Along with this there was a *green martyrdom* which consisted in 'the mortification of their desires by privations and hardships in order to repent and do penance'[28]. The spiritual arms of prayer and works of penance were taken up enthusiastically by the Irish monks, that through these means they might share in the glory of Christ, aided by his grace and by the merits of the saints.

The hymn *Sacratissimi martyres* appears to be earlier than the rhythmical collects in honour of the martyrs, if we are to judge from the absence of rhyme in it. It is also probably anterior to the prose collects on the martyrs, all of which were probably introduced into Ireland in the seventh century, as we shall see. I would date it to a sixth-century Irish monastery, possibly Bangor itself. Its rhythmical form gives us further evidence of the fusion of native Irish tradition with the new Latin learning and life of the Church in the second half of the sixth century. The old Irish rhythmical form appears here in a new Latin medium, in as much as (in G. Murphy's words):

(a) 'each short line . . . contains two or three stressed feet';
(b) 'the final foot in each line commonly has the rhythm - (though not in all examples)'; the exceptions here are: *glória, saéculo* (5,2 − 3), *mártyres, víncerent* (6,2 − 3);
(c) 'a line of slightly different build may be used to mark off a section'.

Whatever further light may be cast on the nature and structures of this accentual type of Irish verse, it is clear that *Sacratissimi martyres* is not an imitation of a Greek model but, rather, the utilization of an ancient Irish metre for the praise of the Christian martyrs and of Christ, their King and leader.

CHAPTER EIGHT

THREE BANGOR HYMNS

Three hymns in the Antiphonary deal explicitly with Bangor and its abbots. There is one in honour of St Comgall; another, which is very like the first in form and language, in honour of the first fifteen abbots of Bangor; and the third, a poem in praise of Bangor itself.

1. COMGALL'S HYMN

This is a long alphabetical hymn of twenty-three stanzas, with eight lines in each stanza; there is also an introductory stanza of eight lines, followed by a refrain of four lines, two of which are repeated alternately after each stanza of the hymn.[1] Metrically, it is a rhythmical version of the iambic dimeter: each line has eight syllables and ends in a proparoxytone.[2]

The chief interest of the hymn lies in the author's artistry with regard to rhyme and metrical form. The rhyme is of the 'chain' variety:[3] all the lines of a stanza end in an identical vowel or syllable (*a, e, em, um, us, o, os,*). An attempt was also made to commence each line with the leading letter of the particular stanza, but this attempt was completed successfully only in stanzas A and D; in stanzas O and Q every second line commences with O and Q respectively.

The language is tedious and repetitive, and the hymn is lacking in inspiration. The author was so taken up with the formalities of metre and rhyme that he often chose words for those reasons alone, at the expense of meaning and clear development of thought, as in this stanza:

3. Contemptum mundialium
voluntatum praesentium
vitiorum firmissimum
infirmos devastantium
verborum cogitaminum
parte leva versantium
continebat per viscerum
secreta vigilantium.

St Comgall is named in the introduction to the hymn,[4] but in the whole extent of it we are not given any historical information about his life and activity. We find, instead, numerous expressions of praise for the saint's virtue, his learning, apostolic zeal and eternal reward, with constant repetition of the same stereotyped forms.[5]

Comgall was founder and first abbot of Bangor, and he died around the year 602. This hymn was written in the seventh century by a monk at Bangor and it testifies, at least, to the esteem with which he was remembered by his community. The artistry of the rhyme indicates a date rather late in seventh century. In spite of its great length, it is the least interesting of all the hymns of the Antiphonary.

2. THE ABBOTS OF BANGOR

The author of Comgall's hymn without doubt also composed this hymn 'in memory of our abbots'.[6] It is identical in form: lines of eight syllables, which end in proparoxytones.[7] There is an introductory stanza of eight lines, and then four stanzas of six lines each in alphabetical arrangement; the last line of the fourth stanza, being the twenty-fourth line, is beyond the alphabetical arrangement.[8] There follows a concluding stanza of eight lines. The refrain which follows the first stanza is repeated throughout, except apparently after the concluding stanza.

The rhyme is again rich and of the chain type: *a* at the end of each line in the introductory and concluding stanzas, *um* at the end of each line in stanzas 2 and 3, *us* at the end of the lines in stanzas 4 and 5. The language is as stereotyped as in Comgall's hymn, and the difficulty is increased here by the insertion of fifteen abbots' names within a few lines; for example,

2. Amavit Christus Comgillum,
bene et ipse dominum;
carum habuit Beognoum;
domnum ornavit Aedeum;
elegit sanctum Sinlanum,
famosum mundi magistrum.[9]

Certain parallel expressions are found in this and in Comgall's hymn.[10] The hymn is important especially in that it helps us to date the MS as a whole. It is the last item in the Antiphonary and it was composed between 680 and 691, while Cronán was abbot. It also gives the names of the first fifteen abbots of Bangor; they are known from other sources also.[11]

3. IN PRAISE OF BANGOR

Benchuir bona regula is a beautiful poem in which the author expresses his love and admiration for the community of Bangor, for the holiness and strictness of its 'divine' rule, and the virtues of the monastic life in Bangor.[12] Metrically it is a rhythmical imitation of iambic dimeter catalectic: a line of seven syllables, which concludes with a paroxytone and in which trisyllabic paroxytones are avoided in the first and middle positions.[13] There are ten stanzas, with four lines in each stanza.

The rhyme is varied and most perfect.[14] Each line ends in *a* and, on top of this, there is disyllabic alternating rhyme or assonance in the final syllables: *ecta*, *ata*, *erta*, *ata*, and so on throughout the hymn.

The introductory stanza praises the rule of Bangor:

Benchuir bona regula
recta atque divina,

stricta sancta sedula
summa iusta ac mira.

The remaining nine stanzas are devoted to praise of the Bangor community, *munther Benchuir*.[15] It is praised for its faith, hope and charity (stanza 2). The author draws on the biblical symbols for the Church[16] when he compares the community to a ship (3), a bride prepared for her marriage to the king (3), a house full of delights founded on rock (4), a fortified city (5), the arc of the covenant (6), the queen clothed in the light of the sun (7), the sheepfold of Christ (8), virgin and mother (9). The language is simple and direct, and the well-chosen words have a truly lyrical quality about them:

3. Navis nunquam turbata,
quamvis fluctibus tunsa,
nuptis quoque parata
regi domino sponsa.

4. Domus delicis plena
super petram constructa,
necnon vinea vera
ex Aegipto transducta.

The final stanza looks forward to the blessed life that awaits the family of Bangor, in union with all the saints:

10. Cui vita beata
cum perfectis futura,
deo patre parata,
sine fine mansura.

If we are to judge from the perfection of the rhyme, this hymn was composed at Bangor in the second half of the seventh century, not long before its incorporation into the Antiphonary.

CHAPTER NINE

CONCLUSION

The foregoing separate analysis of each of the hymns contained in the Antiphonary was necessitated by the variety of subject matter, sources of inspiration, structure and authorship with which they confront us. But, however interesting and necessary this journey into the original sources and bye-ways of history may have been, we cannot afford to ignore the fact that when we first meet these hymns they are united in the pages of one book, a book of prayer for the celebration of the divine office at Bangor in the seventh century. They can, from this point of view, be considered as a unit. It is not our purpose here to go into all the detail such a study of the Antiphonar, as a book of prayer, would merit.[1] But we can offer some guidelines and attempt a synthesis of the results of this part of our enquiry.

These hymns were those used by the Bangor community in their liturgical prayer, perhaps not all the hymns they knew but at least the ones most commonly used. They were not the most extensive part of the monk's prayer, which, in terms of quantity, consisted above all in psalmody, but they express better than anything we now possess the spirit of that prayer, its Christian dimension and content.

The person of Christ, his salvific work and achievements, are the leading motifs in these early hymns. This is especially true of the two great hymns *Hymnum dicat* and *Praecamur patrem*, but it is no less true of *Sancti venite*, *Sacratissimi martyres* and, as part of the *fides trinitatis*, of *Spiritus divinae lucis*. Throughout them all there is a strong emphasis on the divinity of Christ, the Creator, the Word Incarnate, the Light sent by the Father into the world, the King enthroned at the right hand of God and the Judge who is to come. But this great God and King is also the Saviour, whose mercy and pastoral care are extended to mankind, whose Holy Spirit is given to his disciples to make them sons of God, sharers in his life, his strength and grace, his struggle and eventual glory. There is in these hymns, at once a strong awareness of the great gifts of God, the grace and power of Christ, and, on the other hand, the need for a generous and enthusiastic response of praise and commitment in the great drama of salvation, the Christian warfare with the devil and with everything opposed to the reign of Christ.

The hymns in honour of St Patrick and St Camelacus and that in honour of all the martyrs give a portrait of the ideal saint: one inspired by the example of Christ, one whose thought and life are nourished by the Scriptures and by the catholic faith, one who practises what he preaches and does mighty works in the strength of Christ, works of prayer and dedication to the needs of the Church, with a great reward in store for him.

The love of the monk for his own *muinter*, his attachment to his community and its founder, is vividly expressed in *Benchuir bona regula*

84

and in the two hymns in honour of the first abbots of Bangor. This is 'the house that is full of delights' (*Benchuir bona* 4,1): delights of virtue and learning which attracted many devoted disciples and students. The hymns which we have in the Antiphonary stem from the golden age of the Irish monastic movement, the years of foundation and consolidation of the monastic *familiae*. Bangor was one of the most renowned of these monasteries and doubtless was appreciated as such by those who belonged to it.

Our investigation of the individual hymns has revealed the impact of the Latin Christian tradition on the developing Irish Church. If the latter was in its beginnings closely associated with Britain and Gaul, wider horizons opened up as time went on, particularly through the missionary expansion of Irish monasticism into Gaul (Luxeuil) and Italy (Bobbio). The Irish showed themselves remarkably keen to assimilate new aspects of the Church's tradition, at least where it did not conflict in practice with their native traditions. They were keen to learn and imitate the works of Christian antiquity, to assimilate the tradition of Christian Latin thought and prayer and adapt it to their own ways of thought and feeling, their own tradition of poetic literature. Rather than use hymns of foreign origin in their liturgy, they preferred to write their own even when this meant following such models as Ambrose, Prudentius and Venantius Fortunatus. The one foreign element among the hymns in the Antiphonary is *Mediae noctis tempus est*, which the monks at Bangor used for the midnight office. All the others are of Irish origin, even though one or two of them may have been composed by Irishmen in foreign parts rather than in Ireland itself. In the case of one, at least, *Ignis creator igneus,* we concluded that it was probably composed by Bobbio; the same may be true of *Spiritus divinae lucis*, but the evidence for this is indecisive.

The great variety of subject matter in these hymns is an expression of the Irish tendency to use verse for every occasion that merited a special composition. The verse-forms range from the quantative metres of Christian antiquity to various forms of rhythmical verse: structural imitations of quantitative models, the peculiar verse-form of Marius Victorinus, and the truly rhythmical or accentual verse-form employed in *Sacratissimi martyres*. The use of a variety of sources and verse-forms shows the willingness of Irish authors to borrow and adapt material which appealed to them, their eagerness to master the various forms of Latin hymnody, to compose hymns for new purposes and integrate the new Latin culture into their own traditional ways of thought and expression.

We will return to the liturgical use of these hymns in our study of the office of Bangor. We now turn our attention to the collects, to analyse and compare them to the liturgical texts of the other Latin liturgies. The results of our investigation so far will in this way be confirmed and further expanded.

PART II

THE COLLECTS OF THE ANTIPHONARY

CHAPTER TEN

INTRODUCTION

We have remarked a number of times on the lack of esteem for prose in the literary tradition of ancient Ireland. The Christian tradition of the Latin West, on the other hand, was expressed almost entirely in prose, and this in all areas of the Church's life, in liturgy, in symbols of faith, theological writings, scriptural commentaries, and so on. Due to the abuse of verse during the period of Gnostic expansion, a certain suspicion towards it set in. It was regarded as being an inadequate medium for conveying the truth of Christian revelation. Besides, the tradition of order and sobriety in the liturgy, so typical of the Roman approach, did not leave much place for the spontaneous, the enthusiastic, the lyrical element in the worship of the Church. Even when St Augustine and St Ambrose perceived the catechetical and devotional potentialities of the hymn, and thereby inaugurated something new and of great importance for popular participation, verse still made no great inroads into the liturgy. The period between the fifth and the seventh centuries is the era of the preface and collect in all the Western liturgies. These were the means though which the great authors of Rome, Milan, Gaul and Spain expressed in sober and dignified prose the great riches of the Church's mysteries of faith, reflected on them and applied them to the practice of the Christian life.

The conversion of Ireland to Christianity presented the early missionaries with quite a different challenge to that which the apostles faced in the Greco-Roman world. The peculiar difficulties of the Irish mission and the special means of evangelization that were demanded in this new situation are highlighted in the different degrees of success of the Roman Palladius and the Briton Patrick. Ireland was not an urbanized civilization and it had no political unity based on a central authority. Society was rural, familiar and tribal. The unifying cultural element was provided by the Order of Poets (*filid*), who were the custodians of the customary law, the traditions and all that affected the religious and secular life of society. Even within this cultural order there was no tradition of speculative thought which might have provided a vehicle for the translation and further development of Christian thought.[1] St Patrick was no philosopher and had no illusions about the quality of his Latin learning and speech. His success was due to his utter conviction in his mission, his holiness of life and the great practical knowledge he had of the Irish situation. He adapted his apostolate to the condition of Irish society and he was received out of the respect and reverence due to any great *fili* or druid. Nevertheless, the Church he established was of necessity similar to the Church everywhere in the West, in organization, faith and liturgy. Latin prose continued to be the language of the liturgy imported by Patrick and

89

by the other early missionaries. The Irish clergy had to be instructed in this entirely new language and in the mysteries of faith and worship conveyed through it. The transition to a Christian society was not as smooth and rapid as the later hagiographers professed to believe. There was a period of tension and opposition between the new learning and the old established order, and the gap between the two was only gradually bridged.[2]

Irish monasticism, a movement of devotion and asceticism, proved to be the means of intergration between the two orders, and it gave to the Irish Church an identity and constitution all its own in the Western world. It was not the highly developed system of organization and liturgy of the urbanized West, but the monastic movement which had its beginings in the deserts of Egypt, that appealed to the new generation of Irish churchmen. The desert was the 'ideal' place for the contemplation of God and for the pursuit of virtue. But the Irish monastic settlements combined this desire for union with God with a love for books and learning, and they became from the start centres for the study of the Latin literature of the Christian West in the measure that books became available to them. The earliest works they composed were in Latin, not in Irish, but the earliest texts which have come down to us, the canonical and penitential literature[3] and certain hymns such as *Sancti venite* and *Hymnum dicat*, show as well the native interest in law and poetry. The writings of Columbanus[4] show a confident mastery of Latin prose and a knowledge of classical and Christian authors which go back ultimately to his training in the Irish schools. The fame of these schools spread abroad and, as Bede testifies,

> many of the nobles of the English and lesser men also had set out thither, forsaking their native island either for the sake of sacred learning or a more ascetic life. And some of them, indeed, soon dedicated themselves to the monastic life, others rejoiced rather to give themselves to learning, going about from one master's cell to another. All these the Irish willingly received and took care to supply them with food day by day without cost, and books for their studies, and teachings free of charge.[5]

In these monastic schools the native preference for verse emerged in many types of Latin hymnody. We have seen examples in our study of the hymns of the Antiphonary. As time went on the Irish language came more and more into use for Christian purposes. Verse was used for new vernacular hymns and poems, for monastic rules, even for such unusual ends as the writing of history and martyrologies. It will be interesting to see further to what extent this preference for verse and the absence of a system of speculative thought affected the composition of Latin prose collects for the liturgy. Did the Latin learning of the schools equip the most learned of Irish authors with an ability to write prose collects comparable to those of the other Latin liturgies? How do the collects of the Antiphonary compare in terms of originality, development of thought and literary execution, with the Latin hymns in the same book?

90

The earliest Latin collects in the Irish liturgy were imported by the early missionaries from Britian and Gaul, possibly even from Rome.[6] Contact between Ireland and Gaul continued from the early days and was strengthened through the mission of Columbanus and the foundation of Luxeuil at the end of the sixth century. Do the collects of the Antiphonary bear out this contact with Gaul and with other areas of the Latin world which came within the scope of Irish *peregrini* in the sixth and seventh centuries?

We will seek answers to these questions through the detailed study of the collects of the Antiphonary. But before we set about this task, we will consider certain 'traces of Hispano-Gallican influence' in the collects of Antiphonary, as indicated by F.E. Warren.[7]

One of these Hispano-Gallican features is the address to Christ which is found in most of the collects. If we take the conclusion *qui regnas* to be an abbreviation of *salvator mundi qui cum aeterno patre. . . regnas,* then there are only two clear exceptions to the address to Christ among these collects. There are:

AB 61. Deus, qui sanctos tuos cum mensura probas, . . . per dominum nostrum Iesum Christum.

AB 86. Lux orta est in luce prima, . . . unigenitus tuus, domine, . . . qui tecum vivit.

The conclusion *qui tecum vivit* is elsewhere used inconsequentially, in prayers expressly addressed to Christ (AB 84, 85). Some of the collects seem to have been originally addressed to the Father and to have been changed subsequently by the simple addition of the conclusion *qui regnas.* This is evidently the case in

AB 122. Domine, sancte pater, omnipotens aeterne deus, . . . misericordiam tuam, domine, ne auferas a nobis, . . . per te Iesu Christe, qui regnas.

The same may be true of other prayers as well; for example:

AB 68. Deus, qui cotidie populum tuum iugo Aegyptio servitutis absolvis, . . . da nobis de vitiorum impugnatione victoriam, . . . salvator mundi, qui cum aeterno.

The conclusion *salvator mundi qui regnas* was also regarded by Warren as a Gallican symptom. The normal conclusion to the collects in the Antiphonary is the abbreviated *qui regnas.* The more specific conclusion *salvator mundi qui regnas* is found after ten collects,[8] but it is found in its complete form only on two occasions (AB 62 and 91). The same conclusion occurs frequently in Ga G, with the same element of fluidity in the wording which is also found in the Antiphonary. The following comparison reveals the close resemblance and relationship between the texts of the conclusion in both these books (s.m = *salvator mundi*).

AB	Ga G
62.91. s.m. qui cum aeterno patre patre vivis dominaris ac regnas cum (una cum aeterno *add* 91) spiritu sancto in saecula saeculorum.	11.129. s.m. qui cum (aeterno *add.* 129) patre (et spiritu sancto *add.*11) vivis dominaris et regnas deus (in unitate spiritus sancti *add.*129)in saecula saeculorum.
68.92.93. s.m. qui cum aeterno (patre vivis *add.*92.93).	15. s.m. qui cum coaeterno patre vivis et regnas.
63. s.m. qui cum patre vivis.	
64.71.73. s.m. qui regnas. 69. s.m.	12. s.m. qui vivis. 151.159... s.m.

The expression *salvator mundi* is used in all the Latin liturgies, especially in association with the nativity of Christ and the testimony given to his coming by John the Baptist.[9] But the conclusion *salvator mundi qui regnas* is peculiar to Irish and Gallican sources.[10] It is interesting to note its absence from Ga C, a manuscript compiled in Ireland in the middle of the seventh century from Gallican and Spanish sources. The absence of the conclusion *salvator mundi qui regnas* from this book is a good indication of its non-Gallican character, because if it were found in the originals it would scarcely have been omitted by the Irish copyist.[11]

Finally, we may note with Warren the Hispano-Gallican incipits of certain collects: *Sancte domine*[12] and *Te.*[13] The former is found in Gallican and Spanish books,[14] but not in the Roman or Ambrosian. Prayers commencing with *Te* are not found, apart from the *Te igitur* of the Canon of the Mass, in Ve or Gr C, but frequently occur in Ge V, Gallican and Spanish books; there is one Ambrosian instance.[15]

These traces of contact with foreign sources are meagre, but we will discover more specific sources for many collects as we proceed.

CHAPTER ELEVEN

RHYTHMICAL COLLECTS FOR THE HOURS

The first set of collects in the Antiphonary introduces us at once into a characteristically Irish monastic setting. We are faced with a series of rhythmical collects for each of the hours of the monastic office.[1] These collects are perfectly regular rhythmical versions of the iambic dimeter: each collect has four lines, each of which has eight syllables and ends in a word which is at least trisyllabic and proparoxytone.[2] The perfection of disyllabic rhyme or assonance in these prayers is a good illustration of the Irish development of this pre-existent feature of continental hymns. The hymns used for the hours of the monastic office at Arles in the time of Caesarius and Aurelian, for example, already admitted a liberal use of rhyme. The Irish took over this practice and developed it in a manner all their own.

Such rhythmical collects are something new in the history of the Latin liturgy, giving us a typical touch of Irish originality in the use of a traditional form, the rhythmical hymn, for a new purpose. That these quatrains are collects is clear from their headings, *Collectio ad secundam* , and so on, as well as from the conclusion, *qui regnas*, which is added to each one of them. We shall now see how these collects are related in form and content to their continental counterparts, the Ambrosian and Gallican hymns for the hours of the office.

1. AB 17. *Collectio ad secundam*

> Te oramus, altissime,
> exorto solis lumine,
> Christe, oriens nomine,
> adesto nobis, domine,
> qui regnas in saecula.

We can see here the hymn used for *duodecima* at Arles (AH 51, 21):

> 1. Christe, qui lux es et dies,
> noctis tenebrae detegis,
> LUCIFER, lucem praeferens,
> lumen beatum praedicans.

> 6. Memento nostri, domine,
> in gravi isto corpore,
> qui es defensor animae,
> ADESTO NOBIS, DOMINE.

2. AB 18. *Ad tertiam*

> Christe per horam tertiam
> deprecamur clementiam,
> uti nobis perpetuam
> suam tribuat gratiam,
> qui regnas.

The author may have been influenced here by the Ambrosian hymn for terce, also used at Arles (AH 50, 12):

1. Iam surgit HORA TERTIA
qua Christus ascendit crucem;
nil insolens mens cogitet,
intendat affectum precis.

4.Hinc iam beata tempora
coepere CHRISTI GRATIA,
fidei replevit veritas
totum per orbem ecclesias.

3. AB 19. *Ad sextam*

Tuis parce suplicibus
sexta hora orantibus,
qua fuisti pro omnibus,
Christe, in cruce positus,
qui regnas.

The use of the expression *in cruce positus* is fairly widespread,[3] as is the commemoration of the crucifixion at the sixth hour.[4]

4. AB 21. *Ad vespertinam*

Vespertino sub tempore
te invocamus, domine;
nostris precibus annue,
nostris peccatis ignosce.[5]

Such invocations for pardon are a commonplace in the collects and hymns for evening prayer. The hymn used for nocturns at Arles, *Rex aeterne domine* (AH 51, 5), uses comparable language:

12. Tibi NOCTURNO TEMPORE
hymnum deflentes canimus,
ignosce nobis, domine,
IGNOSCE confitentibus.

5. AB 22. *Collectio ad initium noctis*

Noctis tempus exigimus,
Christe, in tuis laudibus;
miserearis omnibus
te ex corde precantibus,
qui regnas.

This collect appears to be directly related to a late-sixth-century Gallican hymn (AH 51, 7):

1. TEMPUS NOCTIS surgentIBUS,
LAUDES DEO DICENTIBUS,
Christo Iesuque domino
in trinitatis gloria.

2. Choro sanctorum psallIMUS,
cervices nostras flectIMUS,
vel genua prosternIMUS,
PECCATA CONFITENTIBUS.

But it has also some resemblance to a Spanish hymn for compline (AH 27, 107):

1. NOCTIS tetrae PRIMORDIA
IN LAUDIBUS TRANSEGIMUS:
nunc te precamur, trinitas,
ut praecinentes audias.

2. Tu omnibus da gratiam,
tu fessa quoque alleva,
errata dele crimina,
exclude iuge scandalum.

Similar expressions occur in some of the *completuriae* for the Spanish monastic *Ordo ad nocturnos*:

Hor 162 Domine Ihesu Christe, qui NOCTURNIS HORIS IN LAUDIBUS tuam misericordiam laudant, quique DE TOTIS PRECORDIS maiestatem tuam UT EIS PARCAS IMPLORANT, benignus concede quae postulant, et, ut tibi placeant, corda eorum spiritu sancto inlumina.
Hor 164 NOCTIS huius SPATIA quiescentes (vigiliam *vel* laudationis officium?) PEREGIMUS, te adiuvante, domine, ut. . . .

6. AB 25. *Ad matutinas*

Gallorum, Christe, cantibus,
te deprecor, sonantibus,
Petri ob quondam fletibus
nostris intende precibus,
qui regnas.

This is the central theme of Ambrose's hymn, *Aeterne rerum conditor (AH 50, 11):*

2. Praeco diei iam SONAT,
noctis profundae pervigil,
nocturna lux viantibus,
a nocte noctem segregans,

4. Hoc nauta vires colligit
pontique mitescunt freta,
HOC IPSE PETRA ECCLESIAE
CANENTE CULPAM DILUIT.

7. Iesu, labantes respice
et nos videndo corrige;
si respicis, lapsus cadunt
FLETUQUE CULPA SOLVITUR.

7. AB 26. *Item alia ad matutinam*

Deus qui pulsis tenebris
diei lucem tribuis,
adventum veri luminis
tuis effunde famulis,
qui regnas.

The theme of this collect is expressed in many ways in the collects and hymns for the morning office in all the liturgies, and the expression of it in our collect appears original. The word *pellere* and composite forms of it are frequently used by St Ambrose.[6] The expression *lumen verum* is found in all the liturgies, but with greater frequency in the Ambrosian and Spanish texts.[7] The combination *adventus (verae) lucis* occurs in

Rot.Rav.15 Omnipotens et invisibilis Deus, qui mundi tenebras LUCIS TUAE ADVENTU fugasti, sereno nos, quaesumus, vultu circumspice.

- 19 Oriatur, quaesumus, omnipotens deus, in cordibus nostris splendor gloriae, d.n.I. Christus, ut omnem noctis obscuritate sublata, filios nos esse diei VERE LUCIS manifestet ADVENTUS.[8]

This concludes the set of rhythmical collects for the hours. They are manifestly to be taken together as an original unit, and their similarity in form and inspiration is undoubtedly the result of a common authorship. The author was well acquainted with the traditional themes associated with prayer at the different hours, and in particular with the Ambrosian tradition of hymnody in the broad sense. The entire set was most probably composed, if we are to judge from the perfection of the rhyming system, around the middle of the seventh century. At that time adequate examples of the continental hymns and prayers for the hours, by which our author was influenced, could well have been known in Ireland[9] and, specifically, at Bangor, where the entire set was probably written.

The custom of composing rhythmical collects appears to have been established in Ireland before the writing of the present set. We have seen some examples of these collects in the course of our discussion of the hymn *Sacratissimi martyres*. Like the latter, they are rhythmical in the strict sense, being structural imitations of Irish accentual verse. The set of collects we have been just now been considering belongs to another tradition of rhythmical verse, being composed in structural imitation of quantitative Latin metres. The author wished to compose a set of collects that would express the traditional themes associated with the various hours, but he chose this type of rhythmical verse rather than prose as his medium. We discovered his model and source of inspiration in the continental hymns for the hours and we have seen how he brought this type of verse to further perfection with regard to the use of rhyme. He succeeded admirably in his purpose, which was to provide an Irish community with a set of collects which would at once please their taste for poetry and enrich their prayer with traditional themes expressed in simple language.

CHAPTER TWELVE

PROSE COLLECTS FOR THE HOURS

The set of rhythmical collects which we have studied in the last chapter is followed by another set in prose for the same hours. Special prayers for the end of the day and a formulary of intercessory prayers have also been included in it.[1] The entire set is thus much more extensive than the first and the prose collects themselves are more in line with the traditional collects for the hours found in the other Latin liturgies.

1. AB 27. *Item ad secundam*

> Exaudi nos, domine, supplices tuos, qui in hac hora prima diei referimus tibi gratias, domino deo nostro, qui nos redemisti (de: *add.corr.*) tuo sancto sanguine, ut preces ac petitiones nostras vice primitiarum tibi oblatas pie clementerque suscipias, qui regnas.

There is no collect comparable to this one in any of the other Latin liturgies. The profusion of themes and rather loose structure, the identification of Christ as *dominus deus noster*, the repetition *domine... domine,* can all be taken as indications of Irish origin. The expression *sanguis sanctus* is peculiar to the Gallican and Irish books.[2] It is used with the verb *redimere* in three other texts of the Antiphonary:

> AB 8 Sancti venite, Christi corpus sumite,
> sanctum bibentes quo redempti sanguine.
>
> AB 34 Redemisti nos, domine, deus veritatis, in tuo sancto
> sanguine.
>
> AB 41 Miserere, domine, ecclesiae tuae catholicae quam redemisti
> in tuo sancto sanguine.

If we compare the expression *redimere sanguine sancto* with related expressions, we get the following break-down of usages:

(a) *redimere sanguine sacro,* found only in Spanish texts;[3]

(b) *redimere sanguine pretioso,* found in the prayers of all the Western liturgies, apart from the Irish and Gallican;[4]

(c) *redimere sanguine sancto,* found only in Gallican and Irish texts. Among the Gallican texts we find an interesting parallel to the text we have given from AB 41; it is an *ad pacem* collect which has the Irish conclusion *salvator mundi,* so that the parallel may be due to Irish influence:

> Deus, qui ECCLESIAM TUAM CATHOLICAM, QUAM TUO SANCTO SANGUINE REDEMISTI, nunquam derelinquas, nobisque indignis... criminum indulgentiam placatus concedas.... salvator (Ga G 320).

The reference to the *primitiae* offered in the Old Law (Ex.29, 38 – 39) may have been suggested by the concluding part of ps.50, which, as we shall see, was said in the office of *secunda*.[5] The *Apostolic Tradition* of Hippolytus attaches to the hour of terce the commemoration of the daily morning sacrifice of the temple, as a figure of the perfect sacrifice of Christ.[6] It is difficult to say whether the text of Hippolytus influenced our prayer in any way; but another prayer in this series shows a close affinity with the *Tradition* and both these cases may not be altogether due to chance.

2. AB 28. *Ad horam tertiam*

Tibi subnixis precibus,[7] Christe domino, supplicamus, qui in hora tertia diei spiritum sanctum apostolis orantibus emisisti: eiusdem gratiae participationem nobis poscentibus iubeas concedi, qui regnas.[8]

The language of this collect owes nothing to the Ambrosian and Spanish collects for terce, even though the descent of the Holy Spirit is commemorated in them also. But the central ideas and expressions are found in two Ambrosian hymns. First, in Ambrose's hymn for terce (AH 50, 12):

1. Iam surgit HORA TERTIA
qua Christus ascendit crucem,
nil insolens mens cogitet,
intendat affectum PRECIS.

2. Qui corde Christum suscipit
innoxium sensum gerit,
VOTISQUE PERSTAT SEDULIS
SANCTUM MERERI SPIRITUM.

4. Hinc iam beata tempora
coepere CHRISTI GRATIA,
fidei replevit veritas
totum per orbem ecclesias.

The same ideas are found in this later Ambrosian hymn[9] (AH 51, 98):

1. Iam Christus astra ascenderat,
regressus unde venerat,
promisso patris munere
SANCTUM DATURUS SPIRITUM.

2. Solemnis urgebat DIES
quo mistico septemplici
orbis volutus septies
signat beata tempora,

3. Cum HORA cunctis TERTIA
repente mundus intonat,
APOSTOLIS ORANTIBUS
deum venisse nuntians.

The author of our collect, who was without doubt an Irishman, was well aquainted with these Ambrosian hymns. His collect is a worthy and balanced composition, which evidences a good command of the Latin prose style of the collect and a familiar grasp of the theme associated with the hour of terce.

3. AB 29. *Ad horam sextam*

Omnipotens aeterne deus, qui nobis magnalia fecisti, sexta hora crucem (sanctam: *add.corr.*) ascendisti et tenebras mundi inluminasti: sic et corda nostra inluminare digneris, qui regnas.

This collect is related to the Ambrosian prayer for sext:

Am M II 452 (Be 1583) Sanctum et terribile nomen tuum, OMNIPOTENS AETERNE DEUS, humiliter deprecamur: ut qui HORA DIEI SEXTA gloriosissimum filium tuum d.n.I. Christum IN CRUCEM ASCENDERE voluisti, ut nos a potestate hostis nequissimi liberares, praesta, quaesumus, ut eius cruce redempti, tibi domino iugiter sine offensione omni tempore serviamus, per eundem.

This Ambrosian collect appears to be itself partly the result of Irish tinkering with the collect given in AB 29. There are a number of indications that this is the case. Firstly, the Ambrosian modifications appear in part in the version of the Irish collect found in Ge A 1893 (Ge G 326,8):

Sanctum et terribile nomen tuum, domine, qui pro nobis magnalia fecisti, sexta hora crucem sanctam ascendisti, tenebras mundi inluminasti: ita et corda nostra inluminare digneris, per.

The insertion of *sanctum . . . tuum* looks very much like being the work of an Irish corrector, who wished to insert a favoured psalm versicle (ps.110,9) before the invocation. And this collect is only one of a number of modified collects from the Antiphonary to appear again in the eighth-century Gelasians.[10] Secondly, the style of the collect in the Ambrosian books is too diffuse, repetitive and disjointed to be genuinely Milanese. In accounting for its origin and present form in the Ambrosian books, two possibilities suggest themselves. The nucleus of the collect may be Ambrosian. This could have been elaborated on in an Irish context[11] and the amended version could then have been received back to Milan, displacing the original. The original collect may have been something along these lines:

Omnipotens aeterne deus, qui hora diei sexta gloriosissimum filium tuum d.n.I. Christum in crucem ascendere voluisti, ut nos a potestate hostis nequissimi liberares, praesta, quaesumus, ut eius cruce redempti tibi sine offensione omni tempore serviamus, per eundem.

There is one internal difficulty posed by this text, the fact that the ascent of Christ on the cross is associated with the hour of terce, not sext, in the Ambrosian tradition. Another possiblity, which I regard as preferable, is suggested. The collect in the Ambrosian books may have been taken over from an Irish source and slightly modified by a Milanese hand; in particular, the address *omnipotens aeterne deus* was felt in the Ambrosian context to be more appropriate to the Father than to the Son. This possibility of Irish influence on the Ambrosian collects for the (monastic) day offices is confirmed by other evidence, which we consider in its place.[12]

The collect in the Antiphonary has itself been strongly influenced by Ambrosian sources. The expression *ascendere crucem* was very probably inspired by Ambrose's hymn for terce (AH 50, 12):

> Iam surgit hora tertia
> qua CHRISTUS ASCENDIT CRUCEM

Again, the phrase *sic et corda nostra illuminare digneris* is found in two Ambrosian collects for terce and vespers:

> Am M II 452 (Be 1584) ut sicut tertia hora apostolos filii tui visitatione sancti spiritus confirmasti, ITA CORDA NOSTRA, eo adveniente, ILLUMINARE et custodire DIGNERIS.
>
> - 442 (Be 1607) petimus clementiam tuam, ut sicut nos huius luminis claritate circumvallas, ITA spiritus sancti tui luce CORDA NOSTRA ILLUMINARE DIGNERIS.

But the Irish origin of our collect is suggested by the unusual address to Christ as *omnipotens aeterne deus* and by the equally unusual attachment to sext of the theme of light, in view of the Gospel account that darkness reigned over the whole world from the sixth to the ninth hour.[13] The author of this collect may well have been the same as the one who wrote the preceding collect, *Tibi subnixis precibus*. Here again there is a marked Ambrosian influence and the author had a good ability to compose in a disciplined prose style. The theme is one which is usually associated with terce rather than sext, but we can expect an original touch from an Irish hand.

4. AB 30. *Ad horam nonam*

> Nona agitur diei hora ad te, domine, directa supplicatione, qua cultoribus tuis divina monstrantur miracula; nostra quoque, eorum imitatione, corda inlumina, qui regnas.

This collect is closely related to the text of the *Traditio Apostolica* which speaks of prayer at the ninth hour:

> Faciant autem etiam MAGNAM PRECEM et magnam benedictionem tempore horae nonae ut scias modum [Botte translates: pour IMITER la maniére]quo anima iustorum benedicit [the Latin MS of Verona resumes at this point] deum qui non mentitur, qui memur fuit sanctorum suorum et emisit verbum suum INLUMINANTEM EOS. Illa ergo hora in latere Christus punctus aquam et sanguem effusit et reliquum temporis diei inluminans ad vesperum deduxit.[14]

The question is, whether the collect in AB was directly or at least indirectly influenced by the text of Hippolytus, or whether it simply reflects another account of the descent of Christ at the ninth hour. I think that the texts are sufficiently close for us to accept the first alternative as very likely; apart from the general similarity, there is explicit mention in both of *prayer*, *imitation* of the saints, *enlightenment* of the saints by Christ. The *cultoribus tuis* of the collect could have been easily suggested by *anima*

100

iustorum benedicit deum, but *divina miracula* perhaps reflects some more explicit account of the descent than is given in Hippolytus's text. The prayer for none in Mo Br 959 also speaks of the descent of Christ, his deliverance of the saints, following the 'glorious miracle' of Christ's triumph on the cross; but the prayer does not have any specific resemblance to our AB collect.[15]

5. AB 31. *Ad vespertinam*

Vespertina oratio nostra ascendat ad aures divinae maiestatis tuae et descendat benedictio tua, domine, super nos, quemadmodum speravimus in te, qui regnas.

This collect is evidently related to the versicle and response which follow the hymn in Saturday vespers of the Roman Breviary. Moreover, the versicle and response themselves appear to have been derived from a prayer which has a typically Irish rhythmical structure:

Vespertína orátio ascéndat ad te, dómine,
et descéndat super nós misericórdia túa.

The collect of AB 31 also appears to be a genuine Irish product. This is suggested by the unusual position of the invocation, *domine*, towards the end, and by the conclusion by means of a psalm versicle.[16] Besides, a number of close parallels to it exist in Irish books:

Ce S 21 Iteramus, omnipotens deus, deprecationem nostram ante conspectum MAIESTATIS TUAE ... pro famulis tuis.... Petitiones eorum ASCENDANT AD AURES CLEMENTIAE TUAE, DESCENDAT SUPER NOS PIA BENEDICTIO, ut sub umbra alarum tuarum in omnibus protegantur.

ILH I 156 ASCENDAT ORATIO NOSTRA usque ad tronum claritatis tuae, domine, et ne vacua revertatur ad nos postulatio nostra.[17]

The concluding prayer for Lauds on ordinary Sundays in the Ambrosian rite has a similar form:

Am M II 417 AD AURES CLEMENTIAE TUAE, Deus, vox nostrae supplicationis ASCENDAT, et tua nos misericordia prosequatur.

The collect *Vespertina oratio* is doutless the original from which these other texts derive. It bears no relationship to the classical evening collects of the other Latin liturgies and it is quite different in style from the two collects which precede it in the Antiphonary. It is of the utmost simplicity in structure and thought.

6. AD 32. *Ad initium noctis*

Deus, qui inextricabiles tenebras inluminas noctium, densitatem caliginis inlustrans, corda nostra in opere mandatorum tuorum, te oramus, domine, custodias, qui regnas.

This is surely another Irish composition. After the elaborate introduction, which deals with the occasion for the prayer, and indirectly praises God as source of light, the petition, which again repeats the invocation, is a *non sequitur*. We should expect the application of the theme which is so well introduced, rather than the generic request for protection. The author has apparently drawn one expression from Cassian,[18] and possibly another from an Ambrosian prayer for vespers.[19] He may be identified with the man who wrote the collects for terce and sext.

7. AB 33. *Ad initium noctis*

> Evolutis nunc diei temporibus, nocturnisque spatiis supervenientibus, dei misericordiam deprecamur, ut suppleti (suppliti MS) divinis sensibus, tenebrarum operibus renuntiare possimus, qui regnas.

The meaning of *suppleti divinis sensibus* is unclear, but it is possibly a reference to the filling of our senses with the divine light, a common theme in the morning and evening prayer. The remainder of the collect is in close contact with certain Ambrosian and Spanish evening prayers:

> Am M II 453 (Be 1595) TRANSACTO DIEI CURSU, gratias nomini tuo referimus, omnipotens Deus; QUAESUMUS MISERICORDIAM TUAM, ut quaecumque in hac die per fragilitatem carnis contraximus, veniam nobis largire digneris.

> Be 1615 ut in fine diei huius, SUPERVENIENTIBUS tenebris, . . . luminis claritatem de tua aeternitate capiamus.

> Be 1616 DECURSU DIEI SPATIO et in vespertina prona vergente, orationis vota solvimus, ut deus a nobis TENEBRAS vitae mortalis abstergat, et lumen perpetuae salutis infundat.

> Be 1619 DIEI LABORE TRANSACTO, te . . ., domine, DEPRECAMUR, ut . . . ad requiem nobis . . . lux sempiterna permaneat.

> Mo Br 699 TRANSACTO DIEI CURRICULO, NOCTURNO APPROPINQUANTE SPATIO, tibi Domine, luminis incensum offerimus vespertinum, suppliciter postulantes magnificentiam tuam, ut quod in nobis obscuratur caligine peccatorum, tui luminis accensione clarescat. . . .[20]

> Br 190 Omnipotens sempiterne Deus, . . . vespertinis laudibus nos dignanter exaudi, ut et placidum SUPERVENIENTIS NOCTIS SPATIUM peragere mereamur, et transacto tenebrarum cursu, . . . sine ulla offensionum macula dies repraesentet exoriens.

> Vesp.Mat.39 TRANSACTO DIEI LUMINE, sacrificium tibi, Domine, vespertinum subnixis genibus exhibentes, dinumeramus intra animum peccata quae gessimus. . . .

> Vesp. Mat.23 Ecce, Domine, rapidus sol diei SPATIA statuta dimersus trahitur in occursum . . ., tuoque nos praesidio exoramus per huius NOCTIS SPATIA conservari.

> B.M., *Addit.MS* 30,845, f.154^v Secies orarum TEMPORIBUS REVOLUTIS, tibi domine deo nostro colla nostra suddentesque sumus. . . .[21]

The authors of these Spanish prayers were influenced by the Ambrosian texts, which first gave expression to this common theme.[22] It appears that the Spanish prayers in turn influenced the author of AB 33, because of the close verbal similarities between them. In the opening antithesis, *temporibus evolutis* of AB corresponds to the Spanish *temporibus revolutis*, and *nocturnis spatiis supervenientibus* corresponds to the Spanish *nocturno appropinquante spatio* or to *supervenientis noctis spatium* (Am *supervenientibus tenebris*). The continuation of our prayer corresponds especially to the Ambrosian prayers; in particular, *dei misericordiam deprecamur* to the Ambrosian *quaesumus misericordiam tuam* or *te, domine, deprecamur*; and *opera tenebrarum renuntiare* to the Ambrosian *tenebras vitae mortalis abstergat.*[23]

The form of the collect, an invitation (*praefatio*) to prayer rather than a direct prayer, is not very peculiar. Similarly constructed evening prayers occur in the Spanish and Ambrosian books, including Am Be 1616 cited above among the parallels to our collect. It is better to regard the collect as an Irish composition than as a direct borrowing from Spain or Milan. Apart from the obscure *suppleti divinis sensibus*, it compares well in structure and theme to its continental prototypes. As the second collect given for the office of nightfall in the series, it may have been designed as an introduction (*praefatio*) to the special prayers for forgiveness and peace which immediately follow.

8.AB 34. *Ad pacem celebrandam*

This formulary consists of two psalm versicles, each of which is followed by a short collect:

> Iniuste egimus. . . (ps.105,6).
> Redemisti nos, domine deus veritatis, in tuo sancto sanguine; nunc adiuva nos in omnibus, Ihesu Christe, qui regnas.[24]

> Pax multa diligentibus. . . (ps.118,165).
> Pax tua, domine rex caelestis, permaneat semper in visceribus nostris, ut non timeamus a timore nocturno, qui regnas.

There are certain parallels to this second collect:

> Ga G 325 Pacem tuam, domine, DE CAELO da nobis et posside nos, ut non hereat IN VISCERIBUS NOSTRIS fraudolentus oculos proditores, sed pax illa, quam tuis reliquisti discipulis, SEMPER inlibata PERMANEAT IN CORDIBUS NOSTRIS.

> Mo LO 367,35 PAX TUA, Christe, cum abundanti dono spiritus sancti MANEAT IN VISCERIBUS FAMULI TUI. . . .

> DE PS. USU II 14 (*Oratio ad completorium*) Pacem tuam, Domine, da nobis DE CAELO, et PAX TUA, CHRISTE, SEMPER MANEAT IN VISCERIBUS NOSTRIS, UT NON TIMEAMUS A TIMORE NOCTURNO.

The author of *De ps.usu* presents a combination of Ga G and AB. Both Ga G and LO collects are well suited to the particular contexts in which they are found, the first being the collect *ad pacem* for the feast of St John the Evangelist, the second being the collect *ad pacem* in the *Ordo votivus de energumeno*. The two collects for celebrating the peace of the Antiphonary are similar in form to those found in the *Oratio communis fratrum* (AB 41 – 56), which we will soon meet. It appears that the second collect, *Pax tua domine*, is an adaptation for this particular occasion of an *ad pacem* prayer such as we have seen in Ga G 325 and LO 367. It is more satisfactory to take it as having been derived from Ga G; *rex caelestis* corresponds to *de caelo* (Ga G) and *permaneat semper* corresponds to *semper inlibata permaneat* (Ga G;*maneat* LO). The conclusion, *ut non timeamus...,*[25] was added so as to adapt it suitably to its new context. These short intercessions were followed by the Apostles' Creed (AB35 *Incipit Symmulum*) and Our Father (AB 36 *Oratio divina*), which concluded the office of nightfall.

9. AB 38. *Ad matutinam*

Tu es, domine, inluminator caliginum, conditorque elementorum, remissor criminum. Misericordia tua, domine, magna est super eos qui te toto corde requirunt. Maiestas tua, domine, mane nos exaudiat et deleat delicta nostra quae tibi non sunt abdita, qui regnas.

This collect consists mostly of biblical citations:

2 Chron.30,18 – 20 oravit pro eis Ezechias, dicens: Dominus bonus propitiabitur cunctis, qui IN TOTO CORDE REQUIRUNT DOMINUM Deum patrum suorum.... Quem EXAUDIVIT Dominus et placatus est populo suo.[26]

Ps.5,4 Quoniam ad te orabo, DOMINE, MANE EXAUDIES vocem meam.

Ps.50,3 Miserere mei, Deus, secundum MAGNAM MISERICORDIAM tuam, et secundum multitudinem miserationum tuarum DELE iniquitatem iniquitatem meam.

Ps.68,6 delicta mea A TE NON SUNT ABSCONDITA.

The author does not appear to have been influenced by any particular continental source.[27] The prayer is an example of the litanic, disjointed type of prayer so frequently found in Irish sources.[28] The theme it touches on, such as God's knowledge of the secrets of the human heart, are found in the prayers of all the liturgies, but usually with more cohesion and development of thought. For example, the psalter collects on ps.68 do not merely repeat the verse of the psalm in question, as does our collect, but tease it out and draw appropriate conclusions.[29]

10. AB 39. *Item ad matutinam*

Tu es spes et salus,
tu es vita et virtus,
tu es adiutor in tribulationibus,
tu es defensor animarum nostrarum,
deus Israhel, in omnibus,
qui regnas.

This collect, which is repeated a little further on (AB 59), is another good example of Irish litanic-type prayer, in which a long row of titles can follow each other without any recognizable connection of thought. The following could serve as further illustrations:

Columban, *Instr.*XIII 3 tu es enim omnia nostra, vita nostra, lux nostra, salus nostra, cibus noster, potus noster, Deus noster.[30]

Basel, *MS A.VII.3*, f.2ᵛ Domine, deus omnipotens, ego humiliter te adoro. Tu es rex regum et dominus dominantium. Tu es arbiter omnis saeculi. Tu es redemptor animarum. Tu es liberator credentium. Tu es spes laborantium. Tu es paraclitus dolentium. Tu es via errantium. Tu es magister gentium. Tu es creator omnium. Tu es amator omnis boni. Tu es princeps omnium virtutum....[31]

This type of prayer would have been unthinkable in the Roman liturgy. What is expressed in AB 39 in lyrical form had to find a more disciplined form in the Roman prayers, so that we read, for example,

Gr C 78,14 Omnipotens sempiterne deus, QUI SALVAS OMNES ET NEMINEM VIS PERIRE, respice ad animas diabolica fraude deceptos....

In the prayers of the Roman liturgy, the invocation is frequently extended by a relative clause which dwells on some aspect of God's saving activity; sometimes, but very rarely, we find absolute attributes used in apposition in these clauses. On the other hand, AB 39 consists entirely of such absolute attributes of God (Christ): He is spoken of as he who *is* salvation, hope, life, and so on, rather than he who *acts* by saving and giving life to those who hope in him. This manner of addressing God is, to an extent, found in all the liturgies and it is frequently met in the psalms.[32] But it is much more characteristic of the Spanish prayers than of those of the other continental liturgies. We do not find in any prayer the exclusive multiplication of absolute attributes that we find in AB 39, but we do find all of its terms used in apposition, sometimes two or three together, in the collects of the various liturgies, particularly in Spain. We are not taking into consideration liturgical hymns and other poetic compositions in which these lyrical expressions occur in a more natural setting.[33] If we limit ourselves to prose collects, we can illustrate how these terms (*spes. salus, etc*) are used as terms of apposition in prayers of the Western liturgies and see how they are of frequent occurrence in Spanish prayers. In order not to overburden our text with references, we will give only one representative of each liturgical tradition and give other references in the footnotes.

Tu es spes:

Ge V 441 Omnipotens sempiterne Deus, spes unica mundi. . . . auge populi tui vota.[34]

Ga B 76 Spes unica vitae nostrae et fidei remunerator, aeterne deus pater omnipotens....[35]

Mo CPs 378 (ps.61) Effundentibus nobis coram te corda in oratione, tu , Domine, qui spes omnium es, exaudi et miserere.[36]

Tu es salus:

Ge V 1350 Deus, refugium pauperum, spes humilium, salusque miserorum....[37]

Ga G 35 Deus, perennis salus, beatitudo inaestimabilis....[38]

Mo CPs 208 (ps.3) Tu es, Domine, salus et tua est salus.[39]

Tu est vita:

Ge V 562 Deus, vita fidelium, gloria humilium, beatitudo iustorum....[40]

Am Be 1336 ut . . . ad te, qui vita es, gratiosus perveniat.[41]

Ga G 358 Deus, inluminatio et vita credentium. . . .
Mo Or 972 Vita fidelium, exultatio sanctorum, indefessa laudatio angelorum, omnipotens Christe. . . .[42]

Tu es virtus:

Gr C 110,4 Deus, incommutabilis virtus et lumen aeternum, respice propitius. . . (Ge V 432; Am Be 525).

Ga G 41 per dominum nostrum Iesum Christum filium tuum, qui est sanctorum omnium virtus et gloria, victoria martyrum et corona pastor ovium et hostia sacerdotum, redemptio gentium et propitiatio peccatorum (Ga B 100).

Mo CPs 18 (ps.17) Virtus nostra, domine, et cornu salutis nostrae. . . .[43]

Tu es adiutor·in tribulationibus:

Ps.45,2 Deus noster refugium et virtus, ADIUTOR IN TRIBULATIONIBUS quae invenerunt nos nimis.

Am Bi 1231 Domine, adiutor noster et protector noster, adiuva nos.[44]

Mo CPs 358 (ps.45) Deus, virtus et refugium nostrum, esto nobis adiutor in tribulationibus.[45]

Tu es defensor animarum:

Ve 862 Populi tui, Deus, defensor et rector, concede. . . .

Mo CPs 320 (ps.3) Domine, gloria nostra, caput nostrum . . . exalta, . . . qui auctor es et defensor nostrae salutis.[46]

The titles by which Christ is addressed in AB 39 are, therefore, found as terms of apposition in the other Western liturgies and they are especially frequent in the Spanish books. But it is only in Ireland that we find prayers consisting entirely of a sequence of such titles. In the case of the collect under consideration, they are combined by rhyme and alliteration. This type of prayer, which stands stylistically somewhere between prose and verse, manifests yet again the lyrical tendencies of Irish authors, their preference for verse rather than sobre prose. It is a style of collect which stands at the opposite pole from the sobriety of form of the Roman collect, but it has something in common with the spirit of the Spanish liturgy.

11. AB 40 – 56. *Oratio communis fratrum*

This is a formulary of intercessory prayers for some fifteen classes of people, a type of litany which was peculiar to the Irish office. Each formula consists of an invitation to prayer[47] followed by an appropriate verse of a psalm, which in turn is followed by a short collect. Two examples will illustrate the structure which is essentially the same throughout:

AB 41 (*Oremus*) *pro baptizatis*
Salvum fac populum tuum, domine, et benedic hereditati tuae, et rege eos et extolle illos usque in saeculum.
Miserere, domine, ecclesiae tuae catholicae, quam redemisti in tuo sancto sanguine.

AB 46 (*Oremus*) *pro blasphemantibus*
Domine, misericordia tua in saeculum, opera manuum tuarum ne dispicias.

106

Domine, deus virtutum, ne statuas illis hoc in peccatum.

This form of prayer had been described by Columban as a series of 'intercessory versicles';[48] he made no explicit mention of the collects, and the classes he mentioned are not as numerous as in the Antiphonary. This may be partly due to his rather summary treatment of the office, but some of the additional classes in the Antiphonary may have been added between his time and the time of writing the Antiphonary. The classes of people prayed for are essentially the same as those prayed for in the litany used at Mass and in the office throughout the West since the fifth and sixth centuries. This litany was inspired in form and content by the Eastern diaconal litany, in which the intentions of various classes were announced by the deacon and the people responded *kyrie eleison* after each announcement.[49] But whereas in the diaconal litany a number of different classes may be included together in one invitation, which is then followed by one *kyrie eleison* (or *domine miserere*), in AB each class has its own appropriate versicle and collect. The versicle and collect replaced the *kyrie eleison* in the *oratio communis* of the office of Bangor. This marked an important stage in the development of the *preces* used since mediaeval times in the various hours of the office.

The relationship between the Columbanian *versiculi* and the Gallican *capitella de psalmis* needs to be clarified, for it has been needlessly confused. Many authors have seen in the *capitella* a peculiarly Gallican form of *preces*: a series of intercessory psalm-verses used in the form of versicles and responses without any bidding.[50] The *preces* of the Breviary would have arisen out of the fusion of the Gallican and Columbanian forms of intercessory versicles; that is, they consist of a series of *capitella* followed by a series of versicles introduced by the bidding *Oremus pro*.[51] But the early evidence for the use of the *capitella* shows that they had nothing to do with the *preces*, that they were, in fact, quite distinct from the litany or its supplication, the *kyrie eleison*, which may have followed them. The Gallican *capitellum* was a *single* verse. In the monastic office it was said after the hymn or reading (and before the *kyrie eleison*, according to Aurelian) to conclude each particular hour.[52] In the cathedral office it was said after the hymn and was immediately followed by the concluding prayer.[53] In reality, there was nothing peculiarly Gallican about the *capitellum*, apart from the name. We find a *versus* between the hymn and *completuria* in the Spanish cathedral matins and vespers,[54] a *capitulum* after the *laudate* psalms in the Ambrosian matins,[55] a *versus* between the hymn and the canticle in the Benedictine matins and vespers,[56] a *versus* between the responsary and readings in the *Regula Magistri*.[57] The use of the verse or *capitellum* was, therefore, widespread, and it always signified a pause, a summing up, and it frequently preceded the concluding element of the office, whether this was a collect, as in the cathedral office of Gaul and Spain, or a litany (or simply the *kyrie eleison*), as at Arles and in some hours of the Benedictine office and of the *Regula Magistri* (if we are to consider the latter's *rogus dei* as a litany). Nowhere do we find a suggestion that the *versus* or *capitellum* was a form of *preces*, of intercessory versicles introduced in place of the litany. On the contrary, it often precedes the litany and is quite distinct from it. Even if this use of a *versus* or *capitellum* originated in Gaul and thence spread to the other liturgies, this only confirms our conclusion that the Gallican *capitellum* was not a form of *preces*. It was a psalm-verse used to conclude the office.

The *oratio communis* of AB 40 – 56 is an Irish transformation of the diaconal litany which, as we have already seen, was widely used in the Western liturgies. It was part of the Mass in Ireland, as well as in Italy and Gaul. At Rome, this litany was also used in the morning and evening offices,[58] and St Benedict depends on the Roman practice when he prescribes it for matins and vespers, whereas for the other hours he prescribes simply the *supplicatio litaniae*, that is, the *kyrie eleison*. We can conclude to the original use of the litany in the morning and evening offices at Milan from the survival of the twelvefold *kyrie eleison* after the hymn in lauds and after the *Magnificat* in some archaic forms of vespers.[59] The Council of Vaison (A.D. 529), which was presided over by St Caesarius, ordered its introduction into the Mass and the offices of matins and vespers in all the churches of southern Gaul, in imitation of Rome and other churches in Italy as well as in the East.[60] This decree of the Council of Vaison does not appear to have had much effect in Gaul, where the only trace of its observance may be seen in Aurelian's prescriptions regarding the *kyrie*.[61]

There is no evidence for the use of this litany in the Irish monastic office, even though it was used in the Mass. Already in the sixth century, according to Columban, the Irish *seniores* had laid down a series of intercessory prayers in the form of versicles said for various classes of people. This practice cannot have been influenced or suggested by a continental source, simply because no parallel or prototype for it existed on the Continent. There the only form of intercessory prayers was the litany, or the manifold *kyrie eleison* at Arles. But the Irish must have discovered the existence of these litanic prayers in the office throughout Italy, and they set about imitating them in their own way, just as the Council of Vaison attempted to do for Gaul in the sixth century. The Irish had a great liking for the psalms and an inclination to use psalm-versicles in their prayers, and even as prayers in their own right.[62] They may have got this idea of the independent use of the *versus* or *capitellum* from the Continent and from Gaul, in particular. But when the idea of intercessory prayers in the office was conceived, the Irish, unlike the Council of Vaison, did not attempt to introduce the litany with its *kyrie eleison* into the office. They saw here an opportunity to give full scope to their liking for versicles, the chance to use them instead of the *kyrie eleison* as the prayer-element of the litany, the *supplicatio litaniae*. This solution permitted a greater variety in the intercessory prayers, not only because the traditional litany with *kyrie eleison* continued to be used in the Mass, but also because in the new form each intention had its own most appropriate versicle.

The classes of people prayed for in this new form correspond roughly to those found in the diaconal litanies used in the Mass and elsewhere in the office. The first class, *pro peccatis nostris*, is preceded by a series of versicles which have a penitential character.[63] This introduction is interesting for this reason, that it shows that what has been regarded as the much later combination of Gallican *capitella* and the Columbanian form of intercessory versicles is already a feature of the *oratio communis* of the Antiphonary. We will now compare the classes prayed for in this *oratio communis* to those found in the litanies with *kyrie eleison*, as used in Ireland and throughout the West generally in the Mass and office.[64] The collects which follow the versicle are very short and must have belonged to the sixth-century form of these prayers. They do not on the whole suggest any contact with the prayers of the other Western liturgies. Most of the intercessions are preceded by biddings; those which are lacking both in the Antiphonary and in Columban, but supplied by Warren, will be given here in brackets.

i. AB 40b. *Pro peccatis nostris* (Columban)

Deus in adiutorium . . . festina (ps.69,2).
Festina, domine, liberare nos ex omnibus peccatis nostris.

This intention is found in Ga 15:

Pro remissione peccatorum vel emendatione morum,

and indirectly in Ir 16:

Sanctorum apostolorum ac martyrum memores simus, ut orantibus eis pro nobis veniam mereamur.

But no doubt the Irish did not need any model for them to give pride of place to this intention.

ii. AB 41. *Pro baptizatis* (*Pro omni populo christiano*: Columban)

Salvum fac populum tuum . . . in saeculum (ps.27,9).
Miserere, domine, ecclesiae tuae catholicae quam redemisti in tuo sancto sanguine, qui regnas.

A corresponding bidding is found in all forms of the litany; for example,

Ir 2 Pro SANCTA ECCLESIA CATHOLICA, quae est a finibus usque ad terminos orbis terrarum.

iii. AB 41b. *Pro sacerdotibus et reliquis . . . gradibus* (Columban)

Exsurge, domine, . . . Sacerdotes tui induentur. . . (ps.131,8 – 9). Laetentur in te, domine, omnes sancti tui, qui sperant in te in omni veritate.

- Ir 4 Pro omnibus episcopis et presbiteris et diaconis et omni clero. - MI[1] 3.4 Pro papa nostro *Illo* et omni clero eius omnibusque sacerdotibus et ministris.

iv. AB 42. *Pro abbate*
There are three versicles (ps.40,3; 120,7 – 8) given here, but no collect; it

was omitted in this case probably because the collects were said by the abbot himself. The corresponding bidding in the litanies is that for the bishop; for example,

Ir 3 Pro pastore N. episcopo.

v. AB 43. (*Pro fratribus*) - AB 44 *Pro fraternitate*

Custodi nos, domine, ut pupillam oculi ... protege nos (ps.16,8). Protegere et sanctificare digneris omnibus, omnipotens deus, qui regnas.

Tu, domine servabis nos ... in eternum (ps.11,8).
Exaudi orationes nostras pro fratribus nostris, ut illis, deus, misereraris.

- Ir 5 Pro hoc loco et habitantibus in eo. -MI[1] 5 Pro civitate hac et conservatione eius omnibusque habitantibus in ea.

vi. AB 45. *Pro pace populorum et regum* (*Pro pace regum*: Columban)

Dominus virtutem ... in pace (ps.28,11).
Pacem praestare digneris omnibus, omnipotens deus, qui regnas.

- Ir 1 Pro altissima pace et tranquillitate temporum nostrorum.
- MI[1] 7 Pro pace ecclesiarum, vocatione gentium et quiete populorum.

Besides, prayers for the emperor and the army are found in all forms of the litany (Ir 6, Ga 6, MI 6, Gel V).

vii. AB 47. *Pro blasfemantibus* (*Pro inimicis*: Columban)

Domine, misericordia tua in saeculum, ... ne dispicias (ps.137,8).
Domine, deus virtutum, ne statuas illis hoc in peccatum.

There is no bidding comparable to this in the litanies.

viii. AB 47. *Pro impiis*

Iudica illos, deus, ... inritaverunt te, domine (ps.5,11). Confundantur illi qui confidunt in se et non nos, domine, qui confidimus in te.

The only bidding that is partially comparable to this is:

Gel X Pro iudaica falsitate aut heretica pravitate deceptis vel gentilium superstitione perfusis, veritatis Dominum deprecamur.

ix. AB 48. *Pro iter facientibus*

O domine, salvum fac, ... prosperare (ps.117,25).
Prosperitatem itineris praesta tuis famulis, qui regnas.

- Ir 11 Pro peregrinantibus et ITER FACIENTIBUS ac navigantibus. MI[1] 11 Pro navigantibus, iter agentibus.... .

x. AB 49. (*Pro gratias agentibus*)

Confiteantur tibi, domine, ... confiteantur tibi (ps.144,10). Tibi gratias agunt animae nostrae pro innumeris beneficiis tuis, domine, qui regnas.

There is nothing comparable in the litanies. Considering its position, after the intercession for those on a journey, and the choice of a versicle from psalm 144, it is probably another intercession *pro iter facientibus* or, rather, a thanksgiving for a safe journey completed.

xi. AB 50. *Pro elimosi(nas facientibus).*

Dispersit, . . . exaltabitur in gloria (ps.111,9)
Elimosinas facientibus in hoc mundo, retribue, domine, in regno sancto tuo.

- Ir 14 Pro his qui in sancta Ecclesia fructus misericordiae largiuntur (MI[1] 14).
-Gel XI Pro operariis pietatis et his qui necessitatibus laborantum fraterna caritate subveniunt.

xii. AB 51. *Pro infirmis*

Et clamaverunt . . . liberavit eos (ps.106,6).
Tribue, domine, tuis famulis sanitatem mentis et corporis.

- Ga 13 Pro his qui infirmantur et diversis languoribus detinentur. - MI[1] 13 Pro his qui diversis infirmitatibus detinentur quique spiritibus vexantur inmundis.

xiii. AB 51b. (*Pro captivis*)

Exsurge, domine, . . . et redime nos propter nomen tuum (ps.43,26).
Adiutorium nostrum in nomine domini (ps.123,8).
Salvare nos digneris per invocationem sancti tui nominis, qui regnas.

- MI[1] 10 PRO CAPTIVIS.

The final section (AB 52 – 56) gives us what I consider to be a double conclusion to the *oratio communis.* Either may have been chosen at liberty, or perhaps on alternate days, or on different occasions. Each conclusion consists of a commemoration of the martyrs, a psalm (which in the first case is followed by a versicle and collect which sums it up), and a collect which concludes the whole *oratio.* We will consider both conclusions together.

(a) Commemoration of the martyrs

Each commemoration consists simply of a collect *de martyribus* (AB 52) or *ad martyres* (AB 55), but they may have been accompanied by one of the antiphons *de martyribus* provided in AB 101 – 104. We will have more to say about these collects later;[65] for the present it will suffice to draw attention to the parallel commemoration of the martyrs at the conclusion of the Irish text of the litany:

Ir 16 Sanctorum apostolorum ac martyrum memores simus, ut orantibus eis pro nobis veniam mereamur.

(b) A psalm of supplication

Only the first words of the psalm are given in each case:[66]

AB 53 Ad te, domine, clamabo: deus meus, ne sileas a me. . . (ps 27,1).
AB 56 Miserere mei, deus, secundum magnam. . . (ps.50,3).

While the two are psalms of supplication, the first is particularly appropriate as a conclusion to the *oratio communis,* since it expresses sentiments of trust that God will hear the prayers of the suppliant and, indeed, rejoices that they have been already heard.[67] It is summed up in a versicle and short collect:

Dominus virtutum nobiscum, susceptor noster deus Iacob (ps.45,8). Adiutor noster deus Iacob, miserere nobis, domine, qui regnas.

(c) Concluding collect

AB 54 *Collectio* (*Collectis*: MS). Sanctus in sanctis, agnus inmaculatus, gloriosus in caelis, mirabilis in terris, praesta nobis, domine, secundum magnam misericordiam tuam, deus, quae te petimus et oramus, qui regnas.

AB 56 Tribue, domine, petentibus te ex fide, secundum magnam misericordiam tuam, deus, qui regnas.

The first of these collects is curiously related to certain Spanish and Gallican prayers. There is a parallel to its first half in:

Mo LS 1287 Vere SANCTUS IN SANCTIS, GLORIOSUS IN CAELIS, MANIFESTUS IN TERRIS dominus noster Iesus Christus.[68]

But the phrase *praesta quae te petimus* is definitely associated with Gallican terminolgy:[69]

Ga Mone 13 Exaudi nos, deus pater omnipotens, et PRAESTA QUAE TE PETIMUS.
- 23 Exaudi nos, domine, et PRAESTA QUAE TE PETIMUS, pacem tuam.
-225 Exaudi nos, deus pater omnipotens, et PRAESTA QUAE PETIMUS.

Ga G 40 Miserere nostri et exaudi nos et praesta, ut possimus . . . fidem tenere.
- 220 (V 12) exaudi nos et PRAESTA, precamur, QUAE corde ROGAMUS.

Ga F 34 Exaudi nos, pie pater, . . . et PRAESTA QUID TE ROGAMUS ET ORAMUS.

Otherwise, the collects are evidently Irish products[70] which were composed for the conclusion of the *oratio communis*.

The subsequent development of this form of intercessory prayer following its transplantation to the continent by Columban and his followers would need to be investigated in a more thorough fashion than we can hope to do here. But the main lines of development appear clear enough. The short collects were abandoned and eventually two main types of *preces* emerged. In one, the biddings were retained and they were answered by the appropriate versicle in each case; this type remained closer to the original Irish form.[71] In the other, the biddings were reduced or entirely eliminated and the versicles, which in many cases were the original Irish ones, were divided so as to form *versicles* and *responses*.[72] This second type, which was only germinally present in the Irish or Columbanian form, eventually gained popularity. The *preces* of mediaeval breviaries generally consist of a series of versicles and responses, followed by a series of biddings and appropriate versicles. The Gallican tradition of the independent use of the *capitellum* may have been a factor in this development of the *preces* as a series of versicles and responses. But it would appear certain from the evidence we have considered that the principle itself as to the use of the versicles for the intercessory prayers was an Irish invention. Gregory of Tours, a near-contemporary of Columban, knows nothing of it. But when it was brought to the Continent by Columban, it found in the tradition of the *capitellum*, still very much alive, a point of contact and a source of further development. Eventually, before the ninth century, the *preces* were introduced into the Romano – Benedictine office of Gaul. A remnant of the old conclusion of this office lived on in the *kyrie eleison* and the Lord's prayer; the *preces* were added to that conclusion and were themselves concluded, as in the original Irish form, by psalm 50 and a collect.

We may now conclude this chapter, in which we have considered the second set of collects and intercessory prayers provided in the Antiphonary for the various hours of the office. All of these prayers are Irish compositions, but some of them manifest their authors' acquaintance with certain continental sources. The collects for terce, sext and *initium noctis* (AB 28 – 29, 32 – 33) are related to certain Ambrosian hymns and collects, while one for the office of nightfall (AB 33) is particularly close to certain Spanish evening prayers. The *Apostolic Tradition* of Hippolytus probably influenced the author of the collect for none (AB 30), at least indirectly by way of another collect or text. These five collects have a certain similarity of style and language and seem to have been composed by one Irish author. He was well acquainted with the style and theme of comparable continental collects and had himself acquired a good ability to write similar ones. He may have written these collects at Bangor, where the continental material on which he based his work could have been available, sent there from Bobbio. But the possibility of his having been a monk at Bobbio itself cannot be absolutely ruled out. It was surely through this Irish foundation that the northern Italian sources[73] discernible here and elsewhere in the Antiphonary became accessible to Irish authors.

The other collects for the hours – those for *secunda* (AB 27), vespers (AB 31), midnight (AB 37) and matins (AB 38 – 39) – are not directly related to continental sources. They have more kinship with the Irish prayers contained in such collections as the *Book of Cerne* than with the classical collects for the office in continental liturgies. They are readily distinguishable from the latter by their asyndetic style, the absence of internal cohesion and development of thought. Even where the ideas are numerous, they are only lightly touched on and the author passes on to a new idea or psalm versicle. A sustained Latin prose style did not come easily or connaturally to an Irish author.

As for the short collects used in the intercessory prayers, we have noted parallels for two of them (AB 34, 41) in two prayers for peace in the *Missale Gothicum* (Ga G 325 and 320, respectively). One of the concluding collects for the *oratio communis* (AB 54) shows a close relationship to one Spanish prayer, while it also reflects the influence of a typically Gallican expression. This collect and certain other factors, notably the exclusive agreement at times between the biddings in the Antiphonary and those in the first Milanese text of the litany, manifest the development of the *oratio communis* between the time of Columban and the date of composition of the Antiphonary. Columban had listed six biddings and, even though his list may not be an exhaustive one, we may safely conclude that certain other biddings, with their versicles and collects, were added to the formulary as time went on.

The few 'Spanish symptoms' we have noted in the collects suggest that some Spanish material was known and used in Ireland. Our investigation will reveal much more in this sense and we will later inquire into the manner of its transmission to Ireland. Contact with Gallican and northern Italian sources is more readily understandable in view of the important Columbanian centres in those regions in the late sixth and seventh centuries.

CHAPTER THIRTEEN

VARIOUS COLLECTS

We include under this general heading a number of collects which are not part of any full set of collects in the Antiphonary. They include a number of collects for different hours, some collects which are addressed to, or speak about, the martyrs, and a number of other pieces.

1. SCATTERED COLLECTS FOR THE HOURS

i. AB 16. *Collectio ad secundam*

Esto nobis protector in ista die, domine, sancte pater, omnipotens aeterne deus, et miserator et misericors et auxiliator et dux nobis et inluminator cordium nostrorum. Custodi, domine cogitationes, sermones, opera, ut possimus placere in conspectu tuo et perficere voluntatem tuam, et ambulare in via recta toto nostrae vitae tempore.

This collect was inserted to fill space left vacant at the end of the first part of the Antiphonary, following the hymn in honour of St Camelacus. It is closely related to the collect said daily at prime in the Roman and Ambrosian offices:

Brev.Rom. Dirigere et sanctificare, regere et gubernare dignare, Domine Deus, rex coeli et terrae, hodie corda et corpora nostra, sensus, sermones et actus nostros in lege tua et in operibus mandatorum tuorum: ut hic et in aeternum, te . auxiliante, salvi et liberi esse mereamur, salvator mundi, qui vivas et regnas in saecula saeculorum.

AmM II 447 – – 448 Dirigere et CUSTODIRE et sanctificare digneris, rex creator caeli et terrae, hodie in die isto corda et corpora nostra, sensus et SERMONES nostros, ACTUS AC COGITATIONES nostras, IN VIA et in lege tua et in opera mandatorum tuorum: UT POSSIMUS PLACERE IN CONSPECTU TUO, et angelus tuus bonus comitetur nobiscum ad dirigendos pedes nostros in viam pacis: ut hic et in aeternum, per te salvi esse mereamur, Ihesu Christe, salvator mundi, qui vivas et regnas, Deus, per omnia saecula saeculorum.

The Ambrosian prayer is closer than the Roman to our AB collect. But both the Ambrosian and Roman texts show traces, even independently of AB 16, of Irish influence in their association of *cogitationes* (*sensus*) *sermones, actus,* and in the expressions *hic et in aeternum* and *salvator mundi qui vivis.*[1] Both prayers must be traced ultimately to an Irish source. The Irish character of AB 16 is further manifest in its multiplication of terms of apposition: *protector, miserator, auxiliator, dux, inluminator.* While individual instances of these terms may be found in the Ambrosian books,[2] such diffusion is an Irish trait and was not retained in the Ambrosian or Roman versions of the collect. The sentiments expressed in the concluding part of the collect are found also in other liturgies, but the expressions are of a general character:

(a) *placere in conspectu tuo et perficere voluntatem tuam*

. Am Bi 1238 ut, te donante, tibi PLACITA cupiat et tota virtute PERFICIAT.

   - 1256 ut te tota virtute diligant et QUE TIBI PLACITA SUNT tota dilectione PERFICIANT.

Mo CPs 10 (ps.10) da nobis ante oculos tuos tibi PLACITA ET PLACITURA PERFICERE.

Gil 78 opera manuum nostrarum IN CONSPECTU TUO DIRIGE PLACITURA.

(b) *ambulare in via recta*

Mo Br 359A ut in via immaculate intelligibiliter ambulemus: quo et misericordiae instinctu intendamus recta et in iudicii metu corrigamus errata.

ii. AB 57. *Ad nocturno*

Média nócte clamóre fácto
ut nós inveniámur paráti spónso,[3]
quo regnas.

This rhyming, rhythmical collect is, evidently, an Irish product. It is the first of a number of collects inserted in the MS at the end of the second complete set for the hours. The others are: three collects for the morning office (AB 58 – 60, two of which are repeated elsewhere, AB 39 = 59 and AB 120 = 58) and one *de martyribus* (AB 61).

iii. AB 58 (120). *Ad matutinam*

Deus, deus noster, ad te de luce vigilare debemus, et tu excita de gravi somno et libera de sopore animas nostras, et in cubilibus nostris conpungamur, ut tui esse memores mereamur, qui regnas.

This collect is a patchwork of scriptural texts:

Ps.62,1 Deus, Deus meus, ad te de luce vigilo.
Sir.22,8 Qui narrat verbum non audienti, quasi qui excitat dormientem de gravi somno.
Ps.4,5 in cubilibus vestris compungimini.
Ps.62,7 Si memor fui tui super stratum meum...

iv. AB 60. *Ad matutinam*

O qui altis habitas et humilia respicis in caelo et in terra, in mari et in omnibus abissis: de profundo cordis te deprecamur, ut firmes manus nostras ad proelium et digitos nostros ad bellum, quo possimus in matutino interficere omnes peccatores terrae nostrae ac nos [a]indefice mereamur et[a] templum sanctum tuum, . Christe, qui regnas.

a – a: indeficienter mereamur esse, Warren II; indeficere mereamur et ingredi, Franceschini.

This is another interesting example of a 'psalter collect' after the Irish fashion,[4] the combination of a number of versicles from different psalms, all artfully joined together and united in the invocation-conclusion. These are the sources:

116

Ps.112,5 – 6 Quis sicut Dominus Deus noster, qui in altis habitat et humilia respicit in caelo et in terra?

Ps.134,6 Omnia quaecumque voluit dominus fecit, in caelo, in terra, in mari et in omnibus abyssis.

Ps.143,1 Benedictus Dominus Deus meus, qui docet manus meas ad proelium et digitos meos ad bellum.

Ps.100,8 In matutino interficiebam omnes peccatores terrae.

v. AB 121. *Ad horam nonam*

Convenientes, fratres dilectissimi, ad orationem nonam, in quo tempore latro confessus est et regnum paradisum pollicetur ei: ita et nos, domine, confitemur peccata nostra, ut (et: MS) regnum caelorum consequamur et vitam aeternam mereamur, qui regnas.

This collect consists of an unusual combination, that is, an invitation to prayer and a prayer addressed to Christ. But this does not mean that the author actually combined two pre-existing prayers. The structural fault is probably part of the original work of composition by an Irish author. It is corrected, though not without some corruption of the text, in Ge A 1894:

Convenientes ad orationem nonam, fratres karissimi, ita conversus et regnum caelorum pollicitus est: ita et nos confiteamur peccata nostra, ut regnum caelorum ad vitam aeternam consequi mereamur, per.

The collect is similar in content to that given in the Ambrosian books for the same hour:

Am M II 452 (Be 1584) Domine Iesu Christe, qui hora nona in crucis patibulo latronem confitentem intra moenia paradisi transire iussisti, te supplices exoramus, ut paradisi portas nos facias introire gaudentes.

One wonders whether this Ambrosian collect is not itself ultimately traceable to an Irish origin. It is given as an alternative prayer for none in Ge A 1895, where Irish traits and the influence of the collect in AB 121 are more readily discernible:

Domine DEUS Iesu Christe, et hora nona in crucis patibulum confitentem latronem infra moenia paradysi transire iussisti:TE SUPPLICES CONFITENTES peccata nostra deprecantium, ut post obitum nostrum paradysi nobis introire gaudentes concedas, per.

This collect is one of the very few collects for the hours in the Ambrosian books that are addressed to Christ. The others are the collects for prime and compline, of which the former is definitely Irish in origin[5] and the latter may also not unreasonably be regarded as Irish.[6] Having said all this, however, an immediate literary relationship between AB 121 and the Ambrosian collect for none does not appear probable; they both express in their own independent ways a common theme. The author of AB 121 was, however, influenced by two lines of the hymn for none, *Ter hora trina* (AH 51,18):

7. Dicamus ergo proximi
laudes deo cum cantico;

CONFESSUS EST LATRO fidem
QUO est redemptus TEMPORE.

The collect shows yet again the difficulty experienced by Irish authors in the field of liturgical prose. Even though there is a unity of thought in the prayer, the application in the second part of the theme introduced in the first part, there is the structural fault which we have noted and which an author more versed in the euchological tradition would have avoided.

vi. AB 122 *Ad secundam*

> Domine, sancte pater, omnipotens aeterne deus, qui diem clarificas et in lumine luminas, misericordiam tuam, domine, ne auferas a nobis. Redde nobis laetitiam salutaris tui et spiritu principali confirma nos, ut oriatur lucifer in cordibus nostris, per te Iesu Christe, qui regnas.

There is a shorter version of this prayer in Ge A 1888:

> Deus, qui ab hora prima diei lucem in lucem inluminas, misericordiam tuam ne auferas a nobis. Reple nos laetitia salutaris tuae; ne derelinquas nos usquequaque, salva. per.

The first part of the collect in AB has the appearance of being a classical morning prayer, but I have not met elsewhere the expressions *clarificare diem* and *luminare in lumine*. The main source of the collect are:

> Ps.50,13 – 14 spiritum sanctum tuum ne auferas a me; redde mihi laetitiam salutaris tui et spiritu principali confirma me.
>
> 2 Pt.1,19 Et habemus firmiorem propheticam sermonem, cui benefacitis attendentes, quasi lucernae lucenti in caliginoso loco, donec DIES ELUCESCAT et LUCIFER ORIATUR IN CORDIBUS NOSTRIS.

The first text is, as one would expect, reflected in the psalter collects on psalm 50,[7] and the second text influenced certain continental morning and evening prayers;[8] but our collect is not related to any of these. It does express, however, a morning theme that is common to all the liturgies, but in the diffuse and eclectic style that is recognizable as Irish.

2. COLLECTS ABOUT THE MARTYRS

i AB 52. *De martyribus*

> Deus, qui sanctis et electis tuis coronam martyrii praestitisti, te oramus, domine, ut eorum meritis obtineamus veniam, qui tantam gloriam non meremur, qui regnas.

The palimpset *Cod. Aug. CXCV* in Karshruhe contains some leaves which were written by a number of Irish scribes in the eighth and ninth cenuries (ff.19, 32 – 35, 39 – 42) and which appear to contain material for three or four distinct liturgical offices.[9] Two of these leaves (ff.33 and 41), which were written by one Irish hand, contain a collection of prayers in honour of the martyrs, four of which were partially deciphered by A. Dold.[10] We shall see that prayers 1 and 4 of this collection are also found in the Antiphonary and that they are of Spanish origin. He could only read the concluding words of the second prayer: *non mereremur qui regnas*.[11] P. Siffrin was quick to point out that this corresponds to the conclusion of the first collect in honour of the martyrs in the Antiphonary, which we have just cited above (AB 52), and it is highly probable that the collect itself was the same in both manuscripts.

The question arises whether this also is not a Spanish collect. The expression *sancti et electi* is a definite Spanish symptom, which, however, has found its way into a large variety of liturgical books. Most of the relevant texts have been collected by E. Bishop and G Manz.[13] Bishop was inclined to regard it as being originally Irish;[14] but Manz was able to add considerably to the data collected by Bishop, especially from among the Spanish and Ambrosian sources, so that the picture is much more complex than it appeared to Bishop.[15] The expression is found with particular frequency in the prayers for the dead in the Spanish, Ambrosian and Gelasian books, all of which are closely related in this particular area. It is not necessary for us here to trace the development and interaction of these prayers, and the later extension of the expression *sancti et electi*. It will suffice to cite some examples of its use which establish it as an originally Spanish expression.

Mo CPs 290 (ps.118,20) Vide humilitatem nostram et libera nos, Domine, de laqueo mortis et insidiis diaboli, ut . . . sub tua miseratione cum SANCTIS ET ELECTIS aeterna praemia consequi mereamur.

Idalius, *Epist. ad S. Julianum*: Oramus, . . . ut . . . post longissima vitae huius spatia, remissis iniquitatibus tectisque peccatis, cum SANCTIS ET ELECTIS suis coelestia vobis ad possidendum regna concedat.[16]

Isidore, *Sententiarum Liber* I,28,7: Multi posse perire ex eis in die iudicii, qui nunc ELECTI videntur ET SANCTI.[17]

M 12 sup. 7,4 Dignum et iustum est, omnipotens deus, ut gratiarum actionem lingua famulante potentiam tuam loquamur in SANCTIS ET ELECTIS tuis.[18]

These early Spanish testimonies and the frequent use of the expression in all Spanish books, apart from Or, prove that the expression is originally Spanish rather than Irish. Its presence in AB 52 is a strong indication of the Spanish origin of this collect. But the possibility remains that already in the seventh century the Irish had taken over this expression for their own compositions, in which case the collect we are considering might possibly be Irish.

The second half of the collect is associated in its language and thought with certain Gallican and Spanish prayers. The phrase *ut eorum meritis obtineamus veniam qui tantam gloriam non meremur* is peculiar, in as much as the usual request in such collects is that we, through the intercession of the saints, may become partakers in their glory and share in their heavenly reward.[19] The idea that we do not deserve such glory is expressed in another way in AB 67, which says of the martyrs:

ut eorum praecibus adiuvari mereamur, quorum consortes esse non possumus.

We shall see that this collect (AB 67) is of Spanish origin. But for the moment we will concentrate our attention on the peculiar parallels to AB 52. We will not consider the general theme of such intercession of the saints or the various scopes of such intercession, so that in this way attention can be focused on those prayers in which the request is that we may obtain *pardon* for our sins *through the merits* of the saints, even though *we do not deserve to share in the glory* (*crown*) *of martyrdom*.

> Ga G 140 (B 52) Deum, qui sanctae famulae suae Eulaliae gloriosam et inmarcesibilem CORONAM MARTYRII contulit, deprecemur, UT ... IPSIUS PRAECIBUS OBTINEAMUS VENIAM, QUI GLORIAM NON MEREMUR.

There is an obvious literary relationship between this prayer and our collect. But, because of the context in which it is found, it cannot without further textual evidence be very confidently regarded as a purely Gallican prayer.[20]

> Ga G 426 Deus, qui beatum martyrem tuum Laudegarium in agone probasti, ... praesta, ... UT QUI GLORIAM NON MEREMUR, INDULGENTIAM PECCATORUM IPSO INTERVENIENTE ADEPISCI MEREAMUR.

These are the most striking parallels from the Gallican texts, and they express what is in effect a traditional Gallican theme.[21] But the same theme is expressed in a variety of ways in Spanish prayers, none of which, however, is quite as close to the formulation of our collect as are Ga G 140 and 426.

> Mo Or 466 (Br 1016C) ut, si effusione sanguinis CORONAS NON MEREMUR ACCIPERE, ex fructu dilectionis verae perpetuam mereamur apud te hereditatem.

> Or 1051 (Br 1125 – 6) ut, qui corporei sanguinis effusione NON MEREMUR CORONAM, votorum impensione perducamur ad gloriam.

> LS 840 UT EIUS (*scil.* Bartholomei) MERITIS populi tui universitas ... semper tibi serviat, ... que per martyrium NON MERETUR DE HOSTE TRIUMPHUM.

> LS 885 Ille (*scil.* Martinus) per confessionis gratiam MERUIT coronam virtutum: nos EIUS SUFFRAGIIS ... VENIAM ... CONSEQUI MEREAMUR.

These are the nearest Spanish parallels to the expression in our prayer.[22] What conclusion may be drawn from this evidence regarding the origin of our collect? If the author was an Irishman, he was strongly influenced by Spanish and, possibly, by Gallican sources. But this possibility of Irish authorship of the collect does not appear very likely. If we are to choose between Spain and Gaul, then our choice must be Spain, if only because of the use of the expression *sancti et electi*. In this case, the Gallican parallel (Ga G 140) must itself be regarded as having been derived from a Spanish original, either directly or by way of an Irish author. But this possibility is quite acceptable and causes no difficulty. Besides, the collect (AB 52) is the earliest known Irish prayer in which the expression *sancti et electi* occurs, an expression which must have come to Ireland in a Spanish prayer, which may have been none other than the prayer we are now considering. Furthermore, we may anticipate a general conclusion and point out that all the prose collects in honour of the martyrs in the Antiphonary, if we except the one in question now, are either certainly or probably of Spanish origin. Lastly, our collect is one of four collects in the palimpsest fragment, *Cod. Aug. CXCV*: of the other three, two are found in Spanish books and the source of the other is uncertain.[23] For these reasons, we are inclined to regard AB 52 as being probably Spanish in origin, rather than Gallican or Irish.

ii. AB 55. *Ad martyes*

Aeternum virtutis tuae nomen, omnipotens deus, oramus, uti nos martyrum et omnium sanctorum tuorum meritis socios, fide pares, devotione strenuos, passione consimiles, in resurrectione felicium facias coaequari, qui regnas.

This is one of the collects which A. Dold succeeded in deciphering fragmentarily in the palimpsest sacramentary, Ga C.[24] Many of the items in this sacramentary are of Spanish provenance, and, in fact, this collect occurs frequently in the Spanish Breviary and Missal, where we find it adapted to the feast of a particular martyr through the insertion of the name in the phrase *ut nos martyris tui N. meritis socios*. There are some variant readings in all the texts of the prayer in the Spanish books, and the text is often wrongly punctuated and altered slightly as a result. The Breviary texts are closest to the readings in AB. We will indicate the more important variants.[25]

Aeternum[a] [b]tuae virtutis[b] nomen, omnipotens deus, oramus, ut nos martyris tui N. et omnium sanctorum meritis socios, fide pares , devotione strenuos[c], passione [d]consimiles, et in[d] resurrectione felicium facias[e] coaequari.

a. Aeternum] Aeterne M 964; b. tuae virtutis] virtutis tuae Br 1196; c. strenuos] extremos M 827; extrenuos M 856; d. consimiles et in] et consimiles in M 827, similes in M 964; e. facias] nos facias M 964.

There is no reason to doubt the Spanish origin of this prayer. Prayers of a similar structure are found in other liturgies also, but the closest linguistic parallels are found in Spanish sources:

Am Bi 908 VD aeterne Deus: beati etenim martyris tui . . . nascendi lege consortes, fidei societate coniuncti, passionis aequalitate consimiles, in uno semper Domino gloriosi. . . .

Ga B 350 Oramus te, pater sancte, ut nos servos tuos beatissimi martires tui *ill.* iubess esse consortis, in confessione participes, in fide stabiles, in persecutione firmus, in tribulatione pacientes, in consummacione victuris. . . .
Ga G 415 praesta ut similes nos fides martyrio copulet, quos tempus passionis in stadio non relinquit.

Mo M 956 Dominum Deum nostrum . . . poscamus, . . . UT NOS SANCTI EIUS MERITIS CONSORTES effectos, propositum nostrum vitamque consummet. Et cuius sumus hic nostra DEVOTIONE FAUTORES, esse mereamur donante Christo participes (cf. LS 1058).

LS 1432 corde creduli et DEVOTIONE STRENUI.[26]

Isidore, *De ortu et obitu patrum* c.59: Tres pueri, ex stirpe regia clari, memoria gloriosi, scientia eruditi, FIDE PARES, DEVOTIONE STABILES, incorrupti corpore, sobrii mente. . . .[27]

Isidore, *ibid.*, c.64: Machabaei septem fratres, in fide stabiles, in spe fortes ... coronas martyrii meruerunt.[28]

It may be that in AB 55 we have a collect composed by St Isidore himself, one preserved in Spain only in the books of Isidorian tradition.

iii. AB 61. *De martyribus*

Deus, qui sanctos tuos cum mensura probas et sine mensura glorificas...

This is a long collect which asks God for various blessings, through the intercession of the saints; the martyrs are not specifically mentioned. It is found also in Ce S 20 and *Cod. Aug. CXCV*,[29] as well as in Mo LO 314. Its Spanish origin has long been established, as well as the fact that the original has been preserved better in the Irish tradition.[30]

iv. AB 97. *Oratio de martyribus*

Deus, qui martyribus tuis largitas es regnum, nobis autem peccantibus veniam prestare digneris. Hii choronam suam passione per fidem meruerunt: nos autem pro iniquitatibus et praevaricationibus nostris remissionem a te et misericordiam postulamus.

This prayer is found, with some slight variations, in:

M 12 sup. 36,1 Dne qui scis martyribus tuis largitus es regnum, nobis veniam presta. Hii coronam suam fide et passione meruerunt: nos pro iniquitatibus nostris promissione ... misericordiam ... tulamur. per dnm nm.[31]

This collect sets up the same antithesis between the *glory* which the martyrs *merited* and the *pardon* which we hope to receive, that we have already encountered in AB 52: *ut eorum meritis obtineamus veniam qui tantam gloriam non meremur*. We saw that the theme is common to the Gallican and Spanish prayers, even though AB 52 has its closest parallel in Ga G 140 and 426. Here we hope to establish, by concentrating on the expression *coronam passione per fidem* (or *fide et passione*) *merere*, that AB 97 is closely associated with Spanish liturgical terminology . We will leave out of consideration the many prayers which, in all the liturgies, speak about the reward (crown, glory, and so on) given to the martyrs, and concentrate on the expression of the reason for this reward, namely, the faith and suffering of the martyrs.

Ga G 139 Deus, qui sanctae martyre tuae Eulaliae PRO POENA GLORIAM, ... PRO PASSIONE CORONAM tribuisti, praesta, ut veniam te donante consequi mereamur.[32]

Mo Or 126 ut, que (*scil.* Leocadia) apud Deum meruisti DE CONFESSIONE CORONAM, nobis confitetibus obtineas apud ipsum peccatorum nostrorum omnium INDULGENTIAM.

Or 154 ut sicut illa (*scil.* Eulalia) POST PASSIONEM obtinuit CORONAM, ita vos per penitentiam veniatis ad veniam (Br 1278C).

Or 424 Christus Dominus, qui inter vos (*scil.* parvulos innocentes) eminens creditur singulis vobis PRO MARTYRIO tribuisse CORONAS, a nobis, pro merito, QUAS MEREMUS arceat PENAS.

LO 328,31 ut sanctis tuis eorum FIDES ET RECTA CONFESSIO pervenit ad CORONAM, ita istis sua devotio occurrat ad VENIAM.

122

LS 885 Ille (*scil.* Martinus) PER CONFESSIONIS GRATIAM MERUIT CORONAM virtutum: nos eius suffragiis, te donante, VENIAM peccatorum nostrorum consequi mereamur.

LS 1060 qui triumphalem palmam per FIDEI munimenta Christo opitulante PRO-MERUIT obtinere, ... dignetur impendere, ut ipse nobis peccatorum tribuat VENIAM, qui contulit inmortalitatis CORONAM.

LS 1241 dedisti eius FIDEM predicationis et constantiam PASSIONIS. Seviebat in eis gladius tirannorum et coronabant eos praemia regni celorum. Respice per eorum merita preces nostras, ... ut, qui illis adquisitum est regnum ad GLORIAM, nobis opituletur ad VENIAM.

We can conclude with probability that our collect is of Spanish origin. Its presence in *M 12 sup.* ties in with the fact that this MS contains a good amount of Spanish material in a Gallican liturgical setting. The textual difference between the two redactions of the prayer suggest that the Irish did not get it from southern Gaul but rather directly from Spain. The reading of the Irish text, in particular the phrase *nobis autem peccantibus veniam prestare digneris*, is preferable to the truncated and abrupt *nobis veniam presta*. Besides, there is a parallelism in

nos autem pro iniquitatibus et praevaricationibus nostris remissionem a te et misericordiam postulamus

which has been lost in the Gallican transcription.

v. AB 124. *De martyribus*

Sancti et gloriosi, mirabiles atque potentes martires, quorum in operibus gaudet dominus et in congregatione laetatur, intercessores obtimi et fortissimi protectores: mementote nostri semper in conspectu domini, ut domini mereamur auxilium, qui regnas.

This is the third of the martyr-collects to occur both in the Antiphonary and in *Cod. Aug. CXCV.*[33] It is also found, in a slightly variant form, as an *oratio ad matutinum* in the *Ordo de Sanctis* of the mozarabic psalter:

Gil 329 Sancti mirabiles atque potentes, in quorum operibus gaudet dominus et in congregatione sancta letatur, intercessores obtimi, fortissimi protectores: mementote nostri, ut domini auxilium habere mereamur.

There is no peculiarly Spanish expression in the prayer, and it could possibly be understood as an Irish composition, reflecting in particular the opening stanza of the hymn *Sacratissimi martyres*. Gil 329 would then be an adaptation of the prayer, obtained by omitting the reference to the martyrs and changing the conclusion from *semper in conspectu domini ut domini mereamur auxilium* to *ut domini auxilium habere mereamur*. On the other hand, there is no real reason why both texts cannot have been derived from a common Spanish original, and we can take this as being at least equally probable. The original appears to have been better preserved in the Irish text,[34] but, of course, the inevitable Irish conclusion *qui regnas* is out of place and cannot have been in the original.

We will meet more martyr-collects in the various sets of collects for the morning office. At the end of our study of the collects we will consider the question regarding the route by which the Spanish collects reached Ireland. For the moment we can note that of the five collects in honour of the martyrs that we have encountered so far, two (AB 55 and 61) are certainly Spanish and the other three (AB 52, 97 and 124) are probably Spanish also. We have here, therefore, further important evidence of Spanish influence in Ireland and of the ecclectic tendencies of the Irish in the domain of liturgy.[35]

3. OTHER COLLECTS

1. AB 96. *Collectio super hominem qui habet diabolum*

Domini, sancte pater, omnipotens aeterne deus, expelle diabolum et gentilitatem ab homine isto, de capite, de capillis, ... de corpore toto, de omnibus compaginibus membrorum suorum, intus et deforis, de ossibus, ... de omni conversatione eius hic et in futuro. Sed operetur in *te* (!) virtus Christi, in eo qui propassus est ut vitam aeternam mereamur, per d.n.I.C. filium *suum* (!).

This curious exorcism is found also in Ce S 24 and in a few later texts,[36] and it must be regarded as of Irish origin.[37] A shorter form of the exorcism is found in Ce S 31 (Ga B 243):

Operare creatura olei, operare in nomine dei patris omnipotentis et filii et spiritus sancti, ut non lateat hic spiritus immundus, nec in membris nec in medullis (nec in) compaginibus membrorum, sed operatur in *te* (!) virtus Christi filii dei vivi altissimi et spiritus sancti per saecula saeculorum.

A similar exorcism is found in an eleventh-century monastic MS from Milan (Am M I 82):

Ungo *te* oleo sanctificato,... ut non lateat hic spiritus immundus, nec in membris, nec in medullis, nec in ullo compagine membrorum *huius hominis*; sed operetur in *eo* virtus Christi, Filii altissimi.

This Ambrosian formula must be regarded as an attemped adaptation of an exorcism which was ultimately of Irish origin.

ii. AB 123. *Post laudate pueri dominum in dominicorum die* (AB 125. *Item alia post laudate*)

Te patrem adoramus aeternum, te sempiternum filium invocamus, teque spiritum sanctum in una divinitatis substantiae manentem confitemur. [a]Tibi trinitati[a] laudes[b] et gratias referimus. [c]Tibi uni deo incessabilem dicimus laudem. Te patrem ingenitum, te filium unigenitum, te spiritum sanctum a patre et filio procedentem corde credimus. Tibi inaestimabili, inconpraehensibili, omnipotens deus, gratias agimus, qui regnas in saecula[c].
a. Tibi trinitati] Tibi uni deo in trinitate 123; b. laudes] debitas laudes 123; c. tibi ... saecula] ut te incessabili voce laudare mereamur 123.

This collect was meant to follow the chanting of the *Te deum* on Sundays,[38] and it must be regarded as an Irish product, which is largely based on the text of the *Te deum* and on the Creed *Quicumque*.[39] A number of its expressions were familiar to Irish and Spanish authors, as will be seen in the following comparative texts.

(a) *Pater aeternus, filius sempiternus, spiritus manens*

Te Deum: Te AETERNUM PATREM omnis terra veneratur... Tu patris SEMPITERNUS es FILIUS.

Quicumque: aeternus Pater, aeternus Filius, aeternus Spiritus sanctus.

(b) *una substantia divinitatis*

Quicumque: neque substantiam separantes; ... Patris et Filii et Spiritus sancti una est divinitas.

Regensburg 2 VD ... qui coaeternus tibi et in tua atque ex tua substantia MANENS, ... in SUBSTANTIAM DIVINITATIS tuae naturam generis mortalis accipiens, ut quod nostrum est suscipiens commonicaret ille nobis quod suum est.

Mo LS 472 Qui est omnipotens ex SUBSTANTIA DIVINITATIS, det vobis posse suis parere preceptis.

LS 481 Qui est indeficiens ex SUBSTANTIA DIVINITATIS natura, ipse spiritualibus deliciis reficiat infirmitatem vestram.

(c) *unus deus in trinitate*

Quicumque: Fides autem catholica haec est, ut UNUM DEUM IN TRINITATE et Trinitatem in unitate veneremur.

Columban, *Epist.*3,2: CORDE CREDIMUS et ore confitemur UNUM DEUM ESSE IN TRINITATE et trinitatem in unitate.[40]

Mo LO 180,14 Te prestante, summe Deus, qui IN TRINITATE UNUS DEUS gloriaris in secula seculorum.[41]

LS 649 TE, omnipotens Ihesu Christe, tota mentis devotione veneramur. TE omnium Dominum fideli servitutis obsequio excolimus. TE coaeternum sancto Patri et sancto Spiritu, MANENTE in singulis equali sempiternaque DEITATE, UNUM IN TRINITATE DEUM indivise confitentes laudamus.[42]

(d) *deo laudes et gratias referre*

This phrase was widely used, but it was a particular favourite in the Gallican and Spanish prayers.[43]

(e) *pater ingenitus, filius unigenitus, spiritus procedens*

Te Deum: Patrem immensae maiestatis, venerandum tuum verum UNIGENITUM filium, sanctum quoque paraclitum spiritum.

Quicumque: Pater a nullo est factus nec creatus NEC GENITUS; Filius a Patre solo est, non factus nec creatus, sed GENITUS; Spiritus sanctus a Patre et Filio, non factus nec creatus nec genitus, sed PROCEDENS.

The expression *Pater ingenitus* was a favourite one in Spain, both in conciliar and liturgical texts.[44] In many cases it was accompanied by the correlative *Filius unigenitus*.

(f) *deus inaestimabilis (et) incomprehensibilis*

Columban, Instr.XI I Deus omnipotens, invisibilis, incomprehensibilis, inenarrabilis, inaestimabilis de limo hominem fingens, imaginis suae dignitate nobilitavit.[45]

Mo LS 77 VD domine sancte, Pater eterne, omnipotens Deus, inestimabili et incomprehensibili clementiae tue perennes gratias referre.

In conclusion, the collect, in both its versions, must be of Irish origin. Indeed, the use of a collect after the *Te Deum* seems to have been peculiar to the Irish liturgy. The parallelism which we have noted above (c) between it and Mo LS 649 is interesting, but is does not appear sufficient to establish an immediate relationship between them.

iii. AB 126. *Item alia post laudate* (T 18)

Te páter rérum iúre laudámus,
te in ómni lóco fatémur et cólimus,
tíbi famulátu spontáneo ministrámus:
exaúdi nos et praésta éa quae rogámus,
qui regnas.

This rhythmical collect, further embellished with rhyme and a trace of internal consonance (*pater rerum iure*), is evidently Irish. The last phrase is, however, peculiarly Gallican. We have already noted the parallels in connection with another collect,[46] and we will simply repeat one here:

Ga G 220 (V 12) EXAUDI NOS ET PRAESTA, precamur, QUAE CORDE ROGAMUS.

The term *spontaneus* is extremely rare in liturgical texts,[47] and the only parallel for the expression *famulato ministrare* is found in a few Spanish instances of *famulatu (de) servire*.[48]

iv. AB 127. *Ad ceream benedicere*

In nocte tu fuisti columna ignis, domine, ad defendendam plebem tuam a facie Faraonis et exercitus eius: ita digneris, domine, emittere spiritum tuum sanctum et de throno flammeo gemmatoque terribili tuo ad custodiendum plebem tuam. In ista nocte scuto fidei defendas nos, ut non timeamus a timore nocturno, qui regnas in saecula.

Because of the events of the Exodus, it is best to regard this collect as being proper to the Easter vigil, to be used possibly as a collect after the hymn *Ignis creator igneus*. In content, it is based on Scripture,[49] and it must be of Irish origin.

In this chapter we have considered a number of collects dispersed throughout the manuscript. Most of them were composed by Irish authors, as can be easily recognised from such typical Irish traits as the rhythm of the phrases, the use of verses from Scripture, notably from the psalter, and the litanic, asyndetic type of structure which is characteristic of many of them. The collects in honour of the martyrs which we have so far encountered are probably all of Spanish origin. They have quite a different type of structure from the Irish collects we have considered in this chapter and they are very much part of the milieu of the Gallican and Spanish liturgies. Irish borrowing from Spain rather than from Gaul may be difficult to understand or explain. But the Spanish Church of the seventh century was pre-eminent in the West and the borrowing of prayers from there by the Irish may be seen as an implicit recognition that these prayers were better than any the Irish could compose for themselves.

CHAPTER FOURTEEN

THE FIRST SET OF COLLECTS FOR LAUDS

The Antiphonary contains seven sets of collects for various parts of the morning office, which for the sake of convenience and in anticipation of our study of the morning office at Bangor we will call lauds. The first is a complete set of six prose collects, many of which are also found in the Turin Fragment and in other Irish documents.[1]

1. AB 62. *Collectio post canticum*

> Deus, qui exeunti ex Aegypto populo tuo maria divisisti, et suspensis utrimque marginibus in specie muri erigi fluenta iussisti, animas quoque nostras a diluvio peccatorum liberare digneris, ut transire vitiorum gurgitem valeamus, hoste contempo, salvator mundi, qui cum aeterno patre vivis dominaris ac regnas, cum spiritu sancto, in saecula saeculorum.

This collect is not related to the Spanish and Ambrosian collects for the canticle *Cantemus*,[2] and, apart from one expression,[3] it has no special relationship to any known continental prayer. If it is a genuinely Irish product, it is an outstanding achievement among the collects of Irish origin in the Antiphonary. I would not have been surprised to discover it in the Spanish breviary, where it would have been quite at home in style and execution.

2. AB 63. *Collectio post benedictionem puerorum*

> Exaudi praeces nostras, omnipotens deus, et praesta, ut sicut in decantato hymno beata puerorum instituta sectamur, ita tuo munere peccatorum laqueis absoluti aeterni ignis non ambiamur incendiis, salvator mundi, qui cum patre vivis.

Apart from the rare expression *laquei peccatorum* and *incendium ignis*,[4] I have not met anything exactly comparable to this collect in other liturgies. The theme itself is commonly met: the fiery furnace symbolizes the flames of passion and sin and the furnace of eternal fire, from which one hopes to be delivered by God's grace.[5] The general impression given by the collect is the same as that given by the one immediately preceding. It is an uncommon achievement for an Irish author, a prose collect which in internal structure and cohesion of thought can compare well with those found in the other Latin liturgies for the same purpose.

3. AB 64. *Collectio post tres psalmos*

> Te dominum de caelis laudamus (ps.148,1), tibi ut canticum novum cantare mereamur (ps.149,1). Te dominum in sanctis tuis (ps.150,1) venerabiliter deprecamur, ut omnia vota nostra suscipias, peccata dimittas, salvator mundi qui regnas.

The use of versicles from the three psalms is characteristic of most of the *post laudate* collects in the Antiphonary and is a sure sign of their Irish origin. But the conclusion of the present collect was influenced by the peculiarly Spanish combination, *vota suscipere, peccata dimittere,* as can be seen from the following texts:

LO 315,35 Votum nostrum Dominus clementer intendat et PECCATA DIMITTAT.
LO 316,30 eorum VOTA SUSCIPIAS et PECCATA DIMITTAS.
LO 317,9 hanc VOTIVAM OBLATIONEM . . . SUSCIPERE digneris et propitius eorum PECCATA DIMITTAS.
LO 327,35 VOTA propitiatus SUSCIPIAS et PECCATA cuncta DIMITTAS.
LO 330,28 ut VOTUM famulorum tuorum SUSCIPIAS, PECCATA DIMITTAS.

Gil 333 fidem augeat, VOTA SUSCIPIAT, PECCATA DIMITTAT.

M 992C ut . . . eius VOTA propicius SUSCIPIAS, PECCATA DIMITTAS.

The collect as it stands is certainly an Irish product, typical of the eclecticism of the Irish in liturgical matters. The author combined three verses from the psalms in question and concluded with a phrase borrowed from a Spanish prayer.

4. AB 65. *Collectio post evangelium*
This is a Spanish *completuria* for morning prayer, as can be seen from the following parallel; variant readings are indicated by italics.

AB 65	Br 189
Exsultantes gaudio pro	Exultantes gaudio *magno* pro
reddit*a* nobis huius diei luce,	reddit*u* nobis huius diei, luce*m*
omnipotent*i* Deo *laudes*	D*ei Patris* omnipotent*is*
gratiasque referamus, ipsius	*et*
misericordiam *obsecrantes*, ut	misericordiam *deprecemur*, ut
diem dominicae *resurrectionis*	diem dominicae *apparitionis*
nobis sollemniter celebrantibus,	solemniter celebrantibus,
pacem *et* tranquill*itatem*,	pacem tranquill*am*
laetitiam praestare	laetitiam*que specialem* praestare
dignetur: ut a vigilia matutina	dignetur: ut a vigilia matutina
usque ad noctem clementiae suae	usque ad noctem clementiae suae
favore protecti, exultantes	favore protecti, exultantes
laetitia perpetua gaudeamus,	*in Domino* gaudeamus.
per dominum nostrum Iesum	
Christum sanctum.	

Another recension of this prayer, also used as a *completuria* for the morning office, is found in Br 231, Gil 364 and in the Toledo MS, *Biblioteca Capitular,* cod.35.4 (Vesp.Mat.52). I will reproduce here the text of the Toledo MS and add the variant readings of the other manuscripts, including AB and Br 189, at the end; the first part of the collect, given here in square brackets, is not found in AB 65 or in Br 189.

[Dies dominicus, fratres charissimi, nobis[a] pia devotione colendus[b] inluxit, dies resurrectionis et pacis, dies verae lucis et vitae, qua[c] [d]Christus a mortuis, credentium vita, surrexit[d]; uberes] Deo [e]gratias laudesque inmensas[f] referamus[e], orantes[g] ut diem dominicae resurrectionis[h] [i]nostraeque redemptionis[i] sollemniter celebranitbus[j] pacem[k] tranquillam[l], laetitiam[m] spiritualem[n] [o]propitius[p] donare[q] dignetur[o]; ut a vigilia matutina usque ad noctem misericordiae[r] suae favore protecti, ⁵redemptoris nostri ᵗDomini nostri Iesu Christiᵗ munere ᵘper omniaᵘ gaudeamus ᵛet gratia repleamurˢᵛ.

a. nobis] a nobis Br 231, *omit*. Gil; b. colendus] colendus est Br 231; c. quia Gil; d. Christus . . . surrexit] Christus . . . resurrexit Gil, Christus, credentium vita, resurrexit a mortuis Br 231; e. gratias . . . referamus] *omit*. Br 189, laudes gratiasque referamus AB, laudes et gratias referimus Gil; f. inmensas] *omit*. Br 231; g. orantes] *omit*. Br 231, ipsius misericordiam obsecrantes AB, et misericordiam deprecemur Br 189; h. resurrectionis] nobis *add*. AB; i. nostraeque redemptionis] *omit. al.*; j. celebrantibus] celebrantes Gil; k. pacem] nobis *add*. Gil; l. tranquillam] et tranquillitatem AB; m. laetitiam] laetitiamque Br 189; n. spiritualem] *omit*. AB, specialem Br 189, 231, spiritalem Gil; o. propitius . . . dignetur] nobis dignetur offerre Br 231; p. propitius] *omit.*AB, Br 189; q. donare] praestare AB, Br 189; r. misericordiae] clementiae AB, Br 189; s. redemptoris . . . repleamur] exultantes laetitia perpetua gaudeamus AB, exultantes in Domino gaudeamus Br 189; t. Domini . . . Christi] *omit. al.*; u. per omnia] *omit*. Br 231; v. et . . . repleamur] *omit*. Br 231.

The text preserved in the Toledo MS (T 4) and its parallels (Gil and Br 231) goes back to a common original which was itself an adaptation of the collect preserved in AB and Br 189. The originality of the latter, by comparison to the former (T 4), is suggested by its structural unity, its internal cohesion. In contrast to it, there is a sharp transition or break in T 4 precisely at the point where it begins to run parallel to the prayer in AB: *Dies . . . surrexit / uberes . . . referamus*. There is an interruption or faulty transition here which is not found in the AB text, *Exultantes . . . referamus*. It appears that the section following *uberes* in T 4 is a block-insertion taken from the prayer preserved in AB 65. The author of T 4 also adapted the conclusion to his particular purpose. He wished to accentuate the redemptive character of the resurrection of Christ and to this end he inserted *nostraeque redemptionis* in the centre, which in turn prepared for his conclusion, *redemptoris nostri . . . gratia repleamur*.

If we now compare further AB 65 and Br 189, it will appear evident that the original Spanish prayer is better preserved in AB. The reading *lucem . . . et misericordiam deprecamur* of Br is surely a corruption of that given in AB. Besides, the variants found in AB, in comparison with Br 189, have an authentic Spanish character about them: *omnipotenti deo laudes gratiasque referamus,*[6] which is also found in the second recension of the prayer (T 4 and parallels), *pacem et tranquillitatem,*[7] *exultantes laetitia perpetua gaudeamus.*[8] Certain other expressions which they have in common, such as *dies dominicae resurrectionis* and *favor clementiae*, also bear out the Spanish origin of the collect.[9]

This Spanish *completuria* for the morning office on Sunday was brought to Ireland in the seventh century and it was used in Ireland for a new purpose, as the invitatory collect after the Gospel of the resurrection in the Sunday morning office.

5. AB 66. *Super hymnum*

Sancte domine, inluminatio et salus vera credentibus, resurrectio dominicae claritatis, inlumina cor nostrum, ut trinitatis scientia et unitatis cognitione filii lucis et membra Christi ac templum sancti spiritus esse mereamur, qui regnas in saecula saeculorum.

This collect appears to have been written especially for the hymn *Spiritus divinae lucis*,[10] and for this reason it must be regarded as an Irish work. Structurally also it approximates to the litanic types of prayer which the Irish liked to compose, even though there is an element of unity and inter-connection of thought in this prayer and on the whole it makes good sense. The language is associated in certain respects with the liturgical language of Gaul and Spain,[11] but this general association is no more than one would expect in seventh-century Ireland.[12] It is an Irish prayer, brimming over with simple ideas relating to the Trinity and the Christian life, with 'half-said' insight and reference to a verse of a psalm (ps.26,1).

6. AB 67. *De martyribus*

Hii sunt, domine, qui felici cruore perfusi, dum blandientem mundi huius in-lecebram gloriosa passione dispiciunt, mortem morte vicerunt; considerantesque tenebras huius lucis certo termine et fine ruituras, sumpserunt de poena vitam et de morte victoriam. Rogamus te, Christe, ut eorum praecibus adiuvari mereamur quorum consortes esse non possumus, per te, Christe, qui cum patre vivas, dominaris et regnas.

The language of this collect has so many Spanish peculiarities that its Spanish origin appears certain. We will indicate each of these peculiarities and similar turns of phrase in other liturgical families.

(a) *Hii sunt domine*

Prayers beginning in this way are otherwise peculiar to Spain.[13]

(b) *felici cruore perfusi*

Ve 1286 O infinita benignitas, cum pro suo nomine trucidatis etiam nescientibus meritum gloriae perire non patitur, sed proprio CRUORE PERFUSIS et salus regenerationis expletur et inputatur corona martyrii (Am Be 165, Bi 160).

Mo LS 304 Quibus (*scil.* nationibus scelerata scelerum impunitate collectis) max-ima esset religio Romuleos colere manes, fratris CRUORE PERFUSOS (*M 12 sup.* 14,3).

LS 1033 Deum, qui inmortales gloriosissimorum martyrum palmas triumphali CRUORE PERFUDIT . . . exoremus.

LS 1295 (col.587 – 8) Tunc supra parvulorum Maccabeorum dilacerata cor-puscula mater leta conlabitur et FELICI CRUORE PERMIXTA octava in tuis, Iherusalem, ianuis passionis vexilla suspendit (Ga C 114).

(c) *blandiens mundi inlecebra*

I have not seen this expression anywhere else, even though such expres-sions as *blandimenta mundi/saeculi* and *inlecebra(e) mundi/saeculi* are found frequently enough; the singular *inlecebra*, as in our prayer, is found especially in Spain.[14]

(d) *passio gloriosa*

Mo Or 569 ut eodem cum suis satellitibus infirmatis et perditis a facie tua nos semper tua protegat PASSIO GLORIOSA (Br 502B).[15]

(e) *mortem morte vincere*

We have already indicated a few Spanish instances of this phrase, when we encountered it in the hymn *Hymnum dicat* 40:

MORTE carnis quam gerebat MORTEM VINCIT omnium.[16]

(f) *tenebrae huius lucis ... fine ruiturae*

This singular expression occurs nowhere else, to my knowledge; but a parallel use of *haec lux*, in the sense of *this world* or *this life*, is found in the phrase *migrare de hac luce*.[17]

(g) *sumere de poena vitam et de morte victoriam*

Ga G 42 Osanna in excelsis, vere sanctus, vere benedictus dominus noster Iesus Christus, qui sanctus in sanctis PRO MORTE VITAM, PRO POENA GLORIAM, PRO CONFESSIONE VICTORIAM praestare dignatus es.
Ga G 139 Deus qui sanctae martrye tuae Eulaliae PRO POENA GLORIAM, PRO MORTE VITAM, pro infirmitate virtutem, pro passione coronam tribuisti, praesta....[18]

Mo LS 201 quum in martyrii certamine constituti aequisierunt de supplicio gloriam, DE MORTE VICTORIAM.

LS 867 Illis conlata est POST MORTEM VICTORIA; nobis eorum interventu donetur facinorum indulgentia; ... nos indignos eorum gaudiis efficias sine fine consortes.

Br 1049 quibus fuit IN POENA VITAE facta est IN MORTE VICTORIA.

While the construction of the expression is similar in all of these texts, there is a closer agreement between AB and the Spanish prayers in their combination of ideas, so that it is *vita* rather than *gloria* which is opposed to *poena*, and it is likewise *victoria* rather than the more obvious and logical *vita* which is opposed to *mors*.

(h) *consortes esse non possumus*

We have already met this theme in two other collects:

AB 52 ut eorum meritis obtineamus veniam, qui tantam gloriam non meremur.
AB 97 hii coronam suam passione per fidem meruerunt; nos autem ... remissionem a te ... postulamus.

We have seen that while the theme is common to Gallican and Spanish collects, AB 52 is closer to certain Gallican formulations[19] and AB 97 is rather associated with the Spanish tradition of this theme.[20] Here we will note simply that the closest parallel to the expression of the theme in our prayer is:

Mo Or 451 (Br 1055C) cum his tribus martyribus mereamur habere in caelestibus partem, QUIBUS NON PASSIONE SED FIDE DINOSCIMUR CONSORTES EXISTERE.

When our collect in AB 67 says *quorum consortes esse non possumus*, the meaning is evidently *consortes gloriosa passione*, as in Or 451.

In summing up these textual parallels, we may ask whether AB 67 is an Irish composition or a direct borrowing from Spain. It seems to me that it has so many Spanish characteristics that its composition by a Spanish author is the only acceptable explanation. We might explain the presence of any one of these, even the strange *felix cruor*, as being due to the influence of another Spanish source on an Irish author. But the combination of *Hii sunt domine, felix cruor, de poena vita: de morte victoria, quorum consortes esse non possumus* seems to establish beyond doubt the Spanish origin of our prayer.

This brings us to the end of the first complete set of collects for lauds. We have gained some more insights into the activity of the Irish liturgical authors and compilers. Ranging far afield in the seventh century, we see them here drawing particularly on the Spanish liturgy; the collect for the Gospel, that for the martyrs, and the conclusion of the collects for the *laudate* psalms are taken over directly or adapted from Spanish sources. In the absence of any literary evidence to the contrary, the first two collects in the set may be regarded as Irish compositions. If this is the case, they came from the pen of an unusually gifted Irish author, gifted, that is, in the field of that liturgical prose style which was as second nature to the great authors of Italy, Gaul and Spain, but which for the Irish was an entirely foreign medium.

CHAPTER FIFTEEN

THE SECOND SET OF COLLECTS FOR LAUDS

This set contains only three collects, one for each of the canticles and one for the *laudate* psalms.

1. AB 68. *Super cantemus domino gloriose*

> Deus, qui cotidie populum tuum iugo Aegyptiae servitutis absolvis, et per fluenta spiritalis lavacri in terram repromissionis, devicto hoste, transducis: da nobis de vitiorum inpugnatione victoriam, et devictis tenebris nostris deducas hereditatem in sanctuario quod praeparaverunt manus tuae, salvator mundi qui cum aeterno.

This collect corresponds very closely in content to the Ambrosian prayer for the same canticle:

> Am M II 414 (Be 1538) Deus, qui populum tuum ex Aegypto tenebrarum duris operibus aggravatum, Moyse famulo tuo duce, liberare dignatus es: nosque famulos tuos, de huius saeculi caligine liberatos, promissam patribus requiem introire permittas, per.

In comparing these prayers one gets the impression that the Ambrosian prayer is the original.[1] It has a more balanced and cohesive construction than the collect in the Antiphonary. There is a twofold theme introduced in the first part and applied in the second. One is the theme of deliverance from darkness: *ex Aegypto tenebrarum liberasti*, to which there corresponds a new deliverance: *de huius saeculi caligine liberatos*. The second theme is found in the opposition of slavery and rest: *duris operibus aggravatam, promissam patribus requiem*. The author appears to be the original master rather than the second-hand adapter of the Irish collect.

There is less balance and formal perfection in the collect in the Antiphonary, but a greater wealth of theme, more life and dynamism. An Irishman would have had no difficulty in choosing between them, if a choice had to be made. The collect as it is found in AB appears to be an adaptation and development of the Ambrosian prayer, and certain expressions indicate that this adaptaion was carried out in a Spanish milieu. We will now see what these indications of Spanish influence are.

(a) *iugum servitutis Aegyptiae*

While this corresponds in content to the Ambrosian *Aegypto ... duris operibus aggravatum*, the expression itself is found in one Spanish collect for the same canticle:

> Br 627 Repelle a nobis, domine, mortiferam perniciem impii Pharaonis, ut comminuto IUGO SERVITUTIS AEGYPTIAE serviamus tibi in gaudio libertatis aeternae.[2]

(b) *fluenta spiritalis lavacri*

On the face of it the expression *fluenta lavacri* would appear to be connected with the Gallican *fons lavacri*,[3] but I have met it only in a few Spanish texts.

LO 213,25 (M 442B) Que (*scil.* nox) transgressionis maculas FLUENTO LAVACRI salutaris (FLUENTA SALUTARIS LAVACRI M) abstersit.

Isidore comments on the crossing of the Jordan, the second circumcision and the celebration of the passover, and he gives to all of this a spiritual interpretation comparable to that found in our collect:

Quaestiones in V.T. In Iosue c.6: Videamus et consequentia. Post evangelii enim circumcisionem, statim in loco revelationis pascha celebratur, immolaturque Agnus ille pro mundi salute occisus, ac deficiente manna legis, primum commedit populus panem corporis Christi, quem incorrupta REPROMISSIONIS TERRA, id est, mater Domini virgo Maria protulit... Postquam enim sub Iesu Christo duce positi PER LAVACRI FLUENTA TRANSIMUS ac per fidem SPIRITUALI circumcisione signamur, tunc his gradibus pervenientes, celebramus pascha.[4]

(c) *impugnatio vitiorum*

This expression occurs elsewhere only in three Spanish texts.[5]

The collect as it stands, therefore, could quite conceivably have come from a Spanish milieu. But it is not at all like any of the prayers found in the Mozarabic Breviary for this canticle, with the exception of the phrase *iugum servitutis Aegyptiae* in one of these prayers. On the other hand, it differs from its Ambrosian counterpart in a few details only, by means, precisely, of those expressions for which we have noted some Spanish parallels. It appears that the Ambrosian collect was imitated by an author who was imbued with the liturgical language of Spain and that his work has been preserved in AB 68. It is difficult to detemine where precisely the collect was composed. It has left no trace of influence on the Spanish prayers for the same canticle and has not been preserved among the known Spanish sources. But, judging from the conclusion of the collect, it was not written by an Irish author. This conclusion is drawn from v. 17 of the canticle, and the text he had before him or was familiar with agrees with the Old Latin version as used at Milan and in Spain, while it differs from the Irish (Old Latin) and Vulgate texts:

AB 68 deducas hereditatem in SANCTUARIO quod PRAEPARAVERUNT manus tuae.

AB 5 (f.8ᵛ) Induces plantans eos in montem hereditatis tuae, ... SANCTIMONIUM tuum, domine, quod PRAEPARAVERUNT manus tuae.

Am M I 176 Induc et planta eos in monte hereditatis tuae, ... SANCTUARIUM, domine (al. sanctuarium tuum), quod PRAEPARAVERUNT manus tuae.

Mo Br 617, 875 Induc et planta eum in montem hereditatis tuae, ... SANCTUARIUM tuum (domine add. 875) quod PRAEPARAVERUNT manus tuae.

Vulgate: Introduces eos et plantabis in monte hereditatis tuae, ... SANCTUARIUM tuum, domine, quod FIRMAVERUNT manus tuae.

The combination of *sanctuarium* and *praeparaverunt* points to a Spanish or Ambrosian liturgical milieu as the source of our collect. We seem to have here, therefore, a lost Spanish collect for the canticle *Cantemus*, an adaptation and development of the Ambrosian collect carried out in some quarter of the Spanish Church. The following collect for the canticle *Benedicite* seems to have had an identical origin and history.

2. AB 69. *Super benedictionem trium puerorum*

> Sancte domine et gloriose, mirabilium et virtutum effector, qui tribus pueris inter supplicia constitutis quartus adsistes, cui factum facilium (factu facillimum: Franceschini) est ignium temperare naturam et vim quodammodo exustantium coercere flammarum, ut inter incendia frigida ymnum tibi canentes cum magna victoria exultarent: eandem nunc, domine, ad liberandos ac protegendos nos dona virtutem, salvator mundi.

The similarity of this prayer to its Ambrosian counterpart is more pronounced here than in the case of the collect for the canticle *Cantemus*.

> Am M II 414 (Be 1539) Deus, qui tribus pueris in camino positis quartus adesse dignatus es, cuius facillimum est ignium temperare naturas et extinguere flammarum impetus: eandem, domine, ad protegendas et liberandas animas nostras extende virtutem tuam, qui vivis.

Once again there is no reason to doubt that the Ambrosian prayer is the original, of which our collect is a development and enlargement. The Ambrosian prayer is a careful and balanced composition; the expanded invocation speaks of the ease with which God assisted the three children and controlled the flames of the furnace; the conclusion asks for the same power of protection and deliverance. The formal balance has been somewhat disrupted in our collect by the introduction into the first part of more vivid expressions of wonder and praise, along with certain more concrete details of the experience of the three children in the furnace. It is easier to explain this as a development of the Ambrosian prayer than to explain the latter as a curtailment of the collect preserved in the Antiphonary.

The Ambrosian prayer was known in Spain, at least to the author of the prayers in the Spanish office for the feast of St Fructuosus, St Augurius and St Eulogius. The *benedictio* for vespers of the evening before the feast begins:

> Or 477 (Br 1056) Christus Dei filius, QUI TRIBUS PUERIS IN CAMINO POSITIS QUARTUM SE DIGNATUS EST demonstrare, gratia vos suae visionis inluminet.

It was, apparently, in Spain that the adaptation of the Ambrosian collect, which resulted in the collect which we have in AB 69, was carried out. This conclusion may be drawn from the fact that the variant readings of our collect, as compared with the Ambrosian prayer, coincide (or very nearly so) with certain expressions used in the Spanish prayers for the feast of the three saints just mentioned. We will take each variant in turn.

(a) *vim exustantium coercere flammarum* (AB) instead of *extinguere flammarum impetus* (Am):

> Or 461 (Br 1060 B) Deus, qui ministerio discendentis e celo angeli tui trium puerorum FLAMMAS mirifice dispersisti, ut VIM naturae suae in illis URENS ignis

amitteret, qui tuis obtutibus placuissent, redde nos a concrematione vitiorum extraneos.

(b)*inter supplicia constituti* (AB) instead of *in camino positi* (Am):

Or 449 (Br 1057A) Hii tres pro tuo nomine in fornacis medio CONSTITUTI, quaesumus, domine, mereamur pro nobis in camino saeculi CONSISTENTIBUS exaudiri.

Or 454 (Br 1058B) Ecce ad instar trium illorum puerorum, hii quoque matyres tui in igne saeculi positi et in camino pro tuo nomine CONSTITUTI, simili te, domine, devotionis more conlaudant; ... ut a te per ignis SUPPLICIA coronentur, himnum deferunt conscientiae libertate: da ergo nobis, ut ... a futuris mereamur SUPPLICIIS liberari.

Br 1180A INTER FLAMMAS saeculi CONSTITUTI ipsi soli flammescatis per studia sanctitatis.

(c) the addition in AB of the clause *ut inter incendia ... hymnum tibi canentes cum magna victoria exultarent*:

Or 450 (Br 1057B) Tres pueri ... LAUDIS TIBI HOSTIAM ... INTER IGNES positi CECINERUNT... Erue ergo nos,... ut VICTORIAM mereamur ferre de mundo.

Or 452 (Br 1057D) tres illi pueri ... MAGNUM specimen his tuis, domine, martyribus praebuerunt, quibus exemplum praebuit eorum veneranda VICTORIA.

Or 454 (Br 1058B) illi quidem ... canticum tibi concinunt gloriae; ... hi vero ... CONCINENTES laudem offerunt precem, ... HIMNUM (TIBI *add*. Br) deferunt conscientiae libertate.

Isidore, *De ortu et obitu patrum c.59*: Tres pueri INTER horrendas spissa caligine FLAMMAS, HYMNUM APERTIS VOCIBUS CECINERUNT.[6]

There are also certain other traces of Spanish influence in our collect, notably the use of the expression *incendia frigida*:

Isidore, *Sententiarum liber III 7*: Unde et puerorum FRIGIDUS IGNIS fuit, ut Nabuchodonosor Deum verum agnosceret.[7]

This evidence clearly suggests that AB 69 resulted from an elaboration of the Ambrosian collect in a Spanish milieu. There is some evidence in the present case that this particular Ambrosian collect was known in Spain itself and the adaptation of the prayer was, in all likelihood, carried out there, even though it has not been preserved in the Spanish books. The northern tradition of the Spanish liturgy did not, apparently, use any collects after the canticles, so it is difficult to situate the context where the adaptation of the Ambrosian collect took place. However this may be, the two collects for the canticles which we have been considering (AB 68 and 69) were probably composed in Spain under the influence and inspiration of the Ambrosian collects for the same canticles, and were taken from Spain to Ireland at some date in the seventh century.

3. AB 70. *Super laudate dominum de caelis*

This is a purely Irish composition which is based on the three *laudate* psalms. The order of the words is sometimes strange, the grammar faulty and the sense unclear. Structurally, the collect is a sequence of unequal phrases with occasional rhyme:

Quem cuncta canite elementa dominum laudant[a] (ps.148,1 – 12),
cuius confessio sacra eadem in caelo et in terra et pignora Sion (ps.148,14).
Novum tonanti dicite hymnum (ps.149,1),
facturi iudicium nefandis in fine conscriptum (ps.149,9).
Perstrepite diversis spiritales melodias[b] modis (ps.150,3-5),
ut Christum conlaudet spiritus per saecla omnis[c] (ps.150,6),qui cum patre vivit.
a. laudant] laudent MS;b.melodias] melodia MS, spiritalis melodiae Warren II; c. omnis] omnes MS.

This collect makes a marked contrast to the two preceding collects in this set and it serves, indirectly, to confirm their foreign origin and character. It also concludes this short set of collects for the office of lauds.

CHAPTER SIXTEEN

FROM THE THIRD TO THE SIXTH SET OF COLLECTS FOR LAUDS

Most of the collects in this section of the Antiphonary are clearly of Irish origin.[1] The abundant use in them of the rhythmical principle, along with rhyme and alliteration, offers convincing evidence for this. But they are generally too brief to offer us much material for comparison with the prayers of the other Latin liturgies.

1.THE THIRD SET (AB 71 – 75)

The first collect in this set is composed of four rhyming lines, with some alliteration; the lines seem to be of the Irish rhythmical type:[2]

i. AB 71. *Super canticum*

Dèus qui ímpiam Aegýptum dènis corruptiónibus múltas
et divìso mári plànum íter pópulo praéstas:
praéces exaúdi quaésumus nóstras,
ut nos nóstris táliter hóstibus sálva(s),
salvator mundi qui regnas.

The second collect is a typical example of the Hiberno-Latin rhythmical versification. It clearly manifests in its rhythm and alliteration the old Irish vernacular prototype of this type of verse; rhyme is added as a further embellishment, sometimes affecting the half-lines as well as the long lines:

ii. AB 72. *Post benedictionem trium puerorum*

Déus qui púeris fíde fervéntibus
fornácis flámmam frígidam fácis
et tríbus invíctis mórte devícta
    quártus adsístis:
praecámur nóbis aéstibus cárnis
tálem virtútem praéstes adústis,
per te, Iesu Christe, qui regnas.

The author was probably influenced by some expressions in AB 69, especially by *incendia frigida* and *quartus adsistis* in that collect. I have not been able to discover any other literary influence.[3]

The collect for the *laudate* psalms differs from the other *post laudate* collects in the Antiphonary in as much as it is not based on psalms 148 – 150, but refers to the 'solemn vigil', doubtless the Sunday morning vigil, which was concluded by lauds.

iii. AB 73. *Post laudate dominum de caelis*

Deus noster, deus omnium animarum, te adoramus, ut in hac vigilia sollennitatis admissa pervenire praestes, quousque tenebrae iniquitatis nostrae convertantur in lumine, sicut sol in meridie splendescit, salvator mundi, qui regnas.

With its reflection on the associated themes of darkness and light, this collect is comparable to the Ambrosian prayers for the *laudate* psalms; but the resemblance ends there, because no literary relationship is discernible between them.

iv. AB 74. *Post evangelium*

Dominicam, nostrae resurrectionis initium, venerantes, trinitati deo nostro debitas laudes et grates unito referamus affectu, obsecrantes misericordiam eius, ut nobis dominus et salvatoris nostri beatae resurrectionis participium tam in spiritu quam etiam in corpore concedat, qui cum patre vivit.

The first part of this collect is not unlike the Spanish collect preserved in AB 65 as a *post evangelium*:

Exultantes gaudio pro. reddita nobis huius diei luce, omnipotenti DEO LAUDES GRATIASQUE REFERAMUS, IPSIUS MISERICORDIAM OBSECRANTES, ut DIEM DOMINICAE RESURRECTIONIS nobis sollemniter CELEBRANTIBUS, pacem . . . praestare dignetur.

Certain other expression in the prayer also have some Spanish associations:

(a) *initium nostrae resurrectionis*

CPs 473 (ps.3) Confessionem nostram, Domine, post quietem dignam tuis conspectibus effice; ut sicut RESURRECTIO NOSTRA in te sumpsit EXORDIUM, ita vita nostra a te habeat praemium (Br 589).

Or 874 Christe Dei filius,. . . da nobis, ut de sepulcris vitiorum exeamus ad te, lumen verum, qui es RESURRECTIONIS NOSTRAE PRINCIPIUM (Br 619B).

Or 960 Te, Domine, . . . petimus, ut per te hic resurrectionis prime habentes principia, cum sanctis omnibus resurgamus ad gloriam sempiternam.

(b) *participium beatae resurrectionis concedat*[4]

Gr C 96,9 Praesta, . . . ut in resurrectione domini nostri Iesu Christi percipiamus veraciter portionem (Ge V 528; Am Be 550; Ga G 304).

Am Be 538 Celebratis atque perfectis divini baptismatis sacramentis, . . . deo patri omnipotenti indefessas gratias referamus, ipsumque supplices postulamus, uti nos atque omnem familiam suam gloriosae resurrectionis domini nostri Iesu Christi annuat esse participes.

Mo CPs 78 (ps.65) Omnis terra adoret te, Domine, et tibi psallat, vitae PARTICIPIO incorruptae (Br 165, 348, 670).

CPs 241 (ps.53) Deus, exaudi orationem nostram, ut in nomine tuo salvemur; et qui censemur vocabulo Christi, mereamur eius PARTICIPIO perfrui (Gil 28; Br 491)

Or 23 dexterae suae letabundos PARTICIPIO iungat.

LS 619 Dominus Iesus Christus, qui . . . hodie resurrexit a mortuis, ipse vos resurrectione sua mortificet a delictis. Quique per crucis patibulum mortis destruxit imperium, BEATE VITE TRIBUAT PARTICIPIUM. Ut qui RESURRECTIONIS EIUS DIEM dum letitia presenti celebrantis in seculo, sanctorum mereamini in celesti regione consortium.

LS738 ut, quorum predicamenta suscipitis, quorumque nunc memoriam facitis, eorum post transitum PARTICIPIUM habeatis.´

The collect may be an Irish production, influenced by AB 65 and other Spanish material. But it is possible that this *post evangelium*, like AB 65, is also a Spanish prayer.

The third set is concluded by a short collect which is distinguished by a noble simplicity:

v. AB 75. *Post hymnum*

> Respice, domine, ad praeces nostras, qui infirmitates visitasti humanas, et tuam nobis sanctificationem largire et inmortalitatem, Christe, qui regnas.

This may be regarded as a development of the refrain *Respice in me, domine,* of the hymn *Spiritus divinae lucis*; but it owes nothing to the obscure language of the hymn itself.

2. THE FOURTH SET (AB 76 – 80)

i. AB 76. *Post canticum*

> Summerso in mari Faraone liberatur Israel: nos quoque per baptismi gratiam et crucis triumphum ab omni malo quaesumus liberari, per te, Christe.

This is evidently an Irish composition, which in simple and traditional language gives a spiritual application to the deliverance from Pharaoh and the passing of the Red Sea.[5]

The other collects in this set consist of two rhythmical lines, with rhyme at the end of the long lines. For example,

ii. AB 77. *Post benedicite*

> Déus, qui tres púeros de fornáce eripuísti,
> sîc nos erípias de supplíciis inférni,
> qui regnas in saecula,

iii. AB 80. *Post hymnum*

> Resurrectiónem túam, Chríste, venerámur,
> per quám in aetérnam salvári mereámur,
> per omnia saecula.

3. THE FIFTH SET (AB 81 – 87)

All the collects in this set are rhythmical, with rhyme at the end of the lines. All are of Irish origin and their language is not, apart from a few expressions, immediately related to any continental source.

i.AB 81. *Post canticum*

> Christe déus, qui in salútem pópuli túi
> Ísrahel adiútor et protéctor fuísti,
> quem per síccum máre ab Aegýpto duxísti:
> sálva nos hoc módo ab iúgo peccáti,
> qui regnas in saecula.

This collect is based directly on the text of the canticle.[6] The expression *iugum peccati* is also used in Roman and Ambrosian texts, as well as in later Gelasian books.[7]

ii. AB 82. *Post hymnum trium puerorum* (T 5; ILH I 196)

Te enim, omnipotens deus, benedicimus iure,
qui tres pueros liberasti ab igne:
nos quoque de supplicio mortis aeternae
propter misericordiam tuam eripe,
qui regnas.

These rhyming phrases are not so perfectly rhythmical as the other collects in this set; the fourth line is used again in a commemoration of the dead in Ce S 9.

iii. AB 83. *Post laudate dominum de caelis* (T 8; Irish Psalters)

Déus altíssime, réx angelórum,
déus, laús ómnium elementórum,
déus, glória et exultátio sánctorum,
custodi animas servorum tuorum,
qui regnas in saecula.

The first two lines here reflect in general ps.148; the third line is an adaptation of ps.149,5: *exultabunt sancti in gloria*; and the fourth line is drawn from ps.96,10: *custodit dominus animas sanctorum suorum*.[8]

The next collect (AB 84), entitled *Post evangelium*, is out of place here; it is in reality a *Post hymnum* and was meant to follow the *Hymnum dicat*, as it does in T 12 and ILH I 42. We shall meet it again when we treat of the office at Bangor.

iv. AB 85. *Post evangelium*

Dilúculo lúcis auctóre resurgénte,
exultémus in dómino devícta mórte,
quo peccáta possímus sémper obíre
vitaéque ambulémus ín novitáte,
qui tecum vivit.

Like the other *Post evangelium* collects which we have seen (AB 65 and 74), this also has a number of expressions which occur in Spanish prayers; but they are not so singular or peculiar to Spain as those in the other collects mentioned. The expression *diluculo resurgente* is found in

Mo CPs 67 (ps.57) Exsurge, gloria nostra, Deus, exsurge; te RESURGENTE DILUCULO mortalitatis nostrae tenebrae pereunt.

The expressions *lucis auctor* and *novitas vitae* are of more general occurence,[9] and St Paul had already drawn this consequence from the resurrection of Christ: *ita et nos in novitate vitae ambulemus*.[10]

v. AB 86. *Post hymnum*

Lúx órta ést in lúce príma
exórdio diérum antíquo fácta:

142

unigénitus túus, dómine, qui nóstra
ablúere vénit per crúcem peccáta,
qui tecum vivit.

The identification of Christ with the Light which shone on the first day of the new creation, Easter Sunday, is a general theme in Western hymnody.[11] It is expressed in a manner that is closely parallel to our collect by the seventh-century Irish Ps.-Hieronymus:

> *Comment. in Marcum c.16*: Post sabbata tristia felix irradiat dies, quae PRIMATUM IN DIEBUS tenet, LUCE PRIMA IN EO LUCESCENTE, et Domino meo cum triumpho resurgente et dicente: Haec est dies quam fecit Dominus, exultemus et laetemur in ea.[12]

Again, there is a similar expression of the theme in a Spanish *completuria* for lauds on Easter Sunday:

> Or 874 (Br 619) Christe Dei filius, qui venerabilis diei huius excursum, et prius a te conditae luci (lucis Br) et post tue resurrectionis mysterio consecrasti: . . . da nobis ut de sepulcris vitiorum exeamus ad te, lumen verum, qui es resurrectionis nostrae principium.

The phrase *abluere venit peccata* is found in

> Mo LO 76,19 Adiuramus te, inmunde spiritus, per . . . Dei altissimi filium, qui VENIT PECCATA NOSTRA ABLUERE per baptismum et Spiritum sanctum.[13]

vi. AB 87. *De martyribus*

Triumphálium mémores mártyrum tuórum,
qui pro té tolleráre vexílla passiónum,
precámur ut per sáncta mérita ipsórum
nostrórum véniam mereámur peccatórum,
qui regnas.

There are some Spanish parallels for the expression *vexilla passionum:*

> Or 598 Christe domine, . . . concede nobis, . . . ut insignia PASSIONIS TUE VEXILLA ad consequenda nobis emolumenta proficiant sempiterna.

> LS 1295 (col.587 − 8) octava in tuis, Iherusalem, ianuis PASSIONIS VEXILLA suspendit (Ga C 114).

> Br 1154D Deus, qui virginali pudicitiae titulo PASSIONIS VEXILLO beatas virgines et martyres tuas Iustam et Rufinam glorificasti, da. . . .

The conclusion of the prayer, *ut per sancta merita ipsorum . . . veniam mereamur,* is similar to AB 52: *ut eorum merita obtineamus veniam qui gloriam non meremur.*

4. THE SIXTH SET (AB 88 − 90)

This comprises three rhythmical collects, with rhyme at the end of the lines. There is nothing worthy of note in them for comparative purposes, apart possibly from the first:

AB 88 *Post cantemus*

Plébs Ísrahel in figúram nóstri
líberátur in tránsitu mári:
nós érgo per grátiam baptísmi
líbera tú ab éxitis múndi,
qui regnas.

The author of this collect may have read Isidore, *De fide cath. contra Iudaeos III 26.2*:

> Thau quippe littera speciem crucis demonstrat, cuius signaculo praenotati sunt quicumque AB EXITU HUIUS SAECULI LIBERANTUR.[14]

5. CONCLUSION

In these four sets of collects we have a good representative sample of the earliest Irish rhythmical prayers. They are perhaps slightly earlier in date than the set of versified collects for the hours of the day and night (AB 17–26), judging from the greater perfection of rhyme in the latter.[15]

The choice of the accentual principle for these collects allowed their authors a good measure of freedom from the structural laws of the prose collect. Generally, the first two lines of a quatrain describe the event which is being recalled and the second two lines apply the lesson to the situation of the Christian community. The theme of deliverance from sin and from hell is frequently suggested by the deliverance of the Hebrews from Egypt and of the three chlidren from the furnace. The ideas and language are extremely simple and would have come within the scope of the monks educated in the Irish schools of the seventh century. But one prose collect in the third set (AB 74) is possibly Spanish, or at least depends on Spanish originals.

144

CHAPTER SEVENTEEN

THE SEVENTH SET OF COLLECTS FOR LAUDS

There are three collects in this set and they are the longest of all the collects in the Antiphonary.[1] The first two are almost literal transcriptions of two sermons of St Zeno of Verona.[2]

AB 91. *Super cantemus*
Cantemus tibi, domine exercituum,
Christe, orantes ut quemadmodum
exemisti dilectum

populum *tuum* captivitatis
acerrim*ae* iugo,

iter demonstrante eis nubis
columna per diem, eadem ignis
quoque per noctem. Finditur
ergo mare dextera levaque in
abruptum: degestis *acerribus*
stupens unda solidatur. *Tuus*
populus navigat plantis. Mira
res! Iter eius
nec eques potest
sequi nec *ratis*. Maria

tympanum quatit, hymnus
iste canitur, *grex peculius*
tueatur:
ita et nos ab insectatione veteris
inimici et ab omni periculo mundi
liberare digneris, salvator mundi.

AB 92. *Super benedic.*
Tres Hebraei, venerabil*es* nume-
r*o*, sacramento muniti, aetate
teneri, sed fidei soliditate
robusti,
amore divinae religio-
nis regis adorare imaginem
contempserunt, utpote qui ipsum
contempserunt regem; qui, ira

Zeno, *Tract.*II 26

Sicut lectio divina testatur,
in Aegypto a Pharaone populoque
eius Israel
dei populus captivitatis *ingenti*
iugo acerrim*e* premebatur. Hunc
deus praecipit proficisci, duce
Moyseo videlicet et Aaron,
iter demonstrante eis[3] nubis
columna per diem, eadem ignis
quoque per noctem. Finditur
mare *et* dextra laevaque in
abruptum digestis *aggeribus*
stupens unda solidatur. *Dei*
populus navigat plantis. Mira
res! Iter eius barbaris vehemen-
ter urguentibus nec eques potest
sequi nec *navis*. Maria cum mulier-
ibus tympanum quatit; hymnus
canitur; *Dei populus liberatur*
. . . .

Zeno, *Tract.*II 76
Tres Hebraei venerabil*is*[4] nume-
r*i* sacramento muniti, aetate
teneri, sed fidei soliditate
robusti, supplicio suffragante
gloriosi amore divinae religionis regis adorare imaginem
contempserunt, utpote qui ipsum
contempserunt regem. Qui ira

145

sufflatus, solito septies
amplius caminum iussit incendi,
ac
pice et stupa
armatum *citari* incendium.
Aestuantibus globis erubescit
quoque ipsum alienibus ignibus
caelum. Illo praecipitantur
insontes, ibidemque *te* propter
quem praecipitantur inveniunt,
Christe. Taliter nos et tyranni
intellectualis furore et ab
ingenito igni digneris liberare,
salvator mundi.

sufflatus solito septies
amplius caminum iussit incendi
ac, ne quid immanitati saevientis
deesse videretur, pice et stupa[5]
armatum *citatur* incendium;
aestuantibus globis erubescit
quoque ipsum alienibus ignibus
caelum. Illo praecipitantur
insontes ibidemque propter
quem praecipitantur inveniunt....

The sermons of Zeno have been given the minimum of adaptation necessary to turn them into prayers addressed to Christ. There can be no doubt that this adaptation is the work of an Irish hand, and it is unlikely that these works of Zeno were used as collects before they came into Irish hands.[6] The sermons may have been sent to Ireland from Bobbio in the seventh century and our two collects may, in that case, be ascribed to a monk at Bangor. But it is equally probable that the collects were first composed at Bobbio and sent from there to Ireland.[7] They form an original unit with the collect *post laudate* which follows them immediately in the manuscript; we will see whether this offers any further evidence for a precise location.

The collect *post laudate* is based on the three psalms, but it does not consist merely in a selection of verses from each of these psalms. There is some elaboration of the ideas selected from each of the psalms in turn, even though internal unity and cohesion of thought are lacking in the collect as a whole.

AB 93. *Post laudate dominum de caelis*

Laudent te, domine, angeli, virtutes, sidera, potestates (ps.148,2 – 3), et quae ortum suum tibi debent officio tuae laudationis exultent, ut per universitatis armoniam tibimet concinentem fiat ut in caelo ita et in terra voluntas tua (Mt.6,10). Sit tibi, precamur, domine, beneplacitum in populo tuo (ps.149,4), ut per exaltationes tuas in eius faucibus (ps.149,6) collocatas, maneat in singulis et verbi tui armatura qua doceas, et vitae nostrae veritas qua semper aspicias, et salus qua mansuetos exaltes, quia secundum multitudinem magnitudinis tuae te laudamus (ps.150,2), domine, gratia laudationis ostensa immolatione per psalterium, mortificatione per tympanum, congregatione per chorum, exsultatione per organum, iubilatione per cymbalum (ps.150,3 – 5), ut semper misericordiam tuam habere mereamur, Christe, salvator mundi.

This extraordinary prayer has no parallel in any of the Western liturgies. Certain expressions in it, however, which are not direct scriptural citations, are found in a variety of other sources. But before we come to these, we may make a few observations on the type of biblical text with which the author was familiar. The word *sidera* is not found in any known text or psalter-collect as the equivalent of the four categories used in ps.148,3: *sol et luna, stellae et lumen*. But *potestates* occurs as a variant for the Old Latin of ps.150,2: *laudate eum in potentatibus eius*. Here the Verona Psalter alone[8] has: *in potestatibus*; the Vulgate[9] reads: *in virtutibus eius*. The combination *exaltationes in faucibus* (ps.149,6) is also peculiar to the Verona Psalter and the Psalter of St Zeno;[10] the other Old Latin texts read *exultationes in faucibus*, while the Vulgate has *exaltationes in guttere*. But our prayer agrees with all the Old Latin and Vulgate texts against the Verona Psalter in presupposing the reading *beneplacitum est domino in populo suo* (ps.149,4), where the Verona Psalter has *benesensit dominus in populo suo*; again, all texts have *secundum multitudinem magnitudinis eius* (ps.150,2), where the Verona Psalter has *secundum multitudinem magnificentiae eius*. The phrase *iubilatione per cymbalum* of the prayer is based on *laudate eum in cymbalis iubilationis* (ps.150,5); this is opposed to the Psalter of St Zeno, which reads *in cymbalis benetinnientibus*. In conclusion, we can say that while most of the citations of the three psalms in our prayer are found to be identical in the Vulgate and Old Latin texts, the reading *in faucibus* (Vulgate, all texts: *in gutture*) shows that the author was influenced by an Old Latin text. But the words *potestates* and *exaltationes* are not sufficient to identify this as a northern Italian Psalter. In Ireland, the Gallican Psalter was used since the sixth century, but reminiscences of the Old Latin remained for a long time, and this alone could explain the reading *in faucibus*.

We can now illustrate from patristic and liturgical sources some of the other ideas and expressions found in the prayer, ideas which are not immediately taken from the text of the psalms but which were current in the Latin tradition of the time.

(a) *quae ortum suum tibi debent*

The Irish 'Milan Commentary' on the Psalms:[11]

'Laudent nomen domini' (ps.148,12).... Cum caeteris creaturis causa cur necesse sit laudari dominum; quae cuncta cum essent sortita sunt existentiam voluntatis eius imperio.

Mo CPs 467 (ps.148) Te in excelsis, domine, laudant (laudent Br 641) angeli et virtutes, tibi de terra DET LAUDEM OMNE QUOD A TE AUCTORE SUMIT ORIGINEM; et qui supernorum conlaudaris officiis, terrestrium semper delecteris obsequiis; maiestatem ergo tuam nostra simul ac superna honoret devotio, et in omnis creaturae sensibus vigilet tua aeterna laudatio (Gil 148, Br 641).

Br 619. 1087 Laudant te, domine, omnes angeli tui, dum a te se creatos agnoscunt; et cunctam creaturam coelestem atque terrenam te opificem subsistere ac disponi non ambigunt.

M 109 (*Oratio post Gloriam*) Laudamus et, domine, cum angelis, benedicimus te cum virtutibus supernis. Et qui te opificem nostrum nos subsistere non hesimus recte honori tui nominis per officium creaturae creatricem tuam potentiam non negamus. Pro qua re nos facito bone voluntate tue placere servicium....

Vesp.Mat.8 Deus, cuius ordinatione mundi ornamenta persistunt, et ORTUS EORUM seu ocasum TE FACTOREM AGNOSCUNT: in his vespertinis temporibus tuis famulis veniam concede benignus.

(b) *officium laudationis*

The Irish 'Milan Commentary' on the Psalms:[12]

'Laudate dominum de caelis' (ps.148,1). Per spiritum sanctum tantam auctoritatem suscipit ut LAUDATIONIS HUIUS OFFICIUM audeat creaturis potioribus imperare... 'Serpentes et volucres pennatae' (ps.148,10)....Subtili ergo succinctaque sed plena divisione omnia animalia ad LAUDATIONIS conveniunt OFFICIUM.

Mo Hor 165 Deus, qui nocturnis horis nos suscitari iussisti ad referendum nomini tuo LAUDATIONIS OFFICIUM in confessione mirabilium et preceptorum tuorum, descendat....

(c) *harmonia universitatis*

The term *universitas* is often used by Columban in the sense of 'the whole creation'.[13] The Italian psalter collect on ps.150 speaks of the harmony of voices in chant:

I CPs 150 HARMONIAE nostrae suavissimum melos, qui nostri pectoris modulamina nunc flatibus nunc fidibus praecipis exerceri: praesta ut dum illa spiritali adfectu concinimus, perpetualibus choris inserti cum sanctis omnibus conlaudemus.

(d) *mortificatio per tympanum*[14]

Mo CPs 395 (ps.80) Exultamus tibi, domine, ... propter quod etiam tibi iubilamus in desideriis, sumimus in doctrina psalmum, IN MORTIFICATIONE REDDIMUS TYMPANUM (Gil 66, Br 355, 417).

LS 366 Deus, ... fac nos ut te in tympano veraciter laudemus et choro: ut qui te per adtrite carnis abstinentiam in tympano personamus, per concordiam alterne dilectionis in choro una voce cum societate laudemus.

LS 406 Christe, salus omnium, concedi cordi nostro pietatis affectum, quo veridice et carnis nostre tympanum per abstinentiam purgat....

(e) *immolatio per psalterium*

AB 100 *Ant. super laudate*
De caelis dominum laudate,
PSALTERIUM iucundum IMMOLATE,
laudate eum in sono tubae.

The same idea is found in the psalms themselves; for example:

Ps.26,6 IMMOLAVI in tabernaculo eius HOSTIAM VOCIFERATIONIS, cantabo et psalmum dicam domino.
Ps.49,14 IMMOLA Deo SACRIFICIUM LAUDIS.[15]

(f) *congregatio per chorum*

Jerome, *Tractatus de ps.149*: Ubicumque CHORUS est, ibi diversae voces in unum canticum congeruntur. Quomodo enim diversae cordae unam vocem efficiunt cantici, sic et diversae voces, hoc est, cum simul fuerint CONGREGATAE, chorum Domini efficiunt.[16]

148

In conclusion, our prayer is based on pss. 148-150, as these were general-ly interpreted throughout the Latin Church. The sequence of thought is not always clear, but the direct address to Christ is sustained throughout and the task of combining the variety of ideas suggested by the three psalms was not an easy one. There is nothing so peculiar in the language as to indicate any particular source of influence on the author, who does not appear to have borrowed directly from any patristic commentary on the three psalms. Even the expression *mortificatio per tympanum*, to which there is a parallel in Mo CPs 395, corresponds to a widespread interpreta-tion of the timbrel as a symbol of mortification. The collect forms part of an original unit or set with the two collects taken from the writings of St Zeno, and all three appear to be the work of one author. We have no means of deciding where exactly he did his work, but Bobbio or Bangor suggest themselves as equally probable alternatives. The Irish must have discovered the writings of Zeno through the foundation of Bobbio in the early seventh century. There is evidence from a later date for direct rela-tions between Bobbio and Verona,[17] but nothing is more likely than that they existed already in the seventh century.

This final set of collects is followed by a single collect *super cantemus domino* (AB 94). It was probably inserted to fill space left vacant on f.28,[v] between the end of the second section of the Antiphonary and the beginn-ing of the third (f.30). But the vacant space proved insufficient and a short slip (f.29) was inserted so that it could be concluded. The collect is distinguished only by its confused and involved style, probably intended for effect by the author, and by its lack of intelligibility. Warren remarked that 'it appears as if the scribe must have copied a Collect which he did not understand',[18] but it is preferable to regard it as being intentionally 'hisperic'. I have not met anything comparable elsewhere.

CHAPTER EIGHTEEN

CONCLUSION

We began this inquiry into the collects of the Antiphonary with two major questions in mind. One question bore on the influence of the other Latin liturgies on the Irish, precisely in the area of the collects used in the seventh-century Irish liturgy. The other question was related to the ability of the Irish to compose original prayers that could compare to those composed in the other areas of the Latin West between the fifth and seventh centuries.

The expectation of finding foreign elements, imported by Irish *peregrini* or by other means, among the collects of the Antiphonary has not been disappointed. At the same time, the sweeping description of the Antiphonary as a 'purely Gallican document' has been shown to be inadequate and misleading. The great mass of the prayers which it contains is, not surprisingly, of Irish origin. Traces of contact with continental sources are discernible in many of these Irish collects. Thus, for example, the author of the rhythmical collects for the hours of the day and night (AB 17-26) was well acquainted with the hymns used for the various hours in the liturgy of Milan and southern Gaul. These collects are, for all that, genuinely Irish and original. It is among the prose collects that we have discovered the most extensive dependence on continental liturgies, and it will be helpful to give here a synthesis of the various sources of origin or influence. The term 'source' as used here does not necessarily mean that the Irish took the collect in question directly from such a source. It may simply mean that the collect as it stands owes something, in ultimate origin or actual composition, to the source indicated. For further details we refer back to the relevant section of our study.

1. *Gallican Parallels or Sources*

AB		
	34 Pax tua domine rex caelestis permaneat	*supra*, p.103
	41 Miserere domine ecclesiae tuae	p. 97
	52 Deus qui sanctis et electis tuis	p.118
	54 praesta nobis domine . . . quae te petimus	p.112
	126 exaudi nos et praesta ea quae rogamus	p.126

2. *Ambrosian Sources*

AB		
	28 Tibi subnixis precibus	p. 98
	29 Ominpotens aeterne deus qui nobis magnalia	p. 99
	68 Deus qui cotidie populum tuum	p.134
	69 Sancte domine et gloriose	p.136

150

3. 'Spanish Symptoms'

(a) Collects which are certainly Spanish

AB   55 Aeternum virtutis tuae nomen   p.121
          61 Deus qui sanctos tuos cum mensura probas   p.122
          65 Exaltantes gaudio pro reddita nobis   p.129
          67 Hii sunt domine qui felici cruore perfusi   p.131

(b) Collects which are probably Spanish

AB   52 Deus qui sanctis et electis tuis   p.118
          68 Deus qui cotidie populum tuum   p.134
          69 Sancte domine et gloriose   p.136
          97 Deus qui martyribus tuis largitus es   p.122
        124 Sancti et gloriosi mirabiles   p.123

(c) A collect which is possibly Spanish

AB   74 Dominicam nostrae resurrectionis initium   p.140

(d) Collects influenced by Spanish originals

AB   33 Evolutis nunc diei temporibus   p.102
          54 Sanctus in sanctis agnus inmaculatus   p.112
          64 ut omnia vota nostra suscipias, peccata dimittas   p.128

(e) A number of other collects have certain expressions which were favoured in Spain, or have a certain affinity in style with the Spanish liturgical language. Notable among these are:

AB   39 Tu es spes et salus   p.104
          66 Sancte domine inluminatio et salus   p.131
        123 Te patrem adoramus aeternum   p.124

4. Possible influence of the Apostolic Tradition

AB   30 Nona agitur diei hora ad te domine   p.100

5. Two Sermons of St Zeno of Verona

AB   91 Cantemus tibi domine exercituum Christe   p.145
          92 Tres Hebraei venerabiles numero   p.145

This outline shows that Spain was the predominant source of external influence on the Irish liturgy in the seventh century. A number of collects for the martrys, for the Gospel of the resurrection in the Sunday morning office and probably for the canticles were taken directly from Spain; both traditions of the Spanish liturgy are represented in these collects of the Antiphonary. Certain other collects composed by Irish authors show that a good deal of Spanish material was circulating in Ireland in the seventh century. Our study of the hymns revealed that the Irish monks, doubtless through the foundation of Bobbio, were becoming acquainted with northern Italian sources. This, as might have been expected, is again borne out by our study of the collects. Sources of influence here are again quite varied; they include the Ambrosian liturgy, the writings of St Zeno of Verona and, possibly, the Apostolic Tradition of Hippolytus. Gallican sources, on the other hand, were used only very sparingly by the author of the collects preserved in our manuscript, and strictly Gallican elements are reducible to a few isolated phrases. The Irish palimpsest sacramentary, Ga C, show. that abundant Gallican material was also available in Ireland in the seventh century, so that its absence from the Antiphonary is surprising. It is possible that the opposition faced by Columban and his disciples in Gaul and their ultimate expulsion from Luxeuil led to a break in the contact between Bangor and Gaul? Whatever may be the reason, it appears that close relations with Bangor were kept up by Bobbio rather than by Luxeuil.

The intermediary role played by Bobbio in the transmission of northern Italian sources seems obvious enough. The manner of transmision to Ireland of the Spanish collects which we have found in the Antiphonary, and of others besides, is not so easily discovered. There was no Irish foundation in Spain which might have acted as intermediary, and the claims of Bobbio to the position of such an intermediary role between Spain and Ireland have to be assessed. The seventh-century scribes of Bobbio played a significant part in the transmission of the works of St Isidore.[1] B. Bischoff has shown that six manuscripts of Isidore's works were copied at Bobbio in the seventh century.[2] Their exemplars may have come directly from Spain to Bobbio, but the possibility of their having first travelled to Ireland and thence to Bobbio cannot be entirely discounted. The earliest non-Spanish manuscript of Isidore, which is certainly Irish, was written probably in Ireland rather than at Bobbio,[3] and this must be only one survivor of many such manuscripts copied in Ireland in the seventh century. The question regarding the direct line of derivation of these manuscripts from Spain, whether directly or through Bobbio, cannot be resolved simply by a count of the surviving seventh-century manuscripts. As J.N. Hillgarth points out, 'the presence of a Spanish work in a Bobbio manuscript may be explained either by its exemplar having come from Ireland or by its having come direct to Bobbio from Spain or through the South of France. All this is obvious enough. What I feel is dangerous is the view that we sometimes find today that it is, *a priori*, more likely a Spanish work travelled to Bobbio direct from Spain . . . rather than that it arrived at Bobbio . . . by way of Ireland'.[4] He goes on to speak of the evidence which is coming to light today, apart from surviving manuscripts, regarding the literary activity of the Irish at home in the seventh century. Some of their works, mainly biblical commentaries and grammatical texts, made considerable use of Isidore and other Spanish authors. In comparison to

Ireland, 'the number and importance of the works composed at Bobbio or in Northumbria in the seventh century are slight, to say the least'.[5] Furthermore, Hillgarth quotes a letter of B. Bischoff to the effect that 'statistics ... show that the transmission of manuscripts from Ireland to the Continent was certainly far more frequent than transmission from Bobbio to St Gall or to Ireland'.[6]

The transmission to Ireland of the Spanish prayers which we have noted above is only a small item in the field of the literary relationship and output of Spain and Ireland in the seventh century. There is no evidence for the transmission to Ireland of complete Spanish liturgical books. The prayers in question must have been selected from Spanish manuscripts and transmitted to Ireland on special *libelli*. One such selection may have been preserved fragmentarily in the Reichenau palimpsest, *Cod.Aug. CXCV*, a collection of collects in honour of the martyrs written probably in Ireland in the eight century.[7] Of the four collects preserved here, three are found in the Antiphonary; two are also found in Spanish books and the other two are possibly Spanish as well. The question remains: were these prayers selected in Spain and sent direct to Ireland, or were they selected at Bobbio or at least sent to Ireland through Bobbio?

Firstly, it appears that such a selection of Spanish prayers could not have been made at Bobbio, because in the seventh century the necessary liturgical manuscripts were not available there. Many seventh-century Spanish manuscripts, including liturgical books, were brought to Italy by refugees who fled the Arabic Invasion at the beginning of the eighth century,[8] but prior to that the knowledge of Spanish authors by Italian writers seems to have been slight. The wide variety of books from which our collects were selected argues, therefore, clearly in favour of Spain as the place where the selection was made.

Secondly, if this is true, these collects must have been transmitted to Ireland through the same channels as were used for the transportation of other and more complete manuscripts. After sifting all the available evidence, Hillgarth comes to the conclusion that 'it appears they often come direct, not via Bobbio or via England'.[9] He argues that the link between Spain and Ireland was provided by Galicia, which had many points of contact with Ireland in monastic spirit and Church organization.[10] We shall see in our study of the office that the conclusion of the nightfall office at Bangor, a conclusion consisting of prayers for peace followed by the Creed and Our Father, was probably inspired by the parallel rites in the Rule of St Fructuosus of Braga.[11] But the Galician Church in turn was influenced by the Irish monastic movement in the seventh century, notably in its penitential discipline and possibly in the *Sancta Communis Regula*.[12] These cross-influences indicate an exchange of writings and the possibility that some Irish monks may have made their way to Galicia. There is no evidence that the Celtic See of Bretonia in Galicia played any special role in this relationship of Galicia and Ireland,[13] but it is one centre where a number of Irish monks may have gathered. In the seventh century it appears that there was direct contact by sea between this part of Spain, particularly Braga, and Britain and Ireland.[14] This is one route by which Spanish manuscripts would have reached Ireland from Spain in the seventh century and it is probably the route by which the collections of Spanish prayers which provided the Irish liturgy with new material also travelled to Ireland.

At the beginning of this century, E. Bishop was the staunch advocate of the direct transmission of liturgical material from Spain to Ireland, against the exclusively Gallican affiliations of the Irish liturgy advanced by L. Gougaud.[15] Recent research has collaborated his view and the independent contribution of Spain to the Irish liturgy is well established. There are aspects of this relationship between the two Churches which remain obscure or hidden from us, such as the personal contacts, the access to a wide range of Spanish material, and the channels of trade in books between the two countries. But the indications are that there were Irish monks in Spain, possibly indeed that they went there for the purpose of collecting manuscripts for their own librairies, and that these were transmitted direct to Ireland rather than through Bobbio or Luxeuil or any other Irish centre in the Franco-Germanic world.

The number of collects in the Antiphonary drawn directly from Spanish and northern Italian sources comes at most to a dozen. This total includes those two collects (AB 91 and 92) adapted from the sermons of St Zeno of Verona, which, even though they may be styled 'typically Irish', do not merit much consideration in terms of original authorship. It remains for us to offer, by way of synthesis and conclusion, some considerations on the style or 'genius' of those collects which are genuinely Irish. They can be classified, in terms of style and structure, under four main headings. There are twenty − eight collects which may be termed rhythmical or versified in various senses of the word,[16] twelve which are more or less in the mould of the traditional prose collect of the other Latin liturgies,[17] seventeen short petitions,[18] and sixteen collects of the 'litanic, asyndetic type' with frequent use of psalm versicles.[19]

The rhythmical collect, generally a rhyming quatrain, is one of the original features of the Irish liturgy. The Irish adopted this form of prayer because, as a result of their own tradition of rhythmical verse, they were more attracted to the tradition of Latin hymnody in its many forms than to the tradition of liturgical prose. Inspired by a love of poetry, they soon acquired a good ability to write hymns in traditional forms, and they began to introduce the medium of poetry into areas hitherto reserved for the most solemn liturgical prose, such as the blessing of the paschal candle and the presidential collect. They could compose collects in this medium with grace and assurance, expressing what is usually a traditional Christian insight in a simple poetic picture. It may give cause for wonder that an author who could write a morning collect such as AB 26,

Deus, qui pulsis tenebris
diei lucem tribuis:
adventum veri luminis
tuis effunde famulis,

which captures the essential meaning of the morning prayer, could not or
would not express the same theme in a well-knit prose collect. The prose
collects for morning prayer are little more than combinations of psalm versicles or litanic phrases.[20] Perhaps these were felt to be superior to mere
sober prose, which was not held in high esteem in the Irish tradition and
which would appear as an unsatisfactory means of address to the great
King of heaven.

Nevertheless, a number of collects do show that a few Irish authors succeeded to a marked degree in the composition of prose collects. The author
(or authors) of the prose collects for the various hours of the office (AB
27 – 33) was well versed in the spiritual themes associated traditionally
with these hours and in the structural laws of the traditional prose collects.
Two collects for the canticles *Cantemus* and *Benedicite* (AB 62 and 63)
show even in clearer light, if they are genuine Irish prayers, the success
which could be achieved in this form by an Irish author who set his mind
to the task. But, for all that, such collects are relatively scarce in the Antiphonary. The task itself may have seemed unattractive and uncongenial
to the Irish temperament. The need for such collects was felt in some
degree, at least to the extent that some were borrowed from foreign
sources. But no Irish systematic author of sufficient stature arose to im-
press his personality and thought on the Irish liturgy in this area of
liturgical prose.

The Irish genius sought expression in the field of poetry, of rhythm and
rhyme, and in what was the natural prosaic extension of this, the litanic,
lyrical, asyndetic type of composition. The short intercessory collects of
the *oratio communis* did not survive long even in the Irish tradition. But
the diffuse type of Irish prayer, often of an intensely personal and penitential cast, with effusions of the heart and litanic expressions of praise, was to
have a long future. These prayers remained for the greater part on the
margins of the liturgy and are known especially from such collections as
the *Book of Cerne*. But they made a significant impact in the whole process
of adaptation and development to which the Roman books were subjected
in northern Italy and France in the seventh and eighth centuries. The Irish
spirit of devotion was propagated not merely by the Irish missionaries
themselves but by others, such as Alcuin and other Anglo-Saxon missionaries, who were imbued with it and played such an active part in the
Carolingian reform. The presence of some of the collects of the Antiphonary in the Gelasian sacramentaries of the eighth century is just one
sign of the influence of the Irish on the development of the Roman liturgy
during that vital period.

PART 3

THE OFFICE AT BANGOR

CHAPTER NINETEEN

CATHEDRAL AND MONASTIC OFFICE IN IRELAND

We know little enough about the pre-monastic condition of the Church in Ireland, since most of the sources dating from the sixth century and later are of monastic provenance. A century elapsed between the time of St Patrick and the flowering of monastic movement, and the liturgy introduced and established during that century formed the basis for subsequent development in the monasteries. Elements of this pre-monastic or 'cathedral' liturgy can still be discovered in monastic sources such as the Antiphonary. There is also some evidence from earlier sources bearing on the life and liturgy of the Church in pre-monastic Ireland, and it will be of interest to begin with this.

There were monastic communities of men and women in the Irish Church from its early beginnings in the fifth century,[1] but they did not have that predominant place in the life and organization of the Church that they were to have later. The early missionaries organized the Church on a diocesan basis, making the native political unit of the *tuath* into the diocese. The bishop of the diocese would have had a sufficient number of clergy to help him minister to the needs of the scattered rural population in the various little churches of the *tauth*. Instruction of the people, celebration of the sacraments and of common prayer, organization of the Church in its pastoral mission: all of this was and remained the business of the diocesan clergy even well into the period of monastic ascendancy.[2]

The important collection of canons attributed to Patrick, Auxilius and Iserinus, dating from the fifth or early-sixth century,[3] provide the best evidence we have of the condition of the Church in the pre-monastic period. These canons deal with matters of Church life and discipline in the midst of a society which is still largely pagan. The type of Church described in them is similar to the Church elsewhere, with well-defined diocesan boundaries, with a bishop and clergy of varying degrees in charge of the several churches of the community. The canons presuppose an established liturgy and make reference to the usual celebrations, Mass on Sunday, baptism, penance, ordination, consecration of churches, morning and evening prayers in common. The content of this liturgy was determined by the early missionaries and it lacked those elements which can be shown to be developments of the monastic period from the sixth century onwards. The system of penance, for example, was not that envisaged by the Irish Penitentials but rather the system of public penance, with excommunication and reconciliation, which was in force elsewhere in the Church.[4] The daily hours of prayer[5] were those universally observed in the morning and evening as communal celebrations in the cathedral churches; there is no reference here to the strictly monastic hours. We are not told what prayers were said morning and evening, but we can be sure that they included those elements of prayer which were said in the cathedral church of southern Gaul and of the West generally at the same period.[6] The morning office would have included the *laudate* psalms, possibly one or more psalms appropriate to morning prayer, a reading from Scripture and the Our Father. The Old – Latin text of the canticles *Cantemus, Benedicite,* and *Benedictus* in the Antiphonary suggests that they were in liturgical use in Ireland in the pre-monastic period. The first two were being introduced into the morning prayer of the cathedral churches, at least on Sundays and feastdays, from the fourth century onwards, and they may have been used in Ireland also in the Sunday morning office from the fifth century.[7] We do not know whether there was a concluding prayer apart from the Our Father; the collects *ad matutinam* in the Antiphonary are probably of monastic rather than of cathedral origin. We are less well instructed about the content of the cathedral evening prayer at this early period, but it must have included a number of appropriate psalms and the Our Father.

The period of monastic expansion began with extraordinary vigour around the middle of the sixth century. Doubtless the established liturgy continued to be celebrated in the monasteries, but the new movement brought its own inspiration to bear on it. This can be seen above all in the liturgy of penance and of the hours. The question of the origin and development of the Irish monastic office is complex, but we will see in some detail to what extent the Irish were faithful to monastic traditions elsewhere and to what extent they were original. There were differences of observance among the various monastic rules in Ireland and changes continued to be made as the centuries elapsed and as the Irish movement became ever more open to a wide range of influences as it expanded to the Continent. Nevertheless, in spite of the differences prevailing between the various monastic families, we can speak with some justification of an Irish monastic office with its own identity and tradition. It is clear that Irish monks, such as Columban, were very conscious of the traditions established in Ireland in the sixth century and desired to be faithful to them. In this chapter we will simply review the sources that have survived so as to form a general picture of the celebration of the hours of prayer in the Irish monasteries. In this way we hope to establish the general context in which the material set down in the Bangor Antiphonary found its place and get further light on the celebration of the hours at Bangor.

We begin with the clear testimony of the Antiphonary itself. We learn from the two sets of collects for the hours (AB 17 – 39) that there were eight hours celebrated in the daily office at Bangor in the seventh century: *secunda*,[8] terce, sext, none, vespers, nightfall, midnight, and matins.

Columban's description of the office in his Monastic Rule takes us back

160

to the practice at Bangor a century or so prior to the Antiphonary. Columban acknowledges the existence of different traditions in the practice of the
canonical hours[9] and states that according to the tradition laid down by his
predecessors there are three night offices as well as an unspecified number
of daily hours (*horae diurnae*). His three night offices are called *initium noctis* (which has twelve psalms), *medium noctis* (twelve psalms), and
matutinum[10] (from twenty-four to seventy-five psalms). There can be little
doubt that these hours correspond to the three which are called *initium
noctis*, *nocturnum*, and *matutina* in the Antiphonary. The number of daily
hours celebrated by Columban's monks has been put at three or four,[11] but
we can argue from the Antiphonary, again with good probability, that Columban had five hours in mind: *secunda*, terce, sext, none, and vespers.[12]
This inference is partly confirmed by the fact that Donatus, a monk at
Luxeuil in the time of Columban and later bishop of Besancon, names
secunda specifically in his *Regula ad virgines*, which follows the Rule of
Columban in what pertains to the office.[13] The inclusion of vespers among
Columban's *horae diurnae* is justified on the grounds that it is the primitive
cathedral office, which must have been continued in monastic practice. It
is this (cathedral) evening prayer which we find mentioned in other
monastic sources under the name *vespertina* or its Latin and Irish
equivalents.[14]

Columban also speaks in his Rule about another *cursus* observed by certain catholics,[15] one somewhat different from the *cursus* he prescribed for
his own community. It has four night offices and a more rigid attachment
to the canonical number of psalms: nightfall (with twelve psalms), midnight (twelve psalms), cock-crow (twelve psalms), and matins (twelve
psalms on ordinary nights, three times twelve or thirty-six psalms on the
nights preceding Saturday and Sunday). It has been suggested that the
catholics in question were Egyptians,[16] but there is no reason to suggest
that they were anything but Irish.

Going somewhat further back into the sixth century, we come to the
monastic practice at Iona as described in Adomnan's *Life of Columcille*.[17]
Adomnan occasionally uses the names of the canonical hours to indicate
the time of day on which certain events which he describes took place. We
find references to the first hour of the day,[18] to the third hour of the day,[19]
to the sixth hour,[20] to the ninth hour of the day,[21] and to vespers.[22] Only
once does Adomnan give us something more than these bare indications of
the hours. In describing the events leading up to Columcille's death he
speaks of three offices of the community. On the evening of his last day,
during which the saint was occupied in transcribing the psalter, he went to
the church for the office of vespers of Saturday evening, after which he
returned to his cell and reclined on his bed. At midnight he rose and went
to the church, where the brothers soon found him, lying before the altar.
They raised him up; he blessed them and died. Then, when the matin
hymns were ended, the sacred body was carried back from the church to

the cell from which he had come a little while before.[23] We find here that only a little while elapsed between midnight and the completion of the 'morning hymns', that is, the office of matins. The text does not explicity mention a midnight office, but we can conclude that (normally, at least) there was such an office, as distinct from matins. There is, however, no place here for the prolonged vigil which Columban prescribes under the name *matutinum*. There appears to have been only *one* night office at Iona, the midnight office; this seems to have been followed immediately by the 'morning hymns' of matins and the whole celebration took but a little time. The night of Columcille's death was the ninth of June, which at Iona was of extremely short duration. There may have been some seasonal variation comparable to that practised at Bangor. In winter the midnight office may have been followed by a further period of sleep before morning prayer, and the latter may have included a prolonged vigil as well as the 'morning hymns'. However this may be, we must admit that Columcille adopted a much more realistic *cursus* for midsummer than did Columban and the catholics mentioned by the latter. We can conclude by saying that the hours at Iona consisted of prime, terce, sext, none, vespers, midnight, and matins (the latter consisting, at least in summer, simply of the morning psalms, without any vigil).[24]

Some authors have claimed that we can go still further back to a time when prime had not yet been introduced into the Irish arrangement of the hours.[25] Evidence for this, it is claimed, is found in an Irish text, which in turn is used to interpret the limited information provided by Columban regarding his *horae diurnae*. The text in question is a note in a manuscript[26] compiled from various sources in the fifteenth or sixteenth century. The note sets out the reason why celebration is made at certain hours rather than at others. The hours are given in order as follows: terce (*teirt*), sext (*médon lái*), none (*nóin*), vespers (*espartu*) and sext (*medón lái*), midnight (*midnocht*), matins (*iarmérge*). Though only six hours are mentioned here, it seems to me beyond question that seven hours were found in the original and that the repetition of sext (*medón lái*) was a scribal error. The second *medón lái* was written above the line in a space left vacant after the treatment of the first (and genuine) *medón lái*. In the first case the reason given for celebrating sext is convenient and traditional, but in the second case the reason given for celebrating it is elsewhere more conveniently applied to *secunda* (*anteirt*) or prime.[27] Vespers and prime (*anteirt* or *prím*?) are considered here together because they both derive their justification from the sacrifices offered daily, morning and evening, in the temple. In this text, therefore, we find no evidence for an Irish system of hours which still lacked the office of prime (*anteirt* or *secunda*). Whatever may have been the inner content of these hours, in particular of *iarmérge*,[28] we find here a series of seven hours: prime, terce, sext, none, vespers, midnight, and matins. Since there is no mention of compline, this text very probably represents Irish practice in the eighth century or earlier still.

The *Regula cuiusdam Patris ad monachos*, which is related to Columban's Rule and may be of Irish origin, seems to establish a system of six hours in the daily office:

Tribus conventibus diei, totidemque noctis tempore in ecclesia conveniendum: tres psalmi in unoquoque conventu diei canendi sunt, duodecim vero in nocturnis conventibus cantabuntur, praeter illam missam quae celebratur ortu solis.[29]

The question is, what is the *missa* which is celebrated at sunrise? Is it possible that this is the third night office, which, like Columban's *matutinum*, has a longer portion of psalmody than the other two? This seems to me to be unlikely. Columban's *matutinum* is a vigil, which can hardly have been celebrated at sunrise. The *Regula cuiusdam* seems to speak of three night offices, each of which has twelve psalms, *and* of another office which is reckoned neither among the day hours nor the night hours but is regarded as an hour of transition from night to day and is celebrated at sunrise. This corresponds to the position and function that *secunda* has in the Irish sources.[30] The author of the *Regula* seems, then, to have seven hours in mind: prime (*secunda?*), trece, sext, none, nightfall, midnight, and matins. Vespers is a noteworthy omission in this Rule.

The ancient order of the hours in Ireland is also witnessed to by two other Irish texts. The first is an Irish gloss of the eighth century written in an Irish commentary on the psalms (Vatican, *Cod.Pal.lat.*68). It enumerates seven hours in the daily office:

'Septies in die laudem dixi tibi' (ps.118,64), .i. antert, tert, sest, noon, fescer, midnocht, maten quod convenit, quia septies in die cadit iustus.[31]

This explanation of the *septies* differs from that given by Benedict,[32] and it is likely that this series of hours corresponds to that which we have seen in Adomnan's *Life of Columcille*.[33]

The second text gives us no complete enumeration of the hours, but it gives us some interesting insights into some of them. This is the Rule of Ailbe of Emly,[34] in which reference is made to the following hours: *anteirt, uair na tertae, nóin, fescair, midnocht,* and *iarméirge*. Sext is not mentioned. The offices of midnight and matins are two night vigils, corresponding to Columban's *medium noctis* and *matutinum*:

19. Thirty psalms every matin (*iarméirge*), twelve psalms for midnight (*midnocht*).
22. The right matin (*iarméirge*) according to sages is the end of the night, the beginning of the day.

The term *fescair* is evidently derived from *vespertina* and for that reason I am inclined to identify it with vespers rather than with nightfall.[35] Once again we have a system of seven hours: *anteirt*, terce, (sext), none, vespers, midnight, and matins.

This system was changed in due course, apparently through the influence of Benedict's Rule. From the ninth century onwards we find compline mentioned as a regular part of the office, and only one night office is found, whereas in earlier centuries there could have been two, or three, or four. The change can be observed in the ninth – century *Navigatio S. Brendani*.[36] This document gives us very interesting information about the content of the various hours and we will return to it again. For the present it will suffice to note the hours it mentions, namely, terce, sext, none, vespers, compline, vigils (*vigiliae*) united to morning prayer (*laudes matutinae*), and another office celebrated at dawn (prime).[37]

A number of documents have come down to us from the *Céli Dé* reform movement of the eighth and ninth centuries. Three of these, relating to the usages of Tallaght, are of special interest for our present purpose. These texts,[38] which derive from a common original composed *c.* 831 – 840 by a monk of the Tallaght community, give a lot of information about the paraliturgical devotions and ascetic practices of the monks. But little or nothing is said about the canonical hours, apart from the indication of their names. There was a period of sleep between the night vigil, here called *iarmérge*, and the morning office, called *maiten*; there followed: *anteirt, teirt, medón lai, nóin, fescor* (also called *easbart, espartain*), and an office technically called *fadg*, or *urnaigthe dul do chodladh*, or *ceilebradh dul do chodladh*, ('bed – time prayers'). Only once do we get even a partial description of the content of an office, when the author says:

> If anyone happened to take a drink or eat any food later than that (i.e. after the prayers said before retiring to rest), it was necessary for him to say the office of *fadg* from *Cum invocarem* to *Nunc dimittis*.[39]

This is the Benedictine office of compline.

The change from a double vigil to a single vigil seems to be implied in the transferrence of the term *iarmérge* to signify the midnight office, previously called *midnocht*. We find it again in a poem on the virtues of the hours in the Trinity College MS, H.3.18, where the hours are listed in order as *prím, tert, medónlái, nóin, esparta, compléit, iarmérge,* and *tiugnáir*.[40] There are many instances of *iarmérge* in this sense of the vigil, or the midnight office, or nocturns.[41]

We have already spoken about the little note on the hours in the Trinity College MS, H.3.17. A comparison between it and the later and much longer treatise on the hours in the *Leabhar Breac*[42] helps to highlight the change that has taken place in the arrangement of the hours. The prose version of this treatise begins in the same way as the note in H.3.17:

> Why is celebration made at these hours rather than at other hours? Not hard to say. Terce, because it was then Christ was given up by Pontius Pilate and therin grace came upon the Apostles.

But the short note makes no mention of compline, and where it speaks of *midnocht* and *iarmérge* the *Leabhar Breac* speaks of *medón aidhche* and *tiugnáir*. The full list of the hours in the *Leabhar Breac* is: *teirt, medón lái, nóin, fescair, compléit, medón aidhche, tiugnáir,* and *prím*.

This survey of the sources for the liturgy of the hours in Ireland has substantiated Columban's assertion that different traditions existed in this matter. Differences were especially noticeable in the number and content of the night offices, which varied from one to four. The office of nightfall (*initium noctis* or *duodecima*) was observed by Columban's community, by those bound by the *Regula cuiusdam*, and by the 'catholics' mentioned by Columban. We found it again at Bangor in the seventh century, along with the cathedral evening office of vespers. Apart from these sources we find no mention of *initium noctis*. In its place we find compline introduced from the ninth century onwards, but it may have been dropped everywhere before this development took place.[43] Two other night vigils, at midnight (*medium noctis*, *midnocht*) and towards morning (*matutinum*, *iarmérge*), seem to have been common at first, but they were eventually reduced to one (*vigiliae*, *medón aidhche*, *iarmérge*), probably through the influence of the Benedictine office. While these two vigils remained the (cathedral) morning prayer was added to the morning vigil, as part of the one office (*matutinum*, *iarmérge*). Where only one vigil existed, morning prayer (*hymni matutini*, *laudes matutinae*, *maiten*, *tiugnáir*) either followed immediately, as at Iona and in the practice described in the *Navigatio*, or was separated from the vigil by a period of sleep, as at Tallaght.

There is general agreement in the sources regarding the number of day hours. Apart from the *Regula cuiusdam*, which makes no mention of vespers as distinct from *initium noctis*, we find mention everywhere of prime (earlier called *secunda* or *anteirt*), terce, sext, none, and vespers. The peculiar name and function of *secunda* calls for some comment at this stage. Where the hours are given in series, the first hour mentioned tends to be *secunda* or *anteirt*, later *prím*; we find this in the Antiphonary, in *Cod.Pal.lat.*68, and in MS H.3.18 of Trinity College. This seems to reflect the fact that *secunda* marked the end of the night's sleep and the beginning of the working day.[44] While the two night vigils of midnight and towards morning remained, the night's sleep in Irish monasteries was broken up into three parts: between nightfall and midnight, between midnight and the morning vigil, and between the morning vigil and *secunda*. This arrangement was quite peculiar to Ireland, though there were precedents elsewhere for a return to sleep either after the vigil or after the morning office.[45] By naming the office *secunda* rather than *prima* the Irish acknowledged that a certain time elapsed between the morning office and the first of the day hours, and that this time was meant for getting some extra sleep.

We now have a general picture of the hours that were celebrated in Irish monasteries at home and overseas from the sixth century onwards. Something of their inner substance is known to us as well, above all through the Bangor documents. We will consider this in greater detail in subsequent chapters.

CHAPTER TWENTY

STRUCTURE OF THE MONASTIC OFFICE

The Antiphonary does not give us any information regarding the number of psalms to be said at each hour or regarding the manner of their selection and recitation. But this is the sole aim of chapter VII of Columban's Rule, which presupposes the existence of another book, apart from the psalter, containing other elements of the office, such as canticles, hymns, antiphons and collects, or at least the knowledge of these elements as they were in use in his day. He himself had been a monk at Bangor for some thirty years before setting out on his mission to the Continent, where he arrived in the year 591. He always remained deeply attached to his native traditions,[1] and in his chapter on the office he based his prescriptions in an explicit way on the tradition of his elders:

> Inde CUM SENIORIBUS NOSTRIS ab VIII kalendas iulii cum noctis augmento sensim incipit crescere cursus.... Per diurnas terni psalmi horas pro operum interpositione statuti sunt A SENIORIBUS NOSTRIS.[2]

We must recognize, of course, that a century separates Columban's departure and the composition of the Antiphonary (*c.*590 – 690). And from our study so far we know that much of the material in the latter was composed, or borrowed from abroad, in the course of the seventh century. But this material, consisting mainly of collects and hymns, did not necessarily change the basic structure of the hours. The *cursus* established by Columban's elders at Bangor in the sixth century, which Columban in turn transmitted, remained with all probability in force until the late seventh century, when the Antiphonary was written. We will not be far wrong if we take Columban's description of the *cursus* as giving us the structural context in which the material set down in the Antiphonary finds its place. Taken together, the Rule and the Antiphonary give us an almost complete account of the monastic office at Bangor in the seventh century.

The system of Columban's *cursus* has been studied in detail by O. Heiming,[3] and all we need to do is to present it here in outline:

1. *Ad initium noctis*: 12 psalms
2. *Ad medium noctis*: 12 psalms
3. *Ad matutinum*, also called *vigilia*:[4]
   — A. On the 'holy nights' preceding Saturday and Sunday:
     a. From Nov.1 — Jan.31: 75 psalms
     b. From Feb.1 — Apr.30: decrease of 3 psalms per week
     c. From May 1 — June 24: 36 psalms
     d. From June 24 — Oct.31: gradual increase from 36 to
       75 psalms
   — B. On other nights:
     a. From Sept.25 — Mar.24: 36 psalms

b. From Mar.25 — Sept.24: 24 psalms[5]

4. *Horae diurnae*: 3 psalms each[6]

The psalms in the office *ad matutinum*, at least, and possibly in the other two nocturnal offices also, were divided into groups of three. Each group of three psalms consisted of two *psalmi psalliti*, that is, two psalms without antiphons, followed by an antiphonal psalm. This group of three psalms was called a *chora*. Thus on Saturdays and Sundays during winter, the 75 psalms of *matutinum* were divided into 25 *chorae* and included 25 antiphonal psalms. The *psalmi psalliti* may be taken to mean either of two modes of psalmody; they may have been chanted by all together (as *directanei*) or, preferably, chanted by one while all others listened in silence in the Egyptian manner.

The *chora*-system applied possibly to all the hours of the office, since the psalmody in every office consisted of three psalms or a multiple of three.[7] The division of the psalmody into groups of three psalms and the division of each group of three psalms into two parts in the proportion of 2 : 1 is general in Western monastic *ordines*. But this fundamental structure is found with different variations in each monastic Rule. We find, for example, the group of three psalms divided in the proportion of two antiphonal psalms and one responsorial psalm, or two antiphonal psalms without alleluia and one antiphonal psalm with alleluia.[8] Columban's proportion, two psalms recited without antiphon or responsary and one antiphonal psalm, is not found elsewhere, but the nearest thing to it is the division of the *psalmi dicti* during Easter-time at Arles into the proportion of two psalms and one psalm with alleluia.[9]

In the Columbanian office the psalms were probably recited consecutively as they are given in the psalter (*currente psalterio*). There were exceptions to this, as we know from the Antiphonary, but it must have been the operative principle at least in the long night offices. The total number of psalms in the morning vigil on the two 'holy nights' was 150 psalms, 75 on each night.[10] This does not mean that during the Saturday morning vigil pss.1 – 75 were chanted and during the Sunday morning vigil pss.76 – 150. The remark of Columban indicates quantity rather than order;[11] that is, the psalmody at the vigil began where it had left off at the midnight office and 75 psalms were chanted. As for specially chosen psalms, we know from the Antiphonary that pss.148 – 150 were used daily at the conclusion of the morning vigil and ps.89 was assigned to *secunda*. This was without doubt the practice already in Columban's time. We cannot say whether the other day hours had specially chosen psalms, at least from the information given to us by Columban and the Antiphonary. We will have occasion to return to this point and consider what later evidence there is for it. We may note here that, even if the day hours did have specially assigned psalms in Columban's time, this could have happened without prejudice to the *chora*-system on which his office was constructed.

The traditional practice of prayer after each psalm is found also in the Columbanian office. It is silent prayer after Egyptian manner, but now it is not left to each one to formulate his own prayer, which would then be summed up and concluded by the president of the assembly.[12] The silent prayer is itself formulated and there is no mention of the presidential collect:

Reg. Coen. II: Qui humiliationem in synaxi, id est in cursu, oblitus fuerit, haec est humiliatio in ecclesia post finem cuiuscumque psalmi, similiter paeniteat.

Reg. Coen. IX : In commune autem omnes fratres omnibus diebus ac noctibus tempore orationum in fine omnium psalmorum genua in oratione, si non infirmitas corporis offecerit, flectere aequo animo debent, sub silentio dicentes, *Deus in adiutorium meum intende, domine ad adiuvandum me festina*. Quem versiculum postquam ter in oratione tacite decantaverint, aequaliter a flexione orationis surgant, excepto diebus dominicis et a prima die sancti paschae usque ad quinquagesimam diem, in quibus moderate se in tempore psalmodiae humiliantes, genua non flectentes, sedule orent dominum.[13]

Columban's insistence on the uniform practice of this prayer by *all* the brothers, at the end of *every* psalm, in *all* the offices of day and night, and that it be done with equanimity, testifies to the difficulty experienced in carrying it out. At the long morning vigil on Saturday and Sunday mornings this practice would have entailed seventy-five genuflexions.[14] In spite of this difficulty, the custom of silent prayer and genuflexion at the end of the psalms was widespread in the monastic office, until its disappearance around the eighth century,[15] while the psalter collects were taken over and developed in the cathedral office during the same period.

Columban says nothing about readings in the office, and we do not possess any other purely Irish documents which would enable us to fill this lacuna. But the *Regula cuiusdam Patris*, 'which is Celtic in origin or at least inspiration',[16] does indeed prescribe them:

30. Orationes vero et duae lectiones, una de Veteri Testamento et alia de Novo, in singulis noctis conventibus dicendae sunt.[17]

Apart from this basic structure of psalmody and silent prayer (and readings, at least in the night offices), each hour had its own distinctive elements of prayer, such as an appropriate hymn, collect, litany, and so forth. We now turn to consider each of these distinctive features of the hours of the day and of the night.

CHAPTER TWENTY-ONE

FORM AND CONTENT OF THE DAY HOURS

Columban distinguished the daily hours from the three long nocturnal vigils. He did not specify their number, but he probably had in mind the five hours named in the Antiphonary as *secunda, tertia, sexta, nona,* and *vespertina.* By combining the data of both sources we get the following provisional outline of the structure of each of these hours:

1. Three psalms[1]
2. *Gloria in excelsis*: at vespers[2]
3. Collect
4. *Oratio communis*[3]

We will examine each of these parts in turn.

1. THREE PSALMS

We have seen that this number of psalms for each of the day hours sets the Columbanian office in the broad stream of monastic tradition and distinguishes it clearly from the Gallican tradition.[4] The question now arises as to whether the psalms used at each of these hours were specially chosen and fixed or whether they were constantly changing according to the custom of continuous psalmody (*psalterium currens*). We know that for *secunda*, at least, ps.89 was specially chosen and used constantly without regard for the day or the feast.[5] Apart from this, nothing is said explicitly in the Antiphonary regarding the choice of psalms. But one of the collects for *secunda* suggests that ps.50 was also appointed for this hour,[6] and this us of ps.50 may also be reflected in another collect for the same hour.[7] The collects for the other day hours do not contain references to specific psalms, so they do not give us any clues as to what psalms were used in these hours.

Our question cannot, therefore, be fully answered on the basis of the Rule of Columban and the Antiphonary. But there is one Irish document which offers evidence for a special choice of psalms in all the five daily hours we are now considering, and the evidence of this document agrees with the meagre data of the Antiphonary and Columban on this point. The document in question is the *Navigatio Sancti Brendani,* which was composed by an Irishman probably in the ninth century.[8] It is a narrative of the voyage of Brendan and his companions over the ocean in search of the 'Land of Promise of the Saints'. Among the strange occurrences they were privileged to experience, two are of particular interest to us. In one story[9] we are told that Brendan and his fellow-travellers one day came upon an island where they found the inhabitants divided into three choirs, who were occupied in singing in turn, without ever ceasing, the versicle:

'Ibunt sancti de virtute in virtute et videbunt Deum deorum in Sion'. We now take up the story as it is told in the *Navigatio* and we will divide it into sections for subsequent reference.

I a. Erat hora quarta quando tenuerunt portum insule. Cum autem SEXTA venisset, ceperunt turme cantare simul, dicentes: 'Deus misereatur nostri' (ps.66,1), usque in finem, et 'Deus in adiutorium meum' (ps.69,2); similiter et tercium psalmum 'Credidi' (ps.115,1), et oracionem ut supra.

b. Similiter AD HORAM NONAM alios tres psalmos: 'De profundis' (ps.129,1), et 'Ecce quam bonum' (ps.132,1), 'Laudaque Ierusalem Dominum' (ps.147,1).

c. Et cantabant AD VESPEROS: 'Te decet hymnus Deus in Sion' (ps.64,1), et 'Benedic anima mea Domino, Domine Deus meus' (ps.103,1), et tercium psalmum: 'Laudate pueri Dominum' (ps.112,1). . . .

d. Tunc (*scil.* AD VIGILIAS MATUTINAS) ceperunt turme cantare, dicentes: 'Laudate Dominum de celis' (ps.148,1), deinde 'Cantate Domino' (ps.149,1), et tercium 'Laudate Dominum in sanctis eius' (ps.150,1). . . .

e. At vero cum dies illucessisset . . . cantabant tres psalmos: 'Miserere mei Deus' (ps.50,1), 'Deus, Deus meus ad te de luce vigilo' (ps.62,1), et 'Domine refugium'(ps.89,1).

f. AD TERCIAM alios tres, id est 'Omnes gentes' (ps.46,2), et 'Deus in nomine tuo' (ps.53,1), tercium vero, 'Dilexi quoniam' (ps.114,1) sub alleluia.

The setting of this story is fantastic, but there are a number of reasons why we should regard the office described in it as more than a figment of the writer's imagination. The first indication of the genuine character of the office is found in the way it is confirmed by the second story we referred to. The setting of this second story is even more fantastic than the first. Here we are told of another delightful island, upon which Brendan and his companions chanced on Easter Sunday. The marvel on this occasion is a multitude of singing virds, who have settled on a tree in the island. They are found to be singing versicles at certain hours, and these versicles are taken from one of the psalms which are assigned to the corresponding hour in the first story. We will reproduce the salient parts of the story[10], and will refer in each section to the corresponding section of our first story.

II a. Cum autem VESPERTINA HORA appropinquasset, ceperunt omnes aves que in arbore erant quasi una voce cantare, percutientes latera sua atque dicentes: 'Te decet hymnus Deus in Sion, et tibi reddetur votum in Ierusalem' (ps.64,1). Et semper reciprocabant predictum versiculum quasi per spacium unius hore. . .(cf. I c).

b. Evigilans autem, vir Dei cepit suscitare fratres suos AD VIGILIAS NOCTIS sanctae, incipiens illum versiculum: 'Domine labia mea aperies'. Finita iam oracione sancti viri, omnes aves alis et ore resonabant, dicentes: 'Laudate Dominum omnes angeli eius, laudate eum omnes virtutes eius' (ps.148,2). Similiter et ad vesperas per spacium hore semper cantabant (cf. I d).

c. Cum AURORA refulsisset, ceperunt cantare: 'Et sit splendor Domini Dei nostri super nos' (ps.89,17), equali modulacione et longitudine psallendi sicut et IN MATUTINIS LAUDIBUS (cf. I e).

d. Similiter AD TERCIAM HORAM istum versiculum: 'Psallite Deo nostro psallite, psallite regi nostro psallite sapienter' (ps,46,7 – 8) (cf. I f).

e. AD SEXTAM: 'Illumina Domine vultum tuum super nos et miserere nostri' (ps.66,2) (cf. I a).

f. AD NONAM psallebant: 'Ecce quam bonum et quam iocundum habitare fratres in unum' (ps.132,1) (cf. I b).

The correspondence between the versicles of the second story and the psalms assigned to particular hours in the first story cannot be accidental. We can possibly see in the versicles chanted by the birds the antiphons used at the particular hours. The versicle chanted for the office at day-break (prime), at any rate, is the daily antiphon for *secunda* according to the Antiphonary (AB 108). As for the others, some of them are paraphrases, rather than literal transcriptions, of psalm versicles, and thus are more in the nature of antiphons.[11]

But the office of the Three Choirs has other signs which show it to be a primitive Irish[12] monastic office. The psalms chosen for the various hours are peculiarly suitable, some of them indeed traditionally associated with the same hours.

For the hours at day-break (*cum dies illucessisset* I e; *aurora* II c) we find pss.50,62 and 89, with the antiphon — if it be such — *Et sit splendor*. We have already discovered three of these in *secunda* as celebrated at Bangor in the seventh century: pss.50 and 89, and the antiphon *Sit splendor*. Furthermore, these three pslams are precisely the same, and come in the same order, as those assigned to the *novella sollemnitas matutina* at its institution, on the testimony of Cassian.[13]

The psalms used for terce, sext, and none are well chosen to express the traditional understanding of these hours of prayer as commemorations of the passion, death, descent, and final triumph of Christ.[14] In the psalms for terce (pss.45, 53, 114) the central theme is the glorification of Christ, following this total trust in God throughout his passion and death.[15] We find basically the same theme, the confidence in God of the poor and persecuted man and his final deliverance, in two of the psalms used for sext (pss.69 and 115); ps.66 is a more general psalm of supplication and praise.[16] In the psalms assigned to none, we find again the themes of supplication, trust and praise which are appropriate for the commemoration of the death and descent of Christ, and his final exaltation together with the just, his brothers.[17]

The psalms assigned to vespers (pss.64, 103, 112) have no special thematic relationship to the psalms used for the three preceding hours. But they also, for their part, are peculiarly appropriate for vespers. We find, first of all, some well-known references to evening; and secondly, a special concentration on such favourite evening themes as the work of God and man in creation and praise of God for all his wisdom and bountiful goodness, as manifested in his creation.[18] Besides, the use of three psalms had become traditional in the evening office of the cathedral; we find it in the most primitive type of vespers at Milan, in the Spanish rite, as well as in the monastic office at Arles, where it is clearly distinguished from the monastic evening office of *duodecima*.[19]

Psalms 148 − 150 are assigned in our office of the Three Choirs to the *vigiliae matutinae* (I d; or *matutinae laudes* II e); they were the universally used morning psalms, and were used also at Bangor in the seventh century, on the evidence of the Antiphonary.

Columban assigned three psalms to each of the day hours, but he did not say whether these psalms were specially chosen. We gathered from the Antiphonary that certain psalms were appointed for *secunda* daily. We are now in a position to state that in at least one Irish monastic *ordo* the three psalms said at each of the day hours were specially chosen psalms. The author of the *Navigatio* must have drawn on an Irish tradition, possibly the observance of the hours in one of St Brendan's communities in Ireland, to express what the ideal monastic office should be. The agreement between the two stories we have recounted from it, as well as the manner in which the office there outlined is rooted in tradition, are a firm indication that it is not immaginary office, but one which existed in reality. Apart from the Rule of Columban (and the *Regula cuiusdam*), this is the only document which speaks about the number of psalms used for the day hours in Ireland, so that we cannot be certain how widespread in Ireland was the practice held up for admiration in the *Navigatio*.[20] But the total agreement of this office, on the one hand, and the office of Columban and of the Antiphonary, in so far as they describe the psalmody of the day hours, on the other hand, suggests that the office of the *Navigatio* was not confined to just one monastery, and that possibly the day hours at Bangor in the seventh century were celebrated as described for us in the *Navigatio Sancti Brendani*.

What, then, we may ask, is the origin of this singular office? It would appear to be an insular development of a tradition going back ultimately to the writings of Cassian, and possibly in part to the monastic usages of southern Gaul. The Irish had, at least, the same distinction between vespers and *duodecima* that we find in the monastic office at Arles. Neither Caesarius nor Aurelian gives any indication regarding the identity of the three antiphonal psalms sung at vespers, but say simply: *antiphonae tres* (or *antiphona tria*). But they probably varied from day to day; only the *directaneus parvulus* is explicitly determined by Aurelian as ps.112, which is found in our office as a complete psalm. It is possible that the choice of the three psalms assigned to vespers in our office was influenced by a source in southern Gaul. But we do not know of any Gallican *ordo* which took Cassian as seriously as did the authors of the Irish office described in the *Navigatio*. The office as a whole appears to have been an insular creation, but one which was grounded in the great tradition of the Church, by means especially of the writings of Cassian. The psalms chosen for morning prayer and prime (or *secunda*) were those already assigned to the conclusion of the morning vigil and to the *novella sollemnitas* in the East at the end of the fourth century, as described by Cassian, and the choice of psalms for the hours of terce, sext, and none was determined by the Christian interpretation of these hours, as found in Cassian and in other early authors. Other and more recent influences may have been at work as well, such as the hymns and prayers for the day hours, which continued to give expression to the Christian significance of prayer at the various hours. The Irish office may also have owed more than we can now appreciate, through lack of the necessary sources, to the British monastic centres in the fifth and sixth centuries, notably to the sixth-century Welsh saints like Gildas and David, who were known and admired in Ireland in the sixth century. But whatever may have been the more exact lines of communication between Ireland and continental tradition, a communication which issued in the creation of the office described in the *Navigatio,* the existence of the latter can be regarded as historically certain. Once this is granted, and once we take into account the interrelations and communication that existed between the monasteries of Ireland in the sixth and seventh centuries,[21] we can say with some probability that the office described in the *Navigatio* was widely used, possibly even in Bangor itself.

Having said this much about the psalmody, we will now go on to consider the other elements of the day hours at Bangor.

2. GLORIA IN EXCELSIS DEO

Its precise place in the office of vespers is not indicated, and we are not told whether it was used daily or merely on Sundays. This use of the *Gloria in excelsis* for vespers is quite without parallel in the West, but there is a parallel use of it in the Byzantine office. It is difficult, however, to explain how Byzantine influence could have brought about the double use of the *Gloria* in Ireland, in the morning and evening offices.[22] A parallel of this kind does not necessarily indicate dependence of one on the other. Its use at vespers in Ireland is clear not only from the rubric in AB 116: *Ad vesperum et ad matutinum,* but also from the additional versicle as found in the Irish *Liber Hymnorum*:

Dignare, domine, NOCTE ISTA (die ista AB) sine peccato nos custodire.[23]

Its position in vespers was possibly after the three psalms, parallel to its position after pss.148 – 150 in the morning office of East and West.[24]

3. THE COLLECT

This seems to be the most natural position for the collect, following the psalms or the *Gloria* in vespers.[25] Every hour of the day and night is represented by its own collects in the Antiphonary, and they give a synthesis of the themes proper to the celebration of each particular hour. We will make here some overall, systematic considerations on these collects from the standpoint of their thematic content, that is, the understanding of the daily hours of prayer that is expressed in them. We will not repeat what we have already said regarding their literary relationships to collects in the other Western liturgies, but reference will be made to the latter occasionally, in order to elucidate certain themes.

(a) *Collectio ad secundam* (AB 16, 17, 27, 122)

Reference is made in a few of these collects to the precise time of day at which *secunda* is celebrated:

in hac hora prima diei (27), exorto solis lumine (17).

In this first hour of the day we are called to give thanks to Christ our God for our redemption (27). God (Christ) is the source of light:

Domine, sancte pater, omnipotens aeterne deus, qui diem clarificas et in lumine luminas (122). — Christe, oriens nomine (17),

and we pray for his help, protection, mercy, and light throughout the day:

Adesto nobis, domine (17). — Esto nobis protector in ista die, domine, ... et miserator et misericors et auxiliator et dux nobis et inluminator cordium nostrorum (16). — Misericordiam tuam, domine, ne auferas a nobis; redde nobis laetitiam salutaris tui, ... ut oriatur lucifer in cordibus nostris (122),

so that we may be able to do his will and be pleasing to him all the days of our life:

ut possimus placere in conspectu tuo, domine, et perficere voluntatem tuam et ambulare in via recta toto nostrae vitae tempore (16).

The content of these prayers is, therefore, determined by the associations and tasks of the particular hour, the beginning of the day. There are a few allusions to certain themes associated with the morning hour, themes which we might expect to find in the morning prayers strictly speaking:[26] the symbolism of the rising sun and the light of day in relation to Christ and to the Christian way of life, which should be characterized by truth and holiness of life. In one of the prayers there is also an element of commemoration, probably inspired by the conclusion of the psalm *Miserere*:

Exaudi nos, domine, ... qui nos redemisti tuo sancto sanguine, ut praeces et petitiones nostras vice primitiarum tibi obaltas pie clementerque suscipias (27).

(b) *Collectio ad tertiam* (AB 18, 28)

In this third hour of the day we pray to Christ (18, 28), that he may give us his grace:

uti nobis perpetuam suam tribuat gratiam (18),

that is, a share in that grace which he gave to the apostles when he sent the Holy Spirit on them:

qui in hora diei tertia spiritum sanctum apostolis orantibus emisisti: eiusdem gratiae participationem nobis poscentibus iubeas concedi (28).

This was the classical theme for terce since the time of Tertullian and

Cyprian, and it is also found in the Ambrosian and Spanish prayers for terce.[27]

(c) *Collectio ad sextam* (AB 19, 29)

We pray at the sixth hour because it was then that Christ was crucified:

qua fuisti pro omnibus, Christe, in cruce positus (19). — nobis magnalia fecisti, sexta hora crucem ascendisti (29).

We pray that, just as Christ enlightened the darkness of the world, he may now enlighten our hearts:

tenebris mundi inluminasti: sic et corda nostra inluminare digneris (29).

The tradition that the crucifixion of Christ should be commemorated by prayer at the sixth hour dates back to the time of Hippolytus at least. Hippolytus also associated it with the darkness that prevailed from the sixth to the ninth hour, but his development of this theme is somewhat different from that found in our prayer no.29, which speaks of the illumination of the darkness at the sixth hour and is quite singular in this respect.[28]

(d) *Collectio ad nonam* (AB 20, 30, 121)

Prayer is again addressed to Christ at the ninth hour, and there are a number of reasons given for this in our collects. First of all, because it is the hour of Christ's descent, when great wonders were revealed to the saints:

qua cultoribus tuis divina monstrantur miracula (30),

and we pray that like them our hearts also may be enlightened (30). Again, because it was at this hour that the thief confessed and gained paradise, and this invites us to pray like him:

ita et nos, domine, confitemur peccata nostra, ut regnum caelorum consequamur et vitam aeternam mereamur (121).

Thirdly, because it was at this hour that Christ visited Cornelius, which gives us confidence that our prayers also will be heard at this hour (20).

There is no direct reference in our collects to the traditional motif of the death of Christ at this hour,[29] but the other events commemorated in them are all found in early sources which deal with prayer at this hour.[30]

(e) *Collectio ad vespertinam* (AB 21, 31)

A prayer for pardon of the sins committed during the day (21) is a natural and traditional evening theme. It figured already in the evening prayer of Basil's monastic community[31] and it continued to be expressed in the evening prayers of the West, alongside the great evening themes of thanksgiving for the day, meditation on the symbolism of light and darkness, and prayer for deliverance from danger during the night.[32]

The second prayer (31):

Vespertina oratio nostra ascendat ad aures divinae maiestatis tuae et descendat benedictio tua, domine, super nos, quemadmodum superavimus in te reflects, like many Ambrosian and Spanish evening antiphons and prayers,[33] the influence of the evening psalm *par excellence*:

> Dirigatur oratio mea sicut incensum in conspectu tuo, elevatio manuum mearum sacrificium vespertinum (ps.140,2).

It is impossible to say whether ps.140 was used as an evening psalm at Bangor before the psalmodic part of the office. There is no reference to it in the Irish sources and our prayer on its own does not warrant a positive conclusion regarding the use of the psalm.

4. AD HORAS DIEI ORATIO COMMUNIS (AB 117)

Two formularies of the *oratio communis* are given in the Antiphonary. The first and more extensive formulary (AB 40 – 56) follows two collects *ad matutinum* (AB 38 – 39) at the end of the set of prose collects for the hours. This set of collects also includes special intercessions for peace, identical in form with those of the *oratio communis*, after two collects for the office of nightfall (AB 32 – 33). Just as the intercessions for peace were meant for the conclusion of the office of nightfall, so also those of the *oratio communis* (AB 40 – 56) must have come at the conclusion of the morning office. The second and much briefer formulary of the *oratio communis* (AB 117) is found between the *Gloria in excelsis* and a mixed collection of prayers for certain hours, in the third section of the Antiphonary. This second formulary, as its title indicates, was meant for use at the day hours.

There was a certain development of the *oratio communis* between the time of Columban and the end of the seventh century. Columban speaks of only one formulary of intercessory prayers and he attaches it, exclusively, it appears, to the day hours:

> Per diurnas terni psalmi horas pro operum interpositione statuti sunt a senioribus nostris, cum versiculorum augmento intervenientium pro peccatis primum nostris, deinde pro omni populo christiano, deinde pro sacerdotibus et reliquis deo consecratis sacrae plebis gradibus, postremo pro elemosinas facientibus, postea pro pace regum, novissime pro inimicis.[34]

The seven classes (including the 'class' *pro peccatis nostris*) named by Columban are readily recognizable in the long formulary found in the Antiphonary.[35] It is this long formulary of intercessory versicles (and prayers) which, according to Columban, was added to the daily hours, not the short formulary, which he does not mention and which in any case caters for only three classes: *pro peccatis nostris, pro abbate nostro,* and *common oroit dun.*[36] If we were to ignore the evidence of the Antiphonary and rely exclusively on Columban's text, strictly interpreted, we would be forced to conclude that the long formulary in AB 40 – 56 was meant for the day hours and the short formulary meant possibly as 'a short alternative set for occasional use'.[37] But Columban's treatment of his subject, here and elsewhere in the same chapter VII of his Rule, is summary in the extreme, and there is a danger of interpreting his words too rigidly. I should imagine that if the daily hours had their intercessory versicles in Columban's day, surely and *a fortiori* these must also have been found in the morning office.[38] The development which took place during the course of the seventh century included not only the addition of further intercessions, but also the restriction of the long formulary to the morning office and the selection of a very few intercessions for the day hours.

The short formulary is specially suitable for the day hours because of its brevity and special content. It is introduced by a series of versicles not found in the long formulary and then it includes the three aforementioned intercessions for the community, the versicles and collects for which have been extracted from the long formulary. It is concluded by the Lord's Prayer, which does not figure in the long formulary.[39] It is, therefore, a self-contained unit of prayer which has the daily needs of the community in mind. The general supplications for the Church and the world, which formed the substance of the diaconal litany, were reserved for the morning office.

We have considered the day hours together on the basis of Columban's distinction between the three night offices with their extensive psalmody and the *horae diurnae* with their three psalms each. It is probable that Columban was talking about the same day hours as we find a century later in the Antiphonary and in other Irish sources. We find a full description of the psalms used in these hours in the *Navigatio S. Brendani*. The psalms chosen for the office of prime (*secunda* in the Antiphonary) and for the morning office are highly traditional and confirm the authentic nature of the office described in the *Navigatio*, while those chosen for the other hours are particularly suitable to the character of each particular hour, as understood in the tradition of the Church. The collects also developed the themes peculiar to each hour and can compare in this respect to the prayers for the day hours in the Ambrosian and Spanish rites. Each hour was concluded by a short formulary of intercessory versicles and collects for the community, and by the Lord's Prayer.

CHAPTER TWENTY-TWO

NIGHTFALL AND MIDNIGHT OFFICES

These two offices have a basic structural similarity, but they also have some distinctive features and we will consider them in turn.

I. THE OFFICE OF NIGHTFALL

The structure of this office, known as *initium noctis* or *duodecima*,[1] was as follows:

1. Twelve Psalms
2. Collect
3. Devotional appendix:
   a. Intercessions for peace
   b. Apostles' Creed
   c. Our Father

We will again take each of these parts in turn and consider what they entailed.

1. *Twelve Psalms*

The canonical number of twelve psalms which, according to Columban, was said at this office, had its original source in the Egyptian evening office.[2] We have seen that in Ireland the psalms were divided into groups of three (a *chora*) and that the silent prayer after each psalm took the form of a versicle, *Deus in adiutorium....* The psalms were probably chanted *currente psalterio* and were probably also followed by two readings.

2. *Collectio ad initium noctis* (AB 22, 32, 33)

The collects express, even more fully than those assigned to vespers (AB 21, and 31), themes which are characteristic of the evening prayers in the liturgies of East and West. This transference to the monastic evening office of themes derived from the cathedral evening office (vespers) is a practice also found in the Ambrosian and Spanish rites, where the collects used at compline continue to express the evening themes more proper to the collects of vespers.[3]

We find here, first of all, a classical reference to the occasion of the office of nightfall:

Evolutis nunc diei temporibus, nocturnisque spatiis supervenientibus (33).

As night comes down, we pray to God the source of light:

Deus qui inextricabiles tenebras inluminas noctium, densitatem caliginis inlustrans (32),

and we ask him for help to overcome the works of darkness and to act in accordance with his commandments:

ut suppleti divinis sensibus tenebrarum operibus renuntiare possimus (33). —

corda nostra in opere mandatorum tuorum, te oramus, domine, custodias.

The Church's daily struggle with the works of darkness is one of the great evening themes, a struggle that is carried on in the awareness of the presence of Christ, the light of the world, in our time, even at night.[4]

3. *Devotional Appendix*

The office of nightfall was concluded by intercessory prayers for peace (AB 34: *Ad pacem celebrandam*), followed by the Apostles' Creed (AB 35) and the Our Father (AB 36).[5] We find a very similar custom in Spanish monastic communities:

Isidore, *Reg. mon. 6*: Ante somnum autem, sicut mos est, peracto completorio, VALEDICTIS INVICEM FRATRIBUS, cum omni cautela et silentio requiescendum est.[6]

Fructuosus, *Reg. mon. 2*: Nocturno igitur tempore prima noctis hora . . . consummanda in Ecclesia est. Deinde VALEFACIENS INVICEM, et reconciliationi ac satisfactioni alterutrum insistentes, LAXANT MUTUO DEBITA, et pietate prona, qui segregati a coetu fraterno ob negligentiam suam fueraṅt merentur indulgentia. Cum demum pergentes ad cubilia, atque in unum cuncti coeuntes OB PERFEC-TIONEM PACIS ET REORUM ABSOLUTIONEM, cantatis tribus psalmis iuxta morem cum laude et benedictione, SYMBOLUM CHRISTIANAE FIDEI communi omnes reci-tent voce, ut fidem suam puram coram Domino ostendentes, si quod dubium non est fieri vel accidere, ut nocturno quisquam tempore evocetur a corpore, commen-datam iam fidem suam et expiatam ab omni scandalo conscientiam proferat ante Deum. Post deinde . . . pergat ad lectulum suum, ubi tacite ORATIONI INSISTENS, psalmosque recensens, ultimo orationem suam quinquagesimi psalmi recita-tionem atque orationem consummet.[7]

The first part of the rite described by Fructuosus comprised two parts: the exchange of the peace, followed by mutual forgiveness and reconcilia-tion. At Bangor, these parts reappear in the form of intercessory versicles and short collects, first of all for the forgiveness of sins (*primum pro peccatis nostris!*, as in the *oratio communis*) and secondly for peace:

Iniuste egimus. . . (ps.105,6). — Redemisti nos, domine, deus veritatis, in tuo sancto sanguine; nunc adiuva nos in omnibus, Ihesu Christe, que regnas.

Pax multa diligentibus. . . (ps.118,165). — Pax tua, domine rex caelestis, per-maneat semper in visceribus nostris, ut non timeamus a timore nocturno.

The Irish probably derived this rite from Spain,[8] but they fashioned it to suit their own peculiar form of intercessory prayers. They also introduced a change in the meaning of the rite. Where Fructuosus speaks of the mutual reconciliation and forgiveness of the monks, and their exchange of peace, the Bangor rite is a confession of sinfulness made *to Christ* and a supplication of his pardon, his help and his peace. Indeed, as G. Morin has pointed out, the Bangor formulae do not necessarily presuppose the rite of peace at all;[9] this, however, clearly existed in Spain. The reference to ps.90,5 in the second prayer adapted it to the occasion, but it does not necessarily mean that ps.90 was actually said.

The Apostles' Creed, with its peculiarly Irish text,[10] was probably recited by all together, as it was by the community of Fructuosus. The final prayer of the day was the Our Father.

II.   THE OFFICE OF MIDNIGHT

The structure of the midnight office was as follows:

1. Twelve psalms
2. Hymn
3. Collect

We again find the same canonical number of psalms as for the office of nightfall, but there was no such Egyptian precedent for this midnight office as there was for the first night office. Indeed the Irish monastic rules stand quite apart from the common tradition of monasticism with their double nocturnal vigil, at midnight (*medium noctis, nocturnum, midnocht*) and towards morning (*matutinum, vigilia, iarmérge*). Columban, the *quidam catholici* spoken of by him, the *Regula cuiusdam Patris*, and Ailbe are all in agreement on this. The number of psalms assigned to midnight by all of them is twelve; the number of psalms for the morning vigil varies, but in all of them it can only be described as gigantic.

In the East in the fourth century the office of midnight was organized as a public celebration in monastic communities of men and women. We find it described by St Athanasius and St Basil,[11] and it appears clearly as the institutionalization of the private midnight prayer which fervent Christians had been accustomed to practice. This new public office was quite independent of the Egyptian morning vigil, which was adopted by the monks of Palestine and Antioch and united, by way of introduction, to the morning office of the cathedral. The midnight prayer of Athanasius and Basil was strictly a *midnight* office; it consisted for the most part of an extended psalmody and was separated from the morning office by a period of sleep. Their morning office, in turn, corresponded, both as regards the time of its celebration and the prayers it contained, to the cathedral morning office of the time as we know it from contemporary documents. There were, therefore, two types of vigil: the *morning* vigil of the Egyptian and Palestinian monks and the *midnight* vigil of the communities of St Basil and St Athanasius. The two traditions are combined in the Irish office, which has a midnight vigil of twelve psalms and a morning vigil with its prolonged psalmody, which is followed by certain psalms and other prayers which were originally proper to the morning office of the cathedral ('lauds').

In the West the monastic vigil is regularly, in spirit at least, a *midnight* office, and it is recognizable as such where it is followed by a period of sleep until the time for the morning office arrives, as in the *Regula Magistri* and in Isidore's Rule.[12] St Fructuosus of Braga, however, was not content with the midnight office and he instituted another office *ante mediam noctem* and added a third after it:

Reg. mon. 3: Ita ante mediam surgentes noctem duodenos per choros recitent psalmos, secundum consuetutinem... Post pausantes paululum medium noctis persolvant officium, ubi quatuor responsoria sub ternorum psalmorum divisione concinentur. Sic post mediam noctem, si hiemis tempus est, sedentibus cunctis, unus medio residens releget librum.... Ita denique duodenis iterum cantatis psalmis adeant cubilia, paululum quiescentes, gallicinio iam sonante, recitatis tribus psalmis cum laude et benedictione sua matutinum celebrent sacrificium.[13]

Fructuosus's midnight office (*medium noctis officium*) corresponds to Isidore's *vigiliae*;[14] both are midnight vigils, like the Irish midnight office. Fructuosus's *matutinum sacrificium* corresponds to Isidore's *matutina officia*: unlike the Irish morning vigil (Columban's *matutinum*), this was not a vigil but the cathedral morning office. The trebling of the midnight office by Fructuosus bears no relationship, therefore, to the twofold Irish vigil of midnight and morning.

At Arles, the office of nocturns (*nocturni*), with its extensive number of *psalmi dicti* (*i.e.*, psalms recited without antiphons and generally without alleluia), was followed immediately by matins (*matutini*) and prime. The office of matins was parallel to the cathedral morning office of the Ambrosian rite. The entire office of nocturns and matins at Arles had as its ultimate model the Palestinian monastic liturgy, which resulted from the fusion of Egyptian monastic practice with urban and cathedral traditions in Palestine.[15] This model became known in Gaul through the writings of Cassian and indeed it was imitated in new foundations, notably at Marseilles and Lérins.[16]

The Irish office of matins (*matutinum*), a combination of monastic psalmody and cathedral morning prayers, belongs to the same tradition as the combined office of nocturns and matins at Arles, even though its distinct Irish character is revealed in a number of ways, not least by its staggering quantity of psalms. The Irish midnight office, on the other hand, belongs to the other and more universally observed tradition of *midnight* prayer. It is difficult to say whether or not the introduction of this midnight office into Ireland was due to any particular continental influence.[17] It may have been a purely native institution introduced to satisfy the many exhortations to midnight prayer found in the writings of the Fathers, and its psalmody fixed naturally at the canonical number of twelve psalms. The additional night office celebrated at cock-crow by the 'catholics' mentioned by Columban, an office which also had the required canonical number of psalms, must be regarded likewise as a native institution introduced for the same reason.

The motivation for the office of midnight and the themes associated with it are expressed in the hymn and in the collects. The hymn, *Mediae noctis tempus est*, is Gallican in origin and it was probably borrowed from Gaul by the Irish monks in the late sixth or seventh century as an appropriate hymn for their own midnight office. It opens with a general invitation to praise the 'perfect Trinity' at this midnight hour. Various events associated with 'this time' in the history of salvation are narrated and in each case the lesson is applied to the present community. First, there was the deliverance of Israel when the destroying angel brought death and destruction on the Egyptians; this is spiritually applied as follows:

> 6. Nos vero Israel sumus,
> laetamur in te, domine,
> hostem spernentes et malum,
> Christi defensi sanguine.

Next, the parable of the wise and foolish virgins is recalled and the future coming of the bridegroom at midnight is re-affirmed; this is another reason why we should watch at midnight:

> 10. Quare vigilemus sobrii,
> gestantes mentes splendidas,
> adventui ut Iesu
> digni curramus obviam.

Finally, Paul and Silas were delivered when, while bound in prison, they prayed at this hour. We are imprisoned also in this world and we should pray at this hour to be delivered from the bonds of sin and to be worthy of eternal life, where we may praise Christ our God forever.

In the collects (AB 23, 37, 57), midnight is portrayed as the hour of Christ's visitation, in which he will bring deliverance, joy and peace. It is the hour of the nativity of Christ (37), of the deliverance of Peter from prison through the power of Christ's visitation (23), and the hour when we are to expect the return of the bridegroom (57):

> Media nocte clamore facto:
> ut nos inveniamur parati sponso.[18]

CHAPTER TWENTY-THREE

MATINS

We have seen that this office consisted of two parts. The first was the extensive psalmody which was the sole object of Columban's attention when, in chapter VII of his Rule, he described this office, which he called *vigilia* or *matutinum*. This part was probably concluded by a collect, of which many examples are found in the Antiphonary under the heading *ad matutinam* (AB 24, 25, 26, 38, 39, 58, 60). The second part was that known in other early sources as *matutini, laudes matutinae*, or *sollemnitas matutina*. Most of the material in the Antiphonary was meant precisely for this part of the morning office at Bangor, and it belongs, in origin or at least inspiration, to the cathedral rather than to the monastic tradition.

Little further need be added to what we have already said about the psalmody which formed the major part of this office of matins. Its massive extent, ranging from twenty-four psalms on the ordinary nights of Summer to seventy-five psalms on the holy nights of Winter, is a distinctive Irish development of a type of psalmody which was first used in the Egyptian desert, whence it was eventually transplanted to southern Gaul and from there spread to Ireland. There would appear to be no immediate contact, however, between the nocturns of the monks at Arles and the matins-vigil described by Columban. Both represent an independent development of an original common tradition of psalmody.[1]

The collects, all of them Irish compositions, present a variety of ideas, but no real development of the classical morning themes. Some of them (AB 38, 39, 58, 60) draw directly on Scripture, notably on the psalms, without for all that being psalter collects in the strict sense. The psalms referred to or cited in these collects are: 4, 5, 45, 50, 62, 100, 112, 134, and 143. No apparent pattern, such as evidence for the existence of a number of specially chosen morning psalms, is discernible in these scriptural citations. A few of them do contain some reference to the early morning vigil or prayer (Sir.22, 8; ps.5,4; 62,1.7; 100,8), but in general they appear to reflect rather the extensive psalmody used in this office and possibly also the readings which followed the psalmody.

We find in these collects for matins allusions to many figures and themes which constituted the traditional substance out of which was fashioned, in manifold ways, the morning prayer of the Christian communities. We find, for example, references to cock-crow (AB 25), to the coming of day and the banishment of darkness (AB 26), to the morning vigil (AB 58). The community addresses its prayer at this hour to Christ, who is the true light (AB 26), who dwells on high and regards all things that happen on earth (AB 60), who is the hope and salvation, the life and strength of those who pray (AB 39). The community asks him for help (AB 24), light (AB 26), pardon for sins (AB 38), and strength to fight the battle and overcome sinners (AB 60). Of these prayers the rhythmical ones, which express a single insight in a simple and forceful way, are the best. One of them (AB 25) commemorates the tears of Peter at cock-crow and attaches intercessory value to them:

> Gallorum, Christ, cantibus,
> te deprecor, sonantibus:
> Petri ob quondam fletibus
> nostris intende praecibus.

Another (AB 26) is a request for the true light:

> Deus, qui pulsis tenebris
> diei lucem tribuis:
> adventum veri luminis
> tuis effunde famulis.

This last prayer expresses in capsule form the central idea of the morning prayer of the Church. But we do not find in these collects a development of the traditional themes comparable to that which we find in the morning collects of the other Western liturgies. The Irish preferred the poetic picture and the associations of scriptural verses to the laborious development of a liturgical prose style.

The second part of the office of matins, which for convenience we will call lauds, can be reconstructed from the order of collects given in the Antiphonary for the various components of this office. The basic structure was as follows:

1. The canticle *Cantemus Domino* and its collect
2. The canticle *Benedicite* and its collect
3. Psalms 148 – 150 and their collect
4. Gospel reading and its collect
5. Hymn and its collect
6. Commemoration of the martyrs

The *Gloria in excelsis* (AB 116) is also indicated as a hymn for matins and the *Te Deum* (AB 7) is also given as a hymn for Sundays, probably also for matins.

There are seven sets of collects for lauds in the Antiphonary. According to H. Schneider, this means that one set is provided for each day of the week and that the canticles *Cantemus* and *Benedicite* were used daily for lauds in Bangor in the seventh century.[2] But an examination of the collects themselves reveals that we cannot base a conclusion regarding the daily use of these canticles on the fact that there are seven sets of collects provided for them. In fact, if we take each set of collects as a formulary meant for a particular day, we find that four of the seven sets were meant for use on Sunday.

(a) First Set (AB 62 – 67), meant for Sunday:

184

AB 65 *Col. post evang.* Exultantes gaudio, ... ut diem dominicae resurrectionis nobis sollemniter celebrantibus, ... laetitiam praestare dignetur.

AB 66 *Super hymnum.* Sancte domine, inluminatio et salus vera credentibus, resurrectio dominicae claritatis...

(b) Third Set (AB 71 – 75), meant for Sunday:

AB 73 *Post laudate.* Deus noster, ... te adoramus, ut in hac vigilia sollemnitatis admissa pervenire praestas.

AB 74 *Post evangelium.* Dominicam, nostrae resurrectionis initium, venerantes....

(c) Fourth Set (AB 76 – 80), meant for Sunday:

AB 79 *Post evangelium.* Resurgentem in hoc diluculo dominum, deprecamur, ut et nos in vitam aeternam resurgamus.

AB 80 *Post hymnum.* Resurrectionem tuam, Christe, veneramur.

(d) Fifth Set (AB 81 – 87), meant for Sunday:

AB 85 *Post evangelium.* Diluculo lucis auctore resurgente, exultemus in domino devicta morte.

AB 86 *Post hymnum.* Lux orta est in luce prima, exordio dierum antiquo facta.

The other three sets of collects (AB 68 – 70; 88 – 90; 91 – 93) comprise only three collects each, for the two canticles and the *Laudate* psalms. They have no reference to any particular day and may have been meant for ordinary weekdays. In one of them there is a fleeting indication of this daily use:

AB 68 *Post canticum.* Deus, qui COTIDIE populum tuum iugo Aegyptiae servitutis absolvis....

The collects for the *laudate* psalms follow those given for the canticles in all seven sets. This is an indication of the daily use of the two canticles, because the *laudate* psalms were almost certainly in daily use. The two canticles are also found in the Turin Fragment (T), with two collects attached to each of them; these collects are included in two of the Sunday sets of collects in the Antiphonary.[3]

The canticles *Cantemus* and *Benedicite* were the most popular of all the canticles in the early Church, first in the Easter Vigil and later, from the fourth century, in the Sunday and weekday morning office in East and West.[4] Two other canticles are included with them in the Antiphonary: the canticle of Moses (Dt.32,1 – 43; AB 1) and the *Benedictus* of Zechariah (Lk.1,68 – 80; AB 4). The canticle of Moses, *Audite caeli*, had long enjoyed wide popularity in the liturgy, but the earliest known use of the *Benedictus* in the West is in Roman lauds in the fifth century and in the Ambrosian liturgical series of canticles which was completed between the fifth and seventh centuries.[5] It is interesting to observe that the four canticles found in the Antiphonary, and these only, are used in the second part of the morning office at Milan on Sundays and Feastdays. This part of the

Ambrosian morning office, now called lauds, corresponds to the second part of the morning office at Bangor. A comparison of the two reveals their striking similarity. We will give an outline of ordinary Sunday lauds at Milan[6] and set alongside it a possible reconstruction of lauds as celebrated at Bangor. At Milan the *Benedictus* (Lk.1) was replaced by *Audite caeli* (Dt.32) on the Sundays of Advent and on the feasts of the Circumcision and Epiphany.[7] The basis of our reconstruction of the Bangor lauds is provided by the series of collects which always occur in the same order; we can regard the sequence of these elements as certainly corresponding to the actual order of the office. We know also that the *Gloria in excelsis* was part of lauds, and other items of the Antiphonary, such as the *oratio communis* and the canticles of Moses and Zechariah, must also have figured in some part of lauds. These items are included in brackets and placed in the positions they occupy in Ambrosian lauds.

Milan	Bangor
Benedictus or *Audite caeli*	(*Benedictus* or *Audite caeli*)
Collect and *Cantemus*	*Cantemus* and collect
Collect and *Benedicite*	*Benedicite* and collect
Collect and pss.148 – 150	Pss.148 – 150 and collect
	Gospel and collect
Psalmus directus	
Gloria in excelsis	(*Gloria in excelsis*)
Hymn	Hymn and collect
Kyrie 12	(*Oratio communis*)
De ecclesia in baptist. —	
psall.I, Complet., Oratio	
De baptist. in aliud —	*De martyribus*
psall.II, Complet., Oratio	

The Gospel and its collect find no parallel in Ambrosian lauds. This is the Gospel of the resurrection, as can be concluded from collects *post evangelium*, all of which are invitations to rejoice and give thanks on account of the Lord's resurrection or to celebrate the day of his resurrection. This Gospel has been placed in an unusual position in the Irish office, in the centre of the (cathedral) morning office rather than before it. As J. Mateos has shown,[8] the office of the resurrection was originally a cathedral vigil celebrated at cock-crow and separated by a certain interval from the cathedral morning office which was celebrated at day-break. The cathedral vigil consisted essentially of three psalms or canticles, each of which was followed by a prayer; then the Gospel of the resurrection was read by the bishop, and this was followed by a procession to the Cross, to the accompaniment of hymns. The office was then concluded by another psalm and prayer. This special Sunday morning vigil has survived in one form or other in many rites, including the Ambrosian.[9] The Gospel of the resurrection is no longer found in this Sunday vigil at Milan, but it must have been an original part of the office there also. If it remained there in the seventh century, the Irish could well have taken it from its place in the vigil and introduced it into the second part (lauds) of their morning office. It was also part of the special Sunday vigil at Arles, as the first reading among the *six missae* which were added to nocturns on Sunday,[10] and it may have been from a source in southern Gaul that the Irish borrowed the idea.

Apart from the Gospel of the resurrection, there is a basic identity between the Ambrosian and Bangor office of lauds. The canticles *Benedictus* and *Audite caeli* and the hymn *Gloria in excelsis* probably occupied the same positions in the Bangor office as they did at Milan. The Gospel and its collect may have followed the psalms. The collect after the Gospel always takes the form of an invitation to praise and thanksgiving; for example:

> AB 74 Dominicam, nostrae resurrectionis initium, venerantes, trinitati deo nostro debitas laudes et grates unito referamus affectu. . . .

The response to this invitation may have been the *Te Deum*, which is indicated for Sunday use (AB 7 *Hymnus in die dominica*) and which occupied a similar position in matins at Arles, after the *laudate* psalms. However, the response may also be seen in the *Gloria in excelsis*. Or again, the Gospel and its collect may have come after the *Gloria in excelsis*, in which case the response of praise must be seen in the *Te Deum* and its collect rather than in the hymn, which on Sundays was *Spiritus divinae lucis*.

The *oratio communis* in its extended form (AB 40 – 56) corresponds to the litany used at Milan. And perhaps it is not forcing the parallel if we see in the commemoration of the martyrs, towards the end of the *oratio communis*, an imitation of the local devotions at Milan, the processions to the baptistries and their chants and prayers. The *psallendae* and prayers used in these processions are mainly intercessory. And in lauds and vespers of Saints' feasts the processions to the baptistries were replaced by a procession to the particular Saint's church or altar, accompanied by a psalm and a *psallenda*.[11]

The *Te Deum* was not part of the Ambrosian office until the fifteenth century. We are not told at what precise service it was used in Ireland, but it would have served a useful purpose in the morning office in the position it occupied at Arles. A comparison of Sunday lauds at Arles and at Bangor reveals the same basic structure that was also found at Milan, even though there was a more extensive use of the psalms at Arles:

Arles[12]	Bangor
Directaneus parvulus (ps.144)	
Confitemini (ps.117)	
Cantemus Domino	*Cantemus* and collect
Lauda anima mea Dominum (ps.145)	
Benedicite	*Benedicite* and collect
Pss.148 – 150	Pss.148 – 150 and collect
	Gospel and collect
Te Deum	*Te Deum* and collect
Gloria in excelsis	*Gloria in excelsis*
	Hymn and collect

The resemblance in the office of lauds between Arles and Bangor is not so complete as it is between Milan and Bangor; indeed both Bangor and Arles may depend immediately on Milan for this section of the office. We have seen that two collects for the canticles *Cantemus* and *Benedicite* in the Antiphonary correspond closely to the collects used for the same canticles at Milan. Since, however, the Irish probably derived these collects immediately from a Spanish source, we cannot use this parallelism as an argument for an immediate relationship with Milan. The fact, however, remains that the Irish did use collects after the canticles, while there is no mention of them at Arles. Then again, the canticles *Benedictus* and *Audite caeli* were not used at Arles; there is no mention in the Rules of Caesarius or Aurelian of a collect to follow the *laudate* psalms and no mention of a hymn, apart from the *Gloria in excelsis*. All of this as against the ultimate derivation of the office of lauds at Bangor from Arles.

The Bangor office of lauds varied somewhat according to the quality of the day. We will now consider these variations, in so far as we can discern them today.

1. SUNDAY LAUDS

This is the form we have outlined above, setting it alongside the lauds of Milan and Arles. It began with the chanting of canticles. The *Audite caeli* is provided with an invariable response, the repetition of the verse *Audite* after each section of the canticle. The *Benedictus* has neither a response nor an antiphon provided for it, but the two canticles *Cantemus* and *Benedicite* are provided with a number of antiphons (AB 99), some of which are rhythmical and some taken from the text of the canticles themselves. None of them agrees entirely with the antiphons found for the same canticles in the Ambrosian and Spanish rites.[13] The collects which followed each of these two canticles speak of the great deliverance of the people from the slavery of Egypt and of the three children from the fiery furnace, and ask Christ, redeemer and saviour (*salvator mundi*), to deliver his people from sin, from all the evil of this world and from the flames of hell, and to lead them to the promised land prepared for them.

The canticles were followed by the *laudate* psalms, which are chanted, as at Milan, under one antiphon, which is provided in AB 100:

De caelis dominum laudate,
psalterium iucundum immolate,
laudate eum in sono tubae.

The collects after the *laudate* psalms are generally based on the text of the psalms and sum up the praise of God contained in them. One collect, however, is strictly a morning prayer and compares, in this respect, with the Ambrosian collects before the same psalms. It is, once again:

188

AB 73 Deus noster, deus omnium animarum, te adoramus, ut in hac vigilia sollemnitatis admissa pervenire praestes, quousque tenebrae iniquitatis nostrae convertantur in lumine, sicut sol in meridie splendescit, salvator mundi qui regnas.

The Gospel was followed by its collect, which is an invitation to rejoice and give thanks on the Lord's day. It was followed possibly by the *Te Deum* and its collect, which again is a summary of the praise, adoration and supplication contained in that hymn, or by the *Gloria in excelsis*. The hymn on Sunday was *Spiritus divinae lucis*. The collects *post hymnum* are not based directly on this hymn, but there is a general thematic agreement between them and the hymn.[14]

The *oratio communis* followed. The collect *de martyribus*, included towards the end of the intercessory prayers, was probably preceded by an antiphon taken from among the four provided in AB 101 − 104. I have not met these antiphons elsewhere. One of them (AB 102) is taken from Apoc.7,14 (*Hii sunt qui venerunt...*) and in two of them we find, possibly, a hint of the *oratio communis*:

AB 103 In memoria martyrum tuorum, domine, et esto praecibus servorum tuorum, Christe.

AB 104 In invocatione sanctorum martyrum miserere, deus, supplicum tuorum.

Veneration of the martyrs and the desire for martyrdom are among the most striking features of early Irish spirituality, in view of the fact that martyrdom was unknown in Ireland itself. But this special regard for the martyrs fitted quite easily into the spirit of the Irish monastic movement, with its radical asceticism, its renunciation of the world and its quest for those 'deserts' where the ideal Christian life of prayer and penance could be pursued.[15]

In the Turin fragment the commemoration of the martyrs is followed by the *Te deum* and its collects.[16] This *may* have been its position in the office at Bangor as well, even though we have found another place for it in the structure of the office given above. One of the collects *ad matutinam* (AB 24) contains an evident reference to it:

Deus, SUBVENI omnibus
TE TER SANCTUM LAUDANTIBUS
unumque CONFITENTIBUS
sacris HYMNORUM CANTIBUS.

One might conclude from this collect that the *Te Deum* was placed after the long psalmody and readings of the morning vigil, a position which it also occupies in the Benedictine vigil. It appears, however, that the collect we have just cited is not a morning collect at all, that it has been placed by mistake among the morning collects and given a wrong title, and that it was originally meant to follow the *Te Deum*, in whatever position this may have been. All the elements of lauds at Bangor were provided with their own proper collects, and it is in lauds that the *Te Deum* must have been sung, either as a response to the Gospel and its collect or at the end of the office, where it is found in the Turin fragment.

2. SATURDAY LAUDS

It is highly probable that the canticles *Cantemus* and *Benedicite* preceded the *laudate* psalms on Saturday as well as Sunday. The three short sets of collects, each of which contains three collects (*post cantemus, post benedictionem puerorum, post laudate*), were surely meant for some day other than Sunday, if not indeed for daily use. The *Gloria in excelsis*, unlike the *Te Deum*, is not restricted to use on Sundays but is indicated simply for use in vespers and matins (AB 116), and it was probably in daily use. The hymn on Saturday was *Sacratissimi martyres* (AB 11). From these indications we get the following outline of Saturday lauds:

1. *Cantemus domino* with antiphon and collect
2. *Benedicite* with antiphon and collect
3. Pss.148 – 150 with antiphon and collect
4. *Gloria in excelsis*
5. *Sacratissimi martyres* (with collect?)
6. *Oratio communis fratrum*

3. DAILY LAUDS

It is possible, as we have seen, that the canticles and the *Gloria in excelsis* were used daily. The collects for the *laudate* psalms are in all cases preceded by those for the two canticles and this fact indicates that lauds always began with the canticles. The hymn for daily use probably varied, but *Hymnum dicat* was certainly used. In T it is given after the *Laudate* psalms and collects and it is provided with its own collect (T 12 = AB 84):

Cánticis spirituálibus delectáti,
hỳmnos, Chríste, consonántes cánimus tíbi,
quíbus túa maiéstas póssit placári,
obláta laúdis hóstia spiritáli,
qui regnas in secula seculorum.

This collect reflects the tone of the beginning and conclusion of *Hymnum dicat*:

1. Hymnum dicat turba fratrum, hymnum cantus personet; Christo regi concinentes laudem demus debitam.

65. Ante lucem, turba fratrum, concinamus gloriam, qua docemur nos futuros sempiterno saeculo.

69. Inmensamque maiestatem concinamus iugiter, ante lucem nuntiemus Christum regem saeculo.

The hymn *Praecamur patrem* was probably also used in lauds, and the hymns in honour of St Patrick, St Comgall, and St Camelacus may have been used on the festivals of these saints. But, notwithstanding a certain variation in the hymn, we can give the following outline for daily lauds:

1. *Cantemus domino* with antiphon and collect
2. *Benedicite* with antiphon and collect
3. Pss.148 – 150 with antiphon and collect
4. *Gloria in excelsis*
5. *Hymnum dicat* with collect
6. *Oratio communis fratrum*

This brings us to the end of our analysis of the various hours of the Irish monastic office as celebrated at Bangor. In our concluding chapter we will attempt to situate this office in the tradition of the Church and make some observations on its origin, affiliations and distinctive features.

CHAPTER TWENTY-FOUR

CONCLUSION

We have had recourse to the Rule of Columban, in particular to his description of the *cursus* of psalms in chapter VII of his Rule, as well as to such other partial descriptions of the Irish monastic office as have come down to us, in order to determine the context and structure in which the material contained in the Antiphonary was to be brought into use. The office celebrated at Bangor was a monastic office, and this monastic character is revealed above all through the Columbanian *cursus*. Much of the material contained in the Antiphonary, on the other hand, shows the influence of the cathedral tradition on the Irish monastic liturgy. The hymns and collects which we find here show how the Irish Church was being enriched, during the sixth and seventh centuries, both by Irish compositions which drew inspiration from the Western ecclesial tradition and by prayers borrowed directly from the cathedral Churches of the Continent. Indeed, we can be certain that the Irish monastic office incorporated from the beginning the cathedral morning and evening prayers introduced by the early missionaries. Development continued in this direction, as we have seen from our study of the collects for the various hours, which show a living contact with other Western liturgies, and from the similarity which we have noted between the 'cathedral' morning office (lauds) at Bangor and Milan.

The origin of the Irish *cursus* of psalms is something which has never been adequately explained. How far is it an indigenous creation? How much does it depend on Gaul? Answers to these questions will perhaps never be fully satisfactory, but we are not wholly deprived of the historical sources necessary to form a balanced judgement on the matter. It has become the accepted position to grant to Gaul a large measure of influence on the Irish in this area of the *cursus*, even to the point of acknowledging that the Irish *cursus* of psalms was 'substantially' derived from Gaul.

This view is not a new one. It was already advocated in the eighth century by the author of a much-cited document which set out an explanation of the origin and diffusion of the six chief *cursus* used at one time or another in the Church up to that time.[1] The author's attention was directed chiefly to describing the origin and diffusion of the *cursus Scottorum*, which he regarded as unique and distinctive. Briefly, his thesis is that this *cursus* was first used by St Mark and that it came down from him through Gregory of Nazianzen, Basil, Anthony, Paul and other Eastern monks; that Cassian introduced it to Lérins, where it was continued by Honoratus and by other disciples of that monastery who later became bishops, notably Caesarius of Arles, Lupus, and Germanus of Auxerre; that Patrick, taught by Lupus and Germanus, introduced it into

Ireland, where it was taken over by Comgall of Bangor, and that finally, through Vandilocus (?) and Columbanus, it was propagated in many new foundations of men and women in Ireland and abroad.

This artificial reconstruction of the origin of the Irish *cursus* has been pieced together out of various scraps of historical information and popular tradition. But when the account is stripped of its immaginative padding and reduced to its central contention, namely, that the Irish *cursus* is derived ultimately from Lérins through the mediation of the Saints mentioned, it seems to fit the historical situation and it has been regarded by many authorities as substantially true.[2]

We now have to consider whether this account is confirmed or borne out by the documents of the Irish and Gallican monastic liturgies. And here we encounter a major difficulty. St Caesarius of Arles says that his *ordo psallendi* depends in the main on the Rule of Lérins.[3] Yet, actual comparison between this *ordo* and the *cursus* of Columbanus shows that they have very little in common. There are some similarities between them, notably the custom of reciting psalms without antiphons in the Egyptian manner, the functional correspondence between Columban's *matutinum* and the *nocturni* celebrated at Arles (both are morning vigils, after the Egyptian-Palestinian fashion, rather than midnight vigils), and the distinction between vespers and *duodecima* (we take it that Columban included vespers among the day hours). Taking Columban's *cursus*, we notice what can only be described as 'substantial' differences from that of Arles, both as regards the number of hours (his midnight office is not found at Arles), the number of psalms in each hour, and the manner of their recitation (his *chora* is not a feature of the *ordo* at Arles). His *ordo* is closer in certain ways to what Cassian would have liked: three psalms for the day hours and the 'canonical number' of twelve psalms in two night offices. On the other hand, the *ordo* of Caesarius includes the all-night vigil between Friday and Saturday, which is not found in Columban. Judging by the similarities between the *ordo* of Columban and that of Arles, we can grant that there is some truth in the tradition of the dependence of the Irish *cursus* on a Gallican source. But when we take account of the differences between them and even allow for a certain independent development from a common basic nucleus, we can only conclude that Columban's *ordo* was not derived from the same source as that of Caesarius. The two are irreducible. Thus, if the *ordo* of Caesarius was in the truth derived from Lérins, the thesis of the eighth-century author of the *Ratio de cursus* is manifestly false.

The remote source of the Irish *cursus* may have to be sought in another Gallican centre which followed the Oriental model proposed by Cassian more closely than did Lérins. The tradition recorded in the seventh-century Patrician documents, to the effect that St Patrick received his ecclesiastical formation in a monastery founded by St Germanus at Auxerre, is regarded as authentic by some scholars.[4] But we know nothing of the office celebrated by that community at Auxerre and in any case it appears too remote to be a source of influence on sixth-century Irish monastic practice. Canon 18 of the second Council of Tours (567) offers more contemporary evidence and shows at the same time that Gallican usages were not all identical with that of Lérins. This canon deals especially with the number of psalms and their antiphons to be recited at matins by the community which served the basilica of St Martin and the other churches of the diocese. The number of psalms ranges from a minimum of twelve in summer to thirty in winter. More interesting still is the fact that the manner of reciting these psalms in winter quite possibly corresponds to the Columbanian *chora*-system: there is an antiphon to accompany each group of three psalms. From Easter to September, however, there were only two psalms to each antiphon. The canon speaks expressly of feast-day matins, but this may have been only by way of emphasis on these days and there probably were at least twelve psalms on ferial days also.[5] This canon also prescribes six psalms for sext and twelve for *duodecima*, which is apparently distinguished from vespers.[6] Though there were notable differences in the Irish system, it is interesting to see the parallel in the twelve psalms for *duodecima*, as in Columban's rule, and the thirty psalms for matins in winter, as in the Irish Rule of St Ailbe.

Much remains obscure in this area of the origins of the Irish office. Many of its distinctive features must have been native developments and it is not possible to find parallels for all of them in Gallican practice. It has been customary to grant to British monasticism a more or less significant role in the development of the Irish monastic system. Relations between Ireland and Wales appear to have been close in the sixth century, when the authority of St Gildas and St David was much esteemed.[7] But apart from the penitential literature, in which a certain influence on the Irish Penitentials by these British authorities has been recognized, we know nothing of the British liturgy, and its possible influence on the Irish must remain a matter of uncertainty.

The Irish Church in its origins was connected with Britain and Gaul, but the sphere of influence was broadened in the seventh century to include northern Italy and Spain. During this period, while the Irish missionaries were making their contribution to the life of the Church on the Continent, the Irish Church itself was being enriched by the new literature it received from the Continent. We have seen that some of the hymns and collects of the Antiphonary are based on northern Italian sources and must have been adapted for Irish liturgical use after the foundation of Bobbio at the beginning of the seventh century. The structure of lauds at Bangor also appears to be more closely modelled on the Ambrosian morning office than on that of Arles.

Certain features of the Irish office are peculiar to Ireland and can be recognized as native developments. Chief among these are the twofold vigil at midnight and early morning (some had an additional vigil at cock-crow) and the choice of three specially appropriate psalms for each of the day hours. There are many other peculiarities of detail, such as the gigantic number of *chorae* in matins, the use of rhythmical collects, the position of the Gospel of the resurrection in lauds, the use of collects after the Gospel and hymn, the use of versicles in the *oratio communis*, and suchlike. Many of these peculiar features are simply local variations and adaptations of the universal ecclesial tradition, and the office as a whole is deeply attached to that tradition. The eight hours observed at Bangor all have their antecedents in the continental tradition, as have the canonical number of twelve psalms for the offices of nightfall and midnight, and the traditional number of three psalms for each of the day hours. The collects for the hours continue to express the understanding of these hours in relation to the mystery of Christ; as commemorations of his passion and death (terce, sext, and none), as celebrations of his resurrection (lauds), or expectation of his return (midnight). They also express, in common with the other Western liturgies, the situation of the Church in the world, in the constant succession of time, which reveals the need for a constant effort of conversion and sanctification (collects for evening and nightfall), as well as the presence of salvation in hope through Christ, who is the light, hope, and salvation of his people (morning collects). The resurrection of Christ is given special prominence in the Sunday morning office, in accordance with ecclesial tradition. The daily concerns of the Church for the world and peoples' needs are expressed in the *oratio communis* of the morning office. All of these themes are genuinely ecclesial and traditional, even though their presence and expression in the Irish office are frequently original and peculiar. They show to what extent the monastic tradition, as represented by Columban's Rule, and the ecclesiastical tradition, as represented by the Antiphonary, were united in seventh-century Irish monasticism. The latter's life-style is still very much under the influence of the ascetic tradition of 'desert' monasticism, but this is now fully integrated into the life of the Church and enriched by the new devotional forms we have been studying, the hymns and prayers of the Antiphonary. Most of these have grown out of the tradition of the Western Church, or, rather, out of the encounter of that tradition with a new culture, where it is expressed and lived in a way that is congenial to the lyrical, somewhat wayward and unpredictable genius of the Irish spirit. The Gospel had spread beyond the Greco – Roman world and had arrived at the ends of the earth:

In fine mundi post tanta mysteria
adest salvator cum grandi clementia.[8]

NOTES

INTRODUCTION

1. A. A. King, *Liturgies of the Past* (London 1959) 224, 236.

2. K. Gamber, for example, describes it as 'das (auf eine gallikanische Vorlage zurückgehende) irische Antiphonar': *Codices*, 82.

3. Cf. J. Hennig, 'Old Ireland and her Liturgy', in: *Old Ireland*, ed. R. McNally (Dublin 1965) 65 – 67. Recently there has also been a renewal of interest in the Hiberno-Latin biblical commentaries which have survived from the seventh century and following. A catalogue of these Irish works, composed in the seventh and eighth centuries and most of which are still unedited, has been made by B. Bischoff, 'Wendepunkte in der Geschichte der lateinischen Exegese im Frühmittelalter', in: *Mittelalterliche Studien* I (Stuttgart 1966) 205 – 273, and more recently by M. McNamara, 'A Plea for Hiberno – Latin Biblical Studies', *The Irish Theological Quarterly* 39 (1972) 337 – 353.

4. Warren II 72 – 75. The sources indicated are mainly scriptural, but some of the Eucharistic antiphons are found in Gallican, Ambrosian and Spanish books.

5. E. Bishop, 'Liturgical Note', in: *The Book of Cerne*, ed. Kuypers (Cambridge 1902) 234 – 283.

6. G. Manz, *Ausdrucksformen der lateinischen Liturgiesprache* (Beuron 1941).

7. Cf. E. Bishop, 'Spanish Symptoms', in: *Liturgica Historica* (Oxford 1918) 165 – 210. Here he summed up and added to the results of his *Liturgical Note*.

8. Cf. J. N. Hillgarth, 'Visigothic Spain and Early Christian Ireland', PRIA, vol. 62, Section C, no. 6 (1962) 167 – 194.

9. See the fine study by Aubrey Gwynn, 'The Irish Monastery of Bangor', *The Irish Ecclesiastical Record* 74 (1950) 388 – 397. For Bangor's contribution to the growth of the Irish literary tradition, see R. Flower, *The Irish Tradition* (Oxford 1947) 1 – 40.

10. The MS is fully described in Warren I, *Introduction*. Cf. also F. Cabrol, 'Bangor (Antiphonaire de)', DACL II 1 (1910) 183 – 185; Kenney, *Sources*, 707 – 712; Lowe, CLA III (1938) 311. They describe the MS from the point of view of palaeography, structure and composition, contents, time and place of composition. The date of its composition is determined by the last item it contains, a hymn commemorating the first fifteen abbots of Bangor and written during the tenure of office of the fifteenth abbot, Cronán (680 – 691). Kenney points out that this means of dating is not absolutely foolproof, since the hymn could conceivably be later or earlier than the other contents of the MS; but he acknowledges that the margin of error cannot be very great on either side of 680 – 691, since the 'script, ornamentation, abbreviations and orthography are Irish, and are not inconsistent with a seventh-century date' (*Source*, 707). The MS was transferred from Bangor to Bobbio at an unknown date and was taken to Milan in 1606 by Cardinal Federico Borromeo, where it is now preserved in the *Biblioteca Ambrosiana, C. 5 inf.*

11. L. A. Muratori, *Anecdota Ambrosiana* IV (Padua 1713) 119 – 159; *Opera Omnia* XI 3 (Arezzo 1770) 217 – 251 (PL 72, 579 – 606). The title *Antiphonarium Benchorense* given to it by Muratori has been retained in all subsequent editions, even though it is entirely inadequate. For other editions, cf. Kenney, *Sources*, 707.

12. See the abbreviation 'AB' in our list of sources. The first volume is a facsimile edition

with a literal transcription and numerous footnotes which draw attention to the various handwritings and other peculiarities of the text. This is preceded by an introduction (v – xxvii) in which the editor gives a description of the MS and treats of its birthplace, date and history, its script and contents. In the second volume he gives an emended text (1 – 33) and an introduction (ix – xxxix) which deals with the litrugical use of the MS and the biblical text used in it. He also notes 'traces of Eastern origin and connection', (xxii – xxviii), which passed to Ireland through a Gallican channel, and 'traces of Hispano – Gallican influence' (xxvi – xxviii). In his notes on the various items (35 – 82) he occasionally points out the occurrence of the same formula in other Irish or English liturgical or devotional books, but none of them is traced to earlier souces.

13. C. Blume, *Hymnodia Hiberno-Celtica saeculi V – IX*: AH 51 (1908) 259 – 364.

14. E. Franceschini, *L'Antifonario di Bangor*: Testi e documenti di storia e di letteratura latina medioevale IV (Padova 1941). Franceschini criticises Warren's emended text for departing too much from the original , but he recognises the excellence of Warren's facsimile edition — 'una esatissima edizione paleographica del testo' (iv). In his introduction he speaks a number of times (vii – ix) about earlier sources for some of the texts found in the Antiphonary. In particular, he says of the 129 items it contains: 'parecchi di essi ci sono stati tramandati anche da altre fonti, talora più antiche e più autorevoli; altre invece devono la loro conservazione a questo solo manoscritto. Notevole, fra i primi, l'inno attribuito a S. Illario di Poitiers' (viii – ix). In fact, however, the Antiphonary is the earliest MS authority for the *Hymnum dicat*. What the 'many' other items are which are found in other earlier sources he does not say.

15. A. Wilmart and L. Brou, *The Psalter Collects from V – VIth century Sources*: HBS 83 (1949) 230 – 235. Most of the collects in question were meant to follow the *laudate* psalms, and none of them is a psalter collect in the strict sense. In certain Irish psalters we find some of these same collects after each group of fifty psalms, the psalter being divided into 'three fifties'; they are evidently out of place after pss.50 and 100. cf. H. M. Bannister, 'Irish Psalters', *The Journal of Theological Studies* 12 -(1910 – 1911) 280 – 284; L. Brou, *op. cit.*, 236 – 237.

16. W. Meyer, 'Das turiner Bruckstück der ältesten irischen Liturgie', *Nachrichten von . . . Göttingen.* Phil. – hist. Kl. 1903, 163 – 214. The MS, indicated 'T' in our list of sources, is: Turin, *Bibl. naz., Cod. 882 no. 8* (*olim*: F. IV. 1 Fasc. 9).

17. CLA IV (1947) 454.

18. The scribe of T drew on two sets of collects which we find in a slightly more amplified form in AB 62 – 67 (prose collects) and AB 81 – 87 (rhythmical collects), and he attached each collect to its appropriate canticle, or hymn. He follows the order found in AB, but he inserts a few rhymthical collects not found in the latter and omits the *post evangelium* and *post hymnum* collects found in AB 65 – 66 and 85 – 86. It appears that he had a number of distinct *libelli* before him: a collection of canticles and hymns similar to AB 1 – 15, a set of rhythmical collects similar to AB 81 – 87, and a set of prose collects similar to AB 62 – 67.

19. W. C. Bishop, 'A Service Book of the seventh Century', *The Church Quarterly Review* 37 (1894) 337 – 363.

20. L. Gougaud, 'Celtiques (Liturgies)', DACL II 2, 3014 – 3018; *Christianity*, 329 – 334. See also W. Godel, 'Irishches Beten in frühen Mittelalter', *Zeitschrift f. kath. Theologie* 85 (1963) 273 – 281.

21. Gougaud, 'Celtiques (Liturgie)', *ibid.*, 2992.

22. F. Cabrol, 'Bangor (Antiphonaire de)', DACL II 1, 183 – 191.

23. Kenney, *Sources*, 712. This is also Cabrol's opinion: 'Beaucoup de singularités . . . s'expliquent du moment que ce libellus est le livre particulier d'un abbé; les lacunes que l'on y remarque ou la présence de telle prière peuvent être le fait de ses gouts personels' (*loc. cit.*, 190). The purpose of the Turin fragment (T) must have been identical, since it

also includes canticles, hymns and collects. But, unlike AB, all of its material was meant for the office, and it does not contain such singular items as AB 96 *Collectio super hominem qui habet diabolum*, or suchlike.

CHAPTER ONE

1. J. H. Bernard and R. Atkinson, *The Irish Liber Hymnorum*, 2 vols: HBS 13 – 14 (London 1898).

2. ILH I 66 – 83; AH 51, 275 – 278. The hymn, which treats of the great themes of the creation and fall of the angels, the creation of the world, the fall and restoration, the last judgement, heaven and hell, is regarded as being with reasonable probability a genuine work of St Columcille. Cf. Kenney, *Sources*, 264; Szövérffy, *Analen*, 145 – 146.

3. ILH I 162 – 183; II 53 – 80, 223 – 235; other MSS in Kenney, *Sources*, 426. The *Amra* 'can with certainty be ascribed to the time it says it was composed, namely the death of St Columcille in the year 597. It is the oldest definitely datable work in Irish literature' (D. A. Binchy, 'The Background of Early Irish Literature', *Studia Hibernica* 1, 1961, 18).

4. ILH I 43 – 45; AH 51, 330. The author was probably the Colmán mac Murchon who, according to the Annals, was abbot of Moville and died in 736. The hymn is 'a fine example of Hiberno-Latin versification, with rich trisyllabic rimes and frequent use of assonances, alliterations and harmonies' (Kenney, *Sources*, 269).

5. ILH I 32 – 34; AH 51, 305 – 306. Cúchuimne was a monk at Iona and died in 747. His hymn is regarded as 'the finest example extant of Hiberno-Latin versification' (Kenney, *Sources*, 270). The stanzas consist of couplets of 8p + 7pp (cf. *infra*, p.200, n.12), with trisyllabic rhyme binding the couplets and internal rhyme in the second part:

Cantemus in omni die
concinnantes VARIE,
conclamantes Deo dIGNUM
HYMNUM sanctae MARIAE.

6. The learned class are variously described in the sources as *draoi* (druid, often in the pejorative sense of magician, because in pre-Christian times they also had priestly functions), *fili* (seer or poet), *breitheamh* (judge), or *bard* (poet or minstrel). Originally there were no such distinctions of functions, because the entire complex of native learning, which was held together by oral tradition, was the business of the *filid*. On the Order of Poets (*filid*), their special training, their number at any given time, their privileged place in society, and their relationship to the kings, cf. D. A. Binchy, 'The Background of Early Irish Literature', *Studia Hibernica* 1 (1961) 7 – 18, and J. Carney, 'Society and the Bardic Poet', *Studies* 62 (1973) 233 – 250.

7. Cf. D. Green, 'Early Irish Literature', in: *Early Irish Society*, ed. M. Dillon (Dublin 1954) 22 – 35. The expression 'rhythmical patterns' was used elsewhere by Professor Green to describe this early verse: 'In the earlier Irish literature it is often hard to say whether we are dealing with prose or verse, because we do not find regular lines or rhyme — only rhythmical patterns and alliteration when the language is heightened' ('The religious Epic', in: *Early Irish Poetry*, ed. J. Carney, Cork 1965, 73). For further description of this accentual verse, with numerous examples, see G. Murphy, *Early Irish Metrics* (Dublin 1961) 2 – 7, and *infra*, pp. 76 – 77.

8. See J. Carney, 'Three Old Irish accentual Poems', *Eriu* 22 (1971) 23 – 80. These poems are examples of the lyric poetry usually ascribed to monastic milieu. Professor Carney, however, thinks that two of these poems on the coming of summer 'are a type of nature poetry belonging exclusively to the native tradition, and would appear to owe nothing to Christian influences' (*ibid.*, 41). If his judgement is correct, the accepted view regarding the introduction of rhyme into Irish poetry will have to be revised. But even he grants that 'in the remote prehistoric period rhyme would hardly have existed as a systematic feature of verse; indeed, it is absent in a functional sense in what are probably the oldest of the Leinster poems . . . . As Irish poetry developed rhyme made continual inroads on the function of alliteration' (*ibid.*,55).

9. The monastery of Bangor appears to have been foremost as a centre of historical studies in the seventh century and the earliest Irish Chronicle seems to have been written there. On this historical work and its devices, cf. R. Flower, *The Irish Tradition* (Oxford 1947) 1 – 40; K. Hughes, *Early Christian Ireland: Introduction to the Sources* (London 1972) 99 – 148.

10. G. Murphy, *Early Irish Lyrics, eighth to twelfth Century* (Oxford 1956).

11. 'In ancient Ireland . . . verse was the commonest, one might say the common literary medium; not only that, but "the art" *par excellence*, so that *dán* or *ceárd* can be used as synonym for *filidheacht* in the sense of "poetry". The man of letters was a poet; if not in all cases an imaginative one, at least a competent versifier . . . . Once the strict metres had been adopted they were applied to almost every subject thought worthy of study and literary expression, so that we have poems didactic, religious, lyrical, humorous, narrative of various kinds. We have in verse not only native works in history, genealogy, law, toponymy, grammar, theology, but also renderings of Latin and Greek (or at any rate ultimately Greek) treaties on geography, history, biblical exegesis and Latin grammar' (E. Knott, *Irish Classical Poetry*, Dublin 1960, 15 – 16).

12. In the area of the structure of Latin rhythmical verse I have found D. Norberg, *Introduction à l'étude de la versification latine médiévale* (Stockholm 1958), especially helpful. Among other things, I will borrow his formula for describing the metre of rhythmical verse; for example, the rhythmical 'iambic dimeter', or line of eight syllables ending in a proparoxytone word, is indicated as 8pp; the rhythmical 'trochaic tetrameter catalectic', or line of fifteen syllables divided by a caesura into two parts (eight syllables ending in a paroxytone and seven syllables ending in a proparoxytone) is indicated as 8p + 7pp.

13. The best general survey of Western hymnody is Szövérffy's *Analen*. For the dating of Spanish hymns, in particular, I rely on the lists drawn up by him, *loc. cit.*, 150 – 151, 179, 247 – 248, 343 – 344, 385.

CHAPTER TWO

1. A. Feder, *S. Hilarii Opera* IV: CSEL 65 (1916) 217 – 223; also AH 51, 264 – 265; W. Bulst, *Hymni Latini Antiquissimi* (Heidelberg 1956) 133 – 135; other editions indicated by Bulst, p. 197.

2. For the external evidence of favour of Hilary's authorship, cf. A. Feder, 'Studien zu Hilarius von Poitiers III', *Sitzungsberichte der kais. Akad. d. Wiss. in Wien*. Phil. – hist. Kl 169 (1912) 76 – 77; J. H. Bernard, ILH II 126.

3. J. H. Bernard and R. Atkinson, LLH I ix – xiii; II 126.

4. C. Blume, AH 51, 269 – 271.

5. A. S. Walpole, 'Hymns attributed to Hilary of Poitiers', *The Journal of Theological Studies* 6 (1905) 601 – 603; *Early Latin Hymns* (Cambridge 1922) 1 – 15.

6. A. Feder, 'Studien zu Hilarıus', *loc. cit.*, 68 – 80.

7. Kenney, *Sources*, 252.

8. Both employ the archaic type of trochaic tetramater catalectic, which permitted the use of spondees in every foot save the seventh, while the classical type, found, for example, in Prudentius' *Cath*.IX, forbade the use of spondees in the first, third and fifth feet. Again both *Hymnum dicat* and *Adae carnis* agree in observing the dipody law which forbade 'impure endings', that is, it forbade the use of a spondaic word or of a word ending in a spondee to begin the second half of the first and third dipody. Cf. W. Meyer, *Gesammelte Abhandlungen* II (Berlin 1905) 346 – 348.

9. Cf. A. Feder, 'Studien zu Hilarius', *loc. cit.*, p. 78.

10. Regarding the Irish liking for the *Hymnum dicat*, cf. J. H. Bernard, ILH II 127 – 128.

11. Warren II 37.

12. W. Meyer, 'Das turiner Bruckstück der ältesten irischen Liturgie', *Nachrichten von ... Göttingen.* Phil. – hist. Ki. 1903, 207 – 208; 'Die drei arezzaner Hymnen des Hilarius von Poitiers und etwas über Rhythmus', *ibid.*, 1909, 423.

13. M. Simonetti, 'Studi sull'innologia popolare cristiana dei primi secoli', *Atti dell'Accad. naz. dei Lincei.* Memorie, classe di scienze morali, storiche e filologiche, serie VIII, vol. IV, fasc. 6 (Roma 1952) 363 – 365.

14. Meyer's reasoning is not lacking in obscurity. In 'Das turiner Bruckstück', *Nachrichten* 1903, 209, he states that 'der trockene, etwas unbeholfere Ausdruck weist in späte Ziet, ebenso die Metrik', and he refers to his study in the same number of the *Nachrichten*, 'Ein Kapitel spätester Metrik' (*Gesamm. Abhandl.* II 342 – 365), where he distinguishes four types of trochaic tetrameter catalectic, of which the regular archaic type is used in *Hymnum dicat*. But he seems to have overlooked the fact that *Adae carnis* of Hilary belongs to exactly the same type. He clarified his position in 'Die drei arezzaner Hymnen', *Nachrichten* 1909, 423, by pointing out an important metrical distinction between the two hymns: in *Hymnum dicat* there is no secondary caesura in the first half-line, while this is a structural law in *Adae carnis*, so that 'in dem 3. Hymnus des Hilarius und in diesem Hymnus "Hymnum dicat" ist also ein und dieselbe Zeile ganz verschieden behandelt. ... Schon deswegen habte ich es für unmogliche, dass Hilarius von Poitiers den Hymnus "Hymnum dicat turba fratrum" gedichtet hat'.

15. Meyer, *Gesamm. Abhandl.* II, 346.

16. Simonetti, 'Studi', 363: 'Esaminando la compagine stilistica dell' inno (*Hymnum dicat*), vediamo quanto profondamente esse sia diversa da quella degl'inni ilariani: quanto in quelli la forma è tormentata, con continue capricciose trasposizioni e inversioni di termini, tanto in questo la forma è piana e semplice, senza forzature, senza inzappamenti faticosi di expressioni l'una nell'altra'. He further points out that in *Hymnum dicat* the main caesura divides the line not only metrically but also syntactically, whereas in *Adae carnis* the two parts of the line are frequently required together to complete the sense. He concludes, *ibid.*, 365: 'le profonde divergenze stilistiche fra l'*Hymnum dicat* e gli inni ilariani, unite alla divergenza nella versificazione colta del Meyer, mi sembrano tali da far ritenere quasi disperata la possibilità di attribuire l'inno in questione ad Ilario'.

17. A. Feder, 'Studien zu Hilarius', *loc. cit.*, 88 – 90.

18. M. Simonetti, 'Studi', *loc. cit.*, 456 – 467. That the final stanza is to be taken as a ritornello is by no means clear; it has, however, been regarded as a later interpolation by Atkinson (ILH II xii – xiii), Meyer ('Das turiner Bruckstück', *loc. cit.*, 206), Blume (AH 51, 265) and Feder (CSEL 65, 223: edited within parentheses). Simonetti attaches great importance to the ritornello as an Irish symptom — 'elemento tipicamente irlandese, quasi mai riscontrato sul continente' ('Studi', *loc. cit.*, 459) — and he regards it as a clear sign of Oriental influence on the Irish, since Oriental hymnody alone furnishes adequate models for it (*ibid.*, 474 – 5).

19. Simonetti, 'Studi', 463 – 464.

20. Szövérffy, *Analen*, 157; *s. a.*, 'Hymnology', *New Catholic Encyclopedia 7 (1966) 290*: 'a Gallican hymn, wrongly attributed to Hilary of Poitiers'; W. Bulst, *Hymni latini antiquissimi*, 18: 'Seine Zuschreibung an Hilarius ebenso unhistorisch ist wie die in irischen Handschriften daran geknupften Legenden. . . . Dass ein auf dem Continent verschollener Hymnus in irischer Überlieferung allein erhalten ist, besagt nicht mehr als dass Verlust und Erhaltung zufällig einmal zusammengetroffen sind. Die Zuschreibung an Hilarius bewahrt noch eine Erinnerung an continentale Herkunft. . . . Seine Entstehung lässt sich im 5. Jahrhundert in Gallien vermuten'.

21. Bede, *De arte metrica* 23 (PL 90, 173).

22. The others are: Prudentius, *Cathemerinon* IX (*Da puer plectrum choraeis*); Sedulius, *A solis ortus cardine* (AH 50, 58 – 59); Venantius Fortunatus, *Pange lingua gloriosi* (AH 50, 71); AB 3, *Praecamur patrem*; and *Ab ore verbum prolatum* (AH 51, 82 – 84). Hilary's *Adae carnis gloriosae* (AH 50, 8 – 9) does not qualify for consideration here since it is really a hymn about the defeat of Satan through the power and presence of the Son of God. The hymns of Prudentius will be cited by book, hymn and line; they are available in many editions, including CSEL 61 (1926), ed. J. Bergman.

23. Szövérffy, *Analen*, 134 – 135; the two hymns were used in the Good Friday liturgy and both are found in identical MSS. *Ab ore* is a rhythmical imitation of the metre of *Pange lingua* and was probably influenced by it in content as well. It is found only in two eleventh-century MSS and is regarded as a tenth-century Spanish hymn (*ibid.*, 344).

24. More detailed parallels between *Hymnum dicat* and *Ab ore verbum* will be given below. We may note here, in passing, that the author of *Ab ore* has also taken two phrases from the Gallican hymn *Rex aeterne Domine* (AH 51, 5):

8. Nam velum templi scissum est (*Ab ore* 6)
   et omnis terra tremuit (*Ab ore* 9).

25. The expression was used by W. Meyer as an argument against Hilary's authorship, because it could only denote a monastic community ('Die drei arezzaner Hymnen', *loc. cit.*, 423); Bernard also understood it in this sense, while supporting Hilarian authorship (ILH II 126 – 128). Feder countered Meyer's argument by observing that *turba fratrum* may mean 'brothers' in the general Christian sense, as in 1. 57 of the hymn: 'Mox videtur a beatis, quos probavit, fratribus' ('Studien zu Hilarius', *loc. cit.*, 80). The word *turba* returns over and over throughout the hymn: *turba fratrum* (1), *turba martyrum* (17), *turba discumbens* (29), *turbae Iudaeorum* (36), *turbis traditur* (37), *turba fratrum* (65).

26. 'The ejaculatory, litanic, asyndetic type of prayer is peculiarly suited to the Irish genius' (E. Bishop, *Liturgica Historica*, 148).

27. Cf. Prudentius, *Cath.* V, 159 – 160; *Cath.* XI 17 – 20; Venantius Fortunatus (?), *Tempore florigero rutilant* 49 – 50 (AH 50, 77).

28. Orientius, *De Epithetis Salvatoris nostri*, in: *Carmina Orientio tributa*, CSEL 16, 243 – 244. Each of the titles is explained in his *Explanatio nominum Domini* (*ibid.*, 247 – 249). Another early document which defines the titles of Christ is the *Multiformis nominum Christi dispensatio* of the Council of Rome in 382; there seven of our titles are explained: *verbum, mons, agnus, via, lapis angularis, sponsus, leo*; ed. C. Turner, *The Journal of Theological Studies* 1 (1899) 556.

29. Cf. the seventh-century Spanish hymn, *Christi caterva clamitat* (AH 27, 64):

A matre natus tempore,
sed sempiternus a Patre,
duabus in substantiis
persona sola est numinis.

Cf. also, *Verus redemptor Christe* (AH 27, 265).

202

30. Sedulius, *A solis ortus cardine* 3 − 5 (AH 50, 58); Prudentius, *Apotheosis* 104 − 106:

> Ergo Pater passus (quid non malus audeat error?)
> ipse puellari conceptus sanguine CREVIT,
> ipse verecundiae DISTENDIT VIRGINIS ALVUM?

Ambrose, *Intende qui regis* (AH 50, 13):

> Alvus tumescit virginis,
> claustrum pudoris permanet.

31. Cf. R. Atkinson. ILH II xi − xii; C. Blume, AH 51, 266 − 267. The stanza has been edited within parentheses by Feder, *loc. cit.*, 219; Bulst, *op. cit.*, 133, prints it without brackets; Meyer, 'Das turiner Bruckstück', 205, accepts it as genuine: 'denn ein Interpolator ist in der Regel für seine Zeit ein feiner Kopf und schreibt nicht Unverständliches'.

32. The word *merum* is used in the same context by Sedulius, *Carmen Paschale* III 4 − 7 (PL 19, 633 − 644):

> In vinum convertit aquas; amittere gaudent
> Pallorem latices, mutavit laeta saporem
> Unda suum, largita MERUM, mensasque per omnes
> Dulcia non nato rubuerunt pocula musto.

But the sense of the word in our hymn is different: the wedding-feast was *barely* saved from disaster by the miracle of Christ. The phrase *propinando poculo* may have influenced the author of *Ab ore verbum prolatum* (AH 51, 83):

> 5. Exaltatus Iesus Christus in crucis patibulo
> haustu fellis et aceti PROPINATUS POCULO.

It is also used in the hymn in honour of St Patrick, *Audite omnes amantes* (ed. Bieler, 121):

> 67. qui caelesti haurit vinum in vassis caelestibus
> PROPINNANSQUE Dei plebem spiritale POCULUM.

33. Prudentius, *Dittochaeum* 145 − 148:

> Quinque Deus panes fregit piscesque gemellos,
> his hominum large saturavit milia quinque;
> implentur nimio micarum fragmine CORBES
> bis seni aeternae tanta est opulentia mensae.

34. W. Meyer, *Die Preces der mozarabischen Liturgie* (Berlin 1914), p. 52, no. 79 (Mo Br 534); cf. also *ibid.*, p.58-59, no. 90 (Br 593). According to Meyer, *ibid.*, p. 9, the composition of the Spanish collection of rhythmical *preces* cannot have been earlier than the tenth century, but D. de Bruyne has shown that some of them at least were composed in the seventh century at the latest: 'De l'origine de quelques textes liturgiques mozarabes: Les Preces rhythmiques', *Rev. bénédictine* 30 (1913) 431 − 436.

35. *Hymnum dicat* 38:

> impiis verbis gravatur, sputa, flagra sustinet.

Ab ore verbum prolatum (AH 51, 82 − 83)

> 3. Caesus ictu flagellorum sustulit opprobria,
> sputis vultum sordidatus, laureatus vepribus,
> deputatus cum iniquis ad mortem crudeliter.
> 13. Qui pro nobis dira probra sustulit ab impiis.

36. Prudentius, *Cath.* V III − 112:

> Iactatasque animas mille laboribus
> iustorum in patriam SCANDERE PRAECIPIT.

37. AB 67 Hii sunt, domine, qui . . . mortem morte vicerunt (this will be shown to be a

Spanish prayer); Mo Gil 331 ut qui ... invicta fidei virtute pugnantes, mortis mortem vicerunt: Br 593 Qui solus mortem nostri criminis tua morte devicisti.

38. *Ab ore verbum prolatum* (AH 51,83):

> 6. Fugiens sol OBSCURATUR cernens mortem Domini
> luctuosam, infert mundo tenebrae caliginem;
> monumenta patuerunt, velum templi scissum est.

The expression *excitare de sepulchris corpora* (*Hymnum dicat* 44) is found almost identically in the hymn used at Arles for the office of none in the time of Caesarius, *Ter trina hora volvitur* (AH 51, 18):

> 4. Haec hora qua RESUSCITANS
> Iesus SEPULCRIS CORPORA
> prodire mortis libera
> iussit refuso spiritu.

39. V. Buzna, *De Hymnis sancti Hilarii episcopi Pictaviensis* (Coloczae 1911) 78: 'Cum nullo alio in carmine saeculorum VI. − VII — VIII. cogitationem hanc sane singularem atque poeticam simul reperire potuerim, cumque Fortunatus fuerit Episcopus Pictaviensis et scriptor etiam vitae Hilarii, facile in illam inclinabar sententiam hymnum hunc 'Hymnum dicat', qui etiam metro eodem est compositus quo hymnus "Pange lingua", a Fortunato fortasse fuisse confectum, progrediente tamen tempore Hilario Pictaviensi erronee utique adscitum'.

40. The word *spiritus* is sometimes used to denote the common divinity of the three Persons, who are one substance, one *spiritus*. Cf. Walpole, *Early Latin Hymns*, 13, for a number of early texts in this sense, including some from St Hilary of Poitiers. But Walpole does not know of any use of the word *vinculum* for the Holy Spirit before St Bernard.

41. Cyprian, *De dominica oratione* 36, ed. Hartel, CSEL 3, 1, 293 − 294.

42. R. Atkinson regarded the three stanzas as a later addition, because of some metrical errors and some use of rhyme: ILH I xii − xiii. They have been included in parentheses by Feder. But W. Meyer suggested some slight emendations to correct the metre and he thought that only the final stanza was a later addition. 'Das turiner Bruckstück', 205 − 206. W. Bulst, *Hymni latini*, 135, has followed Meyer's suggestion.

43. Cf. *Ab ore verbum prolatum* (AH 51, 83):

> 16. Reddituros rationem CHRISTO REGI DOMINO
> 17. Radii solis ad instar Christus iudex veniet
> COLLATURUS PIIS REGNUM, impiis supplicium.

44. Manz 691. The great majority of the texts is Spanish, with one occurrence in Ga B 488.

45. E Bishop, *Liturgica Historica*, 163.

46. Cf. *supra*, p. 24 − 25.

47. In place of these lines on the Incarnation and birth of Christ, Sedulius, *A solis ortus cardine*, has six stanzas; Prudentius, *Cath.* IX, and Fortunatus, *pange lingua*, each have two stanzas of three lines each. A comparison with Prudentius bears out the simplicity of *Hymnum dicat*:

> 16. Corporis formam caduci, membra morti obnoxia
> induit, ne gens periret primoplasti ex germine,
> merserat quem lex profundo noxialis tartaro.

> 19. O beatus ortus ille, virgo cum puerpera
> edidit nostram salutem feta sancto spiritu
> et puer redemptor orbis os sacratum protulit!

Prudentius then adds two further stanzas of invitation to praise. The statement 'nos monemur credere rem novam nec ante visam' (*Hymnum dicat* 12 – 13) seems to be an expression of the typical Irish interest in 'the first time' such and such an event took place, an interest which often became a mania. See also the next line: '*primi* adorant parvulum'; Walpole notes here that 'this distinction really belongs to the shepherds' (*Early Latin Hymns*, 7), but the Irish author would have been delighted to correct the scholar and point out that the shepherds merely '*found* Mary and Joseph and the infant lying in the manger'. See also line 53: 'feminae *primum* monentur salvatorem vivere'. And cf. B. Bischoff, 'Il monachesimo irlandese nei suoi rapporti col continente', in: *Mittelalterliche Studien* I 201 – 202.

48. Neither Prudentius nor Fortunatus mention the story of the Magi, or Herod, or the flight into Egypt, or the return to Nazareth. Sedulius speaks in four stanzas (7 – 10) of the shepherds, Herod's fear, the Magi and the massacre of the innocents. The more concrete character of *Hymnum dicat* is brought out by a comparison with this stanza of Sedulius (AH 50, 58):

> 9. Ibant magi, qua venerant,
> stellam sequentes praeviam,
> lumen requirunt lumine,
> Deum fatentur munere.

49. The implicit reference to an apocryphal infancy Gospel ties in with early Irish interest in the Apocrypha.

50. K. Meyer, *Ancient Irish Poetry*, cited by M. Dillon, in: *Early Irish Poetry*, ed. J, Carney (Cork 1965) 10 – 11.

51. Cf. W. Godel, 'Irishches Beten im frühen Mittelalter', *loc. cit.*, 430 – 433. Godel did not consider *Hymnum dicat* in his treatment of Irish prayer.

52. The kingship of Christ is not over-stressed, but it is stated from the start: '*Christo regi* concinentes laudem demus debitam' (2); the gifts of the magi are 'digna *regi* munera' (15). The theme returns at the end: 'ante lucem nuntiemus *Christum regem* saeculo, Ante lucem decantantes *Christo regi* domino,... *regnaturi cum eo*' (70 – 72). Cf. R. Culhane, 'The Bangor hymn to Christ the King', *The Irish Ecclesiastical Record* 74 (1950) 201 – 219.

53. Evidence for the teaching of classical metrics in the Irish schools is found in a letter written *c*. 650 by a certain Colmanus to his *eruditissimus filius* Feradad; cf. B. Bischoff, 'Il monachesimo irlandese . . .', *loc. cit.*, 197 – 199. Colmanus gives some instruction on the scansion of hexameters and pentameters, but, according to Boschoff, it is such an elementary nature that the teaching of metrics appears to be still in its infancy at that time. He concludes: 'La necessità di un tale insegnamento elementare dà, a mio parere, il colpo di grazia all' opinione diffusa della ininterotta continuità della tradizione classica nell'isola'. However, we are dealing here not so much with the classics as with the ecclesiastical tradition of hymnody, and it may be that the metres used in this, such as the trochaic tetrameter catalectic and iambic dimeter, were learned quite early in the Irish schools. The ability of Columban to write classical verse (ed. Walker, 184 – 196) may have been acquired during his later life on the Continent. But, however illuminating the letter of Colmanus may be, it is still but one piece of evidence and it leaves open the possiblity that *Hymnum dicat* was written in Ireland at the end of the sixth century.

CHAPTER THREE

1. The hymn *Audite omnes amanted*, entitled *Ymnum Sancti Patrici Magister Scotorum* (AB 3; f. 13^v — 15^v), has been critically edited by L. Bieler, 'The Hymn of St Secundinus', PRIA vol. 55, Section C, no. 6 (1953) 117 – 127. We will use the text of Bieler's edition:

the numbers will indicate the lines. The hymn *Audite bonum exemplum*, entitled *Ymnum Sancti Camelaci* (AB 15, f. 17ᵛ), is found only in this MS; ed. Warren II 19; AH 51, 321. We will use the text of the MS: the numbers indicate the stanzas.

2. Regarding the use of rhyme by the Irish, from once they took it over from the Continent to their subsequent development of it as something most characteristically theirs, cf. W. Meyer, *Gesamm. Abhandl.* I 190 – 193; R. Atkinson, ILH II xiv – xvi. F. J. E. Raby expresses the generally held view when he says that 'to the Irish poets must be given the credit of being the first important innovators in the use of rime, and it is possible to trace a progressive development from the rimeless hymns of the fifth century, through the middle period of incipient rimes in the sixth, to the richer and more exact rimes of the seventh and eighth centuries' (*A History of Christian – Latin Poetry*, Oxford 1927, 138).

3. Cf. D. Norberg, *Versification*, 73.

4. In *Hymnum dicat* we find the following disyllabic line-endings: 5 tu *lapis*; 9 tu *maris*; 10 nasci *iubet*; 18 quo *fluit*; 25 aquam *iubet*; 64 factos *dei*; 67 sentit *diem*; 72 cum *eo*. Most of these disyllables are preceded by a monosyllable, with which they would have been considered as one metric word; but that does not affect the point at issue, the use of disyllables in the final position. In our two hymns the number of final disyllables is also small; *Audite omnes*: 22.46 bonis; 24 bono; 23.28.85 dei; 72 deum; 32 in cruce; *Audite bonum*: 3 deo; 4.5 suum.

5. 'Pour la pluspart des vers employés par Secundinus, nous trouvons sans difficulté des modèles structurels dans le septénaire quantitatif. Les hémistiches *Víri / in Chrísto/ beáti* et *Quómodo / bónum / ob áctum* correspondent par exemple au vers de Prudence *Écce / quem váles / vetústis* et *Córporis / fórmᵤm/ cadúci*' (Norberg, *Verisification*, 113).

6. 'Ou bien il a eu ici pour modèle un poème quantitatif du type archaique, . . . ou bien encore nous avons ici seulement une imitation partielle de structure, ce qui semble plus vraisemblable' (Norberg, *loc. cit.*, 113).

7. Cf. L. Bieler, *The Works of St Patrick. St Secundinus' Hymn on St Patrick*: Ancient Christian Writers 17 (Westminister and Maryland 1953) 59. In Muirchu's seventh-century *Life of Patrick* we are told that Patrick had four peitions to make before his death, petions which an angel promised would be granted. The second was: 'ut quicumque ymnum qui de te compositus est, in die exitus de corpore cantaverit, tu iudicabis poenitentiam eius de suis peccatis' (ed. Stokes, VT II 296). The belief that Patrick would judge the Irish on the day of judgement probably grew out of a line in *Audite omnes*: 92 Cum apostolis regnabit sanctus super Israel. It is further reflected in two lines of Fiach's Hymn, *Genair Patraic* (written *c.* 800), 1. 51 – 52: 'A hymn which thou hast chosen in thy lifetime shall be a lorica of protection for all; around thee on the Day of Judgement men of Ireland will go to Doom' (ed. Stokes, VT II 411). Again, among the *Notulae* appended to Tirechan's seventh-century *Memoir* of Patrick, there are those that deal with the 'four honours' of Patrick:

> 1. Solempnitate dormitionis eius honorari in medio veris per tres dies et tres noctes omni bono cibo praeter carnem, quasi Patricius venisset in vita in hostium. . . .
> 3. Ymnum eius per totum tempus cantari.

8. Stokes, VT I 243 – 247; ILH II 3 – 7. The essence of the story is that Secundinus composed the hymn at Dunshaughlin to praise Patrick and make amends for an insulting remark he had made about him. Patrick came to him in great wrath and drove his chariot over him. But they are reconciled and Secundinus recites his hymn in Patrick's praise. Then he pleads with Patrick to grant a just spiritual recompense to all who would recite it and they finally agree on the terms of the reward.

9. Cf. L. Bieler, *The Life and Legend of St Patrick* (Dublin 1949); s.a., *St Patrick and the Coming of Christianity* (Dublin 1967).

10. J. Carney, *The Problem of St Patrick* (Dublin 1961) 36. Carney himself has apparently abandoned his earlier view, put forward in his *Studies in Irish Literature and History* (Dublin 1955) 399 – 400, which maintained that the hymn was a deliberate forgery written expressly to further the Armagh claims to primacy.

11. *The Martyrology of Oengus*, ed. W. Stokes: HBS 29 (London 1905) 237:

> Nov. 27 A stream of wisdom with splendour
> Sechnall diadem of our Lords
> has chanted a melody — noble profit! —
> a praise of Patrick of Armagh.

In the Antiphonary the hymn is simply entitled *Ymnum Sancti Patrici*.

12. L. Beiler, *Life and Legend, op.cit.*, 38. Notable among others who have defended the authorship of Secundinus are: J. H. Bernard, ILH II 96; C. Blume, AH 51, 344 – 345; E. MacNeill, 'The Hymn of Secundinus in honour of St Patrick', *Irish Historical Studies* 2 (1940) 129 – 153; P. Grosjean, 'Notes d'hagiographie celtiques', *Anal. Bollandiana* 63 (1945) 110 – 111.

13. M. Esposito, 'Notes on Latin Learning and Literature in mediaeval Ireland', *Hermathena* 45 (1929) 220 – 230. Kenny, *Sources*, 259 – 260, thought it unlikely that the hymn was written while Patrick was still alive. J. Carney, *The Problem of St Patrick*, 42 – 45, and D. A. Binchy, 'Patrick and his Biographers', *Studia Hibernica* 2 (1962) 52 – 56, argue for a date in the late sixth or early seventh century.

14. E. MacNeill, *art. cit.*, in particular, developed this argument with great eloquence. P. Grosjean, *art. cit.*, would situate the hymn in the context of the attacks against Patrick that were provoked by Patrick's own severe Letter against Coroticus.

15. 'The miracles that are so abundantly ascribed to Patrick in the later documents, e.g. in the vernacular Hymn of St Fiacc, are conspicuously absent from this; and it is throughout marked by that simplicity and sobriety of tone which characterize the work of a contemporary' (Bernard, *op. cit.*, 96).

16. L. Bieler, 'The Hymn of St Secundinus', *loc. cit.*, 117.

17. 'It is difficult, if not actually impossible, to reconcile the picture of Patrick's triumph ("Gloriam habet cum Christo, honorem in saeculo, / qui ab omnibus ut Dei veneratur angelus") with the saint's own description of his trials and sufferings. . . . The hymn seems to me to be far closer to the glorified Patrick of the biographers than to the Patrick of real life' (D. A. Binchy, 'Patrick and his Biographers', *loc. cit.*, 53).

18. Kenney, *Sources*, 260.

19. Cf. J. Carney, *Studies in Irish Literature and History*, 400 – 401. In the review of this work of Carney, L. Bieler, ' "Patrick and the Kings". Apropos a new chronology of St Patrick', *The Irish Ecclesiastical Record* 85 (1956) 171 – 189, grants that Carney is right in claiming that the hymn is probably based on the Confession of St Patrick and not *vice versa* (*art. cit.*, 185, n.40). But in his latest study, *St Patrick and the Coming of Christianity*, Bieler still holds that no absolutely cogent argument has been produced for or against the authorship of Secundinus. Nevertheless, the argument of dependence on the Confession is a decisive one. If, as Bieler accepts, Patrick wrote his Confession towards the end of his .life (*c.* 460), and if Secundinus died in 447, then the latter could not have known the Confession and he could not have written the hymn which depends on it.

20. E. MacNeill, 'The Hymn of Secundinus', *Loc. cit.*, 144 – 145.

21. Stokes, VT II 333.

22. J. Carney, *The Problem of St Patrick*, 44 – 46. D. A. Binchey, 'Patrick and his Biographers', *loc. cit.*, 55, admits that Carney's suggestion 'may well be correct'.

23. In the first sense we have, in the Antiphonary: *Ymnum S. Patrici* (AB 13), *Ymnum S.*

Camelaci (AB 15), *Ymnum S. Comgilli* (AB 14). In the second sense (authorship) we have: *Ymnum S. Hilari de Christo* (AB 2), *Ymnum Apostolorum ut alii dicunt* (AB 3).

24. 'Patrick's hymn, Colmán Elo recited it in his refectory thrice. Patrick (appeared and) stood in the house-floor. And a certain layman said, "Have we no other prayer but this which we might recite?" And Patrick after that departed' (Stokes, VT I 246 – 247).

25. Cf. D. Pochin Mould, *The Irish Saints* (Dublin and London 1964) 86 – 89. In the *Felire of Oengus* (c. 800) he is remembered with these lines (ed. Stokes, HBS 29, 196):

> Sept.26 Colman from Lann Eala
> with perfection of high studies,
> so that he is, splendid cry,
> the great John of Ireland's sons.

In Adormnan's *Life of Columcille* I 5 and II 15 (ed. Anderson, New York 1961, 222, 356 – 358) we learn about the visit of Colmán to Iona and his subsequent return to Ireland.

26. G. F. Hamilton, *In Patrick's Praise. The Hymn of St Secundinus* (Sechnall), 2nd ed., Dublin 1920.

27. L. Bieler, *Libri Epistolarum sancti Patricii Episcopi* I (Dublin 1952). This edition includes the *Confessio* (56 – 91), the *Epistola ad Milites Corotici* (91 – 102) and the *Dicta Patricii* (104 – 105).

28. Cf. also *Conf.* 38 and 46. In the twelfth-century *Life of St Patrick* written by Jocelin there is a quotation from a letter which Patrick is alleged to have written to a friend, and which J. Carney, *The Problem of St Patrick*, 139 – 140, judges to be genuine. There Patrick pleads that nobody should compare him with the Apostles or other perfect men, thereby suggesting that such a comparison might well be made. It is made by the author of our hymn, the first stanza of which can be seen as an explicit rebuttal of Patrick's own humble opinion of himself. The quotation, which 'has an unmistakable Patrician ring' (Carney, *op. cit.*, 139), is: 'Debit mihi Dominus exiguo virtutem faciendi signa in populo barbaro, qualia nec a magnis Apostolis leguntur facta, ita ut in nomine Domini Dei nostri Iesu Christi resuscitarem a mortuis corpora in pulvere a multis annis resoluta. Nullus tamen obsecro credat me ob ista sive his similia parificandum Apostolis aut ullis perfectis viris, cum sim exiguus et peccator et contemptibilis'.

29. Apart from the first stanza cited above, cf. also:

> 61. Quem pro meretis salvator provexit pontifiem,
> 71. Quem thesaurum emit sanctis perfectisque meritis.

30. The 'fisher of men' idea is also found in *Epist.* 11. J. Carney, *Studies in Irish Literature and History*, 400 – 401, shows how a comparison of the texts of the Confession and the hymn, in their expression of this metaphor, indicates the priority of the Confession. The metaphor is studied and artificial in the hymn, while it is more natural and direct in the Confession. As Bernard had also pointed out (ILH II 101), the text of the hymn also subsequently influenced Muirchu in his *Life of Patrick*: 'dicens ei adesse tempus ut veniret et aevangelico rete nationes feras et barbaras ad quas docendas misserat illum deus ut piscaret' (*Book of Armagh*, f. 2).

31. Patrick speaks of himself in the lowliest terms, in order to extoll the grace given to him for the service of others; thus, especially, in *Conf.* 12 – 13.

32. Cf. *Conf.* 14,38,40,42,50,51; *Epist.* 2,3,7,16,17.

33. Fiacc's hymn, *Genair Patraic* 25, repeats the same idea: 'Hymns and Apocalypse, the three Fifties, he used to say them' (ILH II 33). In Muirchu's *Life* this had grown to: 'omnes psalmos et apocalypsin Johannis et omnia cantica spiritualia scripturarum COTIDIE decantans' (*Book of Armagh*, f. 7; cited by Bernard, ILH II 104).

34. The expression *fides catholica* became a popular one in Ireland. It is used a number of times by Columban in one of his letters, *Epist.* 5, 3. 9. 13. 17 (ed. Walker, pp. 38, 46, 50,

208

52). The *Annals of Ulster* have the following entry under A.D. 441: 'Leo ordinatus CLII Romane eclesiae episcopus et probatus est IN FIDE CATHOLICA Patricius episcopus' (cited by J. Carney, *The Problem of St Patrick*, 34). The expression must have been derived from the Creed *Quicumque*: 'Fides autem catholica haec est . . .', which was known from the sixth century in Ireland; cf. ILH 242.

35. MacNeill understood this stanza as referring to the provision of clergy and material necessities in the churches founded by Patrick. By *caelestis annona* the author would have meant 'the material things necessary for the ritual service of the churches throughout Ireland, so far . . . as these things were not locally supplied' ('The Hymn of St Secundinus', *loc. cit.*, 149). The provision of *vestes* is expressly mentioned; other things hard to come by in the early days would have been oil and wine. The *affatus divini et sacri* are understood by MacNeill to signify the Scriptures (*affatus divini*) and the books of ritual (*affatus sacri*) (*art. cit.*, 151).

36. So in the preface to the hymn in ILH II 3.

37. *Hymnum dicat* 22: 'Praedicans caeleste regnum dicta factis adprobat'; *Audite omnes* 46: 'qui quod verbis docet sacris factis adimplet bonis'. *Hymnum dicat* 26: 'Nuptiis mero retentis propinando poculo'; *Audite omnes* 68: 'propinansque Dei plebem spiritale poculum'.

38. Cf. J. Carney, *The Problem of St Patrick*, 43.

39. Bernard, ILH II 101 − 102: 'It is worth observing that the enclitic *que* is very commonly used in this hymn and in the *Altus Prosator*, but very rarely in other pieces (of the *Liber Hymnorum*)'. It is not used at all, for example, in the long hymn in honour of St Comgall, *Audite pantes ta erga* (AB 14).

40. D.A. Binchy, 'Patrick and his Biographers', *loc. cit.*, 55, argues: 'the shorter composition looks as if it were modelled on the longer and formally more correct poem . . . . The survival of *Audite omnes* in three other manuscripts, whereas the hymns of Camelacus and Comgall are preserved only in the Antiphonary, suggests both an earlier origin and a wider distribution for the first-named'. I think it is an exaggeration to claim that *Audite omnes* is formally more correct. The only metrical error in *Audite bonum*, by comparison with *Audite omnes*, is the omission of a syllable in stanza 2, 2: 'gratias Deo agens', where *dō* may be a simple scribal error for *dñō*. Stanza 6, 1: 'Xps illum insinuavit' has a syllable too many, like the corresponding line in *Audite omnes*. The correct metre is not obtained here by emendation, as Binchy suggests, to *insinuat*; the correct metre demands precisely *insinuávit*, a paroxytone. The possiblity of a common authorship was first suggested by J. Carney, *The Problem of St Patrick*, 43 − 44; it is at least as probable as the dependence of *Audite bonum* on *Audite omnes*.

41. In the Irish *Tripartite Life* he is known as Comlach, *clam Patraic*; cf. Stokes, VT I 84 − 85; II 556. In the earlier traditions recorded by Tirechán, which we will note presently, he was not known as a leper.

42. Stokes, VT II 304; and especially *ibid.*, 310 − 311: 'Et venit (Patricius) per flumen Ethne in duas Tethbias, . . . et mittens CAMULACUM COMMIENSIUM in Campum Cuini digito illi indicavit locum de cacumine Graneret, id est aeclessiam Raithin'. In the hymn he is called Camelacus Cumiensis:

Audite bonum exemplum benedicti pauperis
Camelaci Cumiensis Dei iusti famuli.

What is meant by *Cumiensis (Commiensium)* has not been determined.

43. Cf. D. Pochin Mould, *The Irish Saints* 58 − 59.

44. 'Xps illum insinauvit patriarchae Abrahae'. The use of *insinuare* in this sense is rare. The *Thesaurus Linguae Latinae* indicates Ge V 1628: 'Commendamus tibi, domine, animam fratri nostri illius; . . . PATRIARCHARUM TUORUM SENIBUS INSINUARE non rennuas'. According to A. Chavasse, *Le Sacramentaire Gélasien* (Paris 1957) 59 − 60, this formula is

a Gallican (Irish?) addition to Ge V.

CHAPTER FOUR

1. The hymns are found in no other MS. *Sancti venite* is entitled *Ymnum quando communicarent sacerdotes*, while *Praecamur patrem* has the title *Ymnum apostolorum ut alii dicunt*. We will use the MS text in this study (AB 8: f. $10^v - 11$; AB 3: f. $4^v - 6^v$), sometimes correcting it in the light of Blume's edition (AH 51, 298 – 299, 271 – 275; cf. Warren II 10 – 11, 5 – 7); the numbers indicate stanza and line. In language and content there is no connection between the two hymns, but we take them together for purposes of metrical comparison.

2. Regarding the quantitive iambic trimeter, cf. Norberg, *Versification*, 72; for *Sancti venite* and *Praecamur patrem*, cf. *ibid.*, 112.

3. M. Simonetti, 'Studi sull'innologia popolare christiana dei primi secoli', *loc. cit.*, 463 – 464, judges it to be substantially quantitative.

4. Cf. W. Meyer, 'Die Verskunst der Iren in rhythmischen lateinischen Gedichten', *loc. cit.*, 609: 'Die Beobachtung der gleichen Schlusskadenz ist bei den Iren lange nicht so streng wie die Beobachtung der gleichen Silbenzahl. Ziemlich oft steht unter den proparoxytoner Zeilenschlüssen ein paroxytoner und umgekehrt'. Cf. also, Norberg, *Versification*, 128.

5. Cf. ILH II 5; the preface has been reproduced by Blume (AH 51, 229), who is inclined to the belief that it gives us an historical nucleus of truth. But there are no grounds for regarding it as anything other than fictional. We are told that Secundinus had criticised Patrick for not preaching charity. 'Sechnall had just finished Mass except for going to Christ's body, when it was told him that Patrick was coming to the place in great anger against Sechnall. The latter thereupon left the oblation at the altar and bowed down to Patrick, who drove his chariot over him; but God raised the ground around him *hinc et inde* so that it did not harm him. . . . So they made peace then, Patrick and Sechnall. And while they were going round the cemetery, they heard a choir of angels singing around the oblation in the Church; and what they sang was the hymn beginning, 'Sancit venite Christi corpus', etc.; hence this hymn is sung in Ireland when one goes to the body of Christ, from that time onward'.

6. AB 109 – 115; St Gall, MS 1394 (ed. Warren, *The Liturgy and Ritual of the Celtic Church*, 177 – 178); Ce S 18. We will here indicate these sources as: AB,G, S. Warren II 73 – 75 has indicated some continental sources for the communion antiphons found in AB. The occasion and manner of singing these antiphons is described by Jones, *Vita Clumbani* II 16: 'Quadam entenim die dominico cum . . . iam sacri corporis communione participarentur, quaedam ex his nomine Domna, cum iam corpus Domini accepisset ac sanguinem libasset, et sacro choro inserta, cum comparibus caneret: *Hoc sacrum corpus Domini et salvatoris sanguinem sumite vobis in vitam perennem*, in ore eius globus igneus candido fulgore rutilans micabat' (ed. B. Krusch, *Hannoveriae et Lipsiae* 1905, 266 – 267).

7. Warren II 44 draws attention to an early Gallican communion antiphon preserved in Gregory of Tours, *De Miraculis S. Martini* II 13: 'Venite populi ad sacrum et immortale praesidium et libamen agendum. Cum timore et fide accedamus, manibus mundis paenitentiae munus communicemus, quoniam propter nos Agnus Dei patri sacrificium propositum est. Ipsum solum adoremus, ipsum glorificemus, cum angelis clamantes, alleluia'. This is the *Transitorium* for Easter Sunday in Am M II 214.

8. As Manz 869 has shown, the expression *sacerdos et hostia* is also found in the Gallican, Ambrosian and Spanish liturgical books. Another example of its use in Ireland is found in Ps. – Hilary of Arles, *Expos. in Epist. Canonicas*: 'ut nos offeret Deo' (1 Pt.3, 18), i.e.

nostrum corpus in cruce, a quo circumdatus summus sacerdos, quia ipse est SACERDOS ET HOSTIA' (PLS 3, 97). In the *Leabhar Braec* copy of *Audite omnes amantes* there is a gloss on l. 52, 'pro quibus ut deo dignas inmolatque hostias', which reads: 'ut dicitur Christus, HOSTIA ET SACERDOS' (ILH II 99, where Bernard refers to Augustine, *In ps. Sermo* 155)

9. Columban, *Instr.* 13, 1: 'Iam enim vocat ad se, Fons vivus, Fons vitae, et dicit, "Qui sitit veniat ad me et bibat". Quid bibatis intellegite. Dicat enim Isaias, dicat vobis Fons ipse, "me autem dereliquerunt Fontem aquae vivae, dicit Dominus". Dominus ergo ipse Deus noster Iesus Christus est Fons vitae, et ideo invitat nos ad se Fontem, ut illum bibamus.... Ut panem ergo edamus, ut fontem bibamus eundem Dominum nostrum Iesum Christum, qui seipsum nobis quasi sumendum "Panem dicit vivum, qui dat vitam huic mundo", seque similiter fontem demonstrans ait, "Qui sitit, veniat ad me et bibat", de quo fonte et propheta dicit, "Quoniam apud te est fons vitae"' (ed. Walker, 116). He goes on to affirm the need to return again and again to Christ who is at once the Bread and Font of life; his words echo clearly the language of the *Sancti venite*: "Sitientium enim est, non saturantium, iste fons, et ideo esurientes et sitientes quos alibi beatificavit ad se vocat, quibus n ɲquam bibere satis est, sed quanto plus hauserint tanto plus sitient.... Beati qui esuriunṭ ᵘnc panem et sitiunt hunc fontem; semper enim edentes et bibentes adhuc edere et biberᵉ ᵊsiderant' (Walker, 118). Cf. also the seventh-century Irish Ps.-Jerome, *Comm. in Ev.* (Mk. 15,1): 'Samson noster maxilla verbi sui innumeros catervas Iudaeorum et daemon⸝m hic sternit; et FONTEM PERENNIS VITAE SITIENTIBUS nobis, id est corpori suo aperiet' (PL 30, 636D).

10. For the use of *Alfa et O(mega)* see, for example, Prudentius, *Cath.* IX 12; AH 27, 88 (no. 37,1); AH 51, 103 (no 96,4). In a note on this line of our hymn, Walpole, *Early Latin Hymns*, 346, says: 'Probably *O* was taken to be *ōō* (two syllables) or the verse would be a syllable short. The form *O mega*, which most editors read, is a modern invention and cannot have been the original in this ancient hymn'. Another expression in this line of our hymn reflects the article of the Creed: 'exinde VENTURUS IUDICARE vivos et mortuos' (AB 35).

11. According to Bernard, ILH II 99, it is 'a distinctively Celtic hymn'.

12. *Consilii* is pronounced *consili* (28, 2); then we have *cum gladis* (29, 1), *cum socis* (37,3), *propris* (38,1), *donaris* (40,2: for *donariis*).'Die Irem lesen regelmässig 'ii' als einfaches 'i' ... und schreiben oft auch so' (Blume, AH 51, 274).

13. W. Meyer, 'Die Verskunst der Iren', *loc. cit.*, 622, says of it: 'So scheint mir dies Gedicht ein starkes Beispiel dafür zu sein, mit welcher Ungebundenheit die Iren die Reimgesetze verletzten'.

14. The Latin name *Cincris* had its ultimate source in the Chronicle of Eusebius as translated by Rufinus. Speaking of the 18th dynasty of the Egyptian Kings, he wrote; ACHENCHERES annis XVI. Huius aetate Moses ducem se praebuit Hebraeis ex Aegypto excedentibus' (*Chron, Liber* I; PG 14, 189). In the more complete list of the Kings of the same dynasty which he gives a little futher on, Achencheres is given in the ninth king and is followed in the eleventh position by CHENCHERES. For further Irish use of the word *Cincris*, including also AB 94, cf. Warren II 39 – 40. The Irish may have borrowed this form of the word from a Gallican source, where we find it used by Gregory of Tours, *Historia Francorum* I 17: 'Tempore Moysi ... apud Aegyptios CENCRIS duodecimus, qui et in mare obrutus est Rubro' (ed. Arndt, MGH, *Scrip. rer. merov.* I, 1885, 42).

15. Considering the abrupt transition from stanza 3 to 4, and from 15 to 16, Blume concluded that 'vielleicht also haben wir ein Kinglomerat von drei ursprungliche getrennten Gedichte vor uns' (AH 51, 275), and in his edition he divided the hymn accordingly. M. Simonetti, 'Studi sull'innologia popolare cristiana dei primi secoli', *loc. cit.*, 467 – 468, demonstrated the original unity and organic development of the hymn. In stanza 3 of the introduction the theme of the first main part is introduced, and the second main section is but the realization in history of the action of the Word which was present from the beginning in creation and in the Old Testament.

16. Cf. *Lucis creator optime* (AH 51, 34 – 35), *Immense caeli conditor* (AH 51, 35), *Caeli Deus sanctissime* (AH 51, 36). Gregory's authorship of these hymns, supported by Blume, is not accepted today, or at least is regarded as unproven. According to Szövérffy, *Analen.* 142, the most of them may come from the same author, but he would be of somewhat later date than Gregory.

17. I translate this stanza, with Blume, AH 51, 274: 'Before the true light came forth on this day (*hoc,* scil. *die,* i.e. Christ), mortal hearts were clothed in (*or* covered with) deep ignorance'. Warren II emends the text to : 'Hic quum prodiret vera lux. . .'. It is an original expression of a fairly common theme, the illumination of our hearts through the light of Christ.

18. AH 51, 8:

> 5. Dies dierum, aius, es,
> lucisque lumen ipse es.

19. *Post tergum liquit,* cf. Prudentius, *Cath.* VII 195:

> Explorat arte sciscitator callida
> Deusne membris sit receptus terreis,
> sed increpata fraude POST TERGUM RUIT.

20. PL 30, 604D.

21. The expression *calor fidei* is of fairly widespread occurrence. It is used by Caesarius, *Sermo* 183, 3: 'si forte possit (anima) lacrimarum fomentis vivificata CALORE FIDEI suscitari' (CC 104, 772 – 773); cf. also *Sermo* 197, 3 (*op, cit.,* 797). Maximus of Turin, *Sermo* 24, 3: 'Laurentius has flammas FIDEI CALORE non sentit' (CC 23, 94); the Irish Ps. – Jerome, *Comm. in Ev. Mc.* (Mk. 1,6): 'Pilis vero cameli, divites gentium; et zona pellicea, pauperes mundo mortui, . . . qui stipulas Iudaeis arridas relinquentes, frumenta mystica cruribus trahunt et in CALORE FIDEI saltus inhabitant' (PL 30, 593A; cf. 'in deserto virtutum consistere' of our hymn); Ga G 32 ut dato nobis FIDEI CALORE vel munere ad martyrii nos desiderium amoris sui igne succendat; Mo Or 255 fac nos . . . simili FIDEI CALORE fervescere; LS 983 dominum deum . . . rogemus, ut . . . (nos) CALORE FIDEI faciat ampliari.

22. Cf. Ps.-Jerome, *Expos. IV Evang.* ('while its Irish origin is uncertain, it seems to have been used in Ireland', according to M. McNamara, 'A Plea for Hiberno-Latin Biblical Studies', *The Irish Theological Quarterly* 39, 1972, 343): PL 30, 550A, 555C, 556A, 558C, 559B, 560; Ps.-Hilary of Arles, *Expos. in VII Epist. can.:* PLS 3, 117, 130.

23. PL 30, 593B.

24. Ed. Walker, 52. In our conclusion we shall attempt to explain this relationship between the hymn and the works of Columban. The line *natus. . . . mortali in tegmine* may have been suggested by a Sermon of Caesarius which is the immediate literary source of stanzas 19 – 20 of our hymn; see the citation given in our comment on those stanzas.

25. Ed. G. Morin, CC 104, 786 – 787. B. Bischoff has noted the use of the phrase *fulget in stellis* in the late-eighth-century Irish 'Reference Bible' (*Biblewerk*), which is unpublished. There Christ is identified with the star which led the Magi to Bethlehem: 'Christus selbst sei der Stern gewesen, von dem es heisst: *Fulget in stellis.* Von dem Stern wird bemerkt, dass er "unterhalb der anderen Sterne, aber höher als der Vogelflug" seine Bahn gezogen sei' ('Wendepunkte in der Geschichte der lateinischen Exegese in Frühmittelalter', in: *Mittelalterliche Studien* I (Stuttgart 1966 227). He refers also (*ibid.,* n. 3) to the above *Sermo* of Caesarius.

26. *Tempore florigero* (AH 50, 78):

> 69. Indignum est, CUIUS CLAUDUNTUR CUNCTA PUGILLO,
> ut tegat inclusum rupe vetante lapis.

Quem terra pontus aethera (AH 50, 86 – 87):

1. Quem terra, pontus, aethera
colunt, adorant, praedicant,
trinam regentem machinam
claustrum Mariae baiulat.

4. Beata mater munere
cuius supernus artifex,
MUNDUM PUGILLO CONTINENS,
ventris sub arca clausus est.

Agnoscat omne saeculum (AH 50, 85):

3. Maria ventre concipit
verbi fidelis semine,
QUEM TOTUS ORBIS NON CAPIT
portant puellae viscera.

But a similar phrase occurs in Commodian, *Carmen apologeticum* (PLS 1, 78):

Inde PUGILLO SUO CONCLUDERE CIRCULUM ORBIS.
At tamen cum voluit sciri de se ipso qui esset,...
sumptus est in carnem, quem regio nulla capiebat.

27. *Sapor nectaris* may have been suggested by Fortunatus, *Vexilla regis produent* (AH 50, 74); addressing the Cross, he says:

7. Fundis aroma cortice,
vincis SAPORE NECTARE
iucunda fructu fertili
plaudis triumpho nobili.

Cf. also Prudentius, *Cath.* IX 25 – 27:

Cantharis infusa linfa fit Falernum nobile,
nuntiat vinum minister esse promptum ex hydria,
ipse rex SAPORE TINCTIS obstupescit poculis.

And Sedulius, *Carmen Paschale* III 4 – 8 (PL 19, 633 – 634):

In vinum CONVERTIT AQUAS; amittere gaudent
pallorem latices, mutavit laeta SAPOREM
unda suum, largita merum, mensasque per omnes
dulcia non natu rubuerunt pocula musto.
Implevit sex ergo lacus hoc NECTARE Christus.

28. Cf. Venantius Fortunatus, *Vexilla regis* (AH 50, 74):

4. IMPLETA SUNT QUAE CONCINIT David fideli carmine
dicendo nationibus: regnavit a ligno Deus.

29. Cf. Prudentius, *Cath.* IX 67 – 68:

Omnis aegritudo cedit, languor omnis pellitur,
LINGUA FATUR quam veterna VINXERANT silentia.

30. Cf. Columban, *Instr.* 2, 3: 'Non enim audito lex sanctificat, sed facto PROCUL DUBIO (ed. Walker, 70 – 72)

31. St. 28:

Adversus eum initur consilium
qui magni dictus consilii est nuntius.

Cf. AB 89:

Sic nos PER ANGELUM MAGNI CONSILII
liberare digneris ab igne inferni.

Ps. – Hilary of Arles, *Expos. in VII Epist. can.* (Ja. 2, 21): 'Isaac autem risus interpretatur;

quia secundum historiam, in verbis ANGELI MAGNI CONSILII, Sarra risit. Sic nimirum aec-
claesia per multo tempore DE CHRISTO disperata, in promissione ipsius nimia profert
gaudia' (PLS 3, 73).

32. The morning hymn, *Aeterne lucis conditor* (AH 51, 17):

2. Iam cedit pallens proximo
diei nox adventui,
OBTENDENS LUMEN siderum
adest et clarus lucifer.

The hymn for sext, *Iam sexta sensim volvitur* (AH 51, 17):

3. Hoc namque tempus illud est
quod saeculorum iudicem
iniusta MORTI TRADIDIT
MORTALIUM SENTENTIA.

4. Cum sol repente territus
horrore tanti criminis,
mortem minatus saeculis
diem refugit impium.

The hymn for none, *Ter trina hora volvitur* (AH 51, 18):

4. Haec hora qua RESUSCITANS
Iesus SEPULCRIS CORPORA
prodire mortis libera
iussit refuso spiritu.

The hymn for nocturns, *Rex aeterne Domine* (AH 51, 5):

8. NAM VELUM TEMPLI SCISSUM EST
ET OMNIS TERRA TREMUIT;
tu multos dormientium
resuscitasti, Domine.

The phrase *vivi consurgunt de sepulchris mortui*, however, probably reflects the influence of
the Gospel of Nicodemus, on which the next section of our hymn (st. 33 – 37) depends.
There we read: 'Vero plus admirandum est qui non solus resurrexit a mortuis, sed multos
alios MORTUOS DE MONUMENTIS RESUSCITAVIT VIVOS' (ed. C. de Tischendorf, *Evangelia
Apocrypha*, Hildenschein 1966: Reprographischer Nachdruck der 2. vermehrte Auflage,
Leipzig 1876, 389). I have not met elsewhere the expression *cruci confixus*, but *calvis con-
fixus* is used on two occasions by Venantius Fortunatus, *Vexilla regis* 2 (AH 51, 74) and
Crux benedicta 7 (AH 51, 75).

33. Prudentius, *Cath*. IX 70 – 81, 94 – 102; Venantius Fortunatus (?), *Tempore florigero*
(AH 50, 78). Our hymn was not considered by R. E. Messenger, 'The Descent Theme in
Medieval Latin Hymns', *Transactions and Proceedings of the American Philological Associa-
tion* 67 (1936) 126 – 157.

34. Blume, AH 51, 273, reads *saevis*; but the MS reading is the correct one: *annis fere
milibus senis*.

35. I take *feralibus* as qualifying *nodis* and translate: 'gnawed by the fatal knots of hell'. Cf.
Columban, *Epist*. 5, 3: 'Vigilate, quia mare procellosum est et flabris exasperatur
feralibus' (ed. Walker, 38, who translates: 'whipped up by fatal blasts').

36. The MS is here partly corrupt. Warren II restores it thus: *(Et) protoplaustum
(probr)osa suboli*. But *probrosa* is lacking a syllable, even though it makes better sense than
lacrimosa, which is Blume's reading. On this difficult stanza Blume remarks: '
"lacrimosa" wohl Attribut zu "morte"; "saeva ultrice mâli" Apposition zu "morte" ' (AH
51, 274). We would than presumably translate: 'Then he delivered (*extricat*, st. 33) the
protoplastus, the offspring having been abandoned in tearful death — the cruel avenger of

214

evil'. But this makes little sense and I feel *lacrimosa* is still not a satisfactory restoration; in any case I would expect it to qualify *suboli*, as indicating those offspring who were redeemed with Adam. It would then be death which is rejected or destroyed (*abiecta morte*). Reading *mala* instead of *mali*, we could translate: 'Then he delivered the protoplastus with his (... *mosa*?) offspring, after he had destroyed evil, cruel, avenging death'. The reading *mala* is suggested by the use of *mala mors* in a similar context by the Irish Ps. – Isidore, *Liber de numeris* 6: 'Sic enim sacra Scriptura ait: "Invidia diaboli mors intravit in orbem terrarum"'. . . . Ex iniqua suggestione prava cogitatio intus erupit, prava autem cogitatio delectationem peperit, delectatio consensionem, consensio actionem, actio consuetudinem, consuetudo necessitatem, necessitas MALAM MORTEM, MALA MORS perditionem. Suggestione itaque diaboli per serpentem Eva seducta est, et sic primus homo Adam per Evam seductus praeceptum creatoris sui transgressus est, et in ipsa transgressione laborem et MORTEM INVENIT ET SEMINI SUO POST SE IPSA DERELIQUIT. . . . Ipse cum semine in tenebris et cruciatibus a die mortis suae in prima aetate mundi usque ad resurrectionem Christi detentus est' (PL 83, 1297).

37. The main expression here was evidently borrowed from Cassian, *De. Inst. Coen.* III 3, 6: 'Hora vero nona inferna penetrans ... ANTIQUUM INCOLAM PARADISO pia confessione RESTITUIT' (ed. Petschenig, CSEL 17, 36 – 37).

38. AH 51, 274: *ecclesiam*, but MS reads *aecclesiae*, which makes good sense and may have been intended, even though it is quite unusual to speak of Adam as *caput universi corporis ecclesiae*. This could have been suggested by the text of the Gospel of Nicodemus, where it speaks of the entry into paradise of Adam and his descendants: 'et ingredietur OMNIS GENERIS HUMANI PATER Adam CUM OMNIBUS FILIIS SUIS SANCTIS ET IUSTIS' (cited *infra* at length). In our hymn, the subject of the action is Christ: it is he who raises up the *caput universi corporis (ecclesiae)* and places him in paradise. The reading *ecclesiam* gives a disjointed sense: 'raising up the head of the whole body (*scil.* Adam), he located the Church in the Trinity'.

39. *Evangelii Nicodemi Pars Altera, sive Descensus Christi ad Inferos*, ed. Tischendorf, *op. cit. supra*, p.214, n 32. The Latin A text of the Descent (*op. cit.*, 389 – 416) is the one which provided our author with material for his description.

40. A variant text reads: 'quinque millia nongenti duo anni'. In either case this corresponds to the *annis fere milibus senis* of our hymn.

41. Tischendorf, *op. cit.*, 393 – 394.

42. *Op. cit.*, 397. Compare with our hymn, st. 33: *Conrosum nodis . . . feralibus*; and st. 36: *Exaltans caput . . . in trinitate locavit.*

43. *Op. cit.*, 397 – 399. Compare with our hymn, st. 37: *In hoc caelitus iubet portas principes . . . pandere.*

44. *Op. cit.*, 403. Compare st. 34: *(Lacri)mosa (?) suboli abiecta morte*, and st. 35: *Exaltans caput universi corporis.*

45. *Op. cit.*, 404.

46. *Ibid.*, 405 – 406. Compare st. 35: *Exaltans caput universi corporis, in trinitate locavit ecclesiae.*

47. The language of Prudentius symbolizes the hopeless situation of the lost sheep. It is found in his *Cath.* VIII 33 – 40 (*Hymnus post ieiunium*):

Ille ovem morbo residem gregique
perditam sano, male dissipantem
vellus adfixis vepribus per hirtae
    devia silvae,
impiger pastor revocat lupisque
gestat exclusis umeros gravatus

inde purgatam revehens aprico
    reddit ovili.

This hymn of Prudentius may have been known to our author; we will note a definite parallel phrase in his conclusion.

48. This expression may have been suggested by Prudentius, *Cath.* VIII 49 – 52:

HISCE PRO DONIS tibi, fide pastor,
servitus QUAENAM POTERIT REPENDI?
nulla compensant pretium salutis
    vota precantum.

As Manz 964 has shown, the expression *talia ac tanta* (*talis ac tantus*) is common to Gallican, Spanish and Irish prayers. It is found a number of times in Caesarius of Arles (cf. Manz, *ibid.*), and once in Columban, *Instr.* 4.2: 'Quod si itaque pro temporalibus et incertis *tanta et talia* infatigabiliter tolerantur, quid nos pro aeternis et veris certisque sustinere debemus, quorum finis aeternus est?' (ed. Walker, 80).

49. This conventional expression of a writer's inadequacy to write about a certain subject often precedes a lengthy dissertation on the matter. The term *micrologus* is found twice in Columban's letters with an identical meaning; *Epist.* 1,2: 'Licet enim mihi, nimirum *micrologo*, illud cuiusdam egregium sapientis elogium, quod dixisse fertur quondam videns scortam pictam, "Non admiror artem, sed admiror frontem", ad te clarum a me vili scribendo potest inuri: tamen tuae evangelicae humilitatis fiducia fretus tibi scribere praesumo et mei doloris negotium iniungo' (ed. Walker, 2); *Epist.* 5,1: 'Pulcherrimo omnium totius Europae Ecclesiarum capiti, . . . humillimus celsissimo, minimus maximo, agrestis urbano, MICROLOGUS eloquentissimo, extremus primo, peregrinus indigenae, pauperculus praepotenti, — mirum dictu, nova res, rara avis, — scribere audet Bonifatio Patri Palumbus' (ed. Walker, 36). The Irish may have discovered the word in the Latin translations of Rufinus; cf. *Thesaurus Linguae Latinae, s.v.* According to Walker, it was one of a class of Greek colloquialisms current in Ireland in the time of Columbanus: 'On the use of Greek words in the writings of St Columbanus of Luxeuil', *Archivum Latinitatis Medii Aevi (Bulletin du Cange)* 21 (1951) 127.

50. In the 'Second Vision of Adamnan' (*Leabhar Breac*, f. 258 – 259), mention is made of 'The Hymn of the Apostles'. This hymn is probably that attributed to St Cummain Fota, *Celebra Iuda* (ILH I 18 – 21; cf. *ibid.*, p. xxv). Warren II 39 and E. Hull, 'Hymns (Irish Christian)', *Encyclop. of Rel. and Ethics* 7 (1915) 27, identify it with *Praecamur patrem*.

51. Kenney, *Sources*, 262: 'It is probably of early origin, not later than the sixth century'.

52. Columban wrote his Epistles between 600 and 613. Cf. Walker, *Introduction*, xxxvi – xxxix. The clearest evidence of immediate influence of one on the other is found in *Epist.* 5, written in 613; but already in *Epist.* 1 we noted the use of the word *micrologus* in exactly the same sense as it has in the hymn. So in the alternative we are considering we can take 600 as the *terminus ante quem*.

53. Cf. W. Bulst, *Hymni Latini Antiquissimi*, 17.

CHAPTER FIVE

1. In the Antiphonary (AB 9: f. 11) it bears the title: *Ymnum quando caeria benedicitur*. The hymn was edited from this MS alone, by, among others, Warren II 11; Blume, AH 51, 296; Mercati, *Studi e Testi* 12 (1906) 25 – 27. Another MS of the hymn, Turin, *Bibl. naz.*, G. v. 38, written at Bobbio in the tenth century, was noted by Mearns, *Early Latin Hymnaries* (Cambridge 1913) 40, and by Kenney, *Sources*, 261. The two MSS were used by Walpole for his edition (*Early Latin Hymns*, 346 – 349), which agrees with that of Mercati

and which we will follow here. The title in the second MS corroborates the internal in-dications as to the use of the hymn. It is: *Ymnus in Sabato sancto ad cereum benedicere*, showing that the hymn was meant for the Easter Vigil and not for the ordinary office of vespers or *lucernarium*. Again, as Mercati pointed out (*loc. cit.*, 24), Alcuin cited a stanza of the hymn in order to illustrate the feminine gender of the word *rubus*, and he introduced his citation by saying: 'Item Ambrosius in hymno paschali'. Alcuin probably got to know the hymn at York, where Irish influence must have extended it.

2. G. Mercati, 'Un nuovo inno pasquale di S. Ambrogio?', *loc. cit.*, 12 – 36; in the foot-notes of his edition, 25 – 27, he indicates certain parallels with the vocabulary of Ambrose; these are generally no more than isolated words. Indeed, Mercati put forward his idea of Ambrosian authorship more as a suggestion for further study rather than as a firm conclu-sion; thus especially, *loc. cit.*, 35.

3. Mercati, *art. cit.*, 31 – 32; W. Meyer, 'Die Verskunst der Iren', 625, and already in his *Gesamm. Abhandl.* II 120, note.

4. Meyer, 'Die Verskunst der Iren', 625: 'Irisch kann er nicht sein. Denn er ist noch quan-titirend gebaut'.

5. Kenney, *Sources*, 262, says regarding this hymn that 'it is at least possible . . . that there were clerics in Ireland as well as on the Continent in the fifth or sixth century who could write simple classical verse'. On this question, cf. *supra*, p.205, n. 53.

6. Examples of alliteration: the entire first stanza; indulges *g*eminam *g*ratiam (3,2); ve-nientem *p*lebem *p*rotegis (4,2); e *f*lamma *f*amulum provocas, rubum non *sp*ernis *sp*ineam (5,1 – 2); *car*nem lu*cere cer*eam (6,4). There is some rhyme in almost every stanza, but it is not governed by any constant pattern; this would be consistent with a sixth or early seventh-century date. Generally the last line of a stanza rhymes with another line, which on four occasions is the line immediately preceding: mori, pectori (2); exhibes, porrigis (3); intimas, cellulas (7); sarcinis, pinnulis (8).

7. Cf. Mercati, *loc. cit.*, 30: 'All'ispirazione e al movimento vivo dell'inno, ai trapassi e contrasti efficaci ed arditi, ai tocchi — per dir così — rapidi e sicuri si rivela un autore non volgare'.

8. Following Mercati, M. Simonetti insists on the direct derivation of this hymn from the hymns of Ambrose, not only in metre but in general form and content: 'Già la mossa in-iziale *Ignis creator igneus* richiama l'ambrosiana *Deus creator omnium*, ma poi i punti di con-tatto si moltiplicano: il simbolismo della luce come illuminazione spirituale su cui l'autore insiste fortemente . . . è di schietta origine ambrosiana, e così anche l'accenno iniziale alla particolare occasione cui l'inno era destinato. Le due reminiscenze bibliche si possono riallacciare a quella technica compositiva tipica degli inni per le ore terza, sesta e nona che ha trovato la sua prima espressione nell'inno *Iam surgit hora tertia* di Ambrogio. Anche la parte finale dell'inno nel suo fortissimo simbolismo risente del influsso di Ambrogio'. While this is true in so far as it goes, I would rather broaden the horizon and situate the hymn in the more general context, which is, of course, altogether under the influence of Ambrose.

9. The expression *dator salutis* is found in *Sancti venite* 3: DATOR SALUTIS *Christus filius Dei*; I have not met it elsewhere. As a parallel for *creator igneus* we may note, apart from the other sources to be indicated immediately, *Praecamur patrem* 12:

Summerso saevo Cincri canunt aemulo
certatim deo laudes DUCI IGNEO.

10. For example, in two seventh-century Spanish hymns, one for the feast of St Felix (AH 27, 177):

1. Fons, Deus, vitae perennis,
LUX, ORIGO LUMINIS,

aspice plebem canentem
festa summi martyris.

The second, *Ecce te Christe* (AH 27, 263), was used for the dedication of a basilica:

3. Porta hic caeli pateat redemptis,
clausa damnatis, reserata iustis;
veritas, VITA, via, LUX ET IGNIS,
   influe mitis.

11. Text taken from H. Schmidt, *Hebdomada Sancta* II (Roma 1957) 362. Critical editions of the texts are also given by J. Pinell, 'La benedicciò del ciri pasqual i els seus textos', *Liturgica* 2 (Montserrat 1958) 83 – 119.

12. Mercati, *art. cit.*, 26, note: 'Geminus è usitatissimo in S. Ambrogio: *geminae substantiae, gemina virtus, geminam iniuriam* ecc.'.

13. Mercati, *ibid.*, refers to the Ambrosian blessing of the candle: 'Ecce iam IGNIS COLUMNA resplendet, quae PLEBEM Domini beatae noctis tempore' etc., and to Ambrose, *In ps.* 36,30: 'et cecitate DEPULSA lumen refulsit occulorum', and he adds: '*pellere* e composti sono frequenti in Ambrogio'.

14. Mercati, *ibid.*, cites Ambrose, *Ep.* 67,8: 'illi soli se offerat, qui culpam, non hominem EXURIT', and *Ep.* 63,42: 'Tu rubus, ego ignis. . . Propterea ignis ut tibi LUCEAM'.

15. The 'sign' of the burning bush that was not actually burned is also found in Ennodius, *Benedictio Cerei* II 63: 'Redemptor . . . integritatem diligit quam et nascendo in matre servavit: ut a propheta posset inspici, innocui corpus suscepit incendii, cum frondibus in rubo crepitantibus nulla frutex detrimenta sentiret, cum arida pabulum flammis, dum lamberentur, ligna non fierent' (ed. Schmidt, *op. cit.*, 637). The *gratia luminis* of the Gelasian blessing, which throws light on the *gemina gratia nubis (et) luminis* of our hymn, is found in a different context in the introduction to the *Exultet*, where the deacon prays: '(ut) LUMINIS sui GRATIA infundente, cerei huius laudem implere praecipiat' (ed. Schmidt, *op. cit.*, 641).

16. Mercati, *art. cit.*, 26, note, draws attention to Ambrose, *Grates tibi Iesu novas* 5: 'et ora tersit NUBILA' (AH 50, 17); *Ep.* 63,59: 'iram repellat vel DECOQUAT'; *In Luc. lib.* III 24: 'SANCTO FERVENTE SPIRITU'; *De Cain et Abel* II 6,20: 'significat fidem tuam . . . SANCTO FERVERE SPIRITU''. We may also note, apart from the morning hymn of Prudentius (*Cath.* II), to which we will return in the text, Ennodius, *Ben. Cerei* I 56: 'Christi nostri libamina INFUCATA simplicitate conplentur' (ed. Schmidt, *cp. cit.*, 635).

17. Warren accepts a contemporary correction in the manuscript of AB and writes: *condens favi*, which I think is the best reading. Variants: *condis favi* (AB *manu 1a*, Mercati, Walpole); *condens favis* (Turin MS, Blume).

18. Mercati, *loc. cit.*, 26 – 27, notes, says of *secretis . . . favi* that it is a favourite construction of St Ambrose: *secreta mentium, sapientiae, domus, naturae*, etc; then, in particular, he cites Ambrose, *De interpell. David* II 4,15: 'in INTIMA CORDIS SECRETA'; *Victor Nabor Felix pii* 3: 'sancto REPLEVIT Spiritu', and says that Ambrose particularly liked composite verbs in *re*.

19. According to Blume, AH 51, 309, *praelectum* stands for *prae – electum*, and he gives examples from other Irish hymns of the forms *praelectus* and *lectus* meaning *chosen*. But there is an obvious play on the expression *ore legere*, the classical expression for the procreational activity of the bees. The 'swarm of new offspring' in the Church is chosen/begotten by the word (*ore*, just as Christ proceeded from the mouth of the Father) and the Holy Spirit. There is an immediate contact here between our hymn and the Gelasian blessing.

20. Mercati, *art.cit.*, 27, refers for this stanza to Ambrose, *Intende qui regis Israel* 8: 'lumenque nox spirat NOVUM' (AH 50, 13); *Grates tibi Iesus novas* 1: 'Grates tibi, Iesu, NOVAS, / NOVI repertor muneris' (AH 50,13); *Exaem.* V 21,67: 'Ore suo prolem LEGENTES'; *Ep.* 81,12: 'Quid enim stultius quam relictis coelestibus ad terrena intendisse'.

21. Schmidt, *op. cit.*, 643.

22. Cf. *supra*, p.216, n.l.

23. It may, however, be understood as a further reflection on the themes of the blessing already sung by the deacon; this is suggested by J. Pinell, 'La benedicció del ciri pasqual i els seus textos', *loc. cit.*, 72 – 73.

24. The formula *Deus mundi conditor* appears to be certainly of Roman origin; cf. A. Chavasse, *Le Sacramentaire Gélasian*, 102 – 106; J. Pinell, 'La benedicció del ciri pasqual . . .', *loc. cit.*, 9 – 10, 51 – 52, 67 – 79, 80 – 81. According to Pinell, the earliest blessing is the *Exultet*, written in northern Italy and probably by St Ambrose himself. The author of *Deus mundi conditor* adapted the *Exultet* to the more sober form and euchological style of the Roman liturgy. Subsequently, the *Exultet* preface was radically revised at Milan itself and the original text has come down to us only through Gallican sources. Ennodius, for his part, was influenced by the *Exultet*, the Roman formula, and the Milanese preface. But H. Schmidt takes quite a different view of the origin and relationship of these texts. He says of the Gelasian blessing: 'Origo formulae *Deus mundi conditor* nobis videtur esse non ponenda Romae sed, propter influxum thematum benedictionis cerei Enodii, in Italia septentrionali vel in Gallia meridionali; per hanc viam pervenit in Ge V, quod a sua parte eam traditioni antiquiori Ge s. VIII (scil. Ge G et Ge E) in Gallia tradidit' (*op. cit.*, 638).

25. Cf. A. Chavasse, *Le Sacramentaire Gélasien*, 687 – 689.

26. Sometimes castigated as 'the Old Irish mania for amending, after a fashion, liturgical texts which are quite good in themselves' (E. Bishop, *Liturgica Historica*, 86, n. 19; cf, *ibid.*, 84, n. 6; 102, 105).

27. AB 10 (f. 11^v – 12^v) *Ymnum media noctis*; Warren II 11 – 12; AH 51, 3.

28. M. Simonetti, 'Studi sull'innologia', *art. cit.*, 436 – 440; Szövérffy, *Analen*, 113 – 114.

CHAPTER SIX

1. AB 12 (f. 13) *Ymnum ad matutinum in dominica*; Warren II 13. The hymn is also founa in the Turin Fragment (T: ed. Meyer, 197 – 199). A third MS of the hymn was discovered by H.M.Bannister in Paris (B.N., *MS. lat, 9488*. ff. 75 – 76). These two leaves of the Paris codex are in a script which is 'continental Irish, probably of the eleventh-century, and evidently form a fragment of an Irish hymnal or other service book' (Kenney, *Sources*, 716). The fragment also contains the *Hymnum dicat* and *Te Deum*. Bannister has published their variant readings in his 'Liturgical Fragments. . . C. Irish Hymns', *The Journal of Theological Studies* 9 (1908) 422 – 427.

2. In his introduction to *Hymnodia Hiberno-Celtica* , Blume says of this hymn: 'Da . . . weder Rythmus noch Symmetrie auch nur im mindesten grade in diesem 'Humnus' zu entdecken ist, bleibt es für die Hymnologie belanglos' (AH 51, 260). Cf. Szövérffy, *Analen*, 157, where he gives a list of the hymns in AB.

3. Kenney, *Sources*, 262. W. Meyer remarked: 'Form und Inhalt bleibt mir fast unverständlich. Die absätze zählen 19 28 24 41 47 37 47 29 (28) Silben: also scheint von rythmischer Gliederung keine Rede. Der Inhalt besteht aus Prädikaten der Trinität und bald dieser bald jener Person: meistens wird der Sohn, bisweilen der Vater angesprochen' ('Das turiner Bruckstück,' 197).

4. M. Simonetti, 'Studi sull'innologia', 371 – 375.

5. *Marii Victorini Opera. Pars I. Opera Theologica*, ed. P. Henry et P. Hadot, CSEL 83 (1971). This edition contains the three *Hymni de Trinitate* (285 – 305) and the *Adversus Arium libri IV* (54 – 277). We will cite the *Adv. Arium libri* by book, chapter and line of

the edition; the same division of the text is found in the Paris edition: *Marius Victorinus, Traités Théologiques sur la Trinité.* Part I. Texte établi par P. Henry; Introduction, Traduction et Notes par P. Hadot. Part II. Commentaire par P. Hadot: SC 68 – 69 (1960).

6. Cf. also I 17,24 – 34; I 18,32 – 42; I 55,3 – 11; III 6,23 – 28; III 14, 6 – 17; IV 4,7 – 32; IV 9,8 – 12.

7. Cf. also II 6,24; II 7,3 – 12; II 10,4 – 15; II 11,22 – 40.

8. Apart from the two texts cited, cf. I 24,29 – 41; I 36,5 – 12.

9. W. Meyer, 'Das turiner Bruckstück', 197, note, refers to Eph. 1,15: 'qui predestinavit nos in adoptionem filiorum per Iesum Christum in ipsum'.

10. I have noted the following instances in *Adv. Arium I*: 4,11; 22,7; 29,29; 32,13 – 15; 33,31; 34,21; 57,23; 58,5; 59,13 – 14.

11. Cf. also I 24,40 – 41; I 45,3 – 7.

12. W. Meyer, *loc. cit.*, gives the scriptural references: Col. 1,16; Rom. 11,36. *Cepit*, as Warren II 48 noted, 'is not the perfect of "capio" but the present or perfect of "coepio" '.

13. Cf. Victorinus, *In Gal.* 3,26 – 29 (PL 8, 1173); *In Gal.* 4,4 – 6 (*ibid.*, 1178 – 1179); and this text from his *In Eph.* 1,18: 'Cum enim in adoptionem nos recipiat pietas Dei, in adoptionem filiorum suorum, haeredesque simus; haeredes autem, non ut in mundanis est, ... sed ut in his de bonis ut qui haeredes sunt habeamur; ut quibus bonis Deus utitur, iisdem et nos bonis utamur, simus in gloria, simus aeterni. Haec est haereditas. Nam et cum Christo cohaeredes sumus, et Christus Deus est, ergo cum Deo haeredes divitiarum gloriae eius sumus' (*ibid.*, 1248).

14. Cf. also I 13,14 – 15; I 24,41 48; I 36,5 – 12; III 3,13 – 15; Hymn I 69.

15. Cf. I 8,29 – 32; I 10,20 – 23; I 14,25 – 36; I 21,6 – 39; I 26,20 – 53; I 27,18 – 20; etc; Hymn II 259 – 265 contains an expression of this theme which is close to that used in our hymn:

> Semper cum deo Christus est, iuxta substantiam, etenim vita semper est;
> At quoniam vita actio est, actio autem ut agat INCIPIT, hoc est Christus natus est;
> Ex aeterno autem deus et Christus agit: EX AETERNO igitur DEUS CHRISTUS natus est;
> O beata Trinitas.

16. Cf. Col. 1,18: 'Ipse est caput corporis ecclesiae, ... PRIMOGENITUS EX MORTUIS': Phil. 3,21: 'qui reformabit corpus humilitatis nostrae configuratum CORPORI CLARITATIS suae'; 2 Cor. 4,6: 'Deus... illuxit in cordibus nostris ad illuminationem scientiae CLARITATIS DEI in facie Christi Iesu'; Apoc. 5,13: 'Sedenti in throno et Agno benedictio et honor et gloria et potestas IN SAECULA SAECULORUM'; Apoc. 15,3: 'REX SAECULORUM'. Cf. Victorinus, *In Eph.* 2,16: 'Per resurrectionem, assumendo pugnam atque aeternam carnem atque omne CORPUS DIETATIS, cum omnia spiritus fiant, sicut multis locis et Paulus docet' (PL 8, 1259).

17. P. Hadot, *op. cit.*, *Introduction* (SC 68), 79, gives a synthesis of Victorinus's theology on this point.

18. Cf. also Hymn III 152 – 234, *passim*.

19. Cf. also I 37,26; II 6,20 – 22; IV 29,13 – 25.

20. Cf. IV 31,47 – 49: 'Cum mysterium adventus sui compleret, tum iam passionem sustinuit "ut se exinaniret", ut PERSONAM servi susciperet'. Elsewhere he always uses *formam servi* when citing Phil. 2,7; for example, I 21,31; 22,13; IV 30,22; or *imaginem servi*: IV 42,51.

21. P. Hadot, *Marius Victorinus... II. Commentaire* (SC 69), 744, notes regarding the formula *totus de toto* in this text: 'La formule peut venir au travers du dossier homéousien du Concile des Enceniens; cf., dans Hilaire, *De Synodis* 29; PL 10, 502B: *totum ex toto*'. It also

220

occurs in Prudentius, *Apoth.* 278: 'totus et ex toto Deus est de lumine lumen'.

22. Cf. I 42,26 – 28: 'Isto modo et vita filius a patre, . . . TOTA A TOTA'.

23. Many of these expressions were inserted by him when he came to edit definitively and correlate his various works; cf. Hadot, *op.cit.* I, *Introduction*, 66 – 68. I have counted twenty-two cases of *diximus* in the treatises *ad Candidum*, *Adv. Arium* and *De Homoousio*. Other expressions are also used, for example, *docuimus* (15 times), *(frequenter) dictum (est)* (15 times), *declaravimus* (3 times), and many others.

24. Cf. P. Hadot, *op. cit.* II, 750.

25. Cf. II 4,48 – 54: 'Subsistentia ergo proprie dicitur de ambobus, quod est substantia, quoniam quid est esse principale cum forma, subsistentia dicitur. Haec autem et substantia dicitur. Et ideo dictum est: "de una substantia, tres subsistentias esse", ut id ipsum quod est esse subsistat tripliciter: ipse deus, et Christus, id est logos, et spiritus sanctus'. Cf. also III 4,33 – 39.

26. Cf. *Audite omnes amantes* 87 – 88.

quam legem in trinitate sacri credit nominis
tribusque personis unam docetque substantiam.

27. Warren I, f. 13ᵛ, notes that 'Muratori read these four letters as "semper semper", mistaking the accents for marks of abbreviation; but "se" is an impossible abbreviation for "semper" '; and in vol. II 48 he says that ' "se se" must be either a clerical error for "esse", which however is not wanted, or a late Latin equivalent for "illum" '.

28. Cf. also I 33,23 – 26; I 51,4; I 55,25.

29. Warren II 48.

30. Cf. P. Hadot, *op. cit.* I, *Introduction*, 73, 84 – 88, for the influence on successive writers of the works of Victorinus.

31. Cf. P. Hadot, 'Marius Victorinus et Alcuin', *Archives d'histoire doctrinale et litteraire du moyen âge* 21 (1954) 5 – 19. He notes that the works of Victorinus, at least his works of rhetoric and logic, were present in the library of York in the eighth century, and that Alcuin had read them there in his young days (19, n. 1). It is not unlikely that they came to York through an Irish channel.

CHAPTER SEVEN

1. AB 12 (f. 12ᵛ – 13) *Ymnum in natale martyrum vel sabbato ad matutinum*; Warren II 12 – 13; AH 51, 313 – 314. The MS text will be used in our study.

2. Traces of rhyme or assonance, for example: 4, 1 – 2 mente, morte; 8, 2 – 3 habent, gaudent; 9, 1 – 2 obsecremus, consummemur. Alliteration: 4, 1 – 2 *A*rmis *s*piritalibus *m*unita *m*enta / *a*postoli *s*ancti te *s*unt *s*ecuti.

3. W. Meyer, 'Die Verskunst der Iren', *loc. cit.*, 612 – 616.

4. *Ibid.*, 612: 'Von irisch – lateinischer Rythmik ist hier keine Spur. Kein Reim, keine Alliteration, keine Paarung der Langzeilen. Vor allem: die Langzeilen zählen alle mehr als 8 Silben und sind doch durch keinerlei feste Caesur in feste Kurzzeilen getheilt'.

5. *Ibid.*, 613.

6. *Ibid.*, 614: 'auf dei 3 Accentanapaeste folgt ein umgebogener Anapaest -́-u, so dass genau derselbe Tonfall der Zeile entsteht, welchen ich im Liede des Antiphonars von Bangor festgestellt habe'.

7. *Ibid.*, 616: 'Ich glaube hier die Thatsache bewiesen zu haben, dass ein Ire des 7.

Jahrhunderts es gewagt hat, in lateinischer Sprache den Tonfall einer byzantinischen Melodie nachzuahmen und dabei die damals in Ireland gebräuchlichen Regeln der lateinischen Rythmik wenig zu beachten'.

8. Kenney, *Sources*, 262; Simonetti, 'Studi sull'innologia', 463, 475 – 476; Norberg, *Versification*, 148, n.3.

9. Cf. B. Bischoff, 'Das griechische Element in der abendlandischen Bildung des Mittelalters', in: *Mittelalterliche Studien* II 246 – 275. He shows that in spite of the remarkable interest of the Irish in the 'Three sacred languages', actual knowledge of Greek among them was limited to those words which they gleaned with avidity from the Latin authors, for example, Isidore, Glossaries, and biblical texts in Latin and Greek. He claims (249, n. 12) that even the Irish at Bobbio did not learn Greek, and it was only much later that their love for Greek resulted in their becoming promoters of Greek studies on the Continent. Cf. also R. E. McNally, 'The *tres linguae sacrae* in Early Irish Bible Exegesis', *Theological Studies* 19 (1958) 395 – 403. According to McNally, more often than not the Hebrew and Greek was fictional, 'mere pretentions of learnedness or inventions of Irish fantasy', (396). But more recently W. B. Stanford claims that 'the question is not entirely settled', and that 'further consideration might credit the early Irish scholars with more knowledge of the Greek language than is currently admitted. At any rate, whatever the provenance and extent of their Greek was, they were certainly eager to learn and use as much as they could of it' ('Towards a History of Classical Influences in Ireland', PRIA, vol. 70, Section C, no.3 (1970) 24, 26).

10. Contemporary correcting hands are seen on every page of the MS, including the pages on which our hymn was written.

11. The seven lines which defy correction are:

1,4 victores in caelis deo canantes: alleluia
3,1 Magnifice tu prior omnium passus crucem
4,2 apostoli sancti te súnt secuti
7,1 Manu domini excelsa protecti
7,2 contra diabolum steterunt firmati
8,1 Vere regnantes erant tecum Christe deus

12. The ten corrected lines are as follows, given immediately after the original lines of the MS:

2,3 angelorum ibi et martyrum fulgiens chorus
angelórum et mártyrum fúlgens chorus
3,3 qui devicta morte refulsisti mundo
refulsísti qui múndo devícta mórte
4,1 Armis spiritalibus munita mente
Spiritálibus ármis múnita ménte
5,3 qui cum victores exirent de hoc saeculo
qui victóres exírent cum dé hoc saéclo
6,1 Inlustris tua domine laudanda virtus
Tua dómne illústris laudánda virtus
6,3 qui consternerent zabulum et mortem vincerent
qui constérnerent zábulum mórtem víncerent
7,3 semper trinitati fidem toto corde servantes
trinitáti fidém toto córde servántes
8,3 et centinario fructu repleti gaudent
centinário frúctu repléti gaúdent
9,1 Christi dei gratiam supplices obsecremus
Christi grátiam súpplices óbsecrémus
9,3 et in sanctam Hierusalem civitatem dei
et in sáncta Ierúsalem civitáte

222

13. Cf. Kenney, *Sources*, 262: 'The verse-form of the piece is unique; it is quite different from all other examples of Hiberno-Latin verisfication.'

14. G. Murphy, *Early Irish Metrics* (Dublin 1961) 2 – 3.

15. *Ibid.*, 3. The reference to 'stressed feet' should not be taken to mean that there was a regular succession of iambic or trochaic or any such regular type of 'feet'. It means that the poem is composed of an 'almost identical rhythm' throughout. From the many examples of this type of verse given by Murphy, *ibid.*, 4 – 6, we take one:

> Fo-chèn Cònall / crìde lìcce,
> lòndbruth lòga / lùchair èga
> gùss flànn fèrge / fo chìch chùrad
> créchtaig càthbùadaig.
> At cómsa mac Fíndchoíme frím.

16. Examples are given by G. Murphy, *Early Irish Lyrics* (Oxford 1956) xvi, and J. Carney, 'Three Old Irish accentual Poems', *Ériu* 22 (1971) 23 – 80.

17. Carney, *art. cit*, 53, holds that the popular accentual metres never quite died out during the mediaeval period and that they were revived in the seventeenth century. The new syllabic metres (*nuachrotha*), for their part, were not entirely due to imitation of the Latin metres, but were 'syllabic regularizations and developments of the ancient metres'.

18. J. Carney claims that three stressed syllables may be reducible to two, because 'in certain contexts a syllable that would normally be stressed may lose stress when it precedes another stressed syllable' (*art.cit*, 25). This is not so easily verifiable in the Latin lines we are considering; they have a greater number of syllables than the Irish proto-type and a stressed syllable is never followed immediately by another stressed syllable. But, in cases where a half-line has three stresses, we will distinguish what we regard as secondary stresses from the main stresses.

19. 'The opening verse shows a strength and fervour, which give it a distinctively poetical quality' (F. J. E. Raby, *A History of Christian Latin Poetry*, Oxford 1927, 137).

20. The expression *Deus summus* is common in Irish sources, and is also found in Ambrosian, Gallican and Spanish prayers; cf. Manz 247.

21. 'A line of slightly different build may be used to mark off a section' (G. Murphy, *Early Irish Metrics*, 3). In the other stanzas of the hymn a shorter line is used as refrain: 'tibi sáncti proclámant, allelúia' (2, 3, 8), or 'tibi sáncti canébant, allelúia' (4, 5, 6, 7). In the final stanza the concluding line has the normal four accents: 'trinitáti cum sánctis / dicámus allelúia'.

22. Walker, 56. Cf. also *Epist.* 5,8: 'Sperans in antea videre fortiores peritioresque huius sancti conflictus duces' (*op. cit.*, 44).

23. Ambrose, AH 50, 19:

> 1. Aeterna Christi munera
> et martyrum victorias,
> laudes ferentes debitas,
> laetis canamus mentibus.
>
> 2. Ecclesiarum principes,
> belli triumphales duces,
> caelestis aulae milites
> et vera mundi lumina.
>
> 4. Traduntur igni martyres
> et bestiarum dentibus,
> armata saevit ungulis
> tortoris insani manus.

5. Nudata pendent viscera,
sanguis sacratus funditur,
sed permanent immobiles
vitae perennis gratia.

24. Cf. Ambrose, *Victor Nabor Felix pii* (AH 50, 17):

5. Profecit ad fidem labor
armisque docti bellicis
pro rege vitam ponere,
decere pro Christo pati.

6. Non tela quaerunt ferrea,
non arma Christi milites,
MUNITUS ARMIS ambulat
veram fidem qui possidet.

25. The expression *fides Trinitatis* was well known in Ireland from the time of St Patrick, who desired to preach the Christian message according to the measure of faith in the Trinity, *in mensura itaque fidei Trinitatis* (*Conf.* 14). It is used almost as a refrain in some of the early Irish biblical commentaries, notably by Ps. – Jerome, *Expos. IV* Evv. (PL 30, 537D, 554A, 573B, 576D, 577A, 588C) and Ps.-Hilary, *Expos. in Vii Epist. can.* (PLS 3, 63, 98, 103, 115, 126). It had become the slogan of orthodoxy in the West generally since the fourth century; cf. J. A. Jungmann, 'Fides Trinitatis', in: *Pastoral Liturgy.* (London 1962) 32 – 38.

26. Cf. the hymn *Amici nobiles*, which is contained in the *Book of Cerne* and is possibly Irish (AH 51, 314):

6. Fructum centesimum
a Domino datum,
quae casto corpore
vigent in tempore.

7. Hymnus laetitiae
in virginum ore
cum angelis simul
choroque virginum.

27. It would be wrong to conclude that Irish monasticism consisted entirely in fierce asceticism and loyalty to Christ, that it lacked humanity, joy and mysticism. Our hymn corresponds indeed to the spirit of Columbanus, but the latter's *Regula monachorum* and prayers show as well the joyous and mystical goal which all the asceticism aimed to achieve. In his chapter on obedience Columban writes: 'Let this mind be in you which was also in Christ Jesus, who ... humbled himself, being made obedient to the Father up to death, even the death of the cross. Thus nothing must be refused in their obedience by Christ's true disciples, however hard and difficult it be, but it must be seized with zeal, with gladness' (ed. Walker, 125). Columban had little place for moderation or half-measures. But we should not imagine the asceticism to have been joyless and puritanical; we get quite a different impression from the hymn *Benchuir bona regula*, even in the case of such a strict rule as that of Bangor. Other monastic legislators appear to have been more moderate and humane than Comgall or Columban. Cf. K. Hughes, *The Church in early Irish Society* (London 1966) 57 – 64; *s. a., Early Christian Ireland: Introduction to the Sources* (London 1972) 90 – 94.

28. From an Irish homily of the seventh or eighth century, cited by L. Gougaud, *Devotional and Ascetic Practices in the Middle Ages* (London 1927) 213.

CHAPTER EIGHT

1. AB 14 (f. 15^v – 17^v) *Ymnum sancti Comgilli abbatis nostri*; Warren II 16 – 19; AH 51, 321 – 324. The hymn is found in this MS only. The introductory stanza begins *Recordemur iustitiae*, and the first stanza proper *Audite pantes ta erga*.

2. Cf. W. Meyer, 'Die Verskunst der Iren', 619; Norberg, *Versification*, 108. The metrical form is not fully perfect, because 17 of the 196 lines end in paroxytones, even though these occur in words which are at least trisyllabic; again, the lines begin frequently with trisyllabic proparoxytones, an impossible opening in any quantitative model written in iambic dimeter.

3. Cf. W. Meyer, *art. cit.*, 620 – 621, where it is described as 'Reimketten'.

4. Recordemur iustitiae / nostri patroni fulgidae
   Comgilli sancti nomine / refulgentis in opere,
   adiuti dei flamine / sancto claroque lumine,
   trinitatis celsissimae / cuncta tenentis regmine.

5. Cf. J. Szövérffy, *Analen*, 158: 'Die Beschreibung des heiligen ist ganz stereotyp:

   In Scripturis eruditus
   inspiratus divinitus;
   in sacramentis providus
   canonicis affatibus
   veteris novi actibus
   testamenti praefulgidus,
   fervens spiritu, placidus,
   deo carus et pissimus.

Diese Strophe entspricht dem allgemeinen Eindruch von diesem Hymnus'. Repitition of identical expressions, for example: *contemptus mundi* (st. 3, 10, 14, 16, 19), *deo carus* (5, 9, 19), *floridus* (1, 2, 10), *placitus* (2, 5, 9); *lucidus* (5, 10); various forms of *fulgere* are used: *refulgens* (Introd. st.), *fulgidus* (Introd. st., 20), *praefulgidus* (9), *fulgebat* (6); *viscera* is used in various combinations: *alta viscera* (1), *viscera vigilantia* (3), *confirmatus ex viscere* (6), *collocans sua viscera* (18), *toto ex viscere* (23).

6. AB 129 (f. 36^v) *Memoriam abbatum nostrorum*. There is an introductory stanza, *Sancta sanctorum opera*, followed by the memorial hymn proper, *Amavit Christus Comgillum*. Warren II 33; AH 51, 357 – 358.

7. The proper names of the abbots come at the end of the lines and some of them are paroxytones, as well as *suppremus* (5,3) and *aeterna* (6,7). But all of these concluding words are at least trisyllabic, as in Comgall's hymn.

8. The relationship between this hymn and Comgall's hymn is parallel to that between *Audite bonum exemplum* (Camelacus's hymn) and *Audite omnes amantes* (Patrick's hymn). Here also, apart from identity of form and closeness of language (see below), certain lines in the alphabetical arrangement commence with identical words: *Elegit, Lampadem (lampade), Magnum, Notus, Rexit (rector), Christum (Christo), Ymnum (ymnos)*.

9. Sinlán (d. 610) is credited with being the first Irishman to learn the computus by memory from a Greek. His pupil Mo-Chuaróc of the Dési in Munster, 'whom the *Romani (i.e.* the adherents of the Roman date of Easter in the south of Ireland) style doctor of the whole world', recorded it in writing. Cf. K. Hughes, *The Church in Early Irish Society*, 132 – 133.

10. We will indicate here certain parallelisms; A = Abbots' hymn, C = Comgall's hymn. A 1,8 magna merita. 6,1 sanctorum merita; C 1,8 adlata merita. 16,8 sancta merita. 12,5 perfectum meritum. A 1,7 fulgentia; C – cf. *supra*, n.5. A 2,3 carus; C – cf. *supra*,

supra, ibid. A 4,1 notus vir. 5,2 vir amabilis; C 13,1 notus sanctorum coetibus. 13,6 vir apostolicus. A 5,4 ymnos canens; C 22,1 ymnum immolabat. There is a Greek expression in both: A 5,5 zoen; C 1,1 pantes ta erga.

11. Cf. K. Hughes, *Early Christian Ireland,* 122 – 123.

12. AB 95 (f. 30) *Versiculi familiae Benchuir,* which begins *Benchuir bona regula;* Warren II 28; AH 51, 356 – 357.

13. The quantitative model could not admit trisyllabic proparoxytones in the first or middle positions, for this would mean that the second or fourth syllables would be short; cf. Norberg, *Versification,* 108. The structure of the quantitative model is well imitated in our hymn: 'La structure du modèle quantitatif est, dans l'ensemble, conservés dans le vieux chant irlandais . . . *Versiculi familiae Benchuir,* . . . ou les vers normaux ont la forme *Recta atque divîna, Caritate perfécta, spe / salutis ornáta,* etc. (7p). Quelques vers seulement ne respectent pas la structure: d'une part 4 du type *certe civitas / firma,* avec un proparoxyton au milieu, d'autre part 3 qui se terminent par un proparoxyton: *Benchuir bona régula, Stricta, sancta, sédula,* et *Supra montem pósita'* (Norberg, *Versification,* 127 – 128). W. Meyer thought it was composed in accentual feet on the basis of a pre-existing melody, because 32 of the 40 lines are accentuated $\acute{-} - \acute{-} - - \acute{-} -$: 'Der Dichter hat eine bestimmte Melodie, welche von den 7 Silben die 1. 3. und 6. betonte, als Vorbild genommen und darnach seine Verse betont. Er hat also seine Zeilen mit Accentfüssen gefüllt. Das ist in der Lateinischen Rythmik prinzipielle nicht geschehen' ('Die Verskunst der Iren', 612).

14. It is 'das grösste Reimkunststück, welches uns aus der früheren Zeit des Mittelalters erhalten ist', according to Meyer, *art. cit.,* 611.

15. *Munther Benchuir beata* (2,1). *Munther* is derived from *monasterium;* its subsequent sense of *family* is already current in the seventh century, as we can conclude from the title of the hymn: *Versiculi familiae Benchuir.*

16. A recent study has attempted to show that traditional Marian typology is also very much in the author's mind. See P. O'Dwyer, *A Fresh Look at Versiculi Familiae Benchuir* (Carmelite Publications, Dublin 1975).

CHAPTER NINE

1. A very detailed study of the whole period of Irish prayer has been made by W. Godel, 'Irisches Beten im frühen Mittelalter', *Zeitschrift für kath . Theologie* 85 (1963) 261 – 321, 389 – 439. While it ranges over the whole field and is fully documented, this study is not entirely satisfactory. It suffers especially from over-systematization, with little thought given to the different periods of Irish prayer and little or no distinction or judgement of value being made between the various prayers, hymns and fragments that have come down to us. The result is that a *Sancti venite* and a *Lorica* of Brendan are practically considered as being of equal weight and value for the discovery of the spirit and themes of Irish prayer. *Hymnum dicat,* that most popular of all Irish prayers, should have been taken into consideration, regardless of its Irish or foreign origin.

CHAPTER TEN

1. 'The Celtic peoples, with their literature of poetry and lively dialogue and rhetorical description, and the highly technical language of the law tracts, had no tradition of

philosophical debate comparable to that of the Greeks. In fact, their only major philosopher was the ninth-century genius John Scotus, and he had learned Greek before he conceived his system' (K. Hughes, *The Church in Early Irish Society*, 11).

2. Cf. K. Hughes, *op. cit.*, 45 – 53.

3. Ed. L. Bieler, *The Irish Penitentials: Scriptores Latini Hiberniae* V (Dublin 1963).

4. Ed. Walker, *op. cit.*

5. Bede, *Historia Ecclesiastica* III 27; cf. Gougaud, *Christianity*, 242 – 249.

6. The many Roman texts in the Stowe Missal have been generally regarded as a seventh- or eighth-century stratum superimposed on the original Gallican core of the Irish liturgy of the Mass. A recent suggestion of K. Gamber merits serious consideration, namely, that these Roman texts and the Roman elements in the Ordinary of Stowe go back to the beginnings of the Irish Church with the mission of Palladius from Rome; cf. K. Gamber, 'Die irischen Messlibelli alz Zeugnis für die frühe römische Liturgie', *Römische Quartelschrift* 62 (1967) 214 – 221.

7. Warren II xxvi – xxviii. The term *collectio* is generally used in the titles of the collects in the Antiphonary; one prayer is headed *oratio* (AB 97), the Our Father is entitled *Oratio divina* (AB 36) and the intercessions (AB 40 – 56) are called *oratio communis*. On the Gallican term *collectio*, the Roman *oratio* or *orationes et praeces*, and the Carolingian *collecta*, cf. B. Capelle, 'Collecta', *Revue bénédictine* 42 (1930) 197 – 204.

8. AB 62, 63, 64, 68, 69, 71, 73, 91, 92, 93.

9. Cf. Ve 238, 254, 1271: with parallels in all Western liturgies; Gr C 18,6: with parallels in Ga and Am books; Am Be 680, 1093; Mo LS 357, 1434; M 302.

10. There is one Spanish instance, LO 94,22: *s.m. qui in trinitate*. Cf. the texts collected by Bishop, *Note*, 35; Manz 879. Bishop regarded it as a Gallican peculiarity, but, Manz took it to be one of the marks of Irish influence on the Gallican books (Ga G.V).

11. The usual conclusion in Ga C is *per dominum nostrum*. But traces of Irish tinkering are discernible here and in the conclusions to collects; e.g., Ga C 4 miserere nobis; 124 miserere nobis qui regnat; 143 miserere nobis qui vi. The insertion of *salvator* before *dominus* in 147 *per* SALVATOREM *nostrum Iesum Christum cui cum patre* appears to betray an Irish hand. The conclusion *qui regnas* (*in saecula*) is used twice (57, 150); in one of these cases (57) the conclusion of the parallel collect in Ga G 206 reads *per coaeternum*.

12. AB 66, 69.

13. AB 17,64, 78, 79, 123, 125, 126.

14. Cf. Ga G 226 (V 135); 229; 404; Mo LO 156,26; LS 302 (M722; M 12 sup. 13,2); 1206; Br 1008 (1250); M 12 sup. 38,1; 40,3.

15. Am Bi 131; the examples in Ga and Mo are numerous; some, at least, of the occurrences in Ge V are of Gallican origin: Ge V 792; 1605; 1617 (cf. A Chavasse, *Le Sacramentaire Gélasien*, 32, 59 – 60). The others are: G V 579; 600; 848; 1597; Bishop, *Note*, 258, thought Ge V 598 – 601 to be of Gallican origin, but this is contested by Chavasse, *op. cit.*, 172 – 176.

CHAPTER ELEVEN

1. AB 17 – 26 (f. 18^r18^v); Warren II 19 – 20; AH 51, 288 – 289. Blume judged them to belong to the earliest period of Irish hymnody (*ibid.*, 292).

2. Out of forty lines there is only one paroxytone ending: 21,4 *nostris peccatis ignóse*. This is in accord with the tendency to avoid disyllabic line-endings in the hymns written in iambic dimeter, a tendency which became the established rule in the hymns used at Arles in the time of Caesarius and Aurelian; cf. Norberg, *Versification*, 69 – 70. Another feature of the quantitative model retained here is the avoidance of trisyllabic proparoxytone words at the start of the lines, as well as the freedom shown with regard to accent, apart from the final proparoxytone cadence.

3. Cf. Am Be 157 (Bi 152) quem (scil. Iohannem) dominus ... IN CRUCE POSITUS ... vicarium pro se matri filium ... attribuit. Isidore, *De ortu et obitu Patrum* 67: 'quam (scil. Mariam) dominus ipse IN CRUCE POSITUS ... virgini commendavit discipulo' (PL 83, 148). A hymn, possibly of the fifth century (cf. Szövérffy, *Analen*, 155, n.158), with acrostic ORIENTIUS, *Omnipotenti domino* 7: Iamiam IN CRUCE POSITUS (AH 27, 133). The Irish Ps. – Hilary, *Expos. in VII Epist. can.* (Ja. 5,11): ' "Et finem Domini vidistis", i.e. oculis carnalibus IN CRUCE POSITI' (PLS 3, 81).

4. For example, again, in the Arles hymn for sext, *Iam sexta sensim volvitur* (AH 51, 17):

> 3. Hoc namque tempus illud est,
> quod saeculorum iudicem
> iniusta morti tradidit
> mortalium sententia.
>
> 6. Hanc ad precandum congruam
> salvator horam tradidit,
> cum diceret fidelibus
> patrem rogandum servulis.

5. This is one of the *Orat. ad Vesperas* in Ge G 329 (no. 9).

6. Cf. G. Mercati, *Studi e Testi* 12(1904) 26. For example, in the hymn *Grates tibi Iesu novas* (AH 50, 17):

> 6. LUMEN refulsit illico
> fugitque PULSA CAECITAS.

Again, *In ps. 36,30* (cited by Mercati, *ibid.*): 'et caecitate DEPULSA lumen refulsit occulorum'.

7. Manz 551; to which add Rot. Rav. 34.

8. The expression *adventus verae lucis* was not fully retained in the Spanish tradition of this collect: Vesp.Mat.67 Oriatur, quaesumus, Domine, in cordibus nostris sol iustitiae tuae, ut omni noctis obscuritate sublata, quia non est portio lucis cum tenebris, filios nos esse diei lux vera manifestet.

9. We have some evidence of this in the Antiphonary, which includes the hymn *Mediae noctis tempus*. Another Arles hymn, *Christe qui lux es*, is included in the much later ILH (I 197), but its presence in Ireland may have been as early as the seventh century.

CHAPTER TWELVE

1. AB 27 – 56 (f. 18^v – 22); Warren II 20 – 24.

2. Manz 894; he also gives, apart from Irish and Gallican texts, examples from some eighth-century Gelasians; *sanguis sanctus* occurs in Mo M 628 B, but the parallel LO 242,31 has *sanguis sacer*.

3. Manz 892; add Br 615B; 666D; LS 696.

4. Cf. I Pet. 1,18 – 19: 'scientes quod . . . redempti estis . . . pretioso sanguine quasi agni immaculati Christi'. Ve 520 (with parallels in Ge V and Ga V); Gr C 100,3 (parallels in A m); 159,1 (Am Bi 459. 1029); Am Be 500; 1462; 1544; innumerable Spanish instances.

5. Cf. Ps. 50,21: 'Tunc acceptabis sacrificium iustitiae, oblationes et holocausta, tunc imponent super altare tuum vitulos'.

6. *Trad. Apostolica* 41: 'ora tempore horae tertiae et benedic Deum. . . in hac enim hora . . . in veteri, lex praecepit ut offeretur panis propositionis in omni tempore, ut typus corporis et sanguinis Christi; et immolatio agni irrationalis est typus agni perfecti' (ed. Botte, *La Tradition Apostolique de Hippolyte*, Munster Westfalen 1963, 90).

7. There are a number of Irish, Gallican and Spanish instances of the expression *preces subnixae*, but they throw no light on this collect; cf. Ga G 28; Mo Br 60 (Manz 789).

8. This prayer recurs in a slightly corrupt form in Ge A 1890: Tibi subnixis precibus Christum dominum deprecemur, ut qui in hac hora diei tercia spiritum sanctum apostolis oraverunt emisisti, earumque participatione nos facias esse consortes, per (cf. Ge G 325,5).

9. Blume judged it to be originally Ambrosian, on the basis of form and MS tradition; cf. AH,51, 100.

10. AB 21: Ge G 329,9 (cf, *supra*, p.229, n.5); AB 28: Ge A 1890. G 325,5 (*supra*, n.8); AB 121: Ge A 1894 (*infra*, p.117); AB 122: Ge A 1888 (*infra*, p.118). Apart from Ge A 1893, which we have just cited, another collect in the same book shows further traces of influence from the collect we are now considering (AB 29): Ge A 1892 Domine Iesu Christe, qui dum hora sexta redemptionem mundi CRUCIS ASCENDISTI lignum, universes MUNDUS IN TENEBRIS conversus est. . . (De ps. usu 507; Lib. sac. 463).

11. Examples of such development of Ambrosian collects are found elsewhere in the Antiphonary; cf. *infra*, p. 134 – 137.

12. Cf. *infra*, p.101 – 115. The day hours were part of the monastic office at Milan from the fourth century, according to E. Cattaneo, *Il Breviario Ambrosiano* (Milano 1943) 211. This does not mean that the collects as we have them in the sources are necessarily that ancient.

13. Mt. 27,45; Mk. 15,33; Lk. 23,64.

14. Ed. Botte, *La Tradition Apostolique*, 90 – 91. Hippolytus makes a similar exhortation in connection with the sixth hour: 'orent in illa hora ORATIONE POTENTI, IMITANTES vocem eius qui orabat et creationem omnem fecit tenebras pro incredulis Iudaeis' (*op. cit.*, 90).

15. Mo Br 959 Deus qui pro mundi salvatione nonae horae curriculo in crucis stigmate glorioso triumphasti miraculo, et perempta morte sanctorum animas eruens ab infernali ergastulo, viam nobis reserasti, revertendo ad superos; quaesumus, ut ita nostro complacearis obsequio, quatenus illic post transitum properemus gressu perconcito, quo tu nostra praecessisti vera redemptio.

16. Ps. 32,22: 'Fiat misericordia tua, domine, super nos, quemadmodum speravimus in te'. Apart from the many AB collects composed of psalm-versicles, often selected at random, we may note one structural parallel: AB 34 Pax tua, domine rex caelestis, permaneat semper in visceribus nostris, *ut non timeamus a timore nocturno* (Ps. 90,5: 'ut non timebis a timore nocturno').

17. This collect is found in Am M in the form of a responsary (*Resp. VIII* in *Die tertio de Litaniis*), with some minor changes: M II 265 Ascendat, domine, oratio nostra ad thronum maiestatis tuae, et ne vacua revertatur ad nos postulatio nostra.

18. Cassian, *De Inst. Coen.* III 3,6: 'Hora vero nona inferna penetrans INEXTRICABILES Tartari TENEBRAS corruscatione sui splendoris extinxit'. I have not met elsewhere the expression *densitas caliginis*.

19. Am M II 452 (Be 1584) ita CORDA NOSTRA . . . illuminare et CUSTODIRE digneris. If this

influenced our author, it can only have been by way of reminiscence, because otherwise he would surely have included the more appropriate *illuminare*.

20. The parallelism with the AB collect is here most striking: AB evolutis diei temporibus / Br transacto diei curriculo; AB nocturnisque spatiis supervenientibus / Br nocturno appropinquante spatio; AB dei misericordiam deprecamur / Br postulantes magnificentiam tuam; AB tenebrarum operibus renuntiare / Br obscuratur caligine peccatorum.

21. M. A. Gimeno, *Presentation y contenido de un manuscrito de la liturgia hispana. Disertation la Licentia en el Pont. Inst. de Liturgia de S. Anselmo* (Roma 1970), *Apendice* no. 54.

22. Cf. J. Pinell, 'Vestigis del lucernari a Occident', *loc. cit.*, 122 – 123.

23. Similar expressions can be found in other Spanish evening prayers; for example, Br 702 Adsiduis orationibus culparum nostrarum veniam DEPRECANTES, infinitam Dei Patris omnipotentis MISERICORDIAM vespertinam praeposcamus...; Br 224 Deus, auctor luminis, conditor claritatis, qui submovisti omnia OPERA TENEBRARUM ... respice.

24. Cf. Ps. 30,6: 'Redemisti me, Domine Deus veritatis'; Apoc. 5,9: 'redemisti nos Deo in sanguine tuo'.

25. Cf. Ps. 90,5: 'ut non timebis a timore nocturno'.

26. Cf. 2 Par. 7,1.12 – 14: 'MAIESTAS DOMINI implevit domum... Aparuit autem ei Dominus nocte et ait: ... EGO EXAUDIAM DE CAELO ET PROPITIUS ERO PECCATIS EORUM et sanabo terram eorum'.

27. The expression *conditor elementorum* is a Spanish peculiarity, but it could have become current in Irish usage; Manz 310 gives examples from Mo LO 14,10: 18,38; 19,16; 330,28; the Irish St Gall, MS 1395; Ga B 544; to which list we may add Mo Br 1215 – 1216 (1325A); M 1026A. The expression *delere delicta* is used frequently and almost exclusively in Spanish and Irish sources, according to Manz 236.

28. Many of these prayers are also markedly penitential in tone. For example, there is the following prayer in a number of sources: Rogo te ut deleas universa delicta mea quae tibi non sunt abscondita,.... Rogo te, pater, ... ut exaudias me, et deleas universa delicta mea quae tibi non sunt abscondita (Munich, Clm 14248, ed. Frost, *The Journal of Theological Studies* 30, 1928, 36; the prayer is also included in the *Book of Cerne* and in B.M., MS Royal 2. A. XX).

29. From among many texts we may cite one: Mo CPs 534 (ps. 68) Deus, apud quem delicta nostra non sunt abscondita, cuius oculi non solum exteriora prospiciunt, sed cordis intima insensibili intuitu penetrant: da nobis poenitentiae remedium pro cilicii indumento, da confessionis praeconium pro veniae lucro; da ut effluant oculi pro admissis flumina lacrimarum.... The development of the theme of light in the Spanish morning and evening prayers often includes the idea of God's enlightening the soul and banishing the darkness of sin; for example, Br 232 Defensio nostra et inluminatio copiosa, illumina CORDIS NOSTRI OBSCURA, quae sordis facinus et crassum chaos obnubilat. Illumina arcana pectoris ut contemplare possimus clementiam redemptoris; Vesp.Mat.73 oculi tui ABDITA CORDIS aspiciunt.

30. Walker, 120.

31. F. E. Warren, *The Liturgy and Ritual of the Celtic Church*, 185. For comment on this prayer and on the influence of this type of composition on Alcuin,cf. H. B. Meyer, 'Alcuin zwischen Antike and Mittelalter', *Zeitschrift für kath. Theologie* 81 (1959) 319 – 321. An even more elaborate prayer in similar vein is included in the Irish collections of private prayers; cf. M. Frost, *The Journal of Theological Studies* 30 (1928) 38.

32. Cf. ps. 17,2 – 3: 'Diligam te, Domine, fortitudo mea. Dominus firmamentum meum et refugium meum et liberator meus. Deus meus adiutor meus ... protector meus et cornu salutis meae et susceptor meus'; ps. 26,1: 'Dominus illuminatio mea et salus mea, ... Dominus protector vitae meae'; ps. 34,3; 45,2; 70,3; cf. Jn. 11,25; 14,6.

33. The first of the Mone Masses is a metrical composition which has a number of these titles; for example, the *Contestatio* (Ga V 273):

Dignum aequum ac iustum est tibi nos piae clangere laudes,
lux, via, vita, decus, spes, fons, sator, arbiter, auctor,
gratia, dulcedo, sapientia, gloria, regnum,
qui sine principio praestas, sine fine per eum.

34. Ge V 441: Am Be 529. Bi 492. Cf. also Ge V 1350 (Gr C 201,31; Am Be 742; Ga G 343) Deus refugium pauperum, spes humilium, salusque miserorum.

35. Cf. also Ga B 90; 221; 146 (Deus omnium pie ieiunantium spes, salus, gloria); 448 (Domine Iesu Christe spes et salus humani generis).

36. Mo CPs 378: Br 234. 261. 730. Cf. also CPs 381 (ps. 64): Br 670; CPs 412 (ps. 90); 529 (ps. 64): Gil 40; CPs 535 (ps. 70): Gil 50; LO 115,17; 126,28; LS 148 (Iesus vita mortalium et spes unica redemptorum); 872; Gil 356 (Deus credentium salus, spes et resurrectio mortuorum).

37. GeV 1350: Gr C 201,31. Am Be 742. Ga G 343. Cf. also Ge V 1498; 1539 (Am Be 1393. Bi 1270).

38. Ga G 35: Mo LO 273,11. Cf. also Ga V 44; Ga B 448.

39. Mo CPs 208: Br 116. 1089. Or 757. Other Spanish instances: Or 298: Br 143 Domine Iesu Christe ... salus nostra; Or 727: Br 533 Domine Iesu Christe ... tu es animae nostrae salus; Or 729: Br 534. 957 Domine salus animae; Or 792: Br 475 Tu, Domine, ... salus nostra; LO 51,13 tua est salus et tu es salus; LO 72,12,Iesu vera salus: LO 272,41. 318,27 Deus vita et salus fidelium; LO 273,11 Deus perennis salus; LO 342,25 Christus vita fidelium et salus animarum; LS 376; 406; 602; 668; 1337; 1367 (Christus infirmantium virtus, viventium salus, morientium vita); M 962; 995; Gil 356.

40. Ge V 562: Am Be 1276. Bi 1176; Ge V 621; 727; 1460.

41. Cf. also Am Be 1588; Bi 1097; M II 384.

42. From among many other Spanish instances, which often reflect Jn. 11,25 and 14,6, cf. Or 337; LO 272,41 (318,27); 342,25; 350,16; 404,40; 407,33; 422,21; LS 148; 334; 335; 376; 484; 1022 *bis*; 1121; 1367; 1406; 1425; M 617D; 974B; 996 – 997.

43. There are numerous Spanish instances of the use of *virtus* in apposition; for example, CPs 334 (ps 20): Br 255. 708; CPs 52 (ps. 45): Br 396. 402; CPs 237 (ps. 45); CPs 358 (ps. 45): Gil 16. Br 225. 344; Or 213; 586 (Br 593); 1013 (Br 657); 1020; LO 150,11; 416,23; LS 13; 602; 1367; M 962C; 1009B.

44. Cf. Am M I 82 Domine, sis ei adiutor et protector atque defensor (a prayer found in a monastic ritual).

45. CPs 358: Gil 16. Br 225. The term *adiutor* is used frequently in Spanish prayers as a term of apposition; for example, CPs 28 (ps. 27): Br 340. 1314; CPs 326 (ps. 9): Br 196; CPs 392 (ps. 77): Br 303. 412. 1321; CPs 395 (ps. 80): Gil 66. Br 355. 417; CPs 462 (ps. 141): Gil 66. Br 493; CPs 580 (ps. 123): Br 166. 322. Or 1173; CPs 588 (ps. 144): Gil 145. See also in the Index of Spanish formulae compiled by Férotin, LO 586, the many prayers commencing *Adiutor*.

46. Mo CPs 320: Gil 363. Br 596; cf. also CPs 316 (ps. 3): Br 527; CPs 472 (ps. 3): Br 569. LO 381. And cf. the evening hymn used at Arles in the time of Caesarius, *Christe qui lux es et dies* (AH 51,21):

6. qui es DEFENSOR ANIMAE
adesto nobis domine.

47. The intentions were generally written by the original scribe; some which he omitted have been supplied by Warren II 22 – 23. They are written simply *pro baptizatis, pro abbate*, and so on, and it is almost certain that these headings are not merely titles but bid-

dings pronounced by the officiant: *Oremus pro baptizatis*, and so forth. They have been understood in this sense by W. C Bishop, 'A service Book of the seventh Century', *The Church Quarterly Review* 37 (1894) 362, and by E. Bishop, 'Kyrie Eleison', in: *Liturgica Historica*, 127. There is a much shorter form of of the *Oratio communis* in AB 117, where it is introduced as: *Ad horas diei oratio communis*; cf. *infra*, p. OOO – OOO. The expression itself *oratio communis* is found in the collects of the ordination formularies in Ga F, which were subsequently adopted by the other Western liturgies: Ga F 25 Commune votum, COMMUNIS ORATIO prosequatur (Ge V 155; Mo LO 48); Ga F 31 Sit nobis fratres COMMUNIS ORATIO (Ge V 147; Mo LO 54).Cf. A. Chavasse, *Le Sacramentaire Gélasien*, 12; L. Brou, 'Encore les "Spanish Symptoms" et leur contre-partie', *Hispania Sacra* 7 (1954) 480. The Irish probably also derived the expression from Gaul.

48. Columban, *Reg. mon.* VII: 'per diurnas terni psalmi horas pro operum interpositione statuti sunt a senioribus nostris, cum versiculorum augmente intervenientium pro peccatis primum nostris, deinde pro omni populi christiano, deinde pro sacerdotibus et reliquis deo consecratis sacrae plebis gradibus, postremo pro elemosinas facientibus, postea pro pace regum, novissime pro inimicis, ne illis deus statuat in peccatum quod persecuntur et detrahunt nobis, quia nesciunt quid faciunt' (Walker, 130). The phrase *ne illis deus statuat in peccatum* corresponds to the collect for this class in AB 46, and is a sign that Columban also was acquainted with the collects, even though he speaks only of 'intercessory versicles'.

49. Cf. B. Capelle, 'Le Kyrie de la Messe et le Pape Gélase', *Revue bénédictine* 46 (1934) 126 – 144. The author gives an edition and comparative study of the four texts of the litany used in the West: the Irish text (Ir), the Gallican text (Ga), the Ambrosian text in two forms (MI[1], MI[2]), and the *Deprecatio Gelasii* (Gel) used at Rome. Ir, Ga and MI are closely related and are probably derived from a Latin text of the litany which pre-dated the composition of the *Deprecatio Gelasii* (*art. cit.*, 144)

50. S. Bäumer and R. Biron, *Histoire du Bréviaire* II 430 – 431; F. Cabrol, 'Capitellum', DACL II 2 (1910) 2041 – 2042; H. Leclercq, *Histoire des Conciles* II 2 (Paris 1908) 993 – 994; E. Bishop, 'Kyrie Eleison', in: *Liturgica Historica*, 127 – 128; J. A. Jungmann, 'The Kyrie Eleison of the Preces', in: *Pastoral Liturgy*, 181.

51. E. Bishop, *loc. cit.*, he adduces Ammalarius, *De eccl. rit.* IV 4, as evidence for this fusion and claims that 'Amalar . . . explains how, even before his time, that is by the beginning of the ninth century,the two forms had become combined' (128). I cannot find any indication in Amalar's account that he was speaking about the combination of two forms of *preces*. He explains how the *preces* as a whole fulfill the command of St Paul; the first four versicles are artificially explained as 'obsecrationes, orationes, postulationes, gratiarum actiones'. Then he continues: 'Hucusque oratum est secundum Apostolum "pro omnibus hominibus". Deinde sequitur, "pro regibus et omnibus qui in sublimitate sunt, ut quietam et tranquillam vitam agamus in omni pietate et castitate" ' (PL 105, 1176A). According to J. A. Jungmann also, the *preces* arose out of the fusion of three styles of intercessory prayer: 1) the Roman style, that is, the litany with *kyrie*; 2) the Columbanian style, or versicles used in response to the announcement of intentions (*oremus pro. . .*); 3) the Gallican type, which consisted in stringing along psalm verses, divided into versicles and responses, without any announcement of intentions; cf. *art. cit.*, 181.

52. At Arles, according to the Rules of Caesarius and Aurelian, each office concluded with a *capitellum*; cf. Caesarius, *Reg. mon.*, ed. Morin, *Sancti Caesarii Opera Omnia* II (Maredsous 1942) 153 – 154; *Reg. virg.* 66 – 69, ed. Morin, *ibid.*, 120 – 122; Aurelian, *Reg. mon.* (PL 68, 393 – 396), *Reg. verg.* (*ibid.*, 403 – 406). According to Aurelian, the *capitellum* was always followed by the *kyrie eleison*, said three times at the conclusion of each office and twelve times at the conclusion of ferial matins (*Reg. mon.* 393, 395). He alone on one occasion identifies the text of the *capitellum*: 'Quotidianis igitur diebus ad tertiam . . . capitellum *Fiat Domine*' (*ibid.* 395). It is always a single versicle, 'ein dem Psalter entnommener Schlussversikel des Offiziums' (O. Heiming, 'Zum monastischen Offizium von

Kassianus bis Columbanus', *loc. cit.*, 121). Aurelian makes one reference to *capitella consuetudinaria*, not just one *capitellum*, to be said at the conclusion of compline (*ibid.*, 395); this was the only time on which more than one *capitellum* was said.

53. The Council of Agde (509), presided over by Caesarius, ordained (c. 30): 'in conclusione matutinarum vel vespertinarum missarum, *post hymnos capitella de psalmis dicantur*, et plebs collecta oratione ad vesperum ab episcopo cum benedictione dimittatur' (Mansi VIII 329 – 330). The *capitella* referred to must be understood in the light of what we know was the practice in the monastic office at Arles in the time of Caesarius, that is, *one capitellum* following the hymn (singular!) in *both* matins and vespers. References to the *capitellum* are also found in the writings of Gregory of Tours; its nature and purpose is the same as at Arles: a single versicle which concludes the office. Cf. *De Virtutibus S. Martini* I 5: 'peractoque ex more servitio, CAPITELLUM TANTUM, vobis excitantibus, NON EXPLEVI' (ed. Krusch, MGH, *Script. rer. merov.* I, 1885, 591); *Liber Vitae Patrum VI. De S. Gallo* 7: 'alleluiatico cum CAPITELLO EXPLETO consummavit matutinos' (*ibid.*, 685); *Liber in Gloria Confessorum* 4: 'post effusas preces, DICTO ETIAM CAPITELLO, ait (Martinus): "Benedic . . . mihi, vir Dei" '(*ibid.*, 751). Only once does Gregory speak of a number of *capitella* being said, but this practice was only part of the arrogant behaviour of a certain individual whom Gregory speaks about with disapproval. He refers to a man who claimed to have come from Spain with holy relics and who complained of not being properly received by Gregory; in fact this man was 'valde seductor, qui multos decepit dolositate sua. . . . Et ingressus in oratorio, me postposito, IPSE CAPITELLUM UNUM ADQUE ALTERUM AC TERTIUM DICIT; ipse orationem profert et ipse consummat' (*Hist. Francorum* IX 6, ed. Arndt, *loc. cit.*, 362). This story only confirms the fact that the *capitellum* was a single verse of a psalm, not a type of *preces* in the form of versicles and responses. Jungmann's interpretation of *capitellum*, in the passage from *De S. Gallo* cited above, that it 'can only be what we mean by *preces*', is unacceptable, as is his understanding of the canon of the Council of Agde: 'after the psalms we have the lines of the *preces* once more, now described more exactly as *capitella de psalmis*' ('The Pre-Monastic Morning Hour in the Gallo-Spanish Region in the 6th Century', *loc. cit.*, 134 – 135).

54. Cf. J. Pinell, 'El oficio hispánico visigótico', *Hispania Sacra* 10 (1957) 17, 19.

55. E. Cattaneo, describes the *capitulum* as a 'versetto salmodico, simile al *versus ad repetendum* romano, con particolare funzione di riassumere il persiero dominante nei salmi che lo precedono'(*Il Breviario Ambrosiano*, 185).

56. Benedict, *Reg. mon.* 12, 13, 17; in other hours the *versus* came between the readings and the *kyrie eleison*, as it did at Arles; *Reg.* 9, 17 (ed. Hanslik, CSEL 75, 56 – 67).

57. Cf. A. de Vogüé, *La Régle du Maître* I. *Introduction*: SC 105 (1964) 56 – 57, where he gives an outline of the office; text of the *Regula* bearing on the office *ibid.* II: SC 106 (1064) 172 – 222. In the other hours the *versus* came, as in the Benedictine office, between the readings and *rogus dei*. The Master also spoke of a *versus apertionis* in nocturns (*Reg.* 44,1: *op. cit.*, II 202) and a *versus clusoriae* in compline (*Reg.* 37,1: *op. cit.*, II 194).

58. For the history of the *kyrie* and its litany in the Mass and office, cf. C. Callewaert, 'Des étapes de l'histoire du kyrie. S. Gélase, S. Benoit, S. Grégoire', *Revue d'histoire ecclésiastique 38* (1942) 20 – 45.

59. Cf. P. Borella, *Il rito ambrosiano* (Brescia 1964) 248, 260; he says of the 12 Kyrie: 'é l'avanzo della litania, che, in tutte le antiche liturgie, chiudeva le due grandi ufficiature, matutina e vespertina' (248).

60. Council of Vaison c.3: 'Et quia tam in sede apostolica quam etiam per totas orientales atque Italiae provincias dulcis et nimium salutaris consuetudo est intromissa, ut *Kyrie eleison* frequentius cum grandi affectu et compunccione dicatur, placuit etiam nobis ut in omnibus ecclesiis nostris ista tam sancta consuetudo et ad matutinum et ad missas et ad vesperum Deo propitio intromittatur' (Heffele-Leclercq, *Historie des* Conciles I 1113 – 1114). The *kyrie eleison* must be understood here in the sense of litany with *kyrie*

233

eleison, in imitation of the Churches of Rome and Italy; cf. Callewaert, *art. cit.,* 29.

61. Cf. E. Bishop, 'Kyrie Eleison', *loc. cit.,* 126-133.

62. We will have occasion to see certain collects in AB which have been composed of selected versicles of psalms. The Irish love of psalm versicles was also expressed in the abbreviated 'Psalter', a collection of favourite versicles from all the psalms, artfully strung together so as to form one consecutive prayer. A number of these abbreviated Psalters have survived in Irish and English prayer books. Regarding their origin, E. Bishop claimed: 'After a detailed consideration and investigation of the extant specimens of "Breviate Psalter", it appears to me to be historically a devotion of Irish origin and propagation, and to have been cultivated in England only while the Irish influence was still, from old associations at any rate, a living force' (*Liturgica Historica,* 195 – 196). The Irish attitude to the 'Breviate Psalter' is expressed in the introduction to the exemplar of it in ILH I 144: 'Incipiunt 265 orationes quae beatus papa Gregorius sparsim de toto psalterio deo gubernante et adiuvante congregavit. Si devota mente cantetur vicem ut fertur omnium psalmorum et sacrificii et fidelis animarum commendationis continent'.

63. The verses are ps. 78,8 – 9; 73,19 – 20. Warren II 22 has divided this introductory series of versicles, without reason, into a versicle (ps. 78,8) and *Oratio* (ps. 78,9; 73,19 – 20). Likewise in the shorter form of *Oratio communis* (AB 117) the first intercession (*pro peccatis nostris*) is preceded by a series of versicles which express hope and trust in God: ps. 70,1 – 2; 37,22 – 23. The title or bidding *pro peccatis nostris* is lacking in the MS and has been supplied by Warren (from Columban's list) before the versicle *Deus in adiutorium . . .,* which is found in both formularies immediately after the introductory versicles noted. This versicle (ps. 69,2) begins with a capital *D* in the long formulary, being thereby distinguished from the introductory versicles as the first of the intercessions for particular intentions.

64. The abbreviations used here for the various texts of the litany are those used by Capelle in his edition, *art.cit.*: Ir Ga, MI^1, MI^2, Gel.

65. Kenney, *Sources,* 790, thought their presence here is due to misunderstanding on the part of the scribe or to confusion in his *Vorlage.* But their presence can be seen to be quite in order, if we take them as providing a choice of collects to the martyrs at the conclusion of the *oratio communis.*

66. Warran I f. 21^v – 22^r, notes that each verse is followed by a long mark of abbreviation, which he interprets as indicating 'the rest of ps. 27,1' and 'the remainder of ps. 50,3' respectively. He consequently regarded them as further intercessory versicles, and he gave to the first the bidding *pro tribulantibus* and to the second the bidding *pro poenitentibus.* I think that in both cases the whole psalm was recited; this explains the peculiarly long mark of abbreviation indicated by Warren, and explains the corresponding use of psalms (notably ps. 50) at the conclusion of subsequent continental *preces.*

67. Ps. 27: 'Exaudi, Domine, vocem deprecationis meae, dum oro ad te, dum extollo manus meas ad templum sanctum tuum. . . . Benedictus Dominus, quoniam exaudivit vocem deprecationis meae. Dominus adiutor meus et protector meus, in ipso speravit cor meum et adiutus sum. . . . Dominus fortitudo plebis suae, et protector salvationum Christi sui est. Salvum fac populum tuum, Domine. . . .' (vv. 2, 6, 7, 8, 9).

68. Manz 880 has shown that the expression *sanctus in sanctis* also occurs in Ga G 42, 515, and Mo LS 970.

69. A somewhat similar conclusion occurs in AB 126: exaudi nos et praesta ea quae rogamus. Strangely enough, the combination *petimus et oramus,* with which our prayer concludes, is not found in the Gallican books, apart from Ga B 77, but it occurs in Mo Or 144 and LO 132,8 (Manz 861).

70. The eclectic and rather patchwork character of the first collect, the repetition of the invocation *domine . . . deus* and the reference to psalm 50 (*secundum magnam misericordiam*

tuam) in both, are typical Irish traits.

71. Cf. the 'Orationes maiores sive Preces ad Laudes matutinas et ad vesperas dicendae' edited by Bäumer from a number of codices dating from the eighth and ninth centuries, *Histoire du Bréviaire* II 439 – 441. One of these MSS (Cambridge, *Corpus Christi College*, MS 272, *saec*. 9, from Rheims) has been printed by Warren II 64 – 65.

72. Examples in Ammalarius, *De ecclesiasticis officiis* IV 4 (PL 105, 1175 – 1177); Martène, *De ant. Ecclesiae ritibus* IV (Bassani 1788) 14 – 15: *Capitula per omnes horas*, and p.17: *Capitula ad primam*.

73. The *Traditio Apostolica* was well known in northern Italy and particularly in the region of Aquileia. Cf. CLA IV (1947) 508, where Lowe describes the Verona MS of the *Traditio*: written presumably in North Italy near the end of the fifth century and written over with the *Sententiae* of Isidore in the eighth century; and cf. also Gamber, *Codices*, 74 – 78, for evidence of the influence of the *Traditio* on the liturgy of Aquileia.

CHAPTER THIRTEEN

1. For *cogitationes, verba et facta*, and related groupings, cf. Manz 167; for *hic et in aeternum*, cf. *ibid*. 404; for *salvator mundi qui vivis*, cf. *supra*, p.91 – 92, and Manz 879.

2. Cf. Am Be 1574 Esto nobis, domine, AUXILIATOR et rector, ut viam tuam rectis mentibus ambulemus; Bi 1332 (Ge V 1319) adesto famulis tuis, . . . et per omnem quam acturi sunt viam DUX eis et comes esse dignare; Bi 257 VD aeterne deus, INLUMINATOR et redemptor animarum nostrarum; Be 1154 (Bi 1073) PROTECTOR in te sperantium deus.

3. Cf. Mt. 24,44: 'Ideo et vos estote parati'; 25,6: 'Media autem nocte clamor factus est: ecce sponsus venit, exite obviam ei'.

4. Cf. Wilmart-Brou, *The Psalter Collects from V – VIth Century Sources*, 230 – 235.

5. Cf. *supra*, p.115.

6. The collect for compline has a striking likeness in terminology to that used for none at Milan: DOMINE IESU CHRISTE, salvator omnium et protector, qui separasti lumen a tenebris, TE SUPPLICITER EXORAMUS: ut in hac superventurae noctis caligine tua nos protegat dextera, et in lucis aurora cuncta surgamus gaudentes (M II 454). An Irish parallel can be noted in *Sancti venite* 7 – 9: Lucis indultor et SALVATOR OMNIUM. . . Sanctorum CUSTOS, rector quoque dominus; and ILH I 85: PROTEGAT NOS altissimus de suis sanctis sedibus.

7. Cf. A CPs 50; I CPs 50; Mo CPs 367.

8. Rot. Rav.19 (Mo Vesp.Mat.67) Oriatur, quaesumus, omnipotens deus, in cordibus nostris splendor gloriae, d. n. I. Christus; Vesp.Mat.4 donec lucescat dies, et lucifer verus oriatur in cordibus; Vesp.Mat.68 Oriatur, quaesumus, Domine, in sensibus atque moribus nostris aurora lucis spiritualis.

9. Cf. Gamber, *Codices* 153 – 162; he notes, *ibid*., 149, n.2, that in spite of the different handwritings and the varying extent of the script in a number of leaves, all or at least some may have belonged originally to one liturgical book.

10. A. Dold, 'Liturgie Fragmente aus den beiden Palimpsesten Cod. Aug. CXCV und Clm 14429', *Revue bénédictine* 38 (1926) 273 – 287. He assigned the folio in question (in *Cod. Aug.* CXCV) 'zum mindesten ins frühe 7. Jh.' (274), anterior, therefore, to the composition of AB; but Gamber, *Codices* 153, assigns them to the eighth century.

11. Dold, *loc. cit.*, 275, with note on *mereremur*: 'so falschlich für: *meremur*'.

12. P. Siffrin, 'Eine irische Parallele zum Liturgie-fragment 1 und 2 aus Cod. Aug. CX-CV', *Revue bén.* 40 (1928) 137 – 138.

13. Bishop, *Note* 9; Manz 880.

14. Bishop was able to discover only one Spanish occurrence of the expression. He explained its presence five (in reality six) times in Ge V (III 91; III 105) as due to 'foreign elements . . . introduced in Gaul', and likewise its single ocurrence in Ga G 479 as due to Irish influence. He concluded: 'Whilst Spanish influence on the liturgy of the Irish seems at that period to have been considerable, I am not clear that there was not reciprocity, and that there are not in *Moz.* traces of borrowing from Irish sources. Taking into consideration the whole of the facts I am disposed to think that "sancti et electi" is an Irish contribution to Western liturgical terminology, and its presence is a distinct note of warning of Irish influence, direct or indirect' (244 – 245).

15. Still other Spanish texts could be added to those given to Manz. Without counting parallels to the texts given by him from LS and LO, the following should be noted: CPs 290 (ps. 118,20); LO 125,5 *cum sanctis et patriarchis et electis* (GeV 1615 *cum sanctis et electis*, given by Manz); Br 986D (Am Be 1504, Gr A 209: only the latter is given by Manz); Br 1246B. Other Ambrosian texts: Be 1433; 1504 (Mo Br 986); 1509 (Gr A 211, given by Manz); also numerous, doubtless later, occurrences in M I: 92, 102, 160, etc.

16. PL 96, 459. This text is given by Manz, who points out a number of Spanish peculiarities in it.

17. PL 83, 598.

18. Dold does not indicate any source or parallel for this prayer; but since *sancti et electi* is definitely not a Gallican expression, and no Irish influence is found in this sacramentary, the prayer can safely be regarded as Spanish.

19. Cf. Col. 1,12: 'gratias agentes Deo Patri, qui dignos nos fecit in partem sortis sanctorum in lumine'.

20. Ga G 140 is the *Collectio post nomina* in the Mass for the feast of St Eulalia; the *Praefatio* and *Immolatio* of this Mass have been drawn from the *Illatio* of the Mass for the same saint in Mo LS 96: cf. L. Brou, 'Encore les "Spanish Symptoms" et leur contre – partie', *Hispania Sacra* 7 (1954) 468. The second half of Ga G 140 begins with the expression *cari nostri*, which Manz (101) numbers among 'the specifically Irish expressions', one which found its way into Gallican documents in the seventh century. The question can be asked, therefore, whether the whole formulary Ga G 138 – 142 is not an Irish reworking of Spanish materials?

21. Cf. Ga Mone 75 quo igitur interveniente (S. Germano) . . . pietatis tuae misericordiam postulamus, . . . UT QUI EIUS MERITIS AEQUARI NON POSSUMUS, PSALTIM PECCATORUM NOSTRORUM VENIA CONSEQUI MEREAMUR; Ga F 118 VD . . . quoniam gloria virtutes eorum tu es, quibus . . . gloriam in passione vencentibus contulisti . . .; obsecrantes, ut . . . QUOS VIRTUTES IMITATIONE NON POSSUMUS SEQUI, devitae veneratione coniungamus affectu.

22. Cf. also LS 201 UT EORUM inlustribus MERITIS . . . VENIAM condonare digneris; LS 1060 ut ipse nobis peccatorum tribuat VENIAM, qui contulit inmortalitatis CORONAM; LS 1241 ut qui illis adquisitum est regnum ad GLORIAM, nobis opituletur ad VENIAM; Br 1174C ut quibus virtutum tituli non adscribunt ad gloriam, vitiorum dedecora deleantur, ne veniamus in poenam.

23. Its conclusion, eos ad celum ire praecipisti, quorum etiam suffragia postulamus, illorum fidei et passionis participes esse mereamur (Dold, *loc. cit.*, 275, n.3), is not unlike Mo Or 451 cum his tribus martyribus MEREAMUR HABERE IN CAELESTIBUS PARTEM, quibus non PASSIONE SED FIDE dinoscimur CONSORTES existere. And see below, no. iv of the martyr-collects studied here, AB 97 hii coronam suam PASSIONE PER FIDEM MERUERUNT, and the Spanish parallels adduced there.

24. Ga C 105 A*eter*num virtutis *tuae nu*men, omnipotens ds, . . . mum . . . sco . . . r . . .

no*mine* ... *f*ilio ... li*or* ... f...as ... qu ... (italics denote doubtful readings). It can easily be restored: Aeternum virtutis tuae nomen, omnipotens ds, (oramus, uti nos marty)rum (et omnium) sco (rum tuo)r(um fide pares, de)votione (strenuos, passione consi)miles, (in resurrectione fe)lici(um) f(aci)as (coae)qu(ari).

25 Br 1193A, 1196C, 1203B, 1207C; M 827A, 856B, 964A. In Br it is used as the *Oratio* which follows the second or third antiphon in matins on the feasts of St Bartholomew, St Genesius, St Cyprian, and St Matthew; in M it is the *Oratio post Gloriam* on the feasts of St Bartholomew and St Cyprian, and the *Missa* on the feast of many martyrs. This final text is the farthest removed from ours: M 964 Eterne tue virtutis nomen omnipotens Deus rogamus: ut horum martyrum tyorum N. et N. et omnium sanctorum meritis socios fide, pares devotione, strenuos passione, similes in resurrectione felicium nos facias coaequari.

26. Prayers of a similar structure are found in LS 992; M 984. The expression *nomen aeternum* occurs on Or 53: Deus Dei filius cuius ETERNUM permanet NOMEN.

27. PL 83, 146.

28. PL 83, 148.

29. Cf. A. Dold, 'Liturgie Fragmente aus den beiden Palimpsesten Cod. Aug. CXCV und Clm 14429', *loc. cit.*, 275; he succeeded in deciphering most of this collect.

30. The Spanish parallel for this prayer was discovered by P. Siffrin and published by A. Dold, 'Eine Parallele zum Liturgie-fragment 1 aus Cod. Aug. CXCV in der mozarabischen Liturgie', *loc. cit.*, 135 – 136. In the following year P. Siffrin showed that this prayer and another in the same MS correspond to AB 61 and 52 respectively (for AB 52, cf. supra, no.i of the martyr-collects studied here), and he noted the identity of AB 61 and *Cod. Aug.* 1 as against some variants and paraphrasing in LO: 'Eine irische Parallele gum Liturgie-fragment 1 und 2 aus Cod. Aug. CXCV', *Rev. bénédictine* 40 (1928) 137 – 138. Finally, G. Manz demonstrated the unquestionably Spanish origin of the prayer: 'Die ... Oration ... wird durch die in ihn enthaltenen Ausdrüke "fidei profectus", "fructus bonorum operum", "cultus religionis", und "timor divinus" als wisigotisch erwiesen: es kann nicht zweifelhaft sein, dass Entlehnung seitens der Iren vorliegt" (*Ausdrücksformen*, 24 – 25).

31. The doubtful readings and lacunae can now be supplied with the aid of the AB text: nos pro iniquitatibus nostris remissione(m a te et) misericordiam (pos)tulamus. Dold does not indicate any parallel or source for this prayer.

32. Regarding the questionably Gallican character of Ga 139, cf. *supra*, p. 236, n.20. It has a parallel in Ga G 42: Osanna in excelsis, vere sanctus, vere benedictus dominus noster Iesus Christus filius tuus, qui sanctus in sanctis, pro morte vitam, pro poena gloriam, pro confessione victoriam praestare dignatus es. This in turn is suspect, and appears to have been based on a Spanish source; cf. Mo LS 970: VERE SANCTUS IN SANCTIS, vere in omnibus gloriosus DEI FILIUS, and especially LS 1287: VERE SANCTUS IN SANCTIS, gloriosus in celis, manifestus in terris, DOMINUS NOSTER IESUS CHRISTUS FILIUS TUUS. And cf. Manz 888 (*sanctus in sanctis*).

33. *Cod. Aug.* CXCV, f. 33 (ed. Dold, *loc. cit.*, 275): Sci et gloriosi mirabiles martyres adque potentes (mirabiles adque potentes martires AB), quorum in operibus gaudet (dominus et in congre)gat(ione laetatur), intercessores obtimi et fortissimi protectores....

34. The references to *martyres* appears to have been original, as also the reading QUORUM IN (in quorum Gil) ... OBTIMI ET (et: *omit.* Gil) FORTISSIMI.

35. Cf. E. Bishop, 'Spanish Symptoms', *Liturgica Historica*, 165 – 202.

36. Warren II 71 – 72 gives them in parallel columns.

37. The preoccupation to name every single member of the body and omit none is also a feature of the *Lorica* of Gildas (ILH I 206; AH 51, 358). For the Irish use of *hic et in futuro*, cf. Bishop, *Note* 37; Manz 404.

38. Cf. AB 7 *Ymnum in die dominica*. Laudate pueri dominum, laudate nomen domini. Te deum laudamus. . . . The collect we are considering is also found after the *Te Deum* in ILH I 61.

39. Denzinger – Schönmetzer, *Enchiridion Symbolorum* 75-76; ILH I 203 – 205. Bernard notes (II 242): 'The *Quicumque* was well known in Ireland, and several early manuscripts of it, written by Irish scribes, are extant. . . . The first stanza of the *Altus Prosator* seems to be based on it'.

40. Walker, 24.

41. Similar concluding doxologies: LO 31,25; 49,42; 186,24; 258,19; 272, n.2; 318,24; 336,1; 393,23; LS 317 (454); 371; 398; 453; 463; 491; 496; 544; 582; 638; 730; 747; 748; M 436; 617; 678; 773; 1034.

42. Other texts apart from concluding doxologies: Or 1160 (= Br 1202); LO 120,39; 264,20;391,33; LS 97; 99; 430; 791; 1021; 1357; 1447; M 1031; Br 1296. The expression *permanere in Trinitate* is used in Spanish prayers for each of the three divine Persons; cf. LO 264,20; 278;15; LS 791.

43. AB 65 (Mo Br 189); Ce S 32; Ve 552 (Am Be 854, Ga B 24); Am Be 561 (Bi 525); 1525; Ga Mone 23; Ga G 9; 132; Ga V 60; Ga B 253; Mo LO 63,20; 212,13; 236,38; LS 268; 441; 707; 942 (1189); 1118; 1221; M 278A; Br 616A.

44. The term *ingenitus* was especially favoured in Spain as expressing the exclusive property of the Father. So in the Fourth Council of Toledo (633): 'Patrem a nullo factum vel genitum dicimus, Filium a Patre non factum sed genitum asserimus, Spiritum vero Sanctum,nec creatum nec genitum, sed procedentem ex patre et Filio profitemur' (DS 485); the Sixth Council of Toledo (638): 'Credimus . . . Patrem ingenitum' (DS 490); the Eleventh Council of Toledo (675): 'Patrem quidem non genitum, non creatum, sed ingenitum profitemur . . . . Hic etiam Spiritus sanctus nec ingenitus nec genitus creditur: ne aut si ingenitum dixerimus, duas Patres dicamus' (DS 525 – 527). On the liturgical use of *Pater ingenitus* cf. *supra*, p. 31.

45. Walker, *op. cit.*, 106. It was a favourite practice of St Columban to pile up such negative attributes of God. So in his *Instr.* I 5: 'satis enim ineptum est et impium de fide transire ad tractantis invisibilem, inaestimabilem, inconspicabilem Dominum vacua verba. . . . Trinitatis divinitas ab humanis . . . sensibus incomprehensibilis deprehenditur' (Walker, 64); *Instr.* I, 2 – 4 (*ibid.* 60 – 64). Prayers in which such negative attributes of God as *incomprehensibilis, inaestimabilis, invisibilis, ineffabilis, inerrarabilis* are combined in groups of two or three have been collected by Manz 243 – 245. He gives only AB 125 as an example of the combination of *inaestimabilis* and *incomprehensibilis*.

46. Cf. *supra*, p.112, in connection with the phrase *praesta nobis, domine,* . . . *quae te petimus et oramus* (AB 52).

47. I have seen the word only in Mo M 1002: ut qui te his honorat, in SPONTANEIS votis te largiente ditatur premiis infinitis. The word *famulatus* is very common, and it is qualified by a variety of adjectives (*liber, beneplacitus, debitus, sanctus,* etc), but never, apart from the present instance, by *spontaneus*.

48. Cf. Mo CPs 484 (ps. 21): M 113, Br 206, 601, 725, Or 832; CPs 485 (ps. 22): Br 729; CPs 567 (ps. 103): Or 141; Br 1065.

49. Cf. Ex. 13 – 14; ps. 103,30 (*emittes spiritum tuum*); Ezek. 1,26; Dan. 7,9; and especially, Apoc. 4,5 – 6; 20,11; 22,1; ps. 90,5 (*scuto circumdabit te veritas eius, ut non timeabis a timore nocturno*); Eph. 6,16 (*scutum fidei*).

238

CHAPTER FOURTEEN

1. AB 62 – 67 (f. 22^v – 23^v); Warren II 24 – 25. AB 62 (*Post cantemus*): T 3, ILH I 202, the Vatican MS *Pal. lat.* 65 (Bannister, 'Irish Psalters', *The Journal of Theological Studies* 12, 1910/1911, 283). AB 63 (*Post Benedicite*): T 6. AB 64 (*Post laudate*): T 10 and two Irish Psalters: B.M. *Addit.* MS 36929 and Vatican MS *Pal. lat.* 65 (Bannister, *loc. cit.*). AB 67 (*De martyribus*): T 16. In the title for this and the remaining chapters of this part of our study, we will call these seven sets of collects by the convenient designation 'collects for lauds'.

2. The collects which followed the canticles in Spain were peculiar to that branch of the Spanish rite represented by Br (and *Cod.* 35.5 of the *Biblioteca Capitular* in Toledo). According to A. W. S. Porter, they may owe their origin to a collection of canticles published by Isidore; cf. his 'Cantica mozarabici Officii', *Eph. Liturgicae* 45 (1935) 127 – 128. The collects after the *Cantemus* can be seen in Br 622 – 649. At Milan there was only one collect for each of the canticles *Cantemus* and *Benedicite*; cf. Am M II 414 (Be 1538 – 1539), apart from a proper collect for each on Christmas eve: M II 59: Be 111 – 112.

3. The expression *gurges vitiorum*, used also in Mo CPs 320 (ps. 3): Domine, gloria nostra, caput nostrum, ne *vitiorum gurgite* mergamur, exalta (Br 596, Gil 363; Manz 401).

4. Some examples of *laquei peccatorum* have been collected by Manz 524: Ga G 217 (V 144, Am Be 498), 342; Mo Or 1034 (*peccati laqueos caveamus*). *Incendium ignis* occurs in Ga V 168 (Mo M 466B: *aeterni ignis incendia*, not noted by Manz 449), Mo Or 493.

5. Cf. Ge V 1049 (Gr C 44,8; Ga B 33), Am M II 59. The theme has been especially developed in the Spanish collects for the feast of Saints Fructuosus, Augurius and Eulogius (Or 446 – 468: Br 1055 – 1065). But there is no striking similarity of language between these collects and the one we have in the Antiphonary. With our *beata puerorum instituta sectamur* we may compare Or 454: da ergo nobis, ut, cursum vitae nostrae in pace ducentes, et ab ardoribus libidinum liberi a futuris mereamur suppliciis liberari; or again Or 456: ut . . . placita tibi martyrum tuorum imitantes SEQUAMUR VESTIGIA. With *peccatorum laqueis absoluti* we may compare Or 461: redde nos a concrematione vitiorum extraneos, a diaboli LAQUEIS LIBEROS, et tuis nos martyribus post transitum adsocia coronandos. More interesting is the use of *tuo munere* in our collect and in Or 463: Deus, qui probatione solita pietatis probari sanctos tuos voluisti in terris, nec plus eos temtari permittas, quam quod in eis donum tolerantiae adesse conlatum TUO MUNERE perspicis: erue nos ab omni temtatione; again in Or 466: Deus, qui ineffabili splendore pia tuorum martirum pectora replevisti, ut coronas tuo munere refulgentes, quas hic ex passione spei gratia mercaverunt, illic a te percipere in MUNERE mererentur: fac nos splendere et lucere. The same term is used along with the expression *ignis incendium* (and *ignis incendii*) in Or 493: Benedicimus te, omnipotens Deus, qui beatissimum Vincentium martyrem tuum, sicut quondam tres pueros, ab ignis incendio liberasti; . . . eius ergo precibus, rorem misericordiae tuae nostris infunde visceribus, ut, madefacto igne carnalis incendii, flamma in nobis tapescat peccati; . . . ita gratia naturae subveniat, ut, quod origine non caremus, MUNERE restinguere valeamus.

6. Cf. *supra*, p.239, n.43. Two particularly close parallels to our prayer are: Ce S 32 Refecti spiritualibus escis, . . . deo domino nostro Iesu Christo debitas laudes et gratias referamus, orantes (cf. T 4) indefessam eius misericordiam, ut divini muneris (cf. T 4) sacramentum ad incrementum fidei . . . habeamus; and Zeno of Verona, *Lib. II, Tract.* 44 *Ad neophytis post baptismum* 7: Exultemus, fratres, in Christo, tantique proventus reddito ditati, Deo patri omnipotenti laudes et gratias referamus (PL II, 496).

7. Manz 703 (*pax et tranquillitas*) gives one Ambrosian text (Be 88) and numerous Spanish ones, to which we could add Br 606B; M 567D, 1000A.

8. Cf. CPs 335 (ps. 21) nos hereditariae fac eorum spei succedere, et parilitate horum AETERNA cum eis EXULTATIONE GAUDERE; CPs 551 (ps. 83) ut . . . in te Deo vivo EXULTATIONE PERPETUA GAUDEANT; CPs 564 (ps. 101) In omni die . . . exaudi nos, Domine, . . . ut PERPETUA EXULTATIONE GAUDEAMUS (Gil 91); Or 467 da nobis, ut in utrorumque sanctitate LETANTES, sic victorias martyrum celebremus, ut INFINITA cum eis LETITIA GAUDEAMUS (Br 1065).

9. For *dies dominicae resurrectionis*, cf. Am Be 524 (the *Exultet*, near the end); Mo LS 500 (Easter Sunday); 614 (Easter Sunday); 727 (Fourth Sunday after the octave of Easter); 728; M 109 (First Sunday of Advent). To my knowledge, *favor clementiae* does not occur elsewhere, but some expressions close to it are peculiarly Spanish; Cf. Manz 334 (*favor indulgentiae*), 340 (*favor indulgentialis*), 341 (*favor pietatis*: this also in Ga G 29), 109 (*bonitas clementiae*), 166 (*pietas clementiae*), 164 (*miseratio clementiae*: this also in Roman texts).

10. The hymn also speaks of the Trinity, the resurrection of Christ (obtinens corpus CLARITATEM dei), and our redemption through adoption as sons in association with Christ (FILIUS divinae LUCIS).

11. For the incipit *Sancte domine*, cf. *supra*, p.92. The verse of psalm 26 alluded to, *Dominus illuminatio mea et salus mea*, is also found in Mo CPs 340 (ps. 26); cf. also Or 1053 (Br 1126) Christe, esto inluminatio nostra et salus; LS 532 te, deus, quaesumus, ut sis nobis et inluminatio et salus. The use of the antiphon *illuminatio et salus mea Dominus* for vespers in Milan and in Spain has been described by J. Pinell, 'Vestigis del lucernari a Occident', *loc. cit.*, 112 – 113. Finally, the following text regarding the knowledge of the Trinity may be noted: LS 538 Deus fidelis, . . . tu COGNITIONEM nobis tribue TRINITATIS, ut pacifici conversemur inter filios UNITATIS.

12. The unity and trinity of God were firmly established articles of the *fides trinitatis* in Ireland as elsewhere. A phrase in our collect has a parallel in Columban, *Instr.* I 4: 'TRINITATIS enim SCIENTIA profunditati maris merito comparatur' (Walker, 64), though the Trinity is here the subject of the knowledge in question rather than its object.

13. Or 758; 967; 977; 1208; Br 1113 (M 735); 1146; 1238; M 764. Many other pieces, such as antiphons, commence *Hii sunt*; cf. *Index* compiled by Ferotin, LO 673.

14. *Blandimenta saeculi* occurs, along with *carnis inlecebra*, in Ve 1178 (Ga G 115 and some eighth-century Gelasians), but not elsewhere in the Roman or Ambrosian books; it is found in Mo CPs 273 (ps. 104): Br 247, 325, 366, 427, Gil 96; M 927A; cf. Manz 108. The use of *inlecebra mundi/saeculi* is more frequent, but it is also absent from the Roman books. Examples: Am Be 926 (Bi 858) mundi inlecebrae; Ga G 363 mundi huius inlecebrae; Ga V 13 saeculi inlecebrae; 16 (Ga F 55) mundiales inlecebrae . . . passionum vel divitiarum blandimenta; Ga B 359 blandiciae et inlecebrae mundi huius; Ga B 549 inlecebrae carnes; Mo CPs 187 (ps. 123) mundi inlecebra (Br 338 – 339, 346); CPs 198 (ps. 134) mundi inlecebrae (Br 166, 365, 436). Isidore often uses the word *inlecebra(e)*; for example, *Quaestiones in V.T. In Exodo* 17; 'saeculi illecebrae'; *ibid.* 41: 'mundi illecebrae' (PL 83, 295. 308); *In Josue* 6,2: 'illecebra corporalium vitiorum' (*loc. cit.* 373).

15. Manz 685 gives examples of *passio gloriosa* from the Roman (Ve 335, 339; Ge V 51), Gallican (Ga G 117, 394) and Ambrosian (Be 898, 1012) books, but no Spanish example of it.

16. Cf. *supra*, p.203, n.37.

17. Manz 598 (*migrare de hac luce*) gives an Ambrosian (Be 123) and a Spanish (LO 241,3) instance of this phrase, as well as some examples from Caesarius of Arles and this text from Arnobius Iunior, *Comm. in Ps. 140*: 'sacrificium nostrum vespertinum sit, id est, iuxta FINEM LUCIS HUIUS, qua hora ab HAC LACE migramus' (PL 53, 553A). Cf. also the seventh-century Spanish hymn, *Anni peracto circulo* (AH 27, 269):

> 6. quo LUCIS HUIUS TERMINUM
> immaculatus transeat.

240

18. Regarding the questionably Gallican character of Ga G 42 and 139, cf. *supra*, p. 237, n.32.

19. Cf. *supra*, p.119 – 120.

20. Cf. *supra*, p.122 – 123.

CHAPTER FIFTEEN

1. E. Cattaneo, *Il Breviario Ambrosiano*, 18, would seem to grant a high antiquity to the Ambrosian collects for the canticles and the *laudate* psalms, when he says that they correspond to the original type of prayer during the office, as described by Athanasius and Cassian.

2. The expression *iugum servitutis* (*Aegyptiae*) is also used in Or 233 (Br 214B), 656 (Br 482A), 1053 (Br 1126B); Am Be 548 (Ga B 269).

3. Mone 35, G 198; Ge V 601; Mo LS 809.

4. PL 83, 373.

5. Or 156, 328; LS 437.

6. PL 83, 146.

7. PL 83, 677. Cf. Zeno of Verona, *De Abraham* 3: 'sola enim fides deambulabat inter gladios tuta, . . . IN IGNIBUS FRIGIDA' (PL 11, 427). For prayers begining *Sancte domine*, cf. *supra*, p.92.

CHAPTER SIXTEEN

1. AB 71 – 90 (f. 24ᵛ – 26ᵛ); Warren II 25 – 27. The number of collects in each set varies from seven in the fifth (AB 81 – 87: some of these also occur in T and other Irish sources), to five in the third and fourth sets (AB 71 – 75; 76 – 80), and three in the sixth set (AB 88 – 90). Those in AB 83 – 90 are included in the selection of *Collectae ad varias officii partes* edited by Blume, AH 51, 289 – 291, from a number of Irish sources (AB, T, ILH, Irish Psalters).

2. Regarding native Irish accentual verse, cf. *supra*, p.76 – 80.

3. The expression *morte devicta* is found in all the liturgies and is particularly frequent in Spanish prayers. The word *adurere* is used in the Spanish prayers for the feast of St Fructuosus, St Augurius and St Eulogius; cf. Or 447, 457, 459, not only for the literal sense of the term (*flammis adusti*: Or 457), but also for the metaphorical sense (*temptationum igne aduri*: Or 447).

4. This expression may owe something to Apoc. 20,6: 'Beatus et sanctus qui habet partem in resurrectione prima'. Manz 851 deals with *resurrectio beata* which is of universal use, although *participium beatae resurrectionis* is found only in our text. But cf. Ve 177 *resurrectionis beatae primitiae*; Ge F 2462 *partem beatae resurrectionis obtineat*. In the following selection of texts we concentrate on the word *participium* and associated words. For *partem habere in resurrectione prima* see Manz 852 (*resurrectio prima*).

5. Isidore uses similar terms in another connection: 'Noe per aquam et lignum LIBERATUR; lignum quippe et aqua CRUCEM designat et BAPTISMA. Sicut enim ille cum suis per lignum

et aquam salvatur, sic familia Christi per baptismum et crucis passionem sanatur' (*Quaes-tiones in V. T. In Genesin* 7; PL 83, 229). The expression *crucis triumphus* occurs in Or 703 (Br 477D, M 843B); LS 743. *Triumphus passionis*: Br 502.

6. The Irish text (AB f. 7^r – 8^v) has: Adiutor et protector fuit mihi in salutem. Hic Deus meus et honorificabo eum .... Filii autem Israhel habierunt per siccum per medium mare.

7. Manz 508.

8. The Spanish psalter collects on ps. 96 also contain this line: CPs 418 custodi servorum animas; CPs 109 custodi sanctorum tuorum animas.

9. *Lucis auctor*: Ga G 223; B 573; Am Be 1546; Mo Or 370; LO 147,38; LS p. 89,9; Br 140A; 174D (Manz 544). *Novitas vitae*: Ve 478; Ga F 676; Mo Or 630; LO 35,13; LS 581; 667 (Manz 642).

10. Rom. 6,4; the full expression, *ambulare in novitate vitae*, occurs in the Spanish prayers LS 581 and 667, and in CPs 351 (ps. 39): ut in novitate vitae ambulantes, peccatorum nos inquinamenta non polluant.

11. Cf. the expression of this theme in the first section of *Praecamur patrem* (AB 3), and the parallels used to illustrate it, *supra*, p.51 – 53.

12. PL 30, 640 – 641.

13. There is something similar in Am Be 61: ut ADVENTUS . . . filii tui et PECCATA NOSTRA ABLUAT et populo tuo pacem conferat et salutem (Bi 67, M II 33). Other instances of *abluere peccata* in Manz 26.

14. PL 83, 534.

15. C. Blume thought that both groups, those for the hours and those for lauds, 'zu den ältesten der altirischen Hymnodie gehören' (AH 51, 292). His characterization of the col-elcts for the hours (AB 17 – 26) as 'rhythmical' and those for the morning office (AB 83 – 90) as non – rhythmical 'in Reimprosa abgefassten Collectae' is misleading. The first group can be called rhythmical in as much as they are imitations of the structure of the quantitative iambic dimeter and have, as a result, a regular accentual final cadence. The second group must also be classed as rhythmical, all the more so in that they are built on an accentual principle: the recurrence of a number of stresses (generally two) in each half-line. It now appears certain that the Irish were the first to introduce the truly rhythmical (accentual) principle into Latin hymnody. We have a good sample of such rhythmical verse in *Sacratissimi martyres* and in the collects for the various parts of lauds. Much later there would be a fusion of the two principles of rhythmical verse, notably in the mediaeval sequence, which, on the one hand, has a fixed number of syllables in each line and, on the other hand, is built on the succession of regular (trochaic) accentual feet.

CHAPTER SEVENTEEN

1. AB 91 – 93 (f. 20^v – 28^v); Warren II 27 – 28.

2. *Zenonis Veronensis Tractatus*, ed. B. Löfstedt, CC 22 (1971). The sermons in question are *Tractatus* II 22 (*olim* II 76) *Tractatus Danielis* and *Tractatus* II 26 (*olim* II 54) *Tractatus diei paschae cuius supra*. We will use Löfstedt's text, but we will emend it in a couple of places where the text of the Ballerini edition (PL 11, 509 – 510; 526 – 527) is closer to the text of AB. Differences between the prayer and the text of Zeno will be indicated by italics.

3. Eis] *omit*. Löfstedt.

4. I follow the reading of Löfstedt and J.B. Giuliari (Verona 1883), even though the Ballerini reading is *venerabiles*, in agreement with AB. It seems likely that *venerabilis* should qualify *numeri* rather than *Hebraei*, since Zeno speaks in other contexts also of the sacred number three and of its sacramental character (*sacramentum Trinitatis*).

5. stupa] stuppa: Löfstedt, Giuliari.

6. We know from the marginal liturgical notes in some of the MSS of the sermons that they were used as readings in the liturgy at Verona. See Gamber, *Codices* 058 (84, with n.2); Löfstedt, *Introduction*, 8 – 23; PL II,15 – 17. The sermons were collected and copied precisely for their liturgical usage at Verona, and knowledge of them was, with few exceptions, limited to Verona until the first printed edition appeared (Verona 1508). Until now, the first known citations of Zeno's works were to be found in the writings of Ratherius, bishop of Verona in the tenth century.

7. One slight indication for a northern Italian milieu for the composition of these collects is the expression *insectatio veteris inimici* in the first prayer. It has some resemblance to I CPs 118, 19: 'Deus, qui salutem fidelium a peccatoribus elongasti, . . . humilitatem nostram AB INIQUORUM INSECTATIONE CUSTODI'.

8. Cf. *Le Psautier Romain et les autres anciens Psautiers latins*, ed. R. Weber (Libreria Vaticana 1953). The Psalter of Verona (*Bibl.Capit.* I 1, *saec.*6 – 7) was written 'probably in northern Italy' (*ibid.*, xvii).

9. *Biblia sacra iuxta Latinam Vulgatam Versionem X. Liber Psalmorum ex recensione S. Hieronymi*, cura et studio Monachorum Abbatiae Pont. S. Hieronymi in Urbe (Rome 1953).

10. The Psalter of Zeno (*Vat. lat.* 5359) was written *saec.* 7 – 8 probably in the North of Italy and it belonged at one time to the monastery of St Zeno at Verona (Weber, *op. cit.*, xix).

11. *Il codice irlandese dell'Ambrosiana edito e illustrato*. Vol. I. Il testo e le chiose, ed. G. I. Ascoli (Roma – Torino – Firenze 1878) 606.

12. *Ibid.*, 605, 607 – 608.

13. Columban, *Instr.* I 3: 'Quis aeternum universitatis principium tractare audebit?' (Walker , 62), *Instr.* X 1: 'Quam (*Scil.* iram iudicis) universitatis creator Deus . . . minatur' (*ibid.*, 100); *Instr.* X 2: 'Quid debemus nos reddere, si creator universitatis immerito pro nobis impiis . . . mortuus est?' (*ibid.*, 102); *Instr.* XII 2: 'Beata vigilia qua ad Deum universitatis auctorem . . . vigilatur' (*ibid.*, 112).

14. The timbrel is often interpreted in the writings of the Fathers as a sign of moritfica-tion. Augustine, *Ennar. in Ps.* 149,8: 'Et ipsum mysterium tympani et psalterii non est tacendum. In tympano corium extenditur, in psalterio chordae extenduntur: in utroque organo caro crucifigitur. Quam bene psallebat in tympano et psalterio, qui dicebat: 'Mihi mundus crucifixus est, et ego mundo''! Ipsum psalterium velut tympanum tollere te vult, . . . qui te docet quando tibi dicit: "Qui vult esse meus discipulus, abneget semetipsum et tollat crucem suam et sequatur me''. Non dimittat psalterium suum, non dimittat tym-panum. extendatur in ligno et siccetur a concupiscentia carnis' (CC 40, 2183). Again, *Ser-mo* 363,4: 'Qui enim Iesu Christi sunt, ait Apostolus, carnem suam crucifixerunt cum pas-sionibus et concupiscentiis. Hoc significare congruenter intelligitur tympanum . . . . In ligno enim caro extenditur ut tympanum fiat: et ex cruce discunt suavem sonum gratiae confiteri' (PL 39, 1638). Isidore, *Quaestiones in V.T. In Exodo* 20: 'Fideles, postquam de lavacro conscendunt, hymnum . . . emittunt, dicentes: Cantemus Domino. . . . Quod melius et dignius ille dicit qui habet tympanum in manu sua, sicut Maria, id est carnem crucificaverit cum vitiis et concupiscentiis, et mortificaverit membra sua' (PL 83, 296). Jerome, *Tr. de Ps.* 149: 'Crucifigamus corpora nostra Xpisto, et tali tympano canamus Deo. In tympano et psalterio psallant ei. Tympanum non habet carnes, sed pellem: et nos quamdiu carnei sumus, non sumus tympanum' (CC 78, 349).

15. The antiphon in AB 100 (*psalterium iucundum immolate*) seems to have combined one of these texts with ps. 80,3: 'Sumite psalmum et date tympanum, PSALTERIUM IUCUNDUM cum cithara'.

16. CC 78, 249.

17. There is a poem written by an anonymous Irish monk, *Lamentum Refugae cuiusdam* (ed. Traube, MGH, *Poetae latini Aevi Carolini III, Carmina Scottorum* 7, Berlin 1896, 688 – 689), who fled from Bobbio to Verona when threatened by a severe penance for some misdeed. He prays to St Zeno to intercede with Columbanus on his behalf, so that he may be able to return to Bobbio. Cf. G. Murphy, 'Scotti peregrini', *Studies* 17 (1928) 234.

18. Warren II 68. It goes: Domine, qui Cinchrim fugientes tueris bis senas per invisa tribus emulum itinera, prius fluctibus in binis montium utrimque redactis celsorum, ceu iugis abrupte arentibus talis equore murum quasi et de petra limphas producens: mergatur, ergo, ut olim, piorum supplicium hostis aeterni, quaesumus, statores curruum, quod est cuius affatus actusque cum cogitatu celeri nequam sit Pharaoni rex, Israhelem verum quae unda salvat, ut Christo carmina canat per saecla, qui cum patre vivit.

CHAPTER EIGHTEEN

1. Cf. B. Bischoff, 'Die europäische Verbreitung der Werke Isidors von Sevilla', in: *Mittelalterliche Studien* I 171 – 194.

2. *Op. cit.*, 176.

3. *Ibid.*, 180. This MS is *St Gall* 1399 a l, ed. A. Dold and J. Duft: Texte und Arbeiten 31. Anhang (Beuron 1955). It is dated by Bischoff, Dold and Duft to the mid-seventh century; Lowe assigned it to the seventh century and thought that it was 'written in an Irish centre, presumably on the Continent, possibly at Bobbio' (CLA VIII(1956)995).

4. J. N. Hillgarth, 'Visigothic Spain and early Christian Ireland', PRIA vol. 62, Section C, no. 6 (1962) 173.

5. Hillgarth, *art.cit.*, 174.

6. *Ibid.*, 183.

7. Cf. Gamber, *Codices* 153, and *supra*, p. 118 – 119.

8. 'If we look at the evidence recorded in Professor Lowe's *Codices latini antiquiores* it is clear that most of these manuscripts ... left Spain after the Arabic Invasion, when a number of refugees escaped to Italy, taking with them such precious codices as the famous *Orationale* in Verona. In the seventh century contacts between Spain and Italy were slight' (Hillgarth, *art. cit.*, 179 – 180).

9. *Ibid.*, 189.

10. *Ibid.*, 189 – 191.

11. Cf. *infra*, p. 179.

12. Hillgarth, *art. cit.*, 189.

13. E. Bishop, *Note*, 280, suggested that Bretonia may have been a means of communication with the Irish Church. But he later withdrew the suggestion ('Spanish Symptoms', in: *Liturgica Historica*, 181) in answer to Gougaud's criticism (DACL II 2, 2993). But there must have been some link connecting Spain and Ireland, and Bretonia still suggests itself as a possibility; cf. Hillgarth, *art. cit.*, 189 – 190, with n.118).

14. Hillgarth, *art. cit.*, 175 – 179, discusses the Mediterranean sea routes between the East

and Spain between the fifth and seventh centuries and examines the archaeological evidence which proves that ships coming from the East continued on to Britain and Ireland from northern Spain. He concludes that 'there seems no doubt . . . that ships from the Mediterranean, although probably in smaller numbers, continued to reach the British Isles in the seventh century' (178).

15. Dom Gougaud claimed that the Irish liturgy was Gallican in origin and that there is no evidence of direct influence on it from Spain; see especially DACL II 2, 2993. His position on the origins of the Irish liturgy appeared to E. Bishop to be an oversimplification. It would mean, in effect, as Bishop pointed out, 'that the traces of Hispanism found in the productions of Irish and English circles are to be explained by the fact that they came to our insulars not directly from Spanish circles and sources but only mediately through "la Gaule" . . . I believe this idea to be no more than a fiction' ('Spanish Symptoms', *loc. cit.*, 181).

16. AB 17 − 26, 57, 71 − 72, 77 − 90, 126. For reference to the treatment already given to the collects indicated here and in the following notes, cf. Numbered Index, *infra*.

17. AB 27 − 33, 62 − 63, 73 − 75.

18. AB 34, 40 − 56. These are the short collects which follow the intercessory versicles for various intentions at the conclusion of the nightfall office and in the *oratio communis*.

19. AB 16, 38, 39, 54, 58, 60, 64, 66, 70, 93, 94, 96, 122, 123, 125, 127. I take the description 'litanic, asyndetic type of prayer' from E. Bishop, *Liturgica Historica*. 184. I understand it in a generic sense which admits a great variety among the collects indicated, from the explicitly litanic style of AB: 'Tu es spes et salus. . .' to the more consecutive discourse, though still partly asyndetic, of AB 66: 'Sancte domine, inluminatio et salus vera credentibus. . .'. There are three collects which are irreducible to any of the four classes we have given. Two of them (AB 37, 76) are similar in structure to the collects based on St Zeno's sermons (AB 91 − 92); they consist of mere statements of fact followed by an application: AB 37 Per horam mediae noctis tunc gavisi sunt angeli de nativitate d. n. I. Christi: ita et nos laetari debemus in tua pace, omnipotens deus, qui regnas; AB 76 Summerso in mari Faraone liberatur Israhel: nos quoque . . . quaesumus liberari, per te Christe. The third collect (AB 121) could be termed asyndetic in as much as it is an invitation to prayer followed by an invocation and petition: Convenientes, fratres dilectissimi, ad orationem nonam. . .: ita et nos, domine, . . . mereamur, qui regnas.

20. AB 38, 39, 58, 60. There are three rhythmical collects for morning prayer: AB 24 − 26. One of the collects *post laudate* (AB 73) is, however, a good attempt to construct a prose collect for morning prayer along traditional lines.

CHAPTER NINETEEN

1. St Patrick speaks with admiration in his Confession c.41 of 'the sons and daughters of the Kings of the Irish (who) are seen to be monks and virgins of Christ'; their number is countless (c. 42; Epist.12). See Ryan, *Irish Monasticism*, 82 − 104.

2. Cf. P.J. Corish, *The Christian Mission*: A History of Irish Catholicism I 3 (Dublin 1972).

3. *Synodus I S. Patricii*, ed. Bieler, *The Irish Penitentials* (Dublin 1963) 54 − 59. The attribution of the canons to Patrick, Auxilius and Iserinus is upheld by Bieler, but K. Hughes argues in favour of a sixth-century date, *The Church in Early Irish Society*, 44 − 50.

4. Penance is ordered for a number of crimes which are punished by separation from the

Church or excommunication. On completion of his penance, the penitent is 'freed from his obligation by a priest' (c.14; the term *sacerdos* used here probably means the bishop, according to K. Hughes, *op.cit.*, 48). Excommunication was practised strictly, to the extent that an unrepentant excommunicated person 'shall not enter the Church even on Easter night' (c.18).

5. C.7: 'Quicumque clericus ussus negligentiae causa ad collectas mane vel vespere non occurrerit alienus habeatur nisi forte iugo servitutis sit detentus'.

6. Cf. J.A. Jungmann, 'The pre-monastic morning hour in the Gallo-Spanish region in the sixth century', *loc.cit.*, 122 – 157.

7. Cf. H. Schneider, 'Die biblischen Oden in christlichen Altertum', *Biblica*, 30 (1949) 28 – 65; *Die altlateinischen biblischen Cantica*: Texte und Arbeiten 29 – 30 (Beuron 1938) 89 – 98.

8. The earliest Irish sources speak of *secunda* or *anteirt* (*ante tertiam*) rather than *prima* or *prím*. We shall see that the terms are not entirely interchangeable.

9. Columban, *Reg.mon.*7: 'De synaxi vero, id est, de cursu psalmorum et orationum modo canonico quaedam sunt distinguenda, quia varie a diversis memorie de eo traditum est' (Walker, 128). Columban had been a monk at Bangor for many years before he went to Luxeuil and he speaks of the tradition he had learned there from his predecessors.

10. Columban speaks at length of *matutinum* as a night office or *vigilia*. His objective is to lay down its correct *cursus psalmorum*, which varies from twenty-five to seventy-five psalms, and he says nothing about the (cathedral) morning prayer which must have been celebrated at the end of the vigil.

11. Walker (131, n.5) speaks without hesitation of Columban's system of six Hour-Offices (at the third, sixth, and ninth hours of the day, at nightfall, midnight, and early morning)'. W. Godel says: 'Aller Wahrścheinlichkeit nach bestand der Cursus St Columbanus aus sechs Horen, wie es im 6.Jahrhundert im gallischen Liturgiebereich noch üblich ist' ('Irisches Beten...', *loc.cit.*, 274). Neither he nor Ryan, to whom he refers (*Irish Monasticism*, 335), give this Gallican parallel, although Ryan (336) says that the sixfold division — terce, sext, none, vespers (*sic*!), nocturns, matins — 'agrees with the arrangement recorded in the Life of St Melania the Younger, written about A.D. 451'.J.M. Hanssens says that the number of daily hours in Columban's *ordo* must have been at least three, or perhaps four (*Nature et Genèse de l'Office des Matines*, 88).

12. This is suggested by W.C. Bishop, 'A Service Book of the Seventh Century', *The Church Quarterly Review* 37 (1894) 344. There is reason to suggest, as we shall see (*infra*, p. 177), that Columban also included among the *horae diurnae* the final part of matins, that is, the cathedral office of lauds, with its three *laudate* psalms and series of intercessory versicles.

13. Donatus, *Reg.virg.*, 19 – 20 (PL 87, 281). In his *Life of Columbanus*, Jonas speaks of Bertulfus, abbot of Bobbio, and refers to this same hour: 'Cum quodam in tempore, expleto psallendi officio, una cum fratribus secunda diei hora de ecclesia beati Petri egrederetur, obvium habuit hominem' (*Vita Columbani* II 23, ed. Krusch, 284).

14. When speaking of the time for the main meal, which varies somewhat according to the quality of the day and time of year, Donatus also speaks obliquely of vespers: '... ad sextam reficiant sorores...; ad horam nonam ... prandeant...; ad vesperum reficiant. Ipsa autem vespera sic agatur, ut lumine lucernae non indigeant reficientes, sed luce adhuc diei omnia consummentur' (PL 87, 296 – 297). Vespers evidently precedes nightfall. The distinction made at Bangor between *vespertina* and *initium noctis* is parallel to that made at Arles between vespers and *duodecima*; cf. Caesarius, *Reg. virg.*66, ed. Morin, *Sancti Caesarii ... Opera Omnia* (Maredsous 1942), 120; Aurelian, *Reg.mon.*29: PL 68, 393. According to W. Godel, 'Irisches Beten...', *loc.cit.*, 277 – 278, the office called *initium noctis* in AB and in Columban's *Reg.mon.* and *duodecima* in Columban's *Reg.coen.*III (ed. Walker, 146) is to be identified with vespers. All the prayers and devotions indicated in

246

AB *ad initium noctis* or *ad vesperum* are meant for this office of vespers. The office named *vespertina* in the Antiphonary, on the other hand, would have been equivalent to the *hora undecima* celebrated before the evening meal in commemoration of the Last Supper according to Ga B 181. But there are no grounds for Godel's identification of vespers and *initium noctis*. Vespers is the primitive cathedral office, which must be identified with Bangor's *vespertina* or *vesperum* and with its Irish derivatives (*fescair, espartu*). The evening meal in Irish monasteries was usually taken immediately after none (cf. Ryan, *Irish Monasticism*, 386 – 387). Ryan (*ibid.*, 339), Gougaud (DACL II 2, 3017), and Warren (II xvi – xvii), for their part, wrongly distinguish *initium noctis* and *duodecima*, and identify the latter with vespers.

15. *Reg.mon.*7: 'Sunt autem quidam catholici, quibus idem est canonicus duodenarius psalmorum numerus sive per breves sive per longas noctes, sed per quaternas in nocte vices hunc canonem reddunt: ad initium scilicet noctis, ad mediumque eius, pullorum quoque cantus ac matutinum. . . . Noctibus vero reverentissimis dominicis scilicet vel sabbatis ad matutinum ter idem volvitur numerus, id est ter denis et VI psalmis' (Walker, 132).

16. Walker, 133, n.2, thinks this is suggested by the quotation from Cassian, *De Inst.*II 4 and 12: *canonicus duodenarius psalmorum numerus*. According to J.M. Hanssens, these four offices correspond exactly to the four night offices of the *Egyptian Church Order*; cf. *Nature et Genèse de l'Office des Matines*, 89. But Hanssens makes too easy a transition from the private devotions recommended in the *Church Order*, in which there is no mention of twelve psalms, to public offices of the *catholici*. The question whether or not the night offices of the (Irish) *catholici* owe their existence to any foreign liturgical tradition remains to be solved.

17. *Adomnan's Life of Columba*, ed, A.O. Anderson and M.O. Anderson (London — New York, 1961); see *Introduction*, 121 – 122, for collected references to the hours of the office.

18. 'Alio in tempore sanctus . . . PRIMA DIEI HORA quendam advocans fratrem Lugaidum nomine . . . taliter eum conpellat, dicens: "Praepara cito ad Scotiam celerem navigationem" ' (*op.cit.*, 336).

19. 'HORA vero eiusdem DIEI TERTIA vir venerandus Columbanum advocat prespiterum, dicens: "Ad navigandum te hodie praepara" ' (*ibid.*, 358).

20. '. . . ut sicuti prius exobtavimus post HORAM DIEI TERTIAM ad Iovae portum pervenientes insulae, postea manuum et pedum peracta lavatione HORA SEXTA eclesiam cum fratribus intrantes misarum solempnia pariter celebraremus' (*ibid.*, 458).

21. '. . . post NONAM DIEI HORAM valde fessa et fatigata superveniet' (*ibid.*, 312). 'HORA TRANSACTA NONA, sanctus circumstantibus sic profatus ait . . . ' (*ibid.*, 418).

22. 'Nam ipse sanctus cum paucis fratribus extra regis munitionem dum VESPERTINALES DEI LAUDES ex more celebraret, quidam magi ad eos propius accedentes in quantum poterant prohibere conabantur, ne de ore ipsorum divinae laudis sonus inter gentiles audiretur populos. Quo conperto sanctus xl. et iiii. psalmum decantare coepit' (*ibid.*, 228). It is more likely that psalm 44 is a psalm appropriate for this occasion rather than a regular part of vespers.

23. 'Sanctus ad VESPERTINALEM DOMINICAE NOCTIS MISAM ingreditur eclesiam. Qua continuo consummata ad hospitiolum revertens in lectulo resedet. Tum proinde MEDIA NOCTE pulsata personante cloca festinus surgens ad eclesiam pergit, citiorque ceteris currens solus introgressus iuxta altare flexis in oratione genibus recumbit. . . . Interea post sanctae egresum animae YMNIS MATUTINALIBUS terminatis sacrum corpus de eclesia ad hospitium, unde paulo ante vivens venerat, cum canora fratrum reportatur psalmodia' (*ibid.*, 526 – 536).

24. A rhythmical prayer appended to the hymn *In te Christe credentibus*, which is attributed to Columcille in the ILH, appears to recognize the existence of ten canonical hours in some monastic community (ILH I 85):

Protegat nos altissimus de suis sanctis sedibus
dum sibi ymnos canimus decem statutis vicibus,
sitque nobis propitius diebus atque noctibus.

A gloss on *decem* in the eleventh-century MS says: 'Ten canonical hours Colum Cille used to celebrate, *ut ferunt*, and it is from the history of John Cassian that he got that' (ILH II 170; a similar gloss in a MS of the Amra of Columcille is noted by R.I Best, 'The Lebor Brecc Tractate...', *loc. cit.*, 160). As Gougaud remarked, 'there is nothing in Cassian to support this statement' (*Christianity*, 330), and neither is there in Adomnan. The *catholici* mentioned by Columban come to mind as possible claimants of this practice. If we expand the information he gives us (cf. *supra*, p.247, n.15), filling in the day hours and dividing *matutinum* into its vigil and morning components, we get ten hours: *secunda*, terce, sext, none, vespers, nightfall, midnight, cock-crow, vigil, and morning lauds.

25. Cf. Ryan, *Irish Monasticism*, 336; W. Godel, 'Irisches Beten...', *loc.cit.*, 274.

26. Trinity College, Dublin, MS *H.3.17*, containing Brehon Law Tracts and Miscellania. The note on the hours is found on col.675, edited by R.I. Best, 'The Canonical Hours', *Ériu* 3 (1907) 116.

27. 'Sext, for then Adam sinned and then Christ was placed on the cross. None, for then he yielded up his spirit. Vespers and sext, the same cause of evil therin, for offering used to be made in them according to the law'. Part of the translation given, 'the same cause of evil therin', is tentative, since there is an erasure of four letters in the text (*aenfath uil...*), not noted by Best, who reads *aenfath uilc and*. The sense intended is evidently that the reason for celebrating both these hours is the same, the offering spoken of in Ex. 29, 38 – 39. Compare AB 27 (*ad secundam*): 'qui nos redemisti tuo sancto sanguine, ut praeces ... vice primitiarum tibi oblatas ... suscipias'; and the *Leabhar Braec* treatise: 'At prime everyone was wont to make his offering according to the law' (ed. Best, 147) or 'At prime everyone was wont to make offering according to the law, without unreason (*cin anfath*)' (*ibid.*, 159).

28. The reason given for the celebration of *iarmérge* (literally, after rising), 'for then Peter denied and used to shed tears of blood then always', suggests that it was a combination of vigil and morning prayer such as we have found at Bangor. Compare AB 25 (*ad matutinas*): 'Gallorum, Christe, cantibus, / te deprecor, sonantibus: / Petri ob quondam fletibus / nostri intende precibus'.

29. PL 66, 994; cf. Dekkers, *Clavis Patrum Latinorum* no.1862: 'Haec regula saec. vii pulcherrimum nobis praebet specimen mutuae penetrationis regularum S. Benedicti et S. Columbani. ... Hibernice videtur originis'; Gougaud, *Christianity*, 175.

30. Compare AB 17: 'Te oramus, altissime, / exorto solis lumine, / Christe, oriens nomine, / adesto nobis, domine'; AB 122: 'Domine, ... qui diem clarificas et in lumine lumine luminas, ... ut orietur lucifer in cordibus nostris'. We will return to the function of *secunda* later in this chapter. A. de Vogüé has suggested that the *missa* at sunrise in the *Regula cuiusdam* is another night vigil comparable to that celebrated *ad matutinum* by the *catholici* spoken of by Columban; see *La Règle de S. Benoit*, 456, n.11. A comparison of the texts reveals a certain resemblance, but the fact remains that the *Regula cuiusdam* speaks of only *three* night assemblies.

31. W. Stokes and J. Strachan, *Thesaurus Paleohibernicus* I (Cambridge 1901) 3; Gougaud, *Christianity*, 329 – 330.

32. Cf. A. de Vogüé, *La Règle de S. Benoit*, 511 – 518. Benedict excluded *vigiliae* from the *septies*, which for him consisted of matins, prime, terce, sext, none, vespers, and compline.

33. Martin McNamara, who is editing the commentary for the series *Studi e Testi*, assures me that it has Northumbrian connections, and it thus comes within the ambit of the *paruchia Columbae*. It is interesting to note in this connection the use of the term *maten* instead of *iarmérge* for matins. As used in the earliest texts, *iarmérge* seems to correspond to

Columban's *matutinum*, a combination of (monastic) vigil and (cathedral) morning prayer. In the office celebrated by Columcille at Iona, as Adomnan briefly describes it, matins seems to have consisted simply of the (cathedral) morning prayer, *hymni matutini*. This may explain the use of the term *maten* rather than *iarmérge* in the gloss.

34. Ed. J. O'Neill, *Eriu* 3 (1907) 96 – 109. This metrical rule was not written by Ailbe (*saec*.5 – 6) but in the Old Irish period (*saec.* 7 – 10), though it may owe something to the traditions of the community of Ailbe; cf. Gougaud, 'Inventaire des règles monastiques irlandaises', *Revue d'histoire ecclésiastique* 25 (1908) 177 – 178. References to the hours are found in stanzas 17, 19, 22, 23 (*anteirt*, wrongly translated 'the third hour', by O'Neill, as Best, 'The Lebor Brecc Tractate...', *loc.cit.*, 160, has pointed out), 25[a], 26, 28, 31[a], 39.

35. Stanza 17 prescribes 'a hundred genuflexions every hour of vespers (*cech fescair*)'. This need not be taken to imply a great quantity of psalms, such as Columban prescribed for *initium noctis* (twelve psalms). Stanza 18 also prescribes a hundred genuflexions for matins (*iarméirge*), which has thirty psalms. In stanza 25[a] and 28 mention is made of a vigil (*figill*). This does not appear to be a separate office as distinct from *midnocht* and *iarméirge*.

36. *Navigatio Sancti Brendani Abbatis*, ed. C. Selmer: Publications in Mediaeval Studies XVI (University of Notre Dame Press 1959). The earliest MSS, which are of a Lotharingian-Rhenish provenance, are of the tenth century, and Selmer believes that the Irish author was one of the many *Scotti peregrini* who settled in that area in the ninth and tenth centuries (*op.cit.*, xxvii – xxviii). He describes the *Navigatio* as 'a story of Christian visionary character, combined with adventure-reports of early Irish sea-farers, embellished with tales and sagas of folklore and spiced with classical reminiscences' (xv). It is also an expression of the Irish quest for the ideal monastic life in the deserted islands of the western ocean. J.F. Kenney said that the purpose of the author 'was not solely, or even primarily, to describe the wonders of the ocean. As we note the meticulous care with which he elaborates the precepts of Brendan, and the rules of life, the devotions, the method of observing the canonical hours, the psalms sung, the prayers said, the penances observed among the inhabitants, human and superhuman, of the oceanic islands, we come to realize that the author is painting a picture of the ideal monastic life. The *Navigatio Brendani* is the epic — shall we say the Odyssey — of the Old Irish Church' (*Sources*, 415). Kenney thought it was written 'almost certainly in Ireland' and that 'there is good presumption that it is a product of the ninth century' (*Sources*, 410, 415).

37. The hours are described in chapter 11 and 17 of the *Navigatio (Selmer, 25 – 26, 50 – 52);* the principal texts are cited *infra*, p.170 – 171. Compline, called *opus Dei* in c.11, is mentioned separately in c.12: 'Finitis omnibus secundum ordinem cursus diei, omnes cum magna alacritate festinabant ad completorium. At vero abbas, cum inchoasset predictum versiculum, id est "Deus in adiutorium meum", et dedissent simul honorem Trinitati, incipiebant istum versiculum cantare, dicentes: "Iniuste egimus, iniquitatem fecimus. Tu, qui pius es pater, parce nobis Domine. In pace in idipsum dormiam et requiescam, quoniam tu, Domine, singulariter in spe constituisti me". Post haec cantabant officium quod pertinet ad hanc horam' (*op.cit.*, 34 – 35). The texts of the *Navigatio* were also used in the composition of the Latin Life of St Brendan, ed. Plummer, *Vitae Sanctorum Hiberniae* I (Oxford 1910) 114 – 118, 125.

38. Cf. E.J. Gwynn and W.J. Purton, 'The Monastery of Tallaght', PRIA 29 C (1911) 115 – 179; E. Gwynn, *The Rule of Tallaght*: Hermathena 44, second supplementary volume (Dublin 1927), with references to the hours collected *ibid.*, xxii – xxv.

39. E. Gwynn, *The Rule of Tallaght, loc.cit.*, 57.

40. Ed. K. Meyer, *Zeitschrift für celtische Philologie* 6 (1908) 271. The term *tiugnáir* is generally translated 'matins'; cf. *Contributions to a Dictionary of the Irish Languare*, Royal Irish Academy, Dublin, s.v. In the present text, *tiugnáir* is distinguished from *iarmérge*, and Best takes them both to indicate 'the night vigils' ('The Lebor Brecc Tractate...', *loc.cit.*, 163). They are clearly distinguished also in the tenth-century *Saltair na Rann*, ed.

W. Stokes, *Anecdota Oxoniensia* (Oxford 1883), 1.810: 'between *iarmérge* and *tiugnáir*'. I question the accuracy of describing them as 'the night vigils'. The distinction made between them does not seem to me to be the same as that made in earlier texts between *midnocht* (*medium noctis*) and *iarmérge* (*matutinum*), where two night vigils are intended, even though we cannot always be sure of the exact weight attached to these two either, as we find them used, for example, in an episode of the Life of St Bricín, which relates that an angel held converse with the saint 'between *midnocht* and *iarmérge*' (cf. Best, *loc.cit*, 162). When only one night vigil remained it was called *medón aidhche* or *iarmérge* and the morning office (*laudes matutinae*) was called *tiugnáir* or *maiten*.

41. Examples in Best, *loc.cit.*, 162 – 165; see also *Contributions to a Dictionary of the Irish Language*, *s.v. iarmérge*.

42. Ed. R.I. Best, *loc. cit.*, 142 – 166. This treatise consists of a prose and a metrical version, of which the metrical is the earlier and is assigned to the eleventh or early twelfth century.

43. See Gougaud, *Christianity*, 332.

44. Donatus, *Reg.virg.*19 – 20: 'Exuntes a completoriis nulla sit licentia denuo loqui cuiquam aliquid, usque mane post SECUNDAM celebratam in conventu; quod in loco veniam petentes, singulae confessionem dantes pro cogitationibus carnalibus atque turpibus, vel nocturnis visionibus, demum pariter orantes dicant: "Fiat, domine, misericordia tua super nos, quemadmodum speravimus in te". . . . A secunda hora usque ad tertiam, si aliquis necessitas ut operentur non fuit, vacent lectioni' (PL 87, 281). Apart from this, we have the testimony of the Rule of Ailbe 23: 'Except the ruler and the vice-abbot no one should stir himself until *anteirt*' (*co hanteirt óin nínglúaisea*; ed. O'Neill, 101). The term *anteirt* is of Welsh origin, a fact which could be taken to indicate some influence of British monasticism in the formation of the Irish office; see Best, *loc.cit.*, 165 – 166. In the Penitential of Gildas c.19 we find a mention of *secunda*: 'Si excitatus veniat post misam, quicquid cantaverunt replicet ex ordine fratres. Si vero ad SECUNDAM venerit, caena careat' (ed. Bieler, *The Irish Penitentials*, Dublin 1963, 62). Bieler translates *misa* and *secunda* as 'the reading' and 'the second reading', but perhaps there is a distinction made here between the two hours, morning and *secunda*. The ninth- or tenth-century 'Catalogue of the Saints of Ireland' claims that the second order of Irish Saints *a David et Gilla et a Doco Britonibus missam acceperunt*; see P. Grosjean, 'Edition et commentaire du Catalogus . . .', *Analecta Bollandiana* 73 (1955) 196 – 213, 289 – 322. But, as Grosjean points out, this statement of the Catalogus is pretty worthless as historical evidence.

45. On the widespread practice of a return to sleep in monastic *ordines*, outside of Egypt, see A. de Vogüé, *La Règle de S. Benoit*, 427 – 431. A period of sleep after the morning office was customary in the Orient, according to Cassian, *De Inst*.III 4, and it was canonized by the institution of the *novella sollemnitas matutina* at Bethlehem. Cassian condemns this practice when he finds it in Gaul, because it is a departure from the perfection of Egypt; *De Inst*.III 5. The practice must have continued, because it is forbidden by Aurelian, *Reg.mon.*28: 'Post matutinas orationes ad somnum reverti non liceat; sed completis matutinis statim dicatur prima, deinde usque ad horam tertiam omnes lectioni vacent' (PL 68, 391). But Aurelian makes no mention of this prohibition in his *Reg.virg.*, where he speaks both of *secunda* (c.28) and of *prima* (c.29). This probably means that the office of prime was postponed for the nuns, so that they might have sleep between matins and *secunda*. Cf. de Vogüé, *op.cit*, 594, n.17.

CHAPTER TWENTY

1. This attachment to native traditons can be seen in the four letters Columban wrote to the Popes, the French bishops and to his own monks regarding the Easter controversy (*Epist.* I – IV; ed. Walker, 2 – 36). For the chronology of Columbanus, cf. Walker, x – xix.

2. *Reg. mon.* VII; Walker, 128, 130.

3. O. Heiming, 'Zum monastichen Offizium von Kassianus bis Kolumbanus', *Archiv für Liturgiewissenschaft* 7 (1961) 125 – 131. See also the table given by Walker, 131, n. 3.

4. The *vigilia* does not mean simply the extended *matutinum* of the holy night of Saturday and Sunday. Columban conludes his entire treatment of the *matutinum* office for ordinary nights as well as for the holy nights with the statement: 'Igitur iuxta vires consideranda vigilia est' (Walker, 130). Further on he applies it in particular to the Saturday *matutinum*: 'pluribus (psalmis) . . . semper nocti dominicae ac sabbati vigiliae deputatis' (Walker, 130 – 132).

5. I have modified Walker's table slightly. He indicates: Sept.24 — March 25: 36 psalms; March 25 — Sept 24: 24 psalms. But Sept 24 cannot have both 24 and 36 psalms; the same applies to March 25. Columban decides the issue by assigning 24 psalms to the equinoxes themselves: 'XXIIII autem per totum veret aestatem et usque ad autumnale aequinoctium, id est octavo Kalendas Octobris. In quo similitudo synaxeos est sicut in vernali aequinoctio, id est in VIII Kalendas Aprilis' (Walker, 130).

6. 'Per diurnas terni psalmi horas pro operum interpositione statuti sunt a senioribus nostris' (*ibid.*). Three psalms at the day hours, at least for terce, sext and none, was the universal and constant tradition, with the sole exception of the Gallican practice criticised by Cassian (*De Inst.* II 2,2; ed. Petschenig, 18), but still living at Arles in the time of Caesarius and Aurelian. Prime was also originally drawn up on the basis of three psalms, in imitation of the other day hours (Cassian, *De Inst.* III 4,2; *ibid.* 39).

7. Heiming, *art. cit.*, 130, regards this as a possibility.

8. Cf. A. de Vogüé, *La Règle du Maitre* I: SC 105 (1964) 53 – 54. In the Spanish monastic office of nocturns, the psalms were divided into groups of three named *missae psalmorum*. This *missa* was different from a Columbanian *chora* because the psalms were sung without an antiphon and each *missa* was, according to the *Liber Horarum*, followed by a responsary. In the Spanish cathedral office, on the other hand, the *missa* was a group of three antiphons with their appropriate prayers; after each *missa* a responsary, which in festive offices had its own prayer attached, was sung.

9. The use of alleluia in the *psalmi dicti* is indicated only for Easter terce by Caesarius, *Reg. virg.* 66 (ed. Morin, 120), but Aurelian says that the *alleluiaticum* was used in the hours of terce, sext, none, duodecima and nocturns as the third in each group of three psalms on Easter Sunday (*Reg. mon.*; PL 68, 393). Apart from this use of alleluia, the practice at Arles was to have a block of *psalmi dicti*, a multiple of three, followed by one or three or six antiphonal psalms. But here the proportion of 2 *psalmi dicti* : 1 *antiphona* (antiphonal psalm) was not prescribed; indeed; we find it only for Easter terce: 12 *psalmi dicti* (every third of these being an *alleluiaticum*) followed by 6 *antiphonae*.

10. 'Ita ut totum psalterii inter duas supradictas noctes numerum cantent' (Walker, 130).

11. Cf. O. Heiming, *art. cit.*, 131 – 132. He sees the principle of pure *psalterium currens*, with few exceptions to it, as a constant in monastic *ordines*, until Benedict's adoption of the Roman distribution of the psalter.

12. Cf. Cassian, *De Inst.* II 7, 1 – 3 (ed. Petschenig, 23 – 24).

13. Walker, 146, 158. The rule of Ailbe also orders (st. 20): ' "Deus in adiutorium" at the end of every psalm' (ed. O'Neill, *Eriu* 3, 1907, 101).

14. A total of seventy-five genuflexions would not appear extravagant in the Irish situation at that time. Stories were told about saints who were in the habit of making from two hundred to seven hundred genuflexions daily, while reciting the Psalter or the *Beati* (ps. 118); on this practice cf. Gougaud, *Christianity*, 90 – 92. The rule of Ailbe prescribes (st. 17): 'A hundred genuflexions for him at the "Beati" at the beginning of the day before his questions, thrice fifty (psalms) dearer than (other) works, with a hundred genuflexions every hour of vespers' (ed. O'Neill, *loc. cit.*, 99). Again (st. 18) 'A hundred genuflexions every matin (*iarméirge*) are due in church of a believer' (*ibid.*); however, these may have been combined with the 'thirty psalms every matin (*iarméirge*); prescribed in st. 19.

15. On this question of prayer after the psalms, cf. O. Heiming, *art. cit.*, *passim* and especially 138 – 139; A. de Vogüé, *La Règle de S. Benoit*, 555 – 588. The formulation of the silent prayer in the Columbanian office is regarded by de Vogüé as a weakening of the tradition.

16. Gougaud, *Christianity*, 175.

17. PL 66, 994.

18. Cassian, *De Inst*. II 6: 'Venerabilis patrum senatus . . . decrevit hunc numerum (i. e., 12 psalms) tam in vespertinis quam in nocturnis conventiculis custodiri. Quibus lectiones geminas adiungentes, id est unam veteris et aliam novi testamenti . . . addiderunt' (ed. Petschenig, 22).

19. The Rule of Ailbe (st. 20) speaks of 'Lection and celebration with invocation of the Son of God' and orders (st. 25ᵃ): 'After vigil, with prayer, with confessions without ceasing, the rule of the Gospel let him hear and the gentle rule of the monks' (*loc. cit.*, 101).

CHAPTER TWENTY – ONE

1. Columban, *Reg. mon.* VII; cf. *supra*, p.251, n.6.

2. AB 116 *Ad vesperum et ad matutinum*.

3. AB 117 *Ad horas diei oratio communis*.

4. Cf. *supra*, p.251, n.6. In the offices of prime, terce, sext and none at Arles, the number of *psalmi dicti* was either six or twelve, and they were generally followed by one or more antiphonal psalms (six antiphonal psalms at Easter terce): Caesarius, *Reg. virg.* 66 (ed. Morin, 120); Aurelian, *Reg. mon.* 393; *Reg. virg.* 404. Aurelian sometimes doubled the six *psalmi dicti* of Caesarius; thus at Easter sext and none (*Reg.* mon. 393; *Reg. virg.* 403) and at daily terce and none in the monks' office (*Reg. mon.* 395).

5. AB 98: *Incipit antiphona in natale Domini super Domine refugium ad secundam.* AB 105: *Super Domine refugium in dominicorum die.* AB 108: *Alia cotidiana.*

6. AB 122. Cf. *supra*, p. 118.

7. AB 27. Cf. *supra*, p. 97.

8. Ed. C. Selmer, *op. cit. supra*, p.249, n.36.

9. C. 17; Selmer 50 – 52. The author of the *Navigatio* situates the events about which he speaks in the context of the liturgical year, by dating them from Easter, or Pentecost, or Christmas. The event narrated in this first story happened in October or November, so that the office described is not connected with any special liturgical season.

10. C. 11; Selmer, 25 – 26. The event narrated here is situated on Easter Sunday. But the office described agrees with that in the first story and it has no exclusively Paschal character.

11. Thus the versicle chanted by the birds for *matutinae laudes* (II b), 'Laudate Dominum...', adapts ps. 148,2: 'Laudate eum...'; the versicle for terce (II d) omits part of ps. 46,7 – 8: 'Psallite Deo nostro, psallite, psallite regi nostro (psallite; quoniam rex omnis terrae Deus), psallite sapienter'; the versicle for sext (II e), 'Illumina Domine vultum tuum super nos et miserere nostri' adapts ps. 66,2: 'Illuminet vultum suum super nos et misereatur nostri'. In the Columbanian *chora* the third psalm of each group of three was antiphonal, and this *chora*-system may have applied to all the hours. But the versicles which were chanted by the birds are not all taken from the third psalm in each group, and we cannot be sure whether the three psalms in the first story and the versicles in the second were intended to constitute a (Columbanian) *chora*.

12. There can be no question of its being anything but an Irish office, because there is nothing in any continental rite which compares with it. Some of the psalms assigned here to the day hours are also found as chosen psalms in the office at Milan and Rome, but there is no connection between the Irish and continental use of them. For example, pss. 50, 62 and 89, used here for prime, were used in Roman lauds, pss. 50 and 62 daily and ps. 89 on Thursday; ps. 50 is used in ferial lauds at Milan and ps. 89 is the *psalmus directus* on Saturday. Ps. 53, used here for terce, was used for prime in the Roman and Ambrosian office and as the *psalmus directus* in Monday lauds at Milan. Pss. 66 and 69, chosen here for sext, are found as *psalmi directi* for lauds on Tuesday and Wednesday at Milan, while ps. 66 was used daily in Roman lauds. Ps. 112, chosen here for vespers, was also found among the psalms used for Sunday vespers at Rome (and subsequently Milan) and is the *psalmus directus* of Thursday lauds at Milan. One interesting parallel between the office of the *Navigatio* and a continental usage is found in the use of ps. 112 as one *directaneus parvulus* in the office of *lucernarium* (vespers) during Easter-time at Arles, according to Aurelian. He says: 'ad lucernarium directaneus parvulus, id est, "Regna terrae, cantate Deo, psallite Domino" (ps. 67, 33); alia die, "Laudate pueri Dominum" (ps. 112,1)' (*Reg. mon.* 393).

13. *De Inst.* III 6; ed. Petschenig, 41.

14. Cf. Hippolytus, *Trad. Apostolica* 41 (ed. Bottle, 90 – 92); Cassian, *De Inst.*; III 3; ed. Petschenig, 34 – 38. According to Cassian, the hour of terce is a commemoration of the descent of the Holy Spirit, rather than of the nailing of Christ to the Cross, as it was for Hippolytus. These two themes, the crucifixion and descent of the Holy Spirit, continued in the liturgies to be associated with terce. The hours of sext and none were seen as commemorations of the crucifixion and death of Christ, his triumphant entry into the underworld and his illumination and salvation of the saints. Secondary events of significance may also be recalled, such as the vision of Peter and Cornelius at the sixth hour or the ascent of Peter and John to the temple at the ninth hour.

15. For example, the *glorification* of Christ: 'Omnes gentes plaudite manibus,... quoniam Dominus excelsus, terribilis, rex magnus super omnes terram .... Ascendit deus in iubilo, et Dominus in voce tubae' (ps. 46,2 – 6); his *confidence* in suffering: 'Deus in nomine tuo salvum me fac,... quoniam alieni insurrexerunt adversum me.... Confitebor nomini tuo, Domine, ... quoniam ex omni tribulatione eripuisti me' (ps. 53, 3 – 9); his *death and glorification*: 'Circumdederunt me dolores mortis et pericula inferni invenerunt me.... Eripuit animam meam de morte.... Placebo Domino in regione vivorum' (ps. 114, 2 – 9). One of the key themes is summed up in the antiphon: 'Psallite Deo nostro...'.

16. Themes of supplication in tribulation, followed by thanksgiving for deliverance, in pss. 69 and 115: 'Deus in adiutorium meum intende.... Confundantur et revereantur qui quaerunt animam meam.... Ego vero egenus et pauper sum, Deus adiuva me... Domine, ne moreris' (ps. 69,2 – 7); 'Quid retribuam Domino pro omnibus quae retribuit mihi.... Pretiosa in conspectu Domini mors sanctorum eius...' (ps. 115,12 – 15). The antiphon, if it be such, 'Illumina, Domine, vultum tuum...', may be the explanation for the unusual association of the illumination of the darkness with the sixth hour in the collect AB 29; cf. *supra*, p.99 – 100.

17. 'De profundis clamavi ad te, Domine.... Sustinuit anima mea in verbo eius, speravit

anima mea in Domino' (ps. 129,1 – 5); 'Ecce quam bonum et quam iucundum habitare fratres in unum, quoniam illic mandavit Dominus benedictionem et vitam usque in saeculum' (ps. 132,1 – 3); 'Lauda Ierusalem Dominum. . .' (ps. 147). The central theme here is praise for the blessings of God bestowed on his people and, in particular, for the redemption of the one who trusts in God 'out of the depths'; the dominant note of joy and praise is struck in the antiphon: 'Ecce quam bonum. . .'.

18. On the creation theme, as one of the central themes in vespers in East and West from the fourth century to the seventh, cf. J. Pinell, 'Vestigis del lucernari a Occident', *loc. cit.*, especially 100 – 101, 107 – 108. In each of the psalms assigned here to vespers there is an explicit reference to evening: 'Sol cognovit occasum suum. Posuisti tenebras et facta est nox. . .' (ps. 103,19 – 24); 'A solis ortu usque ad occasum laudabile nomen Domini' (ps. 112,3); 'exitus matutini et vespere delectabis' (ps. 64,9). Each of the psalms speaks about God's wonders in creation and man's work in it. The leading note of praise is found in the antiphon from ps. 64: 'Te decet hymnus. . .'.

19. In the most primitive type of Ambrosian vespers, the psalmodic part after the *lucernarium* and hymn comprised only three psalms: a proper psalm, followed by pss.133 and 116; cf. E. Cattaneo, *Il Breviario Ambrosiano*, 224 – 227; P. Borella, Il Rito Ambrosiano, 259. In Spain, the *ordo* of St Isidore for vespers was: 'primo lucernarium, deinde psalmi duo, responsorius unus, et laudes' (*Reg. mon.* 2; PL 83, 876). The same office of vespers, but in a slightly varied form , is found again in the cathedral office of the liturgical MSS: *vespertinum, antiphona, alleluiaticum, sono* (the latter element corresponds probably to the earlier *responsorius* and *laudes*); cf. J. Pinell, 'El oficio hispánico visigótico', *loc. cit.*, 17 – 18. At Arles the 'cathedral' vespers are clearly distinguished from the monastic evening prayer of *duodecima*. The office of vespers never varied in structure: a *directaneus brevis* (or *parvulus*), followed by three antiphonal psalms, a hymn and the *capitellum*; cf. Caesarius, *Reg. virg.* 66 (ed. Morin, 120,12 – 14; 122,12 – 14); Aurelian, *Reg. mon.* 393, 395.

20. The Rule of St Ailbe (f. *supra*, p.163) makes a reference to the office of none which seems to bear out the evidence of the *Navigatio*. In st. 28 it says: 'A stepping to nones, a crying out with psalms' (ed. O'Neill, 103). This may be a veiled reference to the *gradual* psalm 129, the first psalm for none according to the *Navigatio*, and which begins with the words: 'De profundis *clamavi*. . .'.

21. Cf. J. Ryan, *Irish Monasticism*, 323-327.

22. The Irish use of the *Gloria* for matins and vespers is ascribed to Byzantine influence by A. Baumstark, *Nocturna Laus*, 200.

23. ILH I 51. One MS (T) of the *Liber Hymnorum* has this further versicle: 'Praesta nobis, Domine, ut hanc noctem sine peccato nos transire possimus' (*ibid.*). and the *Leabhar Breac* Preface to the *Gloria* notes: 'at night it is due to be sung' (*ibid.* II 21). *Nocte ista* is glossed in the MS with the note: '.i. huius saeculi', and Bernard concludes from this mystical interpretation that 'it would thus appear probable that this old use of singing the hymn at the night offices (*sic*!) had fallen into desuetude at the time when the glosses were added' (*op. cit.*, II 136).

24. Cf. A. Baumstark, *Nocturna Laus*, 199 – 201.

25. In the Spanish office the *completuria* was separated from the psalms by the hymn and the *supplicatio*; it was also sometimes preceded and always followed by other devotional appendices: *preces, clamores, Pater, petitio, benedictio*; cf. J. Pinell, 'El oficio hispánico visigótico', 17 – 21. In the Ambrosian office, the position of the collect varied: at lauds it immediately preceded the *laudate* psalms, at vespers it followed the psalms, and in the small hours it came at the end, immediately before the three-fold *kyrie*; cf. E. Cattaneo, *Il Breviario Ambrosiano*, 180, 121, 224 – 225.

26. This is a common feature of the collects for prime; cf. J. Pinell, *De Liturgia Laudis* 177 – 178.

27. Tertullian, *De Oratione* 25 (ed. Reifferscheid – Wissowa, CSEL 20, 197); Cyprian, *De dominica oratione* 34 (ed. Hartel, CSEL 3,1, 294); Cassian, *De Inst.* Ill 3,2 (ed. Petschenig, 35); Am M II 452 (Be 1582); Mo Br 947 – 953; Dublin, Trinity College, MS H. 3. 17 (cf. *supra*, p.162): 'Terce, because it was then Christ was given up by Pontius Pilate, and therin *grace came upon the apostles'*.

28. Hippolytus, *Trad. Apost.* 41 (ed. Botte, 90), speaks of the crucifixion and the great darkness and of the need to pray with a powerful prayer in imitation of the prayer of Christ in the midst of darkness; other sources speak of sext as a commemoration of the crucifixion: Cyprian, *De dom. oratione* 34 (ed. Hartel, 292); Cassian, *De Inst.* III 3,3 – 4 (ed. Petschenig, 35 – 36); Am M II 452 (Be 1583); Mo Br 955.

29. Cf. Hippolytus, *op. cit.*, 90 – 91; Cyprian, *loc. cit.*, 292; Cassian, *op. cit.*, III 3, 6 – 7 (36 – 37).

30. The descent of Christ and his deliverance of the saints are commemorated here by Hippolytus, *loc. cit.*; Cassian, *loc. cit.*, Mo Br 959. The revelation to Cornelius is commemorated here by Cassian, *loc. cit.* The confession of the good thief and his admittance to paradise is also found in the collect for none in Am M II 452 (Be 1584); for the possible Irish origin of this Ambrosian collect, cf. *supra*, p.117.

31. *Regulae Fusius Tractatae* 37,4 (PG 31, 1015).

32. Cf. Am M II 435 (Be 1595) Transacto diei cursu, gratias nomini tuo referimus, omnipotens Deus; quaesumus misericordiam tuam, ut quaecumque in hoc die per fragilitatem carnis contraximus, veniam nobis largiri digneris. Cf. also Am M II 440 (Be 1603); Mo Br 702; Vesp.Mat. 8, 9, 19, 22, 25.

33. Cf. J. Pinell, 'Vestigis del lucernari', 119 – 120.

34. Walker, 130.

35. Cf. *supra*, p.106 – 111.

36. *Common oroit dum* — 'A common prayer of ours' (Warren II 80). The versicle and collect are the same as in the long formulary (AB 43), where they have been given the title *pro fratribus* by Warren.

37. Warren II 80; elsewhere he says that 'from the position of these intercessions (AB 40 – 56) in the Bangor Book, . . . it would appear that they were used at the end of Mattins, but the wording of the Rule of St Columbanus . . . implies their attachment to all the Day Hours' (II xvi).

38. Were it not for the fact that Columban speaks explicitly of the interruption of work (*pro operum interpositione*) as a characteristic of the day hours, we might lawfully see in his global designation of three psalms for each of these hours the inclusion also of the *laudate* psalms, by which the vigil was almost certainly concluded. He could, speaking in general terms and *per modum unius*, have included lauds (the conclusion of matins) among those daily hours which had an addition of intercessory versicles. No doubt lauds cannot have entailed an 'interruption of work' and in this sense it is not a 'day-time hour'. But, in as much as it had three psalms and an addition of versicles, it could in Columban's mind, who would not have needed to stress the obvious, have been included among those hours which he speaks of as 'day-time' hours (*horae diurnae*).

39. The Lord's Prayer was used as the conclusion of the hours in certain contemporary rites: in the Roman and Benedictine office, and in the morning and evening offices of the Spanish rite. Cf. J. A. Jungman, 'The Lord's Prayer in the Roman Breviary', in: *Pastoral Liturgy*, 191 – 200. In the Benedictine office it also followed the litany (or *supplicatio litaniae*).

CHAPTER TWENTY – TWO

1. It is called *initium noctis* in AB 22, 32, and 33, and in Columban, *Reg. mon VII*. 'Ad initium vero noctis XII psalmi' (Walker, 130). The term *duodecima* is used for the same office in Columban, *Reg. coen*.III: 'Quod si ex neglegentia . . . perdiderit, longa venia in ecclesia dum duodecim psalmos ad duodecimam canunt . . . paeniteat' (Walker, 146). Some would identify this office (*initium noctis* or *duodecima*) with vespers, in spite of the distinction made at Bangor between *initium noctis* and *vespertina*; cf. *supra*, p.246, n.14. The term *duodecima* may have been borrowed by the Irish on the Continent, to replace the native term *initium noctis*. The distinction between *duodecima* and vespers is found also in the Rules of Caesarius and Aurelian, and in that of Fructuosus of Braga, while the *Regula Magistri* (34,4; ed. de Vogüé, SC 106, 188) identifies them both. Aurelian prescribes 18 *psalmi dicti* for daily *duodecima*, *Reg. mon*. 395. There were also 18 psalms for *duodecima* at Easter (Caesarius, *Reg. virg.* 66; ed. Morin. 120; Aurelian, *Reg. mon.* 393), and on feast days there may have been 12, according to Caesarius: 'Cunctis festis diebus ad duodecimam psalmi qui ad tertiam dicendi sunt' (*Reg. virg.* 68; ed. Morin, 121). It is difficult to follow Fructuosus, *Reg. mon.* 2; he puts *duodecima* before vespers and appears to distinguish both from the *prima noctis hora*: 'Ita quoque in reliquis institutum est hunc servandum esse ordinem horis, tertia, sexta, nona, duodecima videlicet, atque vespera, ut ante et post trinas has legitimas horas peculiares orationes prosequantur obsequia. Nocturno igitur tempore prima noctis hora sex orationibus celebranda est, ac deinde decem psalmorum concentu cum laude ac benedictionibus consummanda in ecclesia est' (PL 87, 1099). The Spanish *Regula mon. comm.* 10 puts vespers among the canonical hours, but makes no mention of *duodecima* or of *prima noctis hora* (PL 87, 118). Fructuosus's *duodecima* is a little office of three psalms; his *prima noctis hora* corresponds substantially to what is known in Arles as *duodecima* and by Columban as *initium noctis* or *duodecima*. Of the three, Columban represents more faithfully the original prototype of this evening prayer, the Egyptian evening assembly. See next note.

2. Cassian, *De Inst.* II 4; 'Igitur per universum . . . Aegyptum et Thebaidem duodenarius psalmorum numerus tam in vespertinis quam in nocturnis sollemnitatibus custoditur' (ed. Petschenig, 20).

3. Cf. J. Pinell, *De Liturgia Laudis*, 177 – 179.

4. Cf. Cyprian, *De domin. orat.* 35 (ed. Hartel, 293).

5. Cf. Warren II 61 – 62; G. Morin, 'Destination de la formule "ad pacem celebrandam" dans l'Antiphonaire de Bangor', *Rev. bénédictine* 12 (1895) 201 – 202; F. Cabrol, 'Baiser', DACL II 1, 124. Both Warren and Morin refer to the existence in the evening service of the East Syrian Church of the rite of the kiss of peace, followed by the Nicene Creed; indeed, Warren regarded the AB formulae as evidence of Eastern affiliations in the Irish liturgy.

6. PL 83, 876.

7. PL 87, 1099 – 1100.

8. Some form of reconciliation rite may have been practised already in Columban's time. In his *Reg. coen.* III we find pardon being obtained through prostration during *duodecima*: 'longa venia in ecclesia dum duodecim psalmos ad duodecimam canunt prostratus nullum membrum movens paeniteat' (Walker, 146). A remnant of the AB formula remained even when compline came to replace the nightfall office; cf. *Navigatio S. Brendani*, cited p.249, n.37.

9. Morin, *art. cit.*, 202.

10. J. N. D. Kelly, *Early Christian Creeds* (London 1960) 402 – 403, shows that it has cer-

tain peculiarities, but is 'broadly similar to T (*Textus receptus*), and where it parts company with it recalls features in the creeds of the Bobbio Missal'.

11. Athanasius, *De Virginitate* c. 20 (PG 28, 275; Basil, *Reg. fusius tractatae* 37,3 – 5 (PG 31, 1013 – 1016); *Epist.* 207,2 – 4 (PG 32, 762 – 766). Cf. J. Mateos, 'Office de minuit et office du matin chez S. Athanase', *Orientalia Christiana Periodica* 28 (1962) 173 – 180; 'L'Office monastique à la fin du IVe siècle: Antioch, Palestine, Cappadoce', *Oriens Christianus* 47 (1963) 74 – 88.

12. *Reg. Magistri* c. 33,7 – 9: 'Sed hoc in hieme agendum est, ut nocturnos iam expletos pullorum cantus sequatur, qui quia noctes sunt grandes, ut digesti a somno fratres vigilandigesto sensu opus Dei, quod dicunt, agnoscant. Et ideo intervallum ponitur, ut prolixa nocte somni gravitas finiatur' (ed. de Vogüé, SC 106, 176 – 178). Isidore, *Reg. mon.* 6: 'Post vigilias autem usque ad matutinum requiescendum' (PL 83, 876). Benedict also saw the vigil as a midnight office, for he understood it as being a fulfilment of the prophetic pronouncement, *Media nocte surgebam ad confitendum tibi* (ps. 118,62; *Regula* c. 16, ed. Hanslik, CSEL 75, 64). For Benedict's adaptation of the theory and practice of the *Magister*, cf. A. de Vogüé, *Le Règle de S. Benoit*, 419 – 431.

13. PL 83, 1100 – 1101.

14. Regarding the office of Fructuosus and its relationship to the other Spanish sources, cf. J. Pinell, 'Las horas vigiliares del oficio monacal hispánico', *Liturgica* 3 (1966) 241 – 245.

15. Cf. J. Mateos, 'L'Office monastique à la fin du IVe siècle', *loc. cit.*, 64 – 69.

16. Cf. S. Bäumer — R. Biron, *Histoire du Bréviaire* I, 209 – 214. Caesarius for his part confesses the dependence of his *ordo* on that of Lérins: 'Ordinem etiam quo modo psallere debeatis, ex maxima parte secundum regulam monasterii Lyrinensis in hoc libello indicavimus inserendum' (*Reg. virg.* 66; ed. Morin, 120). The use of the hymn *Mediae noctis tempus est* at first nocturns against winter at Arles (Caesarius, *Reg. virg.* 69: *loc. cit.*, 121; Aurelian, *Reg. mon.* 394) indicates that nocturns was understood as a midnight office; but in reality it was a morning vigil in the Egyptian and Palestinian tradition.

17. Twelve psalms for the vigil or nocturn are found, with variations affecting the use of alleluia and antiphons, and affecting the proportion of antiphonal and responsorial psalmody, in many monastic Rules: *Reg. Magistri*,c. 44,5 – 7(ed. de Vogüé, 202: 12 'impositions' in summer), *Reg. Benedicti* c. 9 (ed. Hanslik, 53 – 56: 12 psalms); *Ordo monasterii* c.2 (ed. de Bruyne, *Rev. bénéd.* 42, 1930, 319: 12 psalms in summer); *Ordo escurialensis* 6 (ed. de Bruyne, *loc. cit.*, 342) and Isidore, *Reg. mon.* 4 (PL 83, 876): 'tres missae psalmorum', which were preceded by 3 *psalmi canonici* and followed by three canticles; on the Spanish *missa*, cf. *supra*, p.252, n.8.

18. Cf. Hippolytus, *Trad. Apost.*, c. 41 (ed. Botte, 96); Mo Hor 53.

CHAPTER TWENTY – THREE

1. We may note the main differences in so far as they apply to the morning vigil. While Columban's vigil was a simple succession of *chorae* the Arles nocturns had a greater variety: 1) *Directaneus*; 2) 18 *psalmi dicti*, with alleluia during Easter-time with every third psalm; 3) three abbreviated antiphonal psalms; 4) two readings (these were most probably also added to the psalmody in Columban's *ordo*); 5) a hymn; 6) *capitellum*. This structure was doubled in winter at Arles, and a further supplement was added: 3 *missae ad librum*; *antiphona et responsus et alia antiphona*; 4 *missae* (Caesarius, *Reg. virg.* cc. 66, 69: ed. Morin, 120 – 121; Aurelian, *Reg. mon.* 394). The *ordines* of Arles and Columban are both

much developed in comparison with the Egyptian model, with its canonical number of 12 psalms (11 *psalmi dicti* or *psalliti* and one with alleluia), but both retain some appreciation of 'pure psalmody', without the adornment of antiphon or response. Furthermore, Columban's special vigil on the 'holy nights' was only an extended form of the daily *matutinum*; at Arles, there was an all-night vigil in the Palestinian manner between Friday and Saturday (Caesarius, *Reg. virg.* c. 66: ed. Morin, 120; Aurelian, *Reg. mon.*, 394, 396) and an addition of 6 *missae* to Sunday nocturns; a *missa* consisted of three readings, with a prayer after each reading, and each *missa* was followed by an antiphonal psalm, a responsorial psalm, and another antiphonal psalm (Caesarius, *Reg. mon.*: Morin, 153; Aurelian, *Reg. mon.* 394).

2. H. Schneider, *Die altlateinischen biblischen Cantica*: Texte und Arbeiten I 29 – 30 (Beuron 1938) 90: 'Offenbar handelt es sich hier um einen Wochenturnus, bei dem die beiden Cantica unverändert bleiben und nur die Antiphonen und Orationen wechseln'.

3. T 2 = AB 81; T 3 = AB 62; T 5 = AB 82; T 6 = AB 63. Schneider, *op. cit.*, 91, concluded that the canticles were here probably meant for Saturdays and Sundays, firstly, because one of the *laudate* collects is headed *ib felib*, that is, 'on feast days', and another fragmentary prayer is headed *si dominicus dies* (T 21); secondly, because of the penitential character of the second collect for both canticles (T 3, 6). T would thus represent an earlier stage of development than AB. But the arguments adduced by Schneider are inconclusive; for one thing, the collects in T are included in two sets intended for Saturday in AB.

4. Schneider, *op. cit.*, 6 – 17; and especially his study, 'Die biblischen Oden im christlichem Altertum', *Biblica* 30 (1949) 28 – 65.

5. For the Roman series and its evolution, cf. Schneider, *op. cit.*, 46 – 64, and especially as regards the *Benedictus*, 63 – 64. The *Benedictus* was not in use at Milan in the time of St Ambrose, whose canticle-series included Ex. 15, Dt. 32 and Dan. 3 (*op. cit.*, 10), but it is found in the Milan series of canticles in the liturgical MSS, a series which was completed between the fifth and seventh centuries (*op. cit.*, 98 – 102). The fact that the other canticle (Dt. 32) is Vulgate is regarded by Schneider (91) as an indication of its relatively late introduction into the Irish office.

6. Am M II 414 – 417; cf. W. C. Bishop, 'A Service Book of the seventh Century', *The Church Quarterly Review* 37 (1894) 350 – 351; *The Mozarabic and Ambrosian Rites* (London 1924) 102 – 105.

7. Am M II 25, 83, 89.

8. 'La vigile cathédral chez Egérie', *Orientalia Christiana Periodica* 27 (1961) 281 – 312.

9. Cf. Mateos, *art. cit.*, 302 – 310. At Milan we find the three canticles (Is. 26, 1 Sam. 2, Jonah 2 or Hab. 3), followed now by three readings where the Gospel of the resurrection must have come originally. The procession in honour of the Cross is accompanied by the chant of an antiphon, preceded and followed by appropriate canticles (*Benedictus*, *Cantemus*, *Benedicite*).

10. Caesarius, *Reg. mon.*: 'Omni dominica sex missas facite. Prima missa semper resurrectio legatur; dum resurrectio legitur nullus sedeat. Perfectas missas dicetis matutinos' (ed. Morin, 153).

11. Cf. P. Borella, *Il rito ambrosiano*, 248-249.

12. Caesarius, *Reg. mon.* (ed Morin, 153). The material of Caesarius has been expanded by Aurelian, with the addition of more psalms and through making the *directaneus parvulus* a *directaneus* simply; he also has the *Magnificat* instead of the *Te Deum* (*Reg. mon.* 393). On Sunday these psalms and canticles had no antiphons but only alleluia; in Ireland, as at Milan, there are antiphons provided (AB 99 – 100) for the *Cantemus*, *Benedicte*, and *laudate* psalms.

13. Am M II 403; A. W. S. Porter, 'Cantica mozarabici officii', *Ephemerides Liturgicae* 45 (1935) 126 – 145. Most of the rhythmical antiphons in AB have disyllabic rhyme and these have been printed by Blume, AH 51, 292. Of the others, some (99, 11 – 12) are paraphrases of verses in Ex. 15 and Dan. 3; the others are taken more or less directly from the Old Latin text of the canticles (99, 5 – 6, 13 – 20), though one (99, 17) reflects the Vulgate reading: 'Cantemus Domino, gloriose enim magnificatus est (VL honorificatus est)'.

14. There are four of these collects *post hymnum.* AB 66: 'Sancte domine, inluminatio et salus . . .' was meant to follow *Spiritus divinae lucis* (cf. Walker II 67). AB 75: 'Respice, domine, ad praeces nostras. . .' was probably meant for the same hymn (cf. its ritornello: Respice in me domine). AB 80: 'Resurrectionem tuam, Christe, veneramur. . .' consists of two brief phrases and 'does not suggest a connection with any hymn in the Bangor Antiphonary' (Warren II 68). AB 68: 'Lux orta est. . .' was probably intended for *Spiritus divinae lucis,* 'with its "lumen de lumine" (3), "filius divinae lucis" (8), and "unigenitus" (4, 7, 9)' (Warren II 68). Another collect, entitled *post evangelium* (AB 84; cf. *supra,* p.142), was in reality meant to accompany the hymn *Hymnum dicat.*

15. Cf. *supra,* pp.79; L. Gougaud, 'Les conceptions du martyr chez les Irlandais', *Rev. bénéd.* 24 (1907) 360 – 373.

16. Ed. Meyer, 201 – 203. The Irish text of the *Te Deum* began with the words of ps. 112,1: 'Laudate, pueri, Dominum, laudate nomen domini'. The collects which were meant to follow it are, therefore, entitled *Post laudate pueri dominum in dominicorum die* (AB 123, 125).

CHAPTER TWENTY – FOUR

1. The treatise was written probably by an Irish monk in the eighth century; ed. J. Wickham Legg, ' "Ratio de cursus qui fuerunt ex auctores". Speculations on the Divine Office by a writer of the eighth Century', in: *Miscellania Ceriani* (Milano 1910) 149 – 169. The six *cursus* in question are: *cursus romanus, cursus gallorum, cursus scottorum, cursus orientalis, cursus quem refert beatus Augustinus, cursus beati Benedicti qui ipsum singulariter pauco distante a cursu romano.*

2. L. Gougaud agreed with a number of earlier authorities, including Dom Bäumer and F. E. Warren, in regarding this explanation of the origin of the Irish *cursus* as being substantially true: 'Ce qui est rapporté au sujet de la transmission du *cursus* depuis Cassien jusqu'á saint Patrice et saint Colomban par les intermédiaires que nous avons cités est tout à fait conforme à ce que nous savons des rapports du monde religieux insulaire avec la Gaule aux Ve et VIe siècle. . . . Tout compte fait, il semble donc que cet exposé de la genèse du *cursus Scottorum* mérite d'être tenu pour substantiellement vrai' (DACL II 2, 2990 – 2991). A few years later he expressed himself less positively, saying simply that 'this account . . . is not wholly devoid of probability' (*Christianity,* 318).

3. *Reg. virg.,* 66: 'Ordinem etiam quo modo psallere debeatis, ex maxima parte secundum regulam monasterii Lyrinensis in hoc libello indicavimus inserendum' (ed. Morin, 120).

4. Cf. L. Bieler, *St Patrick and the Coming of Christianity* (Dublin 1967) 24 – 27. A *dictum* attributed to Patrick by his seventh-century biographer Tírechán, one which may be genuine (cf. Bieler, *op. cit.,* 11 – 14), speaks of his journey through Gaul: 'Timorem Dei habui ducem iteneris mei per Gallias atque Italiam, etiam in insolis quae sunt in mari Terreno' (ed. Bieler, *Libri Epistolarum S. Patricii Episcopi,* Dublin 1952, 104).

5. 'Itemque pro reverentia domini Martini, vel cultu ac virtute, id statuimus observan-

dum, ut tam in ipsa basilica sancta quam in ecclesiis nostris iste psallendi ordo servetur. Ut in diebus festis ad matutinum sex antiphonae binis psalmis explicentur. Toto Augusto manicationes fiant, quia festivitates sunt et missae sanctorum. Septembri septem antiphonae explicentur binis psalmis, Octobri octo ternis psalmis, Novembri novem ternis psalmis, Decembri decem ternis psalmis, Ianuario et Februario itidem usque ad pascha. Sed ut possibilitas habet, qui facit amplius pro se, et qui minus, ut potuerit. Superest ut vel duodecim psalmi expediantur ad matutinum' (ed. Mansi, *Sacrorum Concil. Collectio* IX 796 – 797). The juggling with numbers, which results in seven antiphons in *September*, eight in *October*, nine in *November*, and ten in *December*, appears artificial and unreal. But no doubt the Synod had some real tradition to rely on drawing up this legislation. With Gregory of Tours' *De Cursu Stellarum Ratio* (ed. Krusch, MGH, *Script. rer. merov.* I 854 – 872) we are, it would seem, in a world of pure fantasy when Gregory discusses the possiblities of psalmody at night according to the course of the stars.

6. 'Patrum statuta praeceperunt, ut ad sextam sex psalmi dicantur cum alleluia et ad duodecimam deodecim, itemque cum alleluia. Si ad duodecimam duodecim psalmi, cur ad matutinum non itemque vel duodecim explicantur? Quicumque minus quam duodecim psalmos ad matutinum dixerit, ieiunat usque ad vesperam' (*op. cit.*, 797).

7. L. Gougaud, *Christianity*, 57 – 70, discusses the beginnings of monasticism in Britian and Ireland, and the constant relations that were kept up between the two. See also J. Ryan, *Irish Monasticism*, 105 – 116. It has, however, recently been pointed out that much of the evidence used to prove the influence of British monasticism on the Irish is of very doubtful value; cf. K. Hughes, *The Church in Early Irish Society*, 71 – 74, and *supra*, p.250, n.44.

8. AB 3: *Praecamur patrem* 16.

BIBLIOGRAPHY

Bäumer, S. and Biron, R., *Histoire du Bréviaire* I (Paris 1905).

Baumstark, A., *Nocturna Laus. Typen frühchristlicher Vigilienfeier und ihr Fortleben vor allem im römischen und monastischen Ritus*: Liturgiewissenschaftliche Quellen und Forschungen 32, herausgegeben von O. Heiming, 2nd ed. (Münster Westfalen 1967).

Beare, W., *Latin Verse and European Song. A Study in Accent and Rhythm* (London 1957).

Best, R. I., 'The Lebor Brecc Tractate on the Canonical Hours', in: *Miscellany presented to Kuno Meyer* (Halle a. S. 1912) 142–166.

Bieler, L., *St Patrick and the Coming of Christianity*: A History of Irish Catholicism I 1 (Dublin 1967).

Bieler, L., *The Life and Legend of St Patrick* (Dublin 1949).

Bieler, L., 'The Hymn of St Secundinus', *P.R.I.A.* 55, Section C, No. 6 (1953) 117–127.

Binchy, D.A., 'Patrick and his Biographers, ancient and modern', *Studia Hibernica* 2 (1962) 7–173.

Bischoff, B., *Mittelalterliche Studien. Ausgewählte Aufsätze zur Schriftkunde und Literaturgeschichte*, 2 vols (Stuttgart 1966–1967).

Bishop, W. C., *The Mozarabic and Ambrosian Rites*: Alcuin Club Tracts 15 (London 1924).

Bishop, W. C., 'A Service Book of the Seventh Century', *The Church Quarterly Review* 37 (1894) 337–363.

Borella, P., *Il Rito Ambrosiano*: Biblioteca di Scienze Religiose III 10 (Brescia 1954).

Bulst, W., *Hymni Latini antiquissimi LXXV. Psalmi III* (Heidelberg 1956).

Cabrol, F., 'Bangor (Antiphonaire de)', *DACL* II 1 (1910) 183–191.

Carney, J., *The Problem of St Patrick* (Dublin 1961).

Cattaneo, E., *Il Breviario Ambrosiano. Note storiche ed illustrative* (Milano 1943).

Chavasse, A., *Le Sacramentaire Gélasien* (Paris 1957).

Cousin, P., 'La Psalmodie Chorale dans la Règle de Saint Colomban', in: *Melanges Colombaniens* (Paris 1951).

de Vogüé, A., *La Règle de Saint Benoît. Tome V. Commentaire historique et critique. Partie IV, L'Oeuvre de Dieu*: SC 185 (Paris 1971), 383–643.

Franceschini, E., *L'Antifonario di Bangor*: Testi e documenti de storia e di letteratura latina medioevale IV (Padova 1941).

Godel, W., 'Irisches Beten im frühen Mittelalter', *Zeitschrift für katholische Theologie* 85 (1963) 261–321, 389–439.

Gougaud, L., 'Celtiques (Liturgies)', *DACL* II 2 (1925) 2969–3032.

Gougaud, L., *Christianity in Celtic Lands* (London 1932).

Hamilton, G. F., *In Patrick's Praise: the Hymn of St Secundinus (Sechnall)*, 2nd ed. (Dublin 1920).

Hanssens, J. M., *Nature et Genèse de l'Office des Matines. Aux origines de la Prière liturgique*: Analecta Gregoriana 57 (Romae 1952).

Heiming, O., 'Zum monastischen Offizium von Kassianus bis Kolumbanus', *Archiv für Liturgiewissenschaft* 7 (1961) 89-156.

Hennig, J., 'Old Ireland and Her Liturgy', in: *Old Ireland*, ed. R. McNally (Dublin 1965), 60-89.

Hillgarth, J. N., 'Visigothic Spain and Early Christian Ireland', *P.R.I.A.* 62, Section C, No. 6 (1962) 167-194.

Hughes, K., *The Church in Early Irish Society* (London 1966).

Hughes, K., *Early Christian Ireland: Introduction to the Sources*: The Sources of History: Studies in the Uses of Historical Evidence, ed. G. R. Elton (London 1972).

Hull, E., 'Hymns, Irish Christian', *Encyclopedia of Religion and Ethics* VII, ed. J. Hastings (New York 1915), 25-28.

Jungmann, J. A., 'The Pre-Monastic Morning Hour in the Gallo-Spanish Region in the Sixth Century', in: *Pastoral Liturgy* (London 1962), pp. 122-157.

King, A. A., *Liturgies of the Past* (London 1959).

MacNeill, E., 'The Hymn of St. Secundinus in honour of St Patrick', *Irish Historical Studies* 2 (1940) 129-153.

Mateos, J., 'La vigile cathédrale chez Egérie', *Orientalia Christiana Periodica* 27 (1961) 281-312.

Mateos, J., 'L'office monastique à la fin du IVe siècle: Antioche, Palestine, Cappadoce', *Oriens Christianus* 47 (1963) 53-88.

Messenger, R. E., *The Medieval Latin Hymn* (Washington 1953).

Meyer, W., *Gesammelte Abhandlungen zur mittellateinischen Rythmik*, 2 vols (Berlin 1905).

Meyer, W., 'Die drei arezzaner Hymnen des Hilarius von Poitiers und etwas über Rythmus', *Nachrichten von der königl. Gesellsch. der Wissensch. zu Göttingen. Phil.-hist. Klasse* (1909) 373-433.

Meyer, W., 'Die Verskunst der Iren in rythmischen lateinischen Gedichten', *Nachrichten der K. Gesellschaft der Wissenschaften zu Göttingen. Phil.-hist. Klasse* (1916) 606-644.

Mulcahy, C., 'The Irish Latin Hymns: "Sancti Venite" of St Sechnall (d. *circa* 447) and "Altus Prosator" of St Columba (521-597)', *The Irish Ecclesiastical Record* 57 (1941) 385-405.

Mulcahy, C., 'The Hymn of St Secundinus in Praise of St Patrick', *The Irish Ecclesiastical Record* 65 (1945) 145-149.

Murphy, T. A., 'The Oldest Eucharistic Hymn', *The Irish Ecclesiastical Record* 46 (1935) 172-176.

Norberg, D., *Introduction à l'étude de la versification latine médiévale*: Acta Universitatis Stockholmiensis. Studia Latina Stockholmiensia V (Stockholm 1958).

O'Laverty, J., *An historical Account of the Diocese of Down and Connor, ancient and modern*. Vol. II (Dublin 1880).

Phillips, C. S., *Hymnody, past and present* (London 1937).

Pinell, J., 'Vestigis del lucernari a Occident', *Liturgica* I: Scripta et Documenta 7 (Montserrat 1956) 91-149.

Pinell, J., 'El oficio hispano-visigótico', *Hispania Sacra* 10 (1957) 385-427.

Pinell, J., 'Las horas vigiliares del oficio monacal hispánico', *Liturgica* 3: Scripta et Documenta 17 (Montserrat 1966) 197-340.

Pinnell, J., *De Liturgia Laudis. Synthesis historica et principia doctrinalia de divino officio*, 3rd ed., *pro manuscripto* (Romae 1968).

Raby, F. J. E., *A History of Christian-Latin Poetry from the Beginning to the Close of the Middle Ages* (Oxford 1927).

Reeves, W., 'The Antiphonary of Bangor', *Ulster Journal of Archaeology* 1 (1853) 168–179.

Ryan, J., *Irish Monasticism. Origins and Early Development* (Dublin 1931).

Schneider, H., *Die altlateinischen biblischen Cantica*: Texte und Arbeiten I 29–30 (Beuron 1938).

Simonetti, M., 'Studi sull'innologia popolare cristiana dei primi secoli', *Atti della accademia nazionale dei lincei, anno CCCXLIX* (Rome 1952). Memorie, Classe di Scienze morali, storiche e filologiche, Serie VIII, vol. IV, fasc. 6, 341–484.

Szövérffy, J., *Die Analen der lateinischen Hymnendichtung. Ein Handbuch. I Die lateinischen Hymnen bis zum Ende des II. Jahrhunderts* (Berlin 1964).

Walpole, A. S., *Early Latin Hymns, with Introduction and Notes* (Cambridge 1922).

Warren, F. E., *The Liturgy and Ritual of the Celtic Church* (Oxford 1881).

NUMBERED INDEX OF ANTIPHONARY ITEMS

ALPHABETICAL INDEX OF ANTIPHONARY FORMULAE

GENERAL INDEX

(Certain expressions of the Latin Liturgies studied in the text are given here, with an indication in brackets of their original source, if this is established).

Cattaneo, E. 229, 233, 241, 254
Cerne, Book of 12, 113, 155, 197, 225, 230
Chavasse, A. 209, 219, 232
Columbanus, St 12, 13, 49, 50, 53, 57, 78, 90, 91, 113,   166-168, 183, 192-193
Columcille, St 13, 20, 21, 38, 57, 161-162
Comgall, St 13, 81-82, 193
Conditor elementorum (Mo) 23 10
Corish, P.J. 254
Culhane, R. 205
de Tischendorf, C. 214, 215
Deus summus 223
de Vogue, A. 233, 248, 250, 251, 257
Dillon, M. 199
Dold, A. 235, 237, 244
Duft, J. 244
Esposito, M. 207
Favor clementiae (Mo) 240
Feder, A 200, 201
Felix cruor (Mo) 131
Filid, order of 20, 89
Flower, R. 197 200
Fluenta lavacri (Mo) 134-135
Fortunatus, Venantius 24-26, 29, 33, 50, 53, 54, 57, 85
Franceschini, E. 198
Frost, M. 230
Fructuosus, St 153, 179-181
Gallican hymns 51, 52, 54, 57, 64-65, 93-94; rite 11, 31,   169, 192-194; sources for AB 150, 152
Gamber, K. 197, 227, 235
Gimeno, M.A. 230
Giuliari 243
Godel, W. 205, 226, 246
Gougaud, L. 11, 14, 154, 198, 224, 245, 247, 248, 249,   252, 259, 260
Green, D. 199
Greek, Irish knowledge of 222
Gregorian hymns, 51, 52
Grosjean, P. 207, 250

Gurges vitiorum (Mo) 239
Gwynn, E.J. 249
Gwynn, Aubrey 197
Hadot, P. 219, 220, 221
Hamilton, G.F. 208
Hanssens, J.M. 246, 247
Heiming, O. 232, 251
Hennig, J. 197
Henry, P. 219
Hic et in futuro (Ce) 237
Hilary of Poitiers, St 22-23, 26
Hillgarth, J.N. 197, 244
Hippolytus, *Apostolic Tradition* of 98, 100, 113
Hughes, K. 200, 224, 225, 226, 246, 260
Hull, E. 216
Impugnatio vitiorum (Mo) 135
Incendia frigida (Mo) 137, 139
Incendium ignis (Mo) 239
Intercessory versicles, see Versicles, *Capitella de psalmis*
Irish *Liber Hymnorum* 19, 36
Irish prayer, themes of 12, 84-85, 144, 174-176, 181-182,   188-189, 195; style of 26, 97, 100-106, 113-118 *passim*,   126-129, 131, 133, 134, 141, 144-149, 144-145, 184;   influence on eighth-century Gelasians 99, 103, 117-118,   155, 228, 229; see also Verse, Ambrosian prayers
Isidore, St, 121-122, 135, 179-181
Iugum peccati 142
Iugum servitutis 134
Jungman, J.A. 224, 232, 233, 246, 255
Kelly, J.N.D. 256
Kenney, notes *passim*
King, A.A. 197
Knott, E. 200
Krusch, B. 210
Laetitia perpetua gaudere (Mo) 240. n.8
Laquei peccatorum 239